Naturalism Without Mirrors

Naturalism Without Mirrors

HUW PRICE

OXFORD
UNIVERSITY PRESS

Oxford University Press, Inc., publishes works that further
Oxford University's objective of excellence
in research, scholarship, and education.

Oxford New York
Auckland Cape Town Dar es Salaam Hong Kong Karachi
Kuala Lumpur Madrid Melbourne Mexico City Nairobi
New Delhi Shanghai Taipei Toronto

With offices in
Argentina Austria Brazil Chile Czech Republic France Greece
Guatemala Hungary Italy Japan Poland Portugal Singapore
South Korea Switzerland Thailand Turkey Ukraine Vietnam

Published by Oxford University Press, Inc.
198 Madison Avenue, New York, New York 10016

www.oup.com

Library of Congress Cataloging-in-Publication Data
Price, Huw, 1953–
Naturalism without mirrors / by Huw Price.
p. cm.
Includes bibliographical references.
ISBN 978-0-19-508433-7 (alk. paper)
1. Philosophy, Australian. 2. Philosophy, Modern—20th century. I. Title.
B5704.P751 2010
199′.94—dc22 2009047836

1 5 7 9 8 6 4 2

Printed in the United States of America
on acid-free paper

Посвящаю Оле

CONTENTS

PREFACE AND ACKNOWLEDGMENTS

This volume brings together thirteen previously published essays, written over a period of more than twenty years. In addition, a new introductory chapter describes the general philosophical program to which the remaining chapters all aim to make some contribution—an exploration of a distinctive brand of pragmatic naturalism, distinguished from popular forms of philosophical naturalism by skepticism about the centrality of *representation*.

As might be expected in essays written over such a long period, there are some variations in terminology, from one chapter to another. And as might be expected in thematically linked essays written by the same author in this particular period—when technology has made it so easy to reuse one's own words—there are some significant overlaps between chapters, of text and arguments as well as of targets and conclusions. I have made some small changes to ameliorate the most egregious of these blemishes, but by and large the essays appear as they were first printed. Indeed, each remains a piece that may be read in isolation from the others—though I strongly recommend the new introduction (chapter 1) to readers approaching the volume in this way.

I am grateful to the editors and publishers who have given their permission to reprint the following pieces. Chapter 2 was first published as H. Price (1992) "Metaphysical Pluralism," *Journal of Philosophy*, 89: 387–409 (Copyright © 1992 by *The Journal of Philosophy*). Chapter 3 was originally published as H. Price (1994) "Semantic Minimalism and the Frege Point," in S. L. Tsohatzidis (ed.), *Foundations of Speech Act Theory: Philosophical and Linguistic Perspectives* (London and New York: Routledge, 132–155). (The present version also includes a postscript added for B. Garrett and K. Mulligan, [eds.], *Themes from Wittgenstein* [Canberra: Philosophy Program, Research School of Social Sciences, ANU, 1993, 15–44].) Chapter 4 first appeared as H. Price (1991) "Two Paths to Pragmatism," in P. Menzies (ed.), *Response-Dependent Concepts (Working Papers in Philosophy, No. 1)* (Canberra: Philosophy Program, Research School of Social Sciences, ANU, 46–82). Chapter 5 was first published as J. O'Leary-Hawthorne and H. Price

(1996) "How to Stand Up for Noncognitivists," *Australasian Journal of Philosophy,* 74: 275–292. (The journal is available at http://www.informaworld.com.) I am grateful to John Hawthorne for his permission to reprint it here. Chapter 6 was my contribution to a two-part symposium with Frank Jackson, originally published as H. Price and F. Jackson (1997) "Naturalism and the Fate of the M-Worlds," *Proceedings of the Aristotelian Society,* Supp. Vol. LXXI: 247–267, 269–282. I am grateful to Frank Jackson for his permission to reprint it here. Chapter 7 originally appeared as R. Holton and H. Price (2003) "Ramsey on Saying and Whistling: A Discordant Note," *Noûs,* 37(2): 325–341. I am grateful to Richard Holton for his permission to reprint it here. The first draft of chapter 8 was written for a conference in honor of Richard Rorty at ANU in 1999. It was subsequently published as H. Price (2003) "Truth as Convenient Friction," *Journal of Philosophy* 100: 167–190 (Copyright © 2003 by *The Journal of Philosophy*). Chapter 9 was originally published as H. Price (2004) "Naturalism Without Representationalism," in David Macarthur and Mario de Caro (eds.), *Naturalism in Question* (Cambridge, MA: Harvard University Press, 71–88) (Copyright © 2004 by the President and Fellows of Harvard College). Chapter 10 was first published as H. Price (2004) "Immodesty Without Mirrors—Making Sense of Wittgenstein's Linguistic Pluralism," in Max Kölbel and Bernhard Weiss (eds.), *Wittgenstein's Lasting Significance* (London: Routledge & Kegan Paul, 179–205). Chapter 11 was originally published as D. Macarthur and H. Price (2007) "Pragmatism, Quasirealism and the Global Challenge," in Cheryl Misak (ed.), *The New Pragmatists* (Oxford: Oxford University Press). I am grateful to David Macarthur for his permission to reprint it here. Chapter 12 first appeared as H. Price (2009) "The Semantic Foundations of Metaphysics," in Ian Ravenscroft (ed.), *Minds, Worlds and Conditionals: Essays in Honour of Frank Jackson* (Oxford: Oxford University Press, 111–140). Chapter 13 was originally published as H. Price (2009) "Metaphysics after Carnap: The Ghost Who Walks?' in D. Chalmers, R. Wasserman, and D. Manley (eds.), *Metametaphysics: New Essays on the Foundations of Ontology* (Oxford: Oxford University Press, 320–346). Finally, chapter 14 was originally published as H. Price (2010) "One Cheer for Representationalism," in R. Auxier (ed.), *Library of Living Philosophers,* Vol. XXXII: *The Philosophy of Richard Rorty* (La Salle, IL: Open Court, 269–289).

As I noted above, these essays span about two decades—years I have had the good fortune to spend with congenial and challenging philosophical colleagues, in Sydney and in Edinburgh. I feel especially privileged to have been a member of the Australian philosophical community, in an era in which it has been one of the nation's quiet treasures; all the more fortunate, perhaps, because my own philosophical dispositions are somewhat un-Australian (at least by the standards of the analytic end of the subject). Many of the essays in this volume were attempts to clarify some aspect or other of my disagreements with distinguished compatriots. How much poorer I would have been to have lacked that incentive. ("The fewer men, the greater spur to rigor," as it were.)

Michael Devitt touches on the Australian philosophical character, in the preface to his *Realism and Truth*:

> Some say Australian philosophers are born realists. I prefer to attribute our realism to nurture rather than nature. David Armstrong has suggested (lightly) that the strong sunlight and harsh brown landscape of Australia force reality upon us. In contrast the mists and gentle green landscape of Europe weaken the grip on reality. (Michael Devitt, *Realism and Truth,* 2nd ed., Oxford: Basil Blackwell, 1991, p. x)

For my part, I think that the step from sunlight to metaphysics pays insufficient attention to the difference between seeing and saying. (The relevant fact about Europeans may not be that they see less but that they talk more.) The basic question that drives metaphysics is less "What are we looking at?" than "What are we talking about (what makes our claims true)?" And this opens the door to an alternative philosophical approach, more anthropology than metaphysics, that takes the interesting question to be, "Why are we talking this way?" My disposition has always been to ask this last question, rather than its metaphysical predecessor (though if there is a single issue underlying these essays, it is about the difference between the two).

Late in his life, Bertrand Russell wrote that until his mid-forties, he had always taken for granted that language is transparent. I think it is important to distinguish two ways in which one might disagree with this assumption. One, with some distant affinity with Armstrong's remark about sunlight, challenges only the transparency (allowing, as an Australian apostle might have put it, that language shows us the world "as through sunnies, darkly"). But a more radical view is that the metaphor itself is misleading: the problem is not that the glass is not fully transparent, but that the glassy metaphor itself is entirely empty. The heresy so generously tolerated by my philosophical compatriots is the latter view.

David Armstrong and Michael Devitt were both still members of the Department of Traditional and Modern Philosophy at the University of Sydney when I first joined it; and in different ways, had each done much to shape the landscape from which I found it so useful to try to differentiate myself. From that period, I am grateful also to Keith Campbell, Lloyd Reinhardt, and Michaelis Michael; and—though by now in a different part of the philosophical landscape—to Paul Redding, from whom I learned a great deal in discussions and joint classes in the 1990s. Among Australian philosophers more generally, I am especially indebted, over many years, to Philip Pettit, Peter Menzies, Frank Jackson and David Braddon-Mitchell. More broadly still, I am especially grateful to Simon Blackburn, Bob Brandom, Paul Horwich, Jenann Ismael, Richard Rorty, and Mike Williams, from all of whom I have not yet learned enough.

I would also like to acknowledge the generous support of the Australian Research Council and the University of Sydney. Some of the research for essays in this collection was originally supported by ARC project grants on *David Hume and Contemporary Pragmatism* (1996–1998) and *The Nature of Naturalism* (2001–2003); and, since 2002, I have had the great privilege of holding two ARC Federation Fellowships, with associated research funding from the University of Sydney.

Finally, warm thanks to Fiona Mackenzie, for much well-judged editorial assistance; to Professor Efim Karpov, of the Vinnitsa National Technical University, for his kind assistance with the cover image; to my mother, Eileen Price, whose intelligent pragmatism has always set me such a fine example; and most of all, as ever, to Nye and to Olga.

Naturalism Without Mirrors

1

Moving the Mirror Aside

1. The Matching Game

Imagine a child's puzzle book, arranged like this: The left-hand page contains a large sheet of peel-off stickers, and the right-hand page shows a line drawing of a complex scene. For each sticker—the koala, the boomerang, the Sydney Opera House, and so on—the reader needs to find the unique outline in the drawing with the corresponding shape. The aim of the game is to place all the stickers in their correct locations, in this sense.

Now think of the right-hand page as the world, and the stickers as the collection of all the statements we take to be true of the world. For each such statement, it seems natural to ask what makes it true—what fact in the world has precisely the corresponding "shape." Within the scope of this simple but intuitive analogy, matching true statements to the world seems a lot like matching stickers to the line drawing.

Moreover, many problems in philosophy seem much like the difficulties the child faces, when some of the stickers are hard to place. In both cases, the difficulties arise from restrictions on the options available on the right-hand side of the game. In the first case, the child has to work within the constraints of the line drawing provided. If she is allowed to draw her own outlines, one for each sticker, the task is bound to be straightforward (engrossing, perhaps, at a certain age, but essentially trivial). In a pre-assigned drawing, however, the required outlines can be concealed or even absent altogether, and hence the puzzle can be difficult or even impossible to complete. Imagine that the drawing is constructed from basic shapes like the segments of an orange, for example. We can see how the Opera House fits in, and perhaps the boomerang, but where do we put the koala?

In the philosophical case, similarly, the game is trivial (and not even engrossing, to most temperaments) if for any true statement "P," we are allowed to say that "P" is made true by the fact that P. It becomes non-trivial when we impose limitations on the facts on the right—restrictions on the available "truthmakers" for the statements on the left.

There are various possible motivations for playing the philosophical version of the game with restrictions of this kind, but let us focus on one in particular—the most influential in contemporary philosophy, I think. It rests on two kinds of intuitions, or theoretical assumptions. The first of these—shared, presumably, with other motivations for the philosophical version of this matching game—is a kind of proto-theory about language, in the light of which the game seems to provide a useful informal model of the relation of language to the world. This proto-theory has to accord a key role to the idea that the function of statements is to "represent" worldly states of affairs, and that true statements succeed in doing so.

It may seem inappropriate to call this assumption a proto-theory. The label "theory" may seem too grand for such an obvious truth, or the label "proto" too tentative for such a well-established canon of philosophy of language. Nothing hangs on the terminology, however. For the moment, the important thing is the role that this assumption—be it trivial truth, proto-theory, or mature canon—plays in giving rise to the most taxing form of the philosophical version of the matching game.

If this proto-theory (or whatever) is to be incorporated into a mature scientific theory of the relation of language to the world, then the matching model needs to fit within the scope of a broadly scientific investigation of ourselves, and of the world we inhabit. After all, as we consider the world as scientists, we see ourselves and our language as one small but (to us) rather significant part of it. Hence the second source of the restriction: if the matching model is to be incorporated into a scientific perspective, the perspective itself seems to dictate the shape of the available facts and truthmakers. Roughly, the available shapes are the kinds of outlines recognized by natural science.

Why does this turn out to be a severe constraint, at least prima facie? Because there seem to be many true statements that don't line up neatly with any facts of the kind uncovered by natural science. Indeed, the problem cases are not just the classic misfits, such as the (apparent?) truths of aesthetics, morality, and other normative matters, or those of consciousness. Arguably, at least, they include matters much closer to a scientist's heart, such as probability, causation, possibility and necessity, and conditional facts of various kinds; and even, hovering above all, the heavenly truths of mathematics itself.

Thus there is a striking mismatch between the rich world of ordinary discourse and the sparse world apparently described by science. A great deal of work in modern philosophy amounts to attempts to deal with some aspect or other of this mismatch. The project is often called simply naturalism. I shall call it Naturalism, for now, with a capital N, so as to reserve the generic term for a more basic view (with which, as I shall explain, Naturalism itself may well turn out to conflict).

The Naturalist's mantra goes something like this: The only facts there are are the kind of facts recognized by natural science. But it is not this mantra alone that commits Naturalists to their restrictive version of the matching game. In principle, one could endorse the mantra without thinking that the matching game provides a useful model of the relation of language to the world. (Quine provides an example, perhaps, at least under some interpretations.) The puzzle stems from combining the mantra with a piece of proto-science: the kind of proto-theory about language and the world for which the matching game offers a crude model. The proto-theory says that our statements "stand for," or "represent," aspects of the world. Big-N Naturalists combine this proto-theory with the mantra's restriction on the available truthmakers, and it is the combination that leads to the puzzles to which they devote so much philosophical energy.

I have emphasized the role of the proto-theory because it reveals an interesting vulnerability in the Naturalist's own position. By the Naturalist's own lights, the proto-theory ought to count as an hypothesis about what it is right to say about language itself, from a naturalistic standpoint. If it turned out to be a bad hypothesis—if better science showed that the proto-theory was a poor theory—then the motivation for the Naturalist's version of the matching game would be undermined. But it would be undermined from *within* a scientific view of language and its place in the world. In that sense, the undermining wouldn't be an anti-naturalist conclusion—on the contrary, it would depend on convicting some self-styled naturalists of sub-optimal science.

If we call the proto-theory (big-R) *Representationalism*, then the possibility just mentioned is the possibility that a good naturalistic account of our own linguistic practice might defeat Representationalism—might reveal it to be a poor theory about the relation between language and the world. The result would be naturalism without Representationalism, or naturalism without mirrors.

In "Naturalism Without Representationalism" (chapter 9), I make these points in terms of a distinction between two kinds of naturalism: "object naturalism," which is the view we've just called simply Naturalism, and "subject naturalism," which is the philosophical viewpoint that begins with the realization that we humans (our thought and talk included) are surely part of the natural world. The key claims of the chapter are that subject naturalism is importantly prior to object naturalism, because the latter depends on an assumption about language that might prove false, from the former's perspective; and that there are good reasons for thinking that the threat is a serious one—that Representationalism might well turn out to be a bad (proto)-theory. If so, then the matching game turns out to be a bad analogy for the task that confronts a philosophical account of the place of language in the natural world.

But what alternative is there? Many of the remaining chapters in this volume offer sketches of an answer to this question. In most of them, my role feels to me something like that of a real estate agent, making brief visits to a neglected property, with various kinds of reluctant clients in tow. Usually, the imagined clients are proponents of some rival theory, and I am attempting to convince them that their needs would be better met, at lower cost, by moving to this alternative.

Most of these rival theories are associated with one or other of various familiar approaches to the puzzle of the matching game—to the problem that we seem to have a lot more true statements than naturalistically respectable truthmakers.

The best way to get a sense of where my alternative fits in is to begin there, with a brief survey of the more familiar options.

2. Placement Strategies

The problem is that of "placing" various kinds of truths in a natural world.[1] We seem to have more truths than truthmakers—more stickers than places to put them. Since that puzzle thus turns on an apparent mismatch between the cardinality of two different sets, it should come as no surprise that there are three basic kinds of solution. One argues that the two sets can be matched, just as they are; that there is some non-obvious mapping that does the trick. The second argues that the problem arises because we have undercounted on the right, and that there are actually more truthmakers available than we thought. And the third argues that we have overcounted on the left, and that actually there are fewer statements in need of truthmakers than we thought.

The first option can be called *reductionism*. A noteworthy recent version of this approach is an account due to Frank Jackson, now commonly called the Canberra Plan.[2] I contrast my approach to Jackson's in two essays in this collection, "Naturalism and the Fate of the M-Worlds" (chapter 6) and "The Semantic Foundations of Metaphysics" (chapter 12). In the latter, especially, I try to exhibit the way in which Jackson's program depends on substantial assumptions about language—in effect, Representationalism—and I argue that these assumptions are problematic, in various ways.

The second option is often felt to embrace two sub-options. One accepts the constraint imposed by Naturalism, but argues that there are more facts within the scope of natural science than we thought.[3] The second argues that the constraint itself is at fault, and that we need to recognize that there are non-natural facts.[4] It is debatable whether the distinction between these two sub-options is more than merely terminological—an issue as to what we call science—but we need not discuss that here. What is relevant is what the sub-options have in common, namely, that they attribute the original puzzle to excessive parsimony in our initial assessment of the available truthmakers on the right-hand side of the model. In the earliest essay in this collection (chapter 2, "Metaphysical Pluralism"), I contrast these "super-additive" or "expansionist" approaches (as I call them there) to what

1. I am not sure where this terminology originates. It is used in this way by Blackburn (1993b), writing about an earlier discussion by McDowell.

2. This label was first coined by John Hawthorne and me, in a predecessor of our joint paper "How to Stand Up for Noncognitivists" (chapter 5), originally presented at the Auckland meeting of the Australasian Association of Philosophy in 1994. As we explain in the published version, the original intent was ironic, though the label became a badge of honor for our Canberra opponents.

3. David Chalmers's (1996) view of consciousness is a familiar example.

4. The classic example is Moore's (1903) view of moral facts.

I argue to be a more economical way of doing justice to similarly pluralistic intuitions. The alternative, which in the essay I associate with Wittgenstein, attributes the plurality in question to diversity in the things we do with language, rather than to some preexisting metaphysical or natural diversity in the world. Most of the essays in this volume can be seen as engaged in the elaboration and defence of this "Wittgensteinian" proposal, in various ways; although only one piece (chapter 10, "Immodesty Without Mirrors: Making Sense of Wittgenstein's Linguistic Pluralism") specifically addresses its Wittgensteinian credentials.

The third option, not surprisingly, is to try to reduce the size of the set on the left—in other words, to try to reduce the number of statements we take to require truthmakers. In this case, there are several sub-options, and it will be worth our while to distinguish them with some care.

Eliminativism

Recall that the stickers on the left of the model are supposed to represent true statements. An eliminativist deals with the excess—that is, with the embarrassing residue, after all the obvious candidates are assigned to their naturalistically respectable places on the right—by saying that we are victims of large-scale error. Large subclasses of the statements we take to be true are actually systematically false. For example, perhaps there simply are no moral facts. If so, then all claims whose truth would depend on the existence of such facts are systematically in error.

Fictionalism

A similar but slightly less drastic view offers the same diagnosis of the apparent mismatch between statements and truthmakers, but with a more irenic conclusion. Eliminativists are inclined to compare the false statements in question to the claims of discarded scientific theories, and to recommend that they be accorded a similar fate. Fictionalists are more mellow about falsehood. They embrace the idea of "useful fictions"—language games in which false claims serve some useful purpose. The practices of making moral or modal claims might be beneficial in some way, for example, despite that fact that the claims concerned are not literally true. If so, we do not need to find truthmakers; nor do we need to dispense with language games in question.

Expressivism

The same lesson—namely, that the "point" of some of the statements on our initial list is not to match worldly facts—is carried a stage further by expressivists.[5]

5. This is not to suggest that expressivism is a descendant of fictionalism. It might be more accurate to say that fictionalists are proto-expressivists, who have not yet realized that there is a live alternative to Representationalism.

Expressivists maintain that some of the uses of language that we take to be statements are not genuine statements at all, but rather utterances with some other point or function. The suggestion is that once these pseudo-statements are pruned away, the apparent imbalance between true statements and worldly truthmakers is eliminated, or at least reduced. The usual version of the puzzle rests at least in part on a kind of mistake about language, in the expressivist's view.

At this point, it is worth noting an important difference between fictionalism and expressivism. To make things concrete, consider the moral case. A fictionalist thinks that moral claims have an everyday use and a literal use. Taken literally (and interpreted as a moral claim), the statement "Harming children is worse than harming dogs" is false. (Why? Because, literally speaking, there are no moral facts to make it true.) Taken in its everyday sense, however—within the fiction in which we all participate—it may well be correctly said to be true.

In contrast, an expressivist has no need to admit that there is any sense in which such a statement is literally false. On the contrary, says the expressivist, taking it to be literally false is making a mistake about what kind of speech act it is. It is not the kind of speech act that *has* a literal truth-value, in the sense that the fictionalist intends.

As a result, an expressivist might hope to agree with everyday moral claims, without having to take anything back—without having to admit (even if only in her study, as it were) that all such claims are literally false. She agrees full voice with the everyday folk, and argues that the attempt to raise further issues—are there *really* any such facts?—rests on a mistake about language. Once we see that moral claims are not genuinely descriptive, we see that such metaphysical issues rest on a category mistake. See things properly, the expressivist assures us, and you see that they simply don't arise.

3. Quasi-realism and Globalization

It might seem that the advantage of not having to say that our moral claims are literally false comes with a countervailing disadvantage. Does the expressivist not have to give up on the idea that there could be some everyday sense in which such a claim is true? Indeed, how is the expressivist going to account for the fact that we call such claims true and false, if they are not really in the business of making claims about how things are?

These issues are best addressed by the version of expressivism called *quasi-realism*, championed over many years by Simon Blackburn (see especially Blackburn 1984; 1993a). Quasi-realism begins where expressivism begins, with the thought that the primary function of certain of our (apparent) statements is not that of describing how things are. But it aims to show, nevertheless, how such expressions earn a right to the trappings of descriptive "statementhood"—in particular, the right to be treated as capable of being true and false.

Blackburn emphasizes that the appeal of quasi-realism is that it provides a way of dealing with some of the hard placement problems—the case of moral and aesthetic discourse, for example—without resorting either to implausible metaphysics or the error theory. If successful, quasi-realism explains why the folk practice of making moral claims is in order just as it is, and explains why further any metaphysical inquiry about whether there are *really* moral facts is inevitably missing the point (in being premised on a mistaken view of what we are doing with moral language).

Quasi-realism is important, in the present context, because the view proposed here can be thought of, in most respects, as a generalized or "global" version of quasi-realism. This way of locating the view is mentioned in many of the essays, and most explicitly in one of the most recent (chapter 11, "Pragmatism, Quasi-realism, and the Global Challenge"). To understand how the generalization proceeds, note first that what expressivism does is to remove some (apparent) commitments from the matching game—to say that the matching model is a bad model of the relation of those commitments to the world. (What quasi-realism in particular adds is an account of why, on the surface, it "looks as if" the matching model is applicable.) In place of the matching model, presumably, expressivism offers some positive account of the use of the parts of language in question—some account compatible with the basic ("subject naturalist") premise that the creatures employing the language in question are simply natural creatures, in a natural environment.

Typically, of course, expressivists do all of this *locally*. They think that some of our claims are genuinely factual, or descriptive (and hence, presumably, characterizable in terms of the matching model, insofar as it works at all). And they think that for any of our claims or commitments, there is a genuine issue of whether it is really factual, or descriptive. (The expressivist's alternative is needed when the answer is "no.") However—and this is a crucial point—the belief that there is such an issue and the belief that some claims are genuinely descriptive play *no role at all* in the positive story, in the case of the commitments that the expressivist regards as not genuinely descriptive. In other words, the expressivist's positive alternative to the matching model does not depend on the claim that the matching model is *ever* a useful model of the relation between natural language and the natural world. So there is no barrier, in principle, to abandoning the matching model altogether and becoming a *global* expressivist.

In essence, this global expressivism is the view that I want to defend. I want to defend it in a version that takes over from quasi-realism a strong emphasis on questions about why parts of language that begin life as expressions and projections should take the form that they do—why, in particular, they should be declarative in form, and capable of being regarded as true or false. But as I will explain, I part company with the quasi-realist on some of the details—necessarily so, perhaps, if the quasi-realist's answers depend on the idea of emulating "genuinely representational" claims, because for me there are no such things.[6]

4. Naturalism Without Representationalism

Approached from this direction, then, the view I want to defend can be regarded as a kind of global expressivism. But it differs from local varieties of expressivism not simply in doing globally what they do only locally, but in a more fundamental respect. Local versions of expressivism accept Representationalism in some domains. Their message is simply that the matching game is not as widely applicable as we tend to assume—some of our statements (or apparent statements) have other, non-representational functions, and hence are not in need of truthmakers. We might imagine an expressivist of this sort raising the possibility of a language in which, as a matter of fact, all the (apparent) statements had this kind of non-representational function. This would be to imagine a language (perhaps even our own language) for which, contingently, a globalized expressivism does turn out to be the right story. But it would be to imagine it while keeping in play the proto-theory, and the notion of genuinely representational language.

I want to go a stage further. I am not proposing merely that genuine representation turns out to be a linguistic function that is not in play in our own language, but that representation (*in this sense*—more on the importance of this qualification in a moment) is a theoretical category that we should dispense with altogether. The right thing to do, as theorists, is not to say that it turns out that none of our statements is a genuine representation; it is to stop talking about representation altogether, to abandon the project of theorizing about word–world relations in these terms. It is a bit like the familiar case of simultaneity: the lesson of relativity is not merely that we live in a world in which absolute simultaneity does not make itself manifest, but that we should abandon the notion of absolute simultaneity altogether, for theoretical purposes.

If representation goes by the board in this way, then there is a sense in which expressivism triumphs by default. After all, the defining characteristic of

6. As I will explain, I think that quasi-realism's commitment to the idea that some statements involve genuine representation has hampered the enterprise of developing an adequate general theory of judgment and assertion. If nothing else, it has obscured the explanandum, by disassociating the issue as to why moral claims (say) take the form that they do from the the deeper question as to why any claims take such a form. Far better, in my view, to begin further back, tackling the deeper question in a manner that does not simply presuppose Representationalism—here Brandom offers an explicit model of the methodology required, I think (see chapter 10, section 8, and chapter 14)—and then hoping to sweep up the problem areas as special cases. "Semantic Minimalism and the Frege Point" (chapter 3 of this volume) offers a similar methodology for responding to the Frege-Geach argument. In each case, the quasi-realist's tactical error is to be too charitable to his opponent, in allowing that the relevant account of genuinely representational statements is already in hand (more on this in section 8).

expressivism is that it offers a non-representational account of the functions of some part of language—and if representation goes by the board, there is nothing else left. Still, there is another sense in which the term "expressivism" is a little unhappy, in this context, because of its associations with familiar local forms of expressivism, which take for granted a representationalist framework. Sometimes, therefore, I call the view "pragmatism"—though this term, too, has mixed associations.

For the moment, I want to emphasize two things about this view, whatever it is called. First, there is a clear sense in which it is naturalistic: it adopts the scientific perspective of a linguistic anthropologist, studying human language as a phenomenon in the natural world. It may reject Naturalism, or "object naturalism," but its own naturalistic credentials are not in doubt.

Second, the view does not claim, absurdly, that there is nothing to be said about the relation of our words to the natural world. On the contrary—and as the example of local forms of expressivism makes abundantly clear—it is likely to allow that there is much to be said about why natural creatures in our circumstances come to use the forms of language in question. What it denies is simply that *representation* turns out to be a useful theoretical category, for saying what needs to be said about word–(natural-)world relations. (This is compatible not only with there being other theoretical vocabularies for characterizing word–world relations, but also—as we shall see in a moment—with the notion of representation having other, more useful, theoretical applications.)

In one sense, this is a familiar idea. There are famous critics of Representationalism in modern philosophy, such as Dewey, Wittgenstein, and Rorty. In another sense, it is a view that can be very hard to bring into focus. For my part, I have long felt that it occupies a peculiar location on the contemporary philosophical map: in one sense almost central, or at least easily accessible from familiar and popular places; in another sense almost invisible, almost unvisited. Part of the reason, presumably, is the strong intuitive appeal of the simple model of language for which the matching game is a metaphor. Representationalism can easily look obvious—more on this in section 12, below—and is deeply embedded in contemporary philosophical theory.

Putting the position on the map, and revealing its virtues and accessibility, is a matter of visiting familiar locations that actually lie close by, and then calling attention to the paths that lead in the right direction. (I have already noted the path from quasi-realism.) In a sense, however, we need to do this from several directions simultaneously. Each path individually can easily seem to be obstructed from another angle. Let us look briefly at some of the angles, and at how they are tackled in the essays in this volume.

5. Avoiding the Wrong Kind of Pragmatism

Pragmatists and expressivists point out that various kinds of commitments seem to have distinctive links to aspects of our own psychology, or to contingent features of our situation more generally. For example, evaluative, probabilistic, and causal commitments have all been held to be distinctively linked to (various aspects of) the fact that we are decision-makers and agents. Facts of this kind—facts about the kinds of creatures we are, and about the relevance of these characteristics, in our relation to our natural environment—are an important part of the raw material for the account that my kind of pragmatist wants to give of the functions and genealogy of particular parts of language. One of the reasons that the representationalist model is a bad theory, the pragmatist wants to say, is that it does not pay enough attention to these factors. It is blind to the "located" character of various bits of language—to their dependence on various contingent features of the circumstances of the natural creatures who use them.

One factor hiding my kind of pragmatism from view, at this point, is that there are views which claim similar sensitivity to the contingent dependencies of language, without ever leaving the familiar comforts of Representationalism. In recent literature, many views of this kind avail themselves of the notion of "response-dependence"—a notion claimed by at least one of its chief proponents (Johnston 1993) to be a step in the direction of pragmatism. Not much hangs on the label, but it is important to see that there is a very different way of giving theoretical voice to similar intuitions about the relation of language to contingent aspects of speakers' circumstances. "Two Paths to Pragmatism" (chapter 4) draws this crucial distinction and argues the cases for the non-representational path.

In my view, the recognition of this kind of contingency-to-speakers'-circumstances, on the one hand, and of the possibility of non-representationalism, on the other, fit together very naturally, and indeed reinforce one another. However, we really need to focus our attention in two places simultaneously, to see the benefits—if we look at one issue or other independently, ignoring the possibility of an unconventional approach to the other, we miss the attractions in question, being blind to the mutual benefits.

6. Keeping the Lid on Metaphysics

Like expressivism in general, quasi-realism motivates a kind of metaphysical quietism about the domains to which it is applied. Given that the commitments in question are not genuine factual commitments, metaphysical questions about (say) whether there are *really* any moral facts are simply misguided. The quasi-realist maintains that they involve a kind of category mistake, a misuse of moral language. However, since this case for quietism rests on the distinction between genuinely factual and not genuinely factual commitments, one might worry that it is unavailable, when that distinction goes by the board.

This concern is actually unwarranted, in my view. The reason that the distinction goes by the board, in my global kind of expressivism, is that Representationalism itself goes by the board. So no commitments at all are treated as genuinely factual, in that sense, because the theoretical category is no longer on the table.

But the expressivist's argument for metaphysical quietism depended only on the fact that it was not on the table, in particular cases—and hence simply generalizes, if it is never on the table.

Still, the more friends the better, and in several of these essays I appeal to the authority of some famous allies, in support of the kind of metaphysical quietism that my view requires and entails. Carnap is one of these allies, but his celebrated attack on metaphysics, in "Empiricism, Semantics and Ontology" (Carnap 1950), is often thought to have been decisively rebutted by Quine (who went on to make the world safe again for metaphysics, according to a popular version of the history of twentieth-century philosophy). This reading is quite misguided, in my view. Not only do Quine's criticisms not touch Carnap's metaphysical quietism, or indeed his pragmatism; but Quine, too, should be read as a quietist and a pragmatist—in most respects, indeed, a more thoroughgoing one than Carnap himself. Chapter 13 deals directly with these matters.[7]

My debt to Carnap is not entirely one-sided, however. The general view defended in these papers offers significant new support to Carnap's position, against Quine's objections. Quine challenges Carnap's entitlement to put fences around linguistic frameworks—to maintain, in effect, that there are several existential quantifiers, each doing different duty in a different framework. Quine argues that once we abandon the analytic–synthetic distinction, the fences disappear. We are left with a single arena, as it were, and a single existential quantifier, bullishly surveying the whole. I think that the key to resisting this objection is to make explicit something that is only a kind of implicit corollary in Carnap's own work, namely, the idea that what distinguishes linguistic frameworks are the kinds of functional and genealogical factors to which expressivists call our attention. Carnap ought to say that the pluralism of linguistic frameworks is a functional pluralism, in this sense.[8]

As I note, this kind of functional pluralism challenges a kind of mono-functional conception of language that seems implicit in Quine's own view—for Quine, *the* significant task of the statement-making part of language is that of recording the conclusions of an activity that is ultimately continuous with natural science. One of the interesting things about the role of this kind of methodological monism is how uncomfortably it sits with other aspects of Quine's views about language. In particular, as other writers have noted, it is hard to reconcile with his deflationary

7. Concerning the interpretation of Quine, see also Price (2007a).

8. As I explain in chapter 13, however, there is an important sense in which Carnap does not need to deny that there is a single existential quantifier—far better to say that we have a single logical device, with a variety of functionally distinct applications. I note that this formulation also defuses Quine's well-known objection to Ryle's pluralism about existential quantification. It also provides a model for a more general feature of the kind of view I want to recommend, namely, that it combines unity or homogeneity at one level in language with diversity at another level. The higher-level forms and structures thus become multi-purpose devices, in a novel sense. More on this in section 9 below.

views about truth and reference. In this respect, too, as we are about to see, Quine really ought to count as an ally of the kind of program I have in mind—an ally who provides his own answer, in effect, to his famous challenge to Carnap's pluralism.

7. Keeping the Lid on Semantics

As the matching game itself illustrates, quietism about metaphysics needs to go hand in hand with quietism about semantics. The game is a metaphor for a linguistically grounded methodology that has come to dominate contemporary metaphysics. Doing metaphysics this way, one begins with statements that we take to be true, and then asks what *makes them true*, or to what their terms *refer*.

However, it is important to notice that there are two ways to take such inquiries, a weak way and a strong way. In the weak way, the semantic terms involved can be understood in a deflationary manner, and what is involved is merely semantic ascent, in Quine's sense. It "looks as if" we're talking about language—asking serious theoretical questions about the semantic relata of sentences and terms—but really we're just talking about the objects. Asking "What makes it true that snow is white?" or "What makes 'Snow is white' true?" is just another way of asking what makes snow white—a reasonable question, in this case, but a question to be answered in terms of the physics of ice and light, not in terms of the metaphysics of facts and states of affairs. There is no additional *semantic* explanandum, and no distinctively metaphysical question.

In general, then, this weak, deflationary view of the semantic terms allows us to read "What makes it true that P?" as something like "Why is it the case that P?," or simply "Why P?" This is a simple, first-order request for an explanation, which makes various and varied kinds of sense, depending on the subject matter concerned. It is not a second-order inquiry revealing a theoretical commitment to a univocal or substantial relation of "truthmaking," of the kind required for linguistically grounded metaphysics. Our theoretical gaze never leaves the world.

Moreover, the term "world" here need not be read as "material world." We saw how the combination of Representationalism and the (reasonable) assumption that language is a natural phenomenon leads Naturalists to want to find natural truthmakers for all true statements. But with Representationalism and that notion of truthmaking out of the picture, here—with all our semantic notions suitably deflated—we can ask "What makes it true that P?" with our gaze on other kinds of matters. We can ask "What makes it true that causing unnecessary harm to animals is wrong?," for example, requesting some sort of moral explanation or elucidation, without feeling any of the Naturalists' pressure to read this as an inquiry about the material world (or, for that matter, *metaphysical* pressure about some other kind of world).[9]

There is another use of weak or deflationary semantic notions that needs to be mentioned at this point, namely, their use in contexts of *interpretation*. If I say that "Schnee is weiß" is true iff snow is white, it might be said that there is a clear sense in which I am talking about language (in this case, German), and not about snow. For the moment, the main point to be made about these contexts is that they, too, don't depend on substantial word–world semantic relations. As a result, once again, they are blind to the considerations that animate our Naturalists. The interpretative stance is blind to the kinds of distinctions marked by expressivists, for example. So even though it is true, in some sense, that in interpretation our gaze falls on language, it does not fall on the relation between words and the world, in the way that supports metaphysics—the way that depends on substantial semantic relations (more on this in section 11).

So much for the case in which the use of semantic terms in metaphysics is read in a weak, or deflationary, sense. When the semantic notions are taken in the strong sense, however, then the metaphysician's theoretical gaze can indeed rest on language. The resulting metaphysical program operates under the assumption that certain linguistic items—sentences, or terms, for example—have substantial semantic properties, or stand in substantial semantic relations. Given this assumption, questions posed about these semantic properties and relations can provide an indirect method of discovering things about the non-linguistic world.

In order to keep the lid on metaphysics—indeed, in order, more basically, to keep a lid on Representationalism itself, which combines with the Naturalist's mantra to give rise to this kind of semantically grounded metaphysics—it is necessary to keep the lid on the kind of substantial, non-deflationary semantics. Semantic deflationism, or minimalism, thus figures very prominently in the essays in this volume.

Here, too, of course, I rest heavily on the shoulders and authority of giants—in this case, the "giant minimalists" of the twentieth century, such as Ramsey, Wittgenstein, and Quine himself. But here, too, the debt is not entirely one-sided.

9. Simon Blackburn makes a similar point about semantic ascent, construed in terms of Ramsey's redundancy theory of truth. Blackburn notes that on Ramsey's view, the move from "P" to "It is true that P"—"Ramsey's ladder," as he calls it—doesn't take us to a new theoretical level. He remarks (1998b: 78) that there are "philosophies that take advantage of the horizontal nature of Ramsey's ladder to climb it, and then announce a better view from the top." In the present terms, the philosophies that Blackburn has in mind are those that fail to see that the fashionable linguistic methods—talk of truthmakers, truth-conditions, denotations, and the like—add precisely nothing to the repertoire of metaphysics, unless the semantic notions in question are more robust than those of Ramsey, Wittgenstein, and Quine. I am in complete agreement with Blackburn on this point, but I want to encourage him to walk his own plank: I think that laying the semantic ladder horizontal defeats the vestige of Representationalism that still distinguishes his quasi-realism from my global view.

The project as a whole offers a new view of the significance of semantic deflationism. It reveals some little-recognized advantages of theorizing about language without substantial word–world semantic relations—in particular, that it leaves room for an attractive kind of pluralism about the roles and functions of linguistic commitments (precisely the kind of pluralism whose denial Naturalism presupposes, in effect). With this picture in view, the contrast between the apparent homogeneity of our talk of truth and the diversity of underlying function cannot help but make it implausible that semantic relations can be characterized in causal–functional terms, in any plausible way. As I say, I take this kind of consideration to provide significant support for semantic deflationism—support that we miss if we miss the pluralism, and think of assertoric language as all doing the same kind of job.

8. The True Role of Truth and Judgment

There are some respects in which I part company with familiar versions of semantic deflationism. In particular, I am sympathetic to the charge that the familiar disquotational versions of deflationism pay insufficient attention to the normative character of the notions of truth and falsity. Disquotational truth seems too "thin" to play its proper role in an adequate theory of the general features of assertion, commitment, and judgment.

One motivation for this view, represented in this collection by my disagreement with Richard Rorty in "Truth as Convenient Friction" (chapter 8), is the feeling that pragmatists have often ignored the resources of their own theoretical standpoint—even, in a sense, their own principles—in seeking to equate truth with something like warranted assertibility. A better alternative, in my view, is to seek to explain *in pragmatic terms* why our notion of truth does not line up neatly with warranted assertibility—in other words, to explain what practical use we have for a stronger notion.[10] In my view, there's a plausible answer to this question to be had in terms of the appropriate norms of assertion and commitment—in effect, roughly, the norms required to make an assertion be a *commitment*, rather than a mere expression of opinion.

This view puts the emphasis squarely on the normative character of truth, and like writers such as Wright (1992), I feel that a merely disquotational account of truth cannot do justice to this normative dimension. Unlike Wright, however, I do not think that this is a reason to abandon deflationism. On the contrary, as I have said, I think that what we need is a pragmatic, explanatory account of the role and

10. As the expressivist analogy ought to make clear, this needn't amount to realism *about* truth, in some metaphysical sense; even if the notion of truth involved is strong enough to count as a "realist" notion, by the lights of someone who divides realists from anti-realists in terms of the kind of truth predicate each takes to be appropriate.

genealogy of the distinctive linguistic norm in question—an expressivist account of a normative notion of truth.[11]

I had come to the same conclusion from a different direction in earlier work. There, one motivation was an issue raised by Bernard Williams (1973): if truth is "thin," or deflationary, why should its application be restricted to assertions? As Williams notes, it is not clear why such a notion of truth should not be used for endorsing other kinds of utterances, such as questions or requests.[12] In *Facts and the Function of Truth* (Price 1988), I proposed an answer in terms of normative structures associated with assertion and commitment, and in particular their role in highlighting disagreement. I suggested that this makes much more sense for some of the things we do with language than for others, and that this is the major constraint on the bounds of assertoric language.

This proposal relied on a thesis about the pragmatic significance of norms of truth and falsity (or, rather, of conversational norms whose roles seem closely approximated, for us, by those of truth and falsity): roughly, the suggestion was that norms of this kind play an indispensable role in making disagreements "matter" to speakers—in helping to ensure that speakers who disagree do not simply "talk past one another" (like customers ordering different meals in a restaurant, to use one of my examples).

In *Facts and the Function of Truth* I argued that this view of truth throws new light on the kinds of intuitions that have often motivated expressivism and non-cognitivism, to the effect that some areas of discourse are less "factual" than others. The book begins with a skeptical examination of the fundamental distinction on which such views rely, between "cognitive" and "non-cognitive" uses of indicative utterances. There are many terms in use to mark this (claimed) distinction—"descriptive" versus "non-descriptive," "belief-expressing" versus "non-belief-expressing," "factual" versus "non-factual," and so on. However, it seemed to me that they were all in the business of taking in each other's washing, and that there was no well-founded distinction to be found.

This may sound as if it were an assault on the foundations of non-cognitivism, but my intentions were more even-handed. I took it that I was criticizing a presupposition that non-cognitivists normally share with their opponents. Both sides presuppose that there is a genuine distinction in language, and disagree only about where it lies. I was arguing that this presupposition is mistaken, and hence disagreeing with both sides.

11. In a paper not included in this collection (Price 1998), I discuss Wright's dispute with Paul Horwich about these matters. I argue that although Wright is right about the need for normativity, deflationism wins the wider battle: as elsewhere, what we need is a deflationary, pragmatic, or expressivist account of the functions and genealogy of the relevant norms. (The positive proposals made in that paper are developed at greater length in chapter 8.)

12. Some writers are tempted to appeal to syntax at this point, arguing that it is "ungrammatical" to attach a truth predicate to anything other than an indicative sentence; but this surely prompts the same question about the grammar.

More importantly, my broader sympathies lay in the non-cognitivist camp. In effect, I was proposing what I am now calling global expressivism. And in the second part of the book, I offered a way of making sense of some of the guiding intuitions of non-cognitivism, in terms of the thesis just described about the dialectical role of truth. I suggested that one could understand such intuitions in terms of various ways in which disagreements might reasonably turn out to have a "no-fault" character (linked to a pragmatic or expressivist understanding of the functional role of the discourse in question). I argued that the resulting classification is a matter of degree—the picture offers no sharp distinction between factual and non-factual uses of language.

In effect, then, a large part of *Facts and the Function of Truth* was an assault on Representationalism, along the vulnerable flank on which—even by its own lights—it needs to mark its borders with non-representational uses of language. The assault was a kind of pincer movement. From one side, I tried to undermine the presupposition that there was a well-founded distinction to be found in the territory in question. From the other, I tried to account for some of the linguistic phenomena that might be considered relevant to the issue—especially the application of the notions of truth and falsity—in a way which led naturally to the conclusion that the distinctions in question were a matter of degree.

As I have explained, many of the chapters in the present volume can be seen as making a more direct assault on the same target. This new attack scales the siege ladder provided by quasi-realism, exploiting semantic and metaphysical deflationism to argue that there is no inner citadel, no genuinely representational core that such a ladder cannot reach—nowhere we need anything but quasi-realism, in effect.

It is easy to be mistaken about where this route leads. As I note in several of the present essays (e.g., chapter 9, section 6), many writers have thought that semantic deflationism provides an easy victory for cognitivism, by making it a trivial matter that moral claims (say) are "truth-apt." They fail to see that putting moral claims on a par with scientific claims need not be a victory for a representationalist view of the former. It can be—and in this case, *is*—a defeat for a representationalist view of the latter; a global reason for rejecting Representationalism itself. This mistake has contributed greatly to the near-invisibility of the global expressivist position in contemporary philosophy, in my view—though expressivists themselves must share some of the blame, in failing to see that the stable response lies at the opposite extreme, in a global version of their own position.

However, it seems to me that once the assault route is clearly in view—its true end-point in sight—it must still be used with caution. For it rests a little too heavily on the horizontal character of Ramsey's ladder, on the thin and universal character of semantic ascent, minimally conceived, and hence is in danger of obscuring some important and substantial matters about assertion and judgment. A conventional quasi-realist might hope that he leaves these matters untouched, at least within the representational core, where presumably they matter most; but that option is no longer available, if there is no such core. The more tortuous route of *Facts and the Function of Truth* had the advantage that it put at least one aspect of these issues center-stage, and proposed a way of reconstructing non-cognitivist insights within the resulting framework.

9. Two-layered Language

As I note in *Facts and the Function of Truth*, my view of truth suggests a distinctive two-level picture of the functional architecture of truth-evaluable uses of language. At the higher level, the picture offers us a certain kind of unity, or univocity: truth is essentially the same conversational norm, in all its core applications. (Contrast this to the *local* quasi-realist's distinction between genuine and "quasi" truth.) At the lower level, however, there is room for a multiplicity of functions—a multiplicity of linguistic tasks or "games," each associated with different aspects of our psychology needs, and situation.

This two-level picture has many attractions, in my view. By prising apart word–natural-world relations from what everything common to the higher level (i.e., from the resources needed for a single, unified account of assertion, commitment, and judgment), it adds a new dimension to linguistic theory, a new degree of freedom for functional variability. The effect is to open up regions of theoretical space that are simply invisible, when these two kinds of factors are squashed together. (Here, think of a child's pop-up book. As we open the page, the model lifts into view, transforming a flat jumble into something with recognizable three-dimensional structure: here is the Opera House, and there is the Harbour Bridge.)

Once again, orthodox forms of expressivism, and quasi-realism in particular, can be seen in hindsight as attempts to occupy these regions, working their way laboriously around the limitations imposed by the lack of the missing dimension. When the two levels are prised apart, and the model expands into the new dimension thus made available, these attempts fit naturally into place, without all the distortion.

The model offered in this volume is admittedly sketchy, at both levels. But at both levels, much of the necessary work has already been done elsewhere. The components are available off the shelf, as it were, as ready-made products of familiar projects in contemporary philosophy. Indeed, what is mainly novel about my proposal is simply the idea of connecting these projects together in this way.

At the lower level, the project in question is that of Blackburn, and other contemporary expressivists in the Humean tradition. As I have said, I think that many of the insights of that tradition plug straight into my framework, once reoriented in the way I recommend.

At the higher level, my proposal about the global conversational role of truth cries out for incorporation into a broader account of the nature and genealogy of assertion, commitment, and judgment—an account built on foundations that do not presuppose Representationalism, of course. I sketch a proposal as to how such an account might go in a couple of the chapters in this volume (e.g., chapter 10, section 9), as well as in *Facts and the Function of Truth* (1988), but more certainly needs to be said. But here, too, I am optimistic about what is already available. I think that much of what I need is to be found in the kind of inferentialist account of assertion developed in detail by Robert Brandom (1994; 2000). The crucial thing, from my point of view, is that Brandom explicitly rejects a Representationalist starting point, offering, as he puts it, an "expressivist alternative" to the "representational paradigm" (Brandom 2000: 10).

There may seem to be a tension in linking my proposal to these two different "expressivisms": Brandom's, on the one hand, and Humean expressivism, on the other. After all, expressivism in the Humean sense relies on "world-tracking" conception of genuine, full-blooded assertion, offering its treatment of particular cases by deliberate contrast with assertions so construed; Brandom, as just noted, explicitly rejects such a view of assertion. My proposal resolves this tension by abandoning the representationalist residue in Humean expressivism. With this gone, we are free to help ourselves to Brandom's view, as an account of what I have called the higher level in a two-level picture of assertoric language—in other words, an account of what all assertoric vocabularies have in common. And this is entirely compatible with also adopting off the shelf, as an account of the lower level, much of what Humean expressivists have to say about the functions of particular concepts and vocabularies.

So there is no real tension here—quite the contrary. But the apparent tension is revealing, in my view. It relies on a bifurcation in the conceptual territory surrounding the notion of representation in contemporary philosophy, which is worth noting and making explicit. (Indeed, I think that much of the appeal of Representationalism rests on a failure to make it explicit.)

10. Two Notions of Representation

Consider, then, the notion of representation, type or token, as it is used in cognitive science, and in contemporary philosophy of language and philosophy of mind. (Imagine a survey of these fields.) My proposal is that we can usefully distinguish two nodes, or conceptual attractors, around which the various uses tend to cluster. One node puts the system–world link on the front foot. It gives priority to the idea that the job of a representation is to *co-vary* with something else—typically, some *external* factor, or environmental condition. The other node gives priority to the *internal* cognitive role of a representation. A token counts as a representation, in this sense, in virtue of its position, or role, in some sort of cognitive or inferential architecture—in virtue of its links, within a network, to other items of the same general kind.[13]

In the grip of Naturalism, one naturally assumes that these two notions of representation go together; that the prime function of representations in the

13. I develop this distinction at greater length in Price (2008), calling the two notions *e-representation* and *i-representation*, respectively.

internal sense is to do the job of representing in the external sense. It takes some effort to see that the two notions might float free of one another, but it is an effort worth making, in my view. The vista that opens up is the possibility that representation in the internal sense is a much richer, more flexible, and more multipurpose tool than the naive view always assumes.[14]

Once the distinction between these internal and external notions of representation is on the table, it is open to us to regard the two notions as having different utilities, for various theoretical purposes. In particular, it is open to us to take the view that at least by the time we get to language, there is no useful external notion, *of a semantic kind*—in other words, no useful, general, notion of relations that words and sentences bear to the external world, that we might usefully identify with truth and reference. This is the conclusion that a semantic deflationist has already come to, from the other direction, as it were. On this view, the impression that there are such external relations will be regarded as a kind of trick of language—a misunderstanding of the nature of the disquotational platitudes. But we can think this without rejecting the internal notion: without thinking that there is no interesting sense in which mental and linguistic representation are to be characterized and identified in terms of their roles in networks of various kinds.

Networks of what kinds? We may well want to distinguish several very different conceptions, at this point. According to one conception, the relevant kind of network is causal (or causal–functional) in nature. According to another, it is normative and inferential. According to a third, at least arguably distinct from the other two, it is computational.[15] But however it goes, the notion of representation

14. Once again, quasi-realism provides a useful stepping-stone. The quasi-realist is already committed to the idea that something can behave for all intents and purposes like a "genuine" belief, even though it has its origins at some "non-cognitive" level.

15. In this case (as I am grateful to Michael Slezak for pointing out to me), Chomsky provides an excellent example of someone who not only thinks of representations in this way, but is explicit that it need not be accompanied by a referential conception:

> As for semantics, insofar as we understand language use, the argument for a reference-based semantics (apart from an internalist syntactic version) seems to me weak. It is possible that natural language has only syntax and pragmatics; it has a "semantics" only in the sense of "the study of how this instrument, whose formal structure and potentialities of expression are the subject of syntactic investigation, is actually put to use in a speech community," to quote the earliest formulation in generative grammar 40 years ago, influenced by Wittgenstein, Austin, and others. [Chomsky 1975: Preface; 1957: 102–103]
>
> In this view, natural language consists of internalist computations and performance systems that access them along with much other information and belief, carrying out their instructions in particular ways to enable us to talk and communicate, among other things. There will be no provision for what Scott Soames calls "the central semantic fact about language, . . . that it is used to represent the world," because it is not assumed that language is used to represent the world, in the intended sense (Soames 1989, cited by Smith 1992 as the core issue for philosophers of language). (Chomsky 1995: 26–27)

involved can be divorced from any external notion of representation, thought of as a word–(natural-)world relation of some kind.

The sticker metaphor is useful again at this point. Think of these internal notions of representation as offering an account of what gives a sticker its propositional shape; what makes it the particular sticker that it is. As just mentioned, there are various possible versions of this internal account, but let us focus on the causal version, for the moment, for definiteness. And let us make explicit that the line drawing on the right-hand page depicts the world as seen by natural science.

The first possibility we need to call into view is that there may be a lot more stickers given shape by their internal causal roles than stickers whose truthmakers may be found on the right-hand page. Once again, quasi-realism is helpful to keep in mind at this point. Presumably, a quasi-realist maintains that our "quasi" beliefs—about morality, chance, or whatever—play very much the same roles in our internal cognitive economy as genuine beliefs (being distinguished mainly by characteristic *additional* functional links, in this case to action). Thus they are well-shaped stickers, despite matching no corresponding shape in the natural world.

Once we have reached this stage, we can progress to the mature view. The key step is a shift in our conception of our theoretical goals, a shift from the project of matching stickers to shapes in the natural world to the project of explaining (in natural world terms) how stickers obtain their characteristic shapes. Freed of the requirement that they must bear semantic relations to the natural world, stickers—or representations in the internal sense—can now occupy a new dimension of their own in the model, orthogonal to the natural world. Like the figures in our pop-up book, they stand up from their bases in the natural world, without being constrained to match or resemble anything found there.

Of course, a pop-up book does all the work for us, as we open the page. For a more illuminating metaphor, let us make the construction into a puzzle: a sort of three-dimensional jigsaw puzzle. We begin with a large collection of shapes or pieces, each one a statement we take to be true, and a large board or playing surface, depicting the natural world (in such a way as to give prominence to our own situation, as creatures with certain attributes and situation, within that world). In effect, our task is then to solve two kinds of puzzle simultaneously. We need to arrange subsets of the pieces into clusters, fitting them together so that, as in an ordinary jigsaw puzzle, the shape of each is defined by its relations to its neighbors (and eventually, perhaps, to the super-cluster of all the pieces). And we need to position each of the resulting clusters in the correct place on the board as a whole, so that its edges bear the right relations to particular features of the situation of the speakers (ourselves, in this case) who are depicted on the board.

Consider the pieces representing probabilistic statements, for example. They need to bear certain internal relations to one another, corresponding to the inferential or causal–functional links that define internal representations and their conceptual components in general. But they also need to bear the appropriate functional relations to the decision behavior depicted on the underlying board, in order to count as *probabilistic* statements at all. (In this case, in fact, the latter constraint is likely to involve an additional complexity. Roughly, the development of probabilistic concepts seems to enable, or perhaps go hand in hand with, a distinctive kind of cognitive architecture—let it be the Bayesian model of belief revision, for the sake of the example. This means that fitting the probabilistic pieces properly into the jigsaw requires that they display the appropriate alignment not simply with the behavior depicted on the board, but also with some general features of the architecture on view throughout the model as a whole.)

At least very roughly, then, the first stage of the puzzle is concerned with what makes a piece of the puzzle a *statement* at all. The second stage is concerned with pragmatic factors about its use that may play a crucial role in determining *what* statement it is—what its *content* is, as we would normally say. Missing altogether is the idea that the latter fact is determined by some matching to a shape already discernible in the natural world.

The upshot is a model in which there is a substantial *internal* notion of representation—a substantial theory as to what gives a piece or a pop-up figure its shape—but no substantial *external* notion of representation. As the model illustrates, moreover, internal notions of representation are not constrained by the cardinality of the natural world. So long as we find a role for pieces which is not that of matching outlines in the natural world, we can happily allow that there are many more pieces than available outlines. In effect, this is the original insight of expressivism and quasi-realism, here given a more attractive home, in a version of the picture in which external representation disappears altogether, for theoretical purposes.

Of course, the model still allows for a deflationary conception of the matching relation. Earlier, we thought of this conception by analogy to the version of the matching game in which the picture on the right was constructed by tracing around the outlines of the corresponding stickers on the left. Each statement identifies its own truthmaker, as Ramsey's horizontal ladder requires, with natural truthmakers in no sense distinguished. This works just as well in the new, richer model, in which the pieces themselves are given their shapes as structured artifacts in a natural world. If we imagine taking a photograph of the whole construction, we will be able to match pieces to that image, one by one. But there is no special role for the natural world, in this case—indeed, there is a much diminished role for the natural world, compared to the project of explaining the shapes and structures of the model in the first place.

11. Matching as Interpretation

There is another "deflationary" version of the matching game, played with two sheets of stickers from different designers. Here the aim is to match the two sets, sticker by sticker. We try to place the Opera House sticker from the left on the

Opera House sticker on the right—or at least on what we take to be the best candidate for an Opera House, in the strange and foreign graphical vocabulary of the stickers on the right.

This version of the game provides an analogy to the project of radical interpretation, as conceived by Quine and Davidson. I have introduced it to note that it, too, is blind to the cardinality difficulty, at least unless the two sheets concerned correspond to languages with very different conceptual resources. Matching sentences to sentences, the interpreter does not care about whether either matches some state of affairs in the natural world (unless it bears in some specific way on the available evidence, at least). Thus an interpretative notion of representation also counts as internal, in the relevant sense—a fact which goes hand in hand with the common view that the project of radical interpretation is compatible with deflationary views of truth and reference.[16]

The case of radical interpretation illustrates a way in which many of the concerns of philosophy of language seem relatively untouched by the kind of viewpoint I am recommending. Representationalism seems to play a less fundamental role than might be assumed at first sight. Consider a model-theoretic standpoint, for example. So long as we construct our models from the inside, as it were, formalizing the structures visible to us already as language users (like a child drawing lines around the outlines of her stickers), the entire process can be blind to the cardinality concerns—blind to the considerations that drive the placement concerns. These concerns only arise if we attempt to transform our model theory into a view of the relation of language to the natural world, in the Naturalist's sense. That transformation rests on Representationalism, but the model theory itself does not.

In a similar way, much of the formal machinery of philosophy of language seems entirely compatible with the present viewpoint, so long as it is thought of in this internal way, as formalizing and describing the structures and relations characteristic of language at the higher, homogeneous, level—the level that is blind to the underlying functional distinctions associated with the origins and roles of particular groups of concepts.

It may seem that a theory of this kind is bound to be a kind of sham. If I am right, after all, then it hides the underlying diversity, and does not speak to the interesting and various relations of language to the natural world. It is indeed bound to seem unsatisfactory, to some philosophical temperaments—to philosophers at home with the contemporary integration of metaphysics and philosophy of language; with the explicit attempt to study reality "through the lens of language," via truthmakers, reference relations, and the like. To philosophers of this temperament I have offered the hypothesis that their viewpoint rests on a mistake about language and its place in the natural world—a deep, first-order,

16. Compare chapter 10, section 5, and Williams (1999).

scientific mistake. (Again, this is just the familiar suggestion made by several generations of expressivists, but now cast in a more general and more stable form.) If the hypothesis is correct, then the approach of these philosophers (next to which the approach described above looks like a sham) is no real alternative at all.

My point is that reaching this conclusion need not mean throwing out the baby of philosophy of language, along with the bathwater of metaphysics. Admittedly, it will not always be easy to say where baby stops and bathwater begins. Finding the boundary is a big project, to which the present conclusions are merely a preliminary. As the case of interpretation illustrates, however, we can be confident that the boundary is there to be drawn, somewhere short of the entire contents of the bathtub.

12. Is Representationalism Obvious?

These distinctions help to clarify what is and is not entailed by a rejection of Representationalism. The guiding principle is that so long as an apparently Representationalist intuition trades only in the deflationary semantic notions, we anti-Representationalists have no reason to reject it.

Clarity on this point can go some way to address the incredulity that tends to greet the denial that language is representational. Frank Jackson, for example, remarks that "[a]lthough it is obvious that much of language is representational, it is occasionally denied," and goes on to observe that he has "attended conference papers attacking the representational view of language given by speakers who have in their pockets pieces of paper with writing on them that tell them where the conference dinner is and when the taxis leave for the airport." Jackson asks how this could happen, and suggests "that it is through conflating the obviously correct view that much of language is representational with various controversial views" (Jackson 1997: 270).

Jackson is quite right, in my view, that there is a danger of conflation, on one side of the case or other. For our part, we anti-Representationalists need to be clear that there is, indeed, a deflationary sense in which language conveys information. *Of course*, a sign affirming "P" may inform us that P. But so long as deflationism is on the table, there is no more reason to think that this fact needs to be explained in terms of robust word–(natural-)world relations—the meat of big-R Representationalism, which is what we anti-Representationalists are opposed to—than there is in the case of the corresponding disquotational platitudes. And it is easy to muster intuitions to the contrary. Imagine a sign, in some bleak campus cafeteria, conveying to conference participants the following information: *Clients are forbidden to place inorganic waste in the green bins*. The sentence mentions a (quasi?) commercial relationship, a color property, a prohibition, and some medium-sized dry(ish) goods: in one sense, then, at least four contributions to the information conveyed. Yet it can't be *obvious*, surely, that the contributions are pragmatically univocal; that an explanation of the information conveyed by the sign will simply bottom-out at the level of content—at the level of differences between clients, colors, prohibitions, and inorganic waste—leaving pragmatic factors no role to play?

Conventional Representationalism combines two assumptions about language and thought. The first (call it the "Content Assumption") is that language is a medium for encoding and passing around sentence-sized packets of factual information—the *contents* of beliefs and assertions. The second (call it the "Correspondence Assumption") is that these packets of information are all "about" some aspect of the external world, in much the same way. For each sentence, and each associated packet of information, there is an appropriately shaped aspect of the way the world is, or could be—namely, the state of affairs, or fact, that needs to obtain for the sentence to be true.

Once both assumptions are in place, it is natural to regard language as a medium for representing these sentence-sized aspects of the external environment, and passing around the corresponding packets of information from head to head. My rival proposal rests on pulling the two assumptions apart, replacing the Correspondence Assumption with a richer, more pluralistic, and non-semantic conception of the role of various kinds of linguistic information in our complex interaction with our environment. However, so long as we distinguish two notions of representation, as I recommended above, and allow the notion of information to go with the former, this proposal involves no challenge whatsoever to the view that language conveys information. About this, I agree with Jackson: it is obviously correct. My point is simply that it does not entail Representationalism, for it does not depend on the Correspondence Assumption—on the contrary, it is quite compatible with global expressivism.

13. A Telescope for Metaphysics?

In criticizing Representationalism, I am arguing, in effect, that would-be metaphysicians need to play close attention to language, for two closely related reasons. First, as expressivists have long urged, issues that seem at first sight to call for a metaphysical treatment may be best addressed in another key altogether. And second, even if metaphysics is thought to provide the right key, it is doubtful whether anything is to be gained by arranging the score for semantic instruments. Concerning both points, one moral is that would-be metaphysicians cannot afford to ignore some deep issues in philosophy of language.

In one sense, then, I am very much on the same page with Timothy Williamson, who, in a recent paper about the role of linguistic issues in philosophy, criticizes metaphysicians who believe they have nothing to learn from the philosophy of language:

> Some contemporary metaphysicians appear to believe that they can safely ignore formal semantics and the philosophy of language because their interest is in a largely extra-mental reality. They resemble an astronomer who thinks that he can safely ignore the physics of telescopes because his interest is in the extra-terrestrial universe. In delicate matters, his attitude makes him all the more likely to project features of his telescope confusedly onto the stars beyond. (Williamson 2004: 127–128)

In another sense, however, I am on a very different page. For Williamson's central metaphor gives vivid and approving expression to the Representationalist conception, which I want to reject. As Brian Leiter glosses Williamson's point, in his introduction to the volume in which Williamson's paper appears, "[l]anguage is for the philosopher what the telescope is for the astronomer: the instrument by which the investigator makes contact with his 'real' subject-matter" (Leiter 2004: 6). With this conception in place, Williamson's and Leiter's lesson is a caution for philosophical practice. We should not take the capabilities of our telescopes for granted—"instruments, unless they are well-understood, can corrupt our understanding of the 'reality' to which they are our means of access" (Leiter 2004: 6–7).

Presumably, the opponents Williamson and Leiter have in mind make one of two mistakes. Either they imagine that we can get at reality "directly," without the need of a linguistic lens; or they think that such a lens is so transparent that no issue of distortion can arise. In the present context, however, it should be clear that there is another opponent in the vicinity, to whom Williamson's metaphor simply turns a blind eye. For the metaphor compares language to a representational instrument; whereas, as we have seen, it is a recurring theme among linguistic philosophers that it is precisely the representational conception which leads philosophy astray, at least in certain cases.

This kind of opponent will endorse the sentiment that linguistic instruments, poorly understood, "can corrupt our understanding of 'reality.'" Indeed, in suggesting that Williamson's and Leiter's own view embodies a misguided conception of the functions of language, she will endorse the sentiment more vigorously than they themselves do. She will allow, presumably, that language is an instrument of some kind, an organ that we humans use in negotiating our physical environment. But she will insist that it does not follow that language is necessarily a *representational* instrument—at least in the manner, and cases, supposedly of relevance to metaphysics.

Of course, some versions of this position—familiar versions of expressivism, in particular—will differ at most in degree from the kind of view that Williamson has in mind. They will allow that language is at least sometimes "telescopic," even if the distortions and projections are more significant and wide-ranging than it seems at first sight. As I've emphasized, however, there's also a more systematic version of the view, holding that the representational conception is unhelpful *tout court*, at least as a tool for metaphysics. From this viewpoint, characterizing language as the telescope of metaphysics looks like a symptom of a fundamental philosophical error.

But if language is not a telescope, then what is it? As Brandom points out, a traditional expressivist option is the lamp.[17] I think that modern technology allows us to make this a little more precise. Think of a data projector, projecting internal images onto an external screen. Even better, helping ourselves to one of tomorrow's metaphors, think of a holographic data projector, projecting three-dimensional images in thin air. This isn't projection *onto* an external, unembellished world.[18] On the contrary, the entire image is free-standing, being simply the sum of all we take to be the case: a world of states of affairs, in all the ways that we take states of affairs to be.

At this point a newcomer (occupying a stance we ourselves cannot take up, perhaps) might notice that the projector contains an internal screen, the shapes on which match those in the external image, and conclude that the device is a telescope. Obviously, this gets things backward, however. The facts seem to resemble the statements because the former are the projected image of the latter, not vice versa—the transparency is that of semantic descent, of Ramsey's ladder.

This may sound like a recipe for implausible idealism, so it is worth emphasizing again its naturalistic credentials. The new model sits squarely within the project of understanding human linguistic usage, as a form of behavior by natural creatures in a natural environment. But to see this, we need to be careful to distinguish the new model from the one we used to depict this explanatory project. The two models line up, more or less, on the left-hand side, where we find the page of stickers, or the projector's internal screen. Here, in each case, we have the raw data of linguistic usage, or at least some suitably selected subset of linguistic

17. Brandom notes that "to the Enlightenment picture of mind as a *mirror*, Romanticism opposed an image of the mind as a *lamp*. Broadly cognitive activity was to be seen not as a kind of passive reflection but as a kind of active revelation" (2000: 8). Brandom here cites M. H. Abrams' classic (1953) study of these two themes in the critical tradition. Abrams himself provides examples of the use of the lamp metaphor not only by Romantic poets such as Coleridge and Wordsworth, but also by the "effusive" Edinburgh essayist, "Christopher North" (John Wilson). Wilson held the Chair of Moral Philosophy at Edinburgh, for which Hume had earlier been thought too irreligious, and seems to have shared Hume's antipathies, in this respect; *The Scotsman* called him a "mocker of the Scriptures," whose appointment would be "an outrage on public decency without parallel since Caligula made his horse a Consul." (Sharing Hume's tastes in another respect, he was a haggis-maker of some repute, whose recipe for "a sauce for meat and game" was preserved by Mrs. Beeton for future generations.) Concerning the mind's lamp-like qualities, Wilson says that, as is "well known, . . . we create nine-tenths at least of what appears to exist externally . . . Millions of supposed matters-of-fact are the wildest fictions—of which we may mention merely two, the rising and the setting of the sun" (Wilson 1832: 721). For present purposes, I think we do better to build on Hume's rather more disciplined projectivism—even if updating his metaphor, too, in the way I shall explain, to cope with the demands of globalization.

18. This is how it differs from Hume's "gilding and staining"—a difference required by the global nature of the present view.

usage, such as the (apparently) assertoric uses, or the statements held true within the community in question.

But the two models differ on the right. In the new model, what lies on the right is the holographic image, a metaphor for the world in the most general sense, *as the language users in question take it to be*—the sum of all they take to be the case (and thus, as the metaphor has it, a projection of their usage). In the relevant naturalistic version of the original sticker model, however, we have something different on the right: the natural world, as viewed from the scientific standpoint—the context within which we seek to *explain* the linguistic behavior displayed on the left.[19]

Crudely put—ignoring, for example, all the obvious grounds for holism—the explanatory project goes something like this. We find our speakers disposed to say "P" (i.e., "P" appears in the list of statements on the left of the model). We now ask, "Why do they say that?"; and in general (without pretending that this distinction is sharp) we look for an explanation that refers both to features of the speakers, and to features of their natural environment. Note that in our own case, this attitude always looks sideways-on, or ironic. We say that P, and then wonder *why* we said so, how we came to be making a claim of that kind—looking for something deeper as an answer, of course, than merely, "'Because we realized that P." (This is the kind of irony characteristic of practitioners of the human sciences, of course, who cannot help but view themselves as examples their own objects of inquiry.)

In a somewhat more abstract form, the project becomes that of explaining the function and genealogy of our (internal) representations—that is, of the linguistic items we characterize as representations in whatever version of the internal sense (e.g., causal–functional, or inferential) we have in play. In the general case, as before, we expect explanatory contributions both from our speakers' own nature and characteristics, and from their natural environment; and a complex, relational story about the significance of the mix. (Again, think of Humean expressivism about value or causation as a model.) As I have emphasized, we should also expect to appeal to some general account of the role and significance of the cognitive or logical architecture, in virtue of which the items in question constitute representations, in the internal sense.

At least in the first place, then, this project regards language not as a telescope for metaphysics, but as the primary explanandum of a first-order scientific investigation: the project of understanding our own linguistic behavior, and associated aspects of our cognitive lives, as characteristics of natural creatures in a natural environment. As we have known (in some sense) since the seventeenth century, this project requires that we consider our own contribution to our own commitments, as well as that of our environment. The project thus has a pay-off, closer to

19. Note that this version of the naturalistic model is different in turn from the Naturalist's version of the original matching game, where the task was to match stickers to *truthmakers* in the natural world.

the traditional concerns of metaphysics. We get a less perspectival view of the world by subtraction, as it were, by asking "What kind of world looks like *this* from *here*?"—where the "this" refers to our commitments, to the holographic image, and the "here" to our natural situation, broadly construed.

In one sense, this sounds a lot like Williamson's and Leiter's project, but it has a rather more ironic flavor. We no longer see the philosopher's task as to join the folk in peering *through* the linguistic telescope (contributing simply a heightened sensitivity to possible distortions). Rather, we treat its folk output as the starting point for a new inquiry, which has both anthropological and physical aspects. The theoretical framework is more rigorously naturalistic, in the explanatory sense, and by its own lights, much less naive. In particular, because governed by a more rigorous naturalism about ourselves, it is less willing to postulate metaphysical primitives, simply to allow us to take our own commitments at (what Representationalism takes to be their) face value. The default assumption is always that they should not be taken at their face value—that their face value is a sum of two components, one grounded in us, the other in the natural world.

14. The Status of Science

We might hope to be able to relax this ironic assumption, at some point. Eventually, perhaps, the human component might be entirely pruned away. We would have carved the world itself from the holographic image, as it were, and be left with a bare description of nature.

In practice, however, I think there are strong reasons for thinking that this limit is out of reach—that the contribution on our side never goes to zero. The deepest reasons are associated with the rule-following considerations. In my view, these considerations reveal that wherever generality matters, our judgments depend on dispositions to "go on in the same way" in some particular way. These dispositions might have been different, and hence constitute an ineliminable contingency in our linguistic standpoint. (These issues arise at several points in these essays, and most extensively in chapter 7.)

What does this mean for science itself? Here, my proposal may seem to confront a dilemma. Either science is privileged, and non-perspectival, in which we seem to recover something like genuine representation after all (thus saving Representationalism, apparently, at least in this pared-down scientific form). Or we have to be ironic and perspectival about science, too; and that might seem to count as some kind of self-undermining, on science's part.

Pushing toward the first horn, it might seem that natural science is automatically privileged in the kind of picture I have been describing. In the case of other frameworks, after all, the project is to explain in naturalistic terms why creatures of our kind, in our circumstances, have come to employ those frameworks: why creatures like us should have come to employ normative vocabulary, for example.

In this case, the explanation is not going to appeal to preexisting norms, presumably. Yet in the case of the frameworks we employ for talking about the natural world itself, things must surely be different—the natural entities themselves get cast in explanatory roles. Is the project not therefore committed to according a special status to these entities, by its own lights?

In my view, the right response to this challenge (see chapter 6, section 5) is to acknowledge that scientific ontology is privileged *from the standpoint of the present project*—how could it not be, since the project involves a first-order scientific reflection on our own linguistic practice?—but to deny that this conclusion has the significance the objector claims for it. Science is only one of the games we play with language. Each game privileges its own ontology, no doubt, but the privilege is merely perspectival. Science is privileged "by its own lights," but to mistake this for an absolute ontological priority would be to mistake science for metaphysics, or first philosophy.

Moreover, science is certainly not privileged in the sense that the project cannot turn its spotlight on the language of science itself. On the contrary, I have already emphasized that the expressivism of my view is intended to be global, and in any case to cast light on such particular matters as the use of modal notions, of general concepts, and of a norm of truth. All of these matters seem at least as much in play in scientific language as in any other.

At this point, however, the second horn of the dilemma may seem threatening. If the language of science is not exempt, does the ironic viewpoint not become self-undermining, unable to take itself seriously? These are difficult issues, but I suspect that the threat is to a particular philosophical conception of science, rather than to the scientific enterprise itself. If we equate science with the perspective-free standpoint, the view from nowhere, then science so conceived is certainly under threat. But why not see this simply as a challenge from within science to a particular philosophical conception of science?

To make the case more concrete, suppose (as I have recommended elsewhere—see, e.g., Price 1991a, 2001, 2007b; Menzies and Price 1993) that we were to accept a perspectival genealogy for causation and related notions. This would be a scientific account of a particular aspect of human cognitive and linguistic practice, explaining its origins and function in terms of certain characteristics of ourselves (especially, the fact that we are *agents*, embedded in time in a particular way). A corollary would be that uses of causal concepts in science (including, indeed, in this very explanation) would be held to reflect the same agentive perspective. Some aspects of current scientific practice would thus be revealed *by science* to be practices that only "make sense" from this embedded viewpoint.

Would this be a fundamental challenge to science, a case of science undermining its own foundations? Not at all, in my view. On the contrary, it would simply be continuous with a long scientific tradition, in which science deflates the metaphysical pretensions of its practitioners, by revealing new ways in which they are less god-like than they thought. Some of the greatest triumphs of science have been new ways of showing us how insignificant we are, from the world's point of view—how idiosyncratic the standpoint from which we attempt to make sense of it. We humans may find these lessons unsettling, but science seems to have thrived on this diet of self-imposed humility. Why should the present case be any different?

True, this is hardly a decisive refutation of the kind of skeptical threat that may seem to lurk in the region of the second horn of our dilemma. It is fair to point out that science has been thought to face such threats before, and pulled through in fine shape. But fair, also, to reply that this time it might be worse. The debate is admittedly inconclusive, but my kind of naturalist has one more card to play. Even if the recommended explanatory program were a deep threat to science, in the way that the skeptic imagines, that could hardly count as a reason for counting its conclusions *false*—deeply regrettable, perhaps, but that is a different matter altogether!

15. Naturalism Without Mirrors

The view proposed in these essays may seem radical, for it is certainly not popular, or well-marked in the contemporary philosophical landscape. In another sense, however, it involves no great departure from familiar ideas, for it is simply the place where some comparatively familiar paths turn out to converge. Indeed, my case for challenging Representationalism may be summarized in four simple steps. First, semantic deflationism already challenges Representationalism, by refusing to allow any substantial theoretical role or content to the semantic properties and relations. Second, the placement problems also turn out to challenge Representationalism, in the sense that expressivism and quasi-realism provide an attractive solution to some of these problems, but a solution of which a challenge to Representationalism turns out to be a consequence, when the considerations in question are pushed to their natural limits.

Third, arguments to the contrary at this point are either misdirected (I am thinking here of the attempt to use semantic deflationism against expressivism, which, as noted in section 8, actually counts against Representationalism), or appeal to theoretical resources that are nowhere in sight, such as a well-grounded criterion for a genuinely "descriptive" statement. Finally, a viable defense of Representationalism would have to rest on an adequate theory of notions such as belief, assertion, commitment, and judgment. But here, too, there are reasons to think that the most promising approaches will not respect Representationalism, being grounded on internal conceptions of representation, in the sense of section 10, rather than external, world-tracking notions.

If there is a single key point, it goes something like this. Insofar as our claims are representational, it seems plausible to assume that they are uniformly representational, whatever the subject matter—in other words, that representation is a univocal notion, in this sense. But if representation is viewed as relation to our natural environment, univocity leads to the placement problem in an acute form. The problem is solved by abandoning the external notion of representation in favor of an internal notion; by recognizing that the grip of the alternative picture rests in large part on the disquotational platitudes; and by insisting that we theorize about our relations to our natural environment in a different, non-semantic vocabulary. So long as we practice our naturalism in another key—in the pragmatic, functional dimension that opens up when we abandon Representationalism—we retain univocity where it matters, while avoiding the placement problems altogether.

So, where do we stand, if we take this approach seriously? In one sense, as I said, we find ourselves among well-known landmarks. Close at hand are the Humean intuition that metaphysical puzzles tend to arise from mistakes about the genealogy of our beliefs and commitments; familiar forms of semantic and metaphysical deflationism; and the resources of an inferentialist account of assertion. Our destination turns out to be easily reached from any of these familiar viewpoints, for it is simply the region on the map where they all intersect. To find it, however, we had to remove the obstacle that has been hiding it from view. We had to move the mirror aside.[20]

20. I am grateful to Bob Brandom, Patrick Greenough, Jenann Ismael, Uriah Kriegel, Luca Moretti, Richard Rorty, Kevin Scharp, Lionel Shapiro, and Michael Williams for comments on earlier versions of this chapter.

2

Metaphysical Pluralism

Hume is the Saint Francis of modern metaphysics, the patron saint of ontological ascetics. The devout Humean takes the pinnacle of metaphysical virtue to be a world in which the only facts are the mundane first-order physical facts about how things actually are—"a vast mosaic of local matters of particular fact, just one little thing and then another," as David Lewis puts it (1986a: ix). Hume's own ontological austerity derives in part from his empiricism, in part from the great medieval Fransciscan metaphysician, William of Ockham, and in part no doubt from canny inclinations of his native land. Whatever its original sources, however, the doctrine remains enormously influential. The Humean ideal continues to exert great force in contemporary philosophy.

However, like prosperous Franciscans, many metaphysicians who pay lip service to the virtues of ontological economy have strayed from the true path. The Hume world has frequently been judged too cramped. Some lapsed Humeans extend the bare Humean structure to fit in modal facts; some extend it to fit in subjective experience or intentional mental states; others to fit in moral facts; and so on. The common theme is that a respectable metaphysics simply cannot survive on the bare regime that Hume prescribes.

Now the galling thing about a prosperous Franciscan is not the fact that he is not suffering the discomforts of poverty, or not this as such. It is his moral inconsistency, the fact that he claims virtue while failing to live according to his own professed conception of the virtuous life. There are two ways to challenge this inconsistency. One is to demonstrate to the Franciscan that he could make do with less, and hence establish that by his own lights he is not leading the pious life. This is in effect the strategy of those who dispute the need for particular extensions to the Hume world, arguing that the purpose such extensions serve can be met in some less extravagant manner.[1] The alternative deflationary strategy is more subtle. It is to accept the case for the extensions, for the Franciscan's additional consumption, but to point out that the consequence of accepting this is to

1. A recent example is Bas van Fraassen's (1990) critique of contemporary non-Humean accounts of modality.

undermine the minimalist conception of a virtuous lifestyle. In accepting that the Franciscan is fully entitled to satisfaction of the normal human appetites, in other words, we undercut his claim to abnormal piety.

It may not be obvious that there is any analogous move in the metaphysical case. In this chapter I want to show that there is, and to suggest that this has profound consequences for our understanding of a range of contemporary metaphysical debates. Roughly, its effect is to undercut the distinction between various non-Humean forms of metaphysical realism and something akin to a Wittgensteinian linguistic pluralism. To the extent that the distinction can be drawn, moreover, the latter is the default position. So not only is this form of pluralism an important and widely neglected option in a range of contemporary metaphysical debates; it actually has claim to be the preeminent option. In a sense I shall explain, it is the philosophical geodesic, the course from which no one is entitled to depart without good reason. The chapter thus presents a challenge to the lapsed Humeans of contemporary metaphysics: Embrace worldly pluralism, or return to the pure faith, for there is no virtuous middle way!

The chapter is in five main sections. Section 1 identifies our target species of pluralism, and distinguishes it from a more common species. In section 2, I consider this target species in relation to a variety of anti-pluralist rivals, including in particular the monist doctrine, which seems to be the intended position of the lapsed Humeans; and I draw attention to the central issue of the chapter, namely as to whether there is actually a tenable distinction between this monist position and our target pluralism. Section 3 argues that despite the avowedly ontological nature of their concerns, these lapsed Humeans cannot avoid reliance on a certain semantic distinction—essentially, the distinction between descriptive and non-descriptive uses of language—and points out that this puts them at least at a prima facie disadvantage compared to the pluralists, who need no such distinction. Section 4 then outlines a case for thinking that the required distinction cannot be drawn, and draws attention to some connections between the resulting sort of pluralism and certain other recent approaches to the same metaphysical topics. And in section 5 I illustrate the advantages and character of such a pluralism with reference to the issue between realists and their instrumentalist critics; perhaps surprisingly, this rather Wittgensteinian pluralism turns out to provide an especially secure brand of realism.

1. Two Kinds of Philosophical Pluralism

One familiar kind of philosophical pluralism is exemplified by Quine's brand of ontological relativity, and perhaps in a different way by other forms of scientific relativism. Here the plurality consists in the possible existence of a range of alternative scientific worldviews, each empirically adequate to more or less the same degree, and none, even in principle, having privileged claim to provide a "truer" description of the world. This form of pluralism itself comes in several varieties or sub-species, of course. The distinction between Quine's variety and Kuhnian scientific relativism may well be a deep one, for example (see Romanos 1983). However, for present purposes what matters is something that these views have in common, namely that the plurality they admit involves a range of different ways of doing the same kind of thing, *of performing the same linguistic task*. There may be many equally valid possible scientific worldviews, but all of them are scientific worldviews, and in that sense are on the same level of linguistic activity. In other words, this is what might appropriately be called *horizontal* pluralism.

Horizontal pluralism is far from confined to this scientific level. It is a product of certain kinds of relativism, and so may be found wherever these flourish. In ethics, for example, it is the familiar thesis that there is a range of equally coherent moral viewpoints, none objectively superior to any other. Why is this a case of *horizontal* pluralism? Again, because the plurality it envisages is confined to a single linguistic plane or level. Different moral systems are all nevertheless *moral* systems. They have something in common, in virtue of which they may be counted to be different ways of performing the same linguistic task. It may be a very nice question how this something in common is to be properly characterized, but it must have an answer, if relativism is not to degenerate into the trivial point that the same words may mean different things for different people.

If these are cases of horizontal pluralism, what would be a vertical pluralism? It would be the view that philosophy should recognize an irreducible plurality of *kinds* of discourse—the moral as well as the scientific, for example. This is the species of pluralism with which we are going to be most concerned. (I shall mainly use the term *discourse pluralism*.) I want to show that it provides a natural if not initially a congenial home for the lapsed Humean.

The plurality of forms of discourse, or "language-games," is a prominent theme in the later Wittgenstein. This remark is typical: "We remain unconscious of the prodigious diversity of all the everyday language-games because the clothing of our language makes everything alike" (Wittgenstein 1968: 224; see §§23–24 for similar remarks). There also seems to be a strong element of discourse pluralism in the American pragmatist tradition, of which Goodman and Rorty are the most prominent recent representatives. True, Goodman and Rorty's pluralism is not exclusively vertical. It also contains a strong horizontal or relativistic element. However, the fact that the vertical component is significant in its own right is manifest in the contrast between the positions of Goodman or Rorty on the one hand, and Quine on the other. Quine at times seems close to a purely horizontal pluralism, to the view that all factual discourse is either eliminable or reducible to physical discourse. This view acknowledges that there might be alternative physical discourses—"alternative physical theories, insusceptible to adjudication," as Quine puts it (1981: 98)—but says that there is nothing else at any other level.

And certainly Quine rejects Goodman's proposal to admit on an equal footing a multiplicity of further "world versions," such as those of art and music, saying that in his view "this sequence of worlds or versions founders in absurdity" (Quine 1981: 97–98).

More accurately, however, Quine himself is non-physicalist to the extent of accepting the existence of certain abstract objects, such as classes and numbers. This is not to say that he intends to be a discourse pluralist. On the contrary, he is critical of the proposal to regard the acceptance of such objects as in some sense radically unlike the acceptance of physical objects:

> There are philosophers who stoutly maintain that "true" said of logical or mathematical laws and "true" said of weather predictions or suspects' confessions are two uses of an ambiguous term "true." There are philosophers who stoutly maintain that "exists" said of numbers, classes and the like and "exists" said of material objects are two uses of an ambiguous term "exists." What mainly baffles me is the stoutness of their maintenance. What can they possibly count as evidence? Why not view "true" as unambiguous but very general, and recognize the difference between true logical laws and true confessions as a difference merely between logical laws and confessions? And correspondingly for existence? (Quine 1960: 27)

Later I want to argue that this point backfires. Discourse pluralism is the default position in this debate, and doesn't need to be defended by appealing to a claimed ambiguity in "true" or "exists." On the contrary, it is the discourse pluralist's opponent who needs to appeal to some suitably "thick" or substantial unity in these notions—and Quine's preferred thin notions are not up to the task. Hence I want to suggest that Quine himself might best be recast as a discourse pluralist about abstract objects. He thus exemplifies what I shall argue to be the predicament of many would-be non-Humean realists in contemporary philosophy. (The striking thing about Quine's case is that his predicament stems from his own minimalism about truth and existence.)

The first task is to mark off discourse pluralism from a range of other ways of dealing with the same philosophical topics.

2. Discourse Pluralism and Its Rivals

As a distinctive philosophical doctrine, discourse pluralism is perhaps best understood in terms of what it denies, in terms of the contrasts it tries to establish with other philosophical treatments of problematic topics. In this section I describe four such contrasts. I distinguish a pluralist treatment of a philosophical topic from four other approaches: reductionism; two forms of irrealism; and lastly a

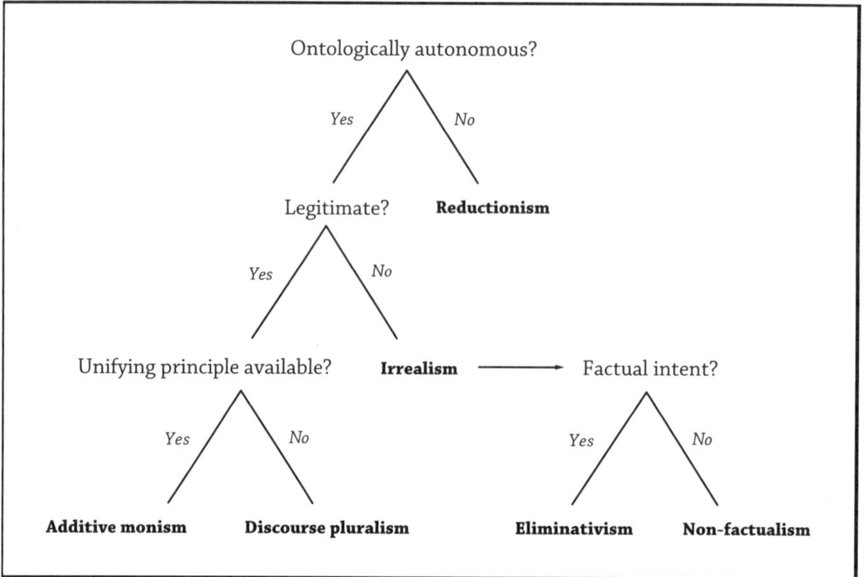

Figure 2.1. **A discourse status quiz.**

view I call *additive monism*, which is the intended position of non-Humean metaphysicians. (Later our main interest will be in the question whether an additive monist can resist reconstitution as a discourse pluralist.)

To establish the general framework, consider a problematic topic against the background of an unproblematic topic—morality against the background of natural science, say. Assume for simplicity that the status of the background topic is not at issue. Our first group of distinctions rest on different combinations of answers to two questions about the status of the problematic topic. First question: Is its (purported) subject matter distinct from that of the background discourse? Second question: Is the problematic topic fully legitimate, again by whatever standards may properly be applied to the background discourse? (What is meant by "legitimate" here will become clearer as we proceed.) In terms of our example then: Is the subject matter of moral discourse distinct from that of natural science?[2] And is it a fully legitimate discourse, or does it in some way fall short?

2. There has been much discussion as to whether there are autonomous levels of explanation in science. Those who argue that there are such levels commonly insist that, nevertheless, physics has ontological priority. Functionalists about the mental will often profess to ontological physicalism, for example, though claiming that psychology involves autonomous modes of description of (certain special arrangements of) physical entities or properties. For present purposes I shall assume that this ontological criterion is capable of bearing the weight, and hence that such a view does count as a form of reductionism in the sense of figure 2.1 (in contrast, say, to Cartesian dualism). If this assumption were to prove untenable, then I think the defenders of multiple levels of description, like those I am calling lapsed Humeans, would be hard pressed to distinguish their view from a discourse pluralism about the scientific hierarchy.

Discourse pluralism answers "yes" to both questions, and hence may be distinguished from views that answer "no" to one or other (and also from the less interesting view, which I won't mention further, which answers "no" to both). The first contrast is therefore with *reductionism*, which concedes autonomy in order to save legitimacy. (We are at the first level in the tree shown in figure 2.1.) The reductionist agrees with the discourse pluralist about the legitimacy of moral discourse, but seeks to secure it by denying the ontological distinctness of its subject matter. On the contrary, the reductionist argues, morality is a branch of natural science—a fact that is obscured, in practice, simply by our usual ignorance of the appropriate identities between moral facts and natural facts. For the reductionist moral discourse is legitimate because it actually is natural discourse, albeit disguised natural discourse.[3] A pluralist wants both autonomy and legitimacy, whereas a reductionist is prepared to sacrifice the former in the interests of the latter. (The reductionist may not view it as a sacrifice, of course.)

Our next contrast is with two views that make the alternative sacrifice, conceding ground on legitimacy in order to preserve autonomy. They concede ground in very different ways, and we shall need to treat them separately. However, the fact that they both do so in some sense is a reason to deal with them under a common heading.

Irrealism thus comes in two main forms. The first is *eliminativism*, the approach famously exemplified in Mackie's *error theory* of moral discourse (1977). In effect, the eliminativist holds that a problematic area of discourse *tries* to be legitimate, as well as autonomous; but that it fails to connect with anything in reality, and so is systematically false. The problematic topic is thus legitimate in intent, but fails in the execution of that intent. Mackie notwithstanding, eliminativism has not been particularly popular among moral philosophers. There are more familiar cases elsewhere, however. It has recently become a prominent approach to intentional psychology, for example. And Quine has long been seen as an eliminativist about meaning (and hence at least in some respects about psychology).

The second form of irrealism—*non-factualism*, as I shall call it—is much more popular. It is the approach that preserves the autonomy of disputed topics by giving ground on their factual character. So whereas the eliminativist holds that moral discourse tries to be factual, but fails to connect, the non-factualist denies that moral claims are ever intended to be factual claims. They don't fail to connect, for their linguistic role is not to attempt to connect. What it is instead is a matter of some interest, of course. In the moral case the traditional options are the *expressive* or *emotivist* view, namely that moral judgments express certain sorts of evaluative psychological attitudes; and the *prescriptivist* view, which treats a moral assertion as something approaching a command.

Non-factualism is a very common doctrine. Apart from the moral case, the approach is also well-known in application to aesthetic judgments, mathematical

3. Bear in mind that the relevant notion of reduction is an ontological one; see the previous note.

statements, theoretical sentences in science, secondary qualities, knowledge claims, psychology more generally, meaning ascriptions, indicative and subjunctive conditionals, and probabilistic, causal, and modal judgments. (No doubt I have missed some.) Not always well appreciated are some of the basic philosophical commitments of any such position. It is clear that such a view is committed to the existence of a significant distinction between factual and non-factual uses of language. Perhaps not so obvious is the obligation that the non-factualist incurs as a result of this, namely to account for the fact that non-factual uses of language can present themselves as factual uses, at least superficially.

The contemporary philosopher who has done most to acknowledge and to try to meet this obligation is Simon Blackburn (see, e.g., Blackburn 1984, 1993a). Drawing on Hume's idea that we project our attitudes and prejudices onto the world, and so see it as populated by seeming facts of our own construction, Blackburn has argued that the non-factualist can explain our conversing as if there really were such facts. He has tried to show that the projectivist is entitled to a notion of truth, and to the other trappings of a realist linguistic practice. Thus projectivism supports *quasi-realism*, as Blackburn calls it. Couched in these terms, the non-factualist's concessions concerning the legitimacy of a disputed topic are now very muted. To be sure, moral discourse (or whatever) is not *really* factual; but it has and is entitled to all the trappings of factuality, all the appearances of legitimacy. So although on this view there is only one real world, only one realm of *genuine* facts, our language quite properly works as if there were many.[4] If this is not already discourse pluralism, then what separates it is the availability of a substantial distinction between factual and non-factual uses of language. If that goes, non-factualism is no longer a distinct alternative to discourse pluralism.

So much for the distinction between discourse pluralism and the various views that differ from it in denying either the autonomy or the legitimacy of a problematic area of discourse. We now turn to a contrast not marked by a disagreement on either of these issues, namely the distinction between discourse pluralism and the doctrine that I call *additive monism*. Additive monism agrees with discourse pluralism in rejecting reductionism and both forms of irrealism, accepting that multiple domains of discourse may each be autonomous and yet fully legitimate. The disagreement is only about how these separate domains are to be construed. The additive monist regards them as sub-domains of a *single* universe of facts—not a single *physical* universe, presumably, for that would be to concede the game to a physicalist reductionism, but single in some sense. What distinguishes additive monism from discourse pluralism is the claim that there is something that unifies the various autonomous discourses; what distinguishes it from reductive physicalism,

4. Why not say "... as if this realm were more inclusive than it actually is," so that the alternative to non-factualism becomes additive monism? Here I anticipate a little—we shall see that the availability of a substantial distinction between factual and non-factual uses of language turns out to be a requirement for the additive monist, as much as for the non-factualist.

the claim that whatever this unifying principle is, it is not that all facts are ultimately physical facts.

It is natural to wonder whether there is a real distinction between discourse pluralism and additive monism, or whether the apparent issue rests on an empty metaphor. And if there isn't a real distinction, how is the single resulting position best described? These neglected questions are of enormous importance to a wide range of current philosophical debates. For additive monism seems the intended home of the lapsed Humeans with whom we began—of contemporary non-Humean approaches to such topics as diverse as causation, modality, the mental, abstract objects, morality, and so on. On the face of it, these accounts argue that there are more kinds of facts in the world than the Hume world admits—facts about causal relations, over and above facts about constant conjunction, for example. The proponents of these views do not think of themselves as Wittgensteinian pluralists, of course. But it is not clear that there is conceptual space for any other position. The additive monist needs to show that something unifies the various autonomous discourses. Failing this, pluralism is the default option—what the would-be monist must fall back to if the distinction cannot be maintained. Thus I want to argue that it is much harder not to be a Wittgensteinian pluralist than many people have assumed. Since a pluralism of this kind explicitly abandons Humean metaphysical minimalism, its effect here is deflationary—it undermines the Humean conception of metaphysical virtue.

The issue turns on the availability of a unifying principle. What might the additive monist appeal to at this point?

3. A Principled Monism?

A first thought might be that supervenience will do the trick. Perhaps additive monism corresponds to the view that a problematic topic is supervenient on a non-problematic background (though not reducible to it); and discourse pluralism to the more extreme version of autonomy involved in denying both reducibility and supervenience between discourses. However, a little reflection shows that this won't do the job. There are counterexamples in both directions. Non-Humean metaphysicians commonly deny that facts about laws, causation, and the like are supervenient on first-order matters of particular fact (see, e.g., Armstrong 1983).[5] Conversely, it is far from clear that a pluralist need deny supervenience. A nice counterexample may be extracted from Blackburn's discussion of moral supervenience (1971, 1984, 1985). Blackburn argues that his projectivist quasi-realism not only accounts for moral supervenience, but is especially well adapted to doing

5. It is my contention that these views would be better explicitly recast in terms of discourse pluralism, but clearly they are not intended as such.

so. It is true that quasi-realism is not a form of discourse pluralism. But I think it differs mainly in assuming that some stronger form of realism is appropriate elsewhere, for (at least some) non-moral topics. So we would have a form of discourse pluralism if we abandoned this assumption, and thus extended quasi-realism "all the way down." At the same time we would still be entitled to Blackburn's account of moral supervenience, for this rests simply on the idea that moral discourse projects evaluative attitudes. Hence it seems that supervenience is independent of the issue between discourse pluralism and additive monism.

With supervenience out of the way, the next suggestion may be that additive monism is primarily a metaphysical doctrine, whereas discourse pluralism is primarily linguistic. The monist maintains that the autonomous domains of facts are all part of a single universe or *metaphysical* totality; whereas the pluralist seems to be denying the unity of factual *language*, opting instead for the view that a variety of different uses of language share certain superficial characteristics—Wittgenstein's common clothing of the diversity of language-games. (What are these characteristics? More on this in a moment.) But although this certainly distinguishes the two doctrines in terms of their natural characterizations, it does not exclude the possibility that they come to the same thing. After all, the pluralist may well take the view that metaphysics itself is a manifestation of the superficial clothing of language, and derives its apparent unity from this very source. Thus if metaphysics is essentially a concern with ontology, with "what there is," and this issue is seen in Quinean terms, then metaphysics and grammar become inseparable. Ontology is a matter of quantification, and this is precisely the sort of linguistic feature that the pluralist might take to be an element of the superficial clothing of language, serving similar grammatical purposes in discourses whose underlying functions in language are widely varied. (Analogous remarks would apply to truth.)

Monists might object at this point that they have a more substantial ontological principle in mind, and that their dispute with discourse pluralism turns largely on the question of our entitlement to some such notion. I think that this is on the right lines, but that it leaves out an important part of the story. The dispute cannot be entirely ontological, but must have a semantic or linguistic dimension. For the metaphysical view requires that there be a non-trivial sense in which the various discourses to which it applies are all serving the same linguistic function. It requires that they are all *descriptive* in the same sense, that they share a common goal of truth, a common concern to portray the facts as they are. It is not enough for the monist that there be a unified world out there; it is also crucial that within each disputed part of language, statements stand in the same relation to the relevant part of the single world. Otherwise, monism is trivial: it is easy to find a unified world to which every use of language relates *in some sense*. The monist requires that it always be *the same sense*. So monism needs a common semantic theory, as well as a unified world.

The monist might simply begin at this semantic level, of course, professing a concern with *truth*, *the facts*, or some such thing (again claiming to construe this semantic notion in a substantial way, incompatible with the pluralist's suggestion that these concepts belong to the superficial common layer of language). However, my point is that even if the commitment does not begin at this semantic level, *it must get there in the end*. In effect, the monist needs a distinction between factual discourse—the kind that does or is intended to describe a part of a metaphysical totality—and non-factual discourse, the kind that is not so intended.[6]

This obligation may seem to fall as much on the discourse pluralist as on the additive monist. However, I think there is an important asymmetry—the onus here lies predominantly with the monist. For *diversity* is obvious, being guaranteed by difference of subject matter (once reductionism is rejected). It is the monist's *unity* that calls for substantial argument. So not only does additive monism turn out to involve a linguistic doctrine after all, its monism requiring or entailing a linguistic characterization; but it also turns out to be a significantly more committed linguistic doctrine than discourse pluralism. The monist must hold that the unity of factual discourse is more than skin deep (or clothing deep, in Wittgenstein's metaphor). Whereas the pluralist can be content with an easy-going linguistic "multifunctionalism"—with the view that under their common syntactic skin the roles of the various discourses in our lives may be as different as, say, those of our various internal organs.[7]

Additive monists thus incur a significant debt in the coin of semantic theory: They owe us a substantial characterization of factual discourse. (We have already noted that the same is true of non-factualism.) I want to exploit this point to argue for the attractions of discourse pluralism over additive monism, or for that matter over its other non-reductionist rivals. In effect, I want to suggest that the debt thus incurred turns out to be impossible to repay in any of the acceptable currencies. We could accept payment in the debt's own currency, accepting the fact–non-fact distinction as an uncashed primitive. However, ordinary scientific economy recommends instead that we give preference to a view that needs no such primitive. Pluralism and perhaps a physicalist reductionism emerge as the economical alternatives.[8]

This line of argument depends on a claim that many readers may find surprising, namely that there isn't a readily available and well-founded distinction between factual and non-factual uses of language. I have defended this claim at length elsewhere (Price 1988), and in the next section I sketch some of the main

6. Strictly, a monist might consistently hold that all discourse is factual (a position that David Lewis adopts in Lewis 1983). What matters is not the factual–non-factual distinction as such, but the characterization of the factual itself.

7. These also exhibit striking superficial similarities, looking to the untrained eye like so much raw meat. Who could have guessed that the kidney was really a filter, the brain a thinker, etc.? The pluralist is suggesting that the functions of language might exhibit a similar diversity and modularity.

8. Physicalism might after all emerge as a degenerate form of discourse pluralism, namely as the view that in fact there is only one autonomous and legitimate discourse, although there could have been many.

points of that argument, and some related advantages of discourse pluralism. However, I think the claim should really not be surprising to a contemporary philosophical audience, for in a sense it is a natural consequence of Quinean scepticism about meaning. Factuality is a semantic property, if anything. It is the property of "statementhood," or that property which is shared by all *assertoric* utterances. Thus it is a particular component of meaning, and Quine's general skepticism about meaning might already have led us to recognize the possibility that there is no such property, in any substantial sense.[9]

4. Truth and Factuality

I have said that discourse pluralism and additive monism are distinguished by the fact that the former makes no appeal to—indeed, explicitly rejects—the assumption that there is a more than superficial category of fact-stating or descriptive uses of language. It may seem perverse to count this a point in the pluralist's favor. For isn't it obvious what such a category consists in? Fact-stating utterances are just those that have genuine truth-conditions, those that have assertoric force, those that express genuine beliefs about that world. Surely these notions are unproblematic?

The pluralist's response to this challenge is to draw attention to the possibility that these commonsense intuitions might rely on nothing more than the superficial features of language, the clothing that covers a more fundamental diversity. Are the notions of truth, fact, assertion, belief, and so on foundational categories, inevitably central to any theoretical account of our use of language? Or are they mere products of language, categories thrown up by language itself, and not therefore presupposed by a proper explanatory theory of language? As a first step, the pluralist asks us simply to acknowledge that the latter answer is at least a conceptual possibility—that common sense is powerless to exclude it. Thus an appeal to common sense is ruled out by the consideration that common usage is the very object of theoretical inquiry here. All sides are agreed that ordinary usage exhibits a superficial unity between the discourses in question. The issue is whether this superficial unity is more than skin deep.

Perhaps surprisingly, it is the pluralist who has the better of the naturalistic high ground in this dispute. The issue concerns the structure of a complete *naturalistic* theory of language use. Roughly, it is the question whether such a naturalistic

9. The odd thing is that Quine himself never seems to notice that his skepticism has this consequence. As we noted at the end of section 1, he takes his minimalist intuitions about truth to support the view that there is a single category of descriptive discourse, contra, for example, those who would take an instrumentalist view of talk of abstract objects. But he fails to notice that this is the sort of "victory" that we achieve by sweeping the pieces from the board. The default position is a kind of pluralism—not the non-factualist's kind, but the Wittgensteinian doctrine that superficial unity of our talk of truth masks wide differences in the functional roles of discourses or "forms of life."

theory reveals a structural feature of language that may be regarded as constituting a fact-stating–non-fact-stating distinction. This doesn't mean that the pluralist must concede that *all* linguistic notions are ultimately naturalistic (which would be to embrace a form of reductionism that the pluralist is in general eager to avoid). The pluralist simply wants us to recognize the possibility that what can be said about language in naturalistic terms might reveal no trace of a substantial factual–non-factual distinction. As a naturalistic question, this not the sort of thing that can be decided a priori. So discourse pluralism is ultimately an empirical doctrine, albeit a highly theoretical one, and one that concerns the linguistic part of the natural world.

The onus lies with the additive monist to show not only that there is a substantial property of factuality underlying ordinary usage, but also that it has a particular distribution. The monist wants to show that the disputed discourses are unified by a common concern to "depict the world," or some such. The discourse pluralist is not denying that scientific utterances and moral utterances are alike in being meaningful speech acts, but simply that there is any more substantial sense in which they are both "statements of fact," or "descriptions of how things are." So a plausible strategy for the pluralist is to try to argue that none of the usual attempts to characterize such a property is capable of settling the issue of distribution; or in particular of excluding the trivializing possibility that all discourse is factual discourse—that is, that statementhood is a property guaranteed to be possessed by any utterance whatsoever. If a proposed analysis of statementhood cannot exclude even this possibility, it is unlikely to convince us that the monist has a defensible claim concerning the factual status of the discourses of interest.

This skeptical attempt to trivialize any proposed analysis of the notion of statementhood is the strategy that I adopted in *Facts and the Function of Truth* (Price 1988). To illustrate, the most common suggestion is that factual discourse is distinguished by its relation to the notion of truth. Genuinely factual utterances are said to be those that are genuinely truth-bearing, or genuinely "aimed at truth," or some such. As several writers have pointed out, however, the notion of truth involved had better be capable of doing the work. One notion that obviously won't do the work is a redundancy or disquotational notion, which depends on nothing more than the standard equivalence principle: the fact that for any sentence P, "P," and "P is true" seem in some strong sense to say the same thing.[10] So if truth is to be invoked at this point, we need what Bernard Williams called a *substantial* theory of truth (1973: 202). I argue in *Facts and the Function of Truth* that there is no such theory to be had. The contenders inevitably fail on one of two counts: either they are like the disquotational theory, in applying equally well to any sort of discourse; or they already assume a fact-stating–non-fact-stating distinction, in some other form.

10. As we have already noted, Quine's minimalist views about truth fall into this category.

One such alternative relies on the psychological distinction between beliefs and other kinds of propositional attitudes. This proposal originates in the kind of emotivism that grounds itself on Humean moral psychology, drawing a contrast between descriptive or belief-expressing language, on the one hand, and expressive or evaluative attitude-expressing language, on the other. The emotivist treatment of moral discourse has provided a model for parallel treatments of other topics. In the process it has given rise, at least implicitly, to a general theory of the nature of the distinction between factual and non-factual language: to the view that factual language expresses belief, whereas non-factual language expresses attitudes of other kinds. The trouble with this theory is that there is very little prospect of drawing the required psychological distinction, in advance of some other solution to the problem that it is supposed to address.[11] We need a substantial notion of belief, but we won't get that until we have a substantial way of drawing the same distinction somewhere else.

The skeptical attempt to drive a conventional doctrine around a logical circle has a famous paradigm in modern philosophy, in Quine's own attack on the analytic–synthetic distinction. And as we have noted, the conclusion itself seems one that Quine might well have endorsed. Quine's irrealism about meaning seems very much at home with the view that there is no substantial unity to the factual, descriptive, or truth-bearing part of language as a whole—no single such semantic category, in any substantial sense. Indeed, this view might be seen as simply doing for semantics what Quine himself does for ontology: insisting that philosophy has no privileged second-order vantage point, but must rather make do with the deliverances of the best first-order theories, taken at face value.

At any rate, the effect of these skeptical arguments is to underline the economical advantages of discourse pluralism, by showing that a useful characterization of factual discourse is not as readily to hand as we have tended to assume. But it might be objected that pluralism incurs costs of its own. For one thing, it owes us an account of what it regards as the superficial unity of language—for example, of the fact that all discourses apparently avail themselves of the same indicative syntax, and of the notion of truth. For another thing, we are entitled to be told in what the underlying *diversity* is supposed to consist—in what dimension the different discourses enjoy their vertical separations. Related to the latter point is the important question as to how we set the limits to pluralistic tolerance. Clearly there are some conceptual conflicts that call for a less tolerant response, for simply discarding one of the alternatives. The obvious thought is that this is appropriate when the theories concerned are attempting to occupy the same linguistic role, or level; but what does this mean, in general?

11. In the original emotivist case, this difficulty has recently been highlighted by the inconclusiveness of several attempts to exclude the possibility that desires or evaluative attitudes might themselves be represented as a special class of beliefs. See in particular Smith 1987; Pettit 1988; Lewis 1988; Collins 1988; Smith 1988; Price 1989; Pettit and Price 1989.

These are real obligations for a discourse pluralist. I think they should not be unwelcome, however. On the contrary, they provide a further opportunity for pluralism to display its comparative creditworthiness, by showing that it has the means to meet such conceptual debts. In *Facts and the Function of Truth*, I tried to provide a suitable account of truth for these purposes—an account that has the potential to explain why diverse uses of language should be alike in being treated as "truth bearing." The basic idea is that despite the diversity of uses of language, different uses tend to be alike in this respect: within each use or discourse, there is some potential utility in noting and resolving disagreements between the members of a speech community. A notion of truth encourages a community to realize this potential. It does so by generating a social value that is negative when speakers disagree and positive when they agree. Disagreement thus becomes socially unstable, and argument, with its long-run benefits, is thereby encouraged.

This approach does not require that argument is always beneficial, of course. Like any evolutionary theory, it keeps its eyes on the long run. Nor, importantly for a pluralist, does it require that the kind of benefit always be the same. The pluralist can thus allow on the one hand that there is no uniform way in which each of the many language-games affects our well-being; and yet on the other that in all or most such games there is *some* benefit in argument, and hence in the availability of a notion of truth. In fact, I think the pluralist can do considerably more than this. For it turns out that our use of the notion of truth is *not* strictly uniform across the range of different domains of discourse. There are significant differences, underlying the predominant pattern. I think that pluralism can do much to account for these variations, by appealing to the different functions or linguistic roles of the different domains concerned. And *only* pluralism has the flexibility to do this: other approaches are tied too rigidly to the existence of a fact-stating–non-fact-stating dichotomy in language.

What are these discourse to discourse variations? They turn on the differential tendency of arguments to be resolved in such a way that neither participant is judged to have been initially mistaken—for example, the kind of thing that may happen when a disagreement about a probability turns out to have stemmed from the fact that the speakers concerned had access to different evidence. This kind of outcome to an argument manifests itself as a sudden reluctance to apply the notions of truth and falsity to the judgments concerned. Such no-fault disagreements occur for different reasons in different parts of language. To a surprising extent, however, it seems to be possible to explain where they do occur in terms of an understanding of the distinctive functional role of the type of discourse concerned, coupled with the general principle that the origins of truth and falsity lie in their role in encouraging useful argument. (In the process, incidentally, it is possible to explain many of the intuitions that have motivated non-factualism—but to do so without the non-factualist's problematic division of language into fact-stating and non–fact-stating categories.)

This approach has affinities with the recent work of Crispin Wright on what might be called the "fine structure" of truth (1992, 1993). Wright has distinguished a number of different components that may, but need not all, be characteristic of the use of truth in association with a particular area of discourse. In effect, he suggests that we may classify a subject matter according to which of the set of these characteristics we take its notion of truth to involve. As I understand it, his concern is mainly descriptive and taxonomic. However, I think there is some prospect that the structure thus discerned will turn out to be explicable as sketched above, in terms of some general account of the function of truth in language. Whether the best general account will be in the terms I outlined earlier remains to be seen. But if it is to be in keeping with Wright's program, I think it will have to be like my account in being *explanatory* rather than *analytic*: its focus will be not on the question "What *is* truth?" but on the question "Why do ordinary speakers have such a notion as truth?"

Interestingly, Wright too takes this stance on truth to support a non-committal metaphysics, at least as the natural fallback position. He characterizes this position as an anti-realist one, in Dummett's sense, on the grounds that the minimal notion of truth it requires can be thought of as derived from assertibility. I disagree at this point, arguing that in practice the minimal notion of truth is already realist in this sense, for reasons to do with the origins of negation (Price 1990). That issue aside, I take the following remark of Wright's to be in much the same vein as my emphasis on the economical advantages of discourse pluralism: "Anti-realism thus becomes the natural, initial position in any debate. It is the position from which we have to be shown that we ought to move. All the onus, everywhere, is on the realist" (1993: 69). Substitute "pluralist" for "anti-realist" and "non-pluralist" for "realist," and these are my sentiments exactly.

The project also has affinities with Blackburn's quasi-realism. The quasi-realist about moral discourse (for example) wants to argue that although moral judgments are not *really* factual, they are entitled to the trappings of factuality, including a respectable notion of truth. So although there is only one domain of *genuine* facts, it is quite proper on this view for ordinary usage (and truth in particular) to work as if there were many. As we noted earlier, what separates this from discourse pluralism is the quasi-realist's assumption that his project is a limited one, bounded in its application by the availability of a substantial distinction between factual and non-factual uses of language. If that distinction lapses, quasi-realism is no longer a distinct alternative to discourse pluralism. Discourse pluralism is again the default position. But so long as a more limited quasi-realism remains a live project, the quasi-realist's interest in explaining why certain discourses should usefully employ an "artificial" notion of truth will apparently coincide with the project described above.

In sum, there are considerable grounds for doubt as to whether a useful principle of semantic unity is available to an additive monist, other than as an *ad hoc* and costly theoretical primitive. And there are considerable grounds for optimism concerning the project to explain what superficial unity we find in language (and the limits of this unity) on foundations that only the discourse pluralist finds congenial. The case is not closed, of course, but it is the additive monist who is on the defensive.

5. Pluralism as Defensible Realism

At this point it may be helpful to emphasize that discourse pluralism is not an irrealist position. The pluralist accepts with all sincerity that there are moral states of affairs, possible worlds, numbers, or whatever. What he or she rejects is the additive monist's attempt to put a further metaphysical gloss on such existential claims. (That gloss turns out to depend on a semantic distinction of questionable standing, or so the pluralist argues.) Without the gloss, discourse pluralism sits quite happily with a non-metaphysical or "minimal" realism.[12]

Perhaps more surprisingly, this species of realism turns out to be particularly well protected against one of realism's traditional opponents. Discourse pluralism has a defense against an instrumentalist challenge, of a kind that continues to be pressed against realists in a number of branches of contemporary philosophy. This defense is simply not available to the monist, for as we shall see, the antidote that the pluralist is able to employ against instrumentalism works equally well against additive monism.

Instrumentalists prey on the Humean tendencies of the modern philosophical public, offering a simple path to ontological asceticism. To avoid the realist's ontological excesses, they tell us, we need simply treat our *talk* of such ontology as a convenient instrument. The talk works just as well when construed this way, and yet in ontological terms it is absolutely free. Thus there are vast ontological savings compared to realism, and at no extra cost elsewhere.

Of course, realists often respond that the offer is too good to be true. There is a cost elsewhere, albeit one that may not be obvious at first sight. What we lose under instrumentalism, the realist claims, is the ability to explain why the instrument works. The need for such an explanation thus becomes a debt that the instrumentalist cannot pay off.

This response is a good deal less effective in some cases than in others, however. Whatever its merits as an objection to instrumentalism about theoretical physics, it is likely to be of little use in defense of realism about possible worlds, for example. Here the realist will typically acknowledge that a proper explanation of why talk of non-actual worlds is useful can only appeal to the actual world—that is, in effect, to acknowledge that such talk would be just as useful if there were no other worlds. Similar considerations might apply in the case of intentional

12. This point was made vivid to me in discussions with John Campbell. Discourse pluralism seems compatible with what Campbell calls the Simple View about entities or properties of a given kind. See, e.g., Campbell 1993.

psychology. Realists might well grant that an adequate explanation of why talk of beliefs and desires is useful could in principle be cast in terms of scientific theories making no reference to intentional states.

In cases such as this, the realist needs a different strategy, and might be tempted to appeal to Quine. For has Quine not taught us that there is no more to the question of whether there are possible worlds (say) than the matter as to whether such things are quantified over in the most serviceable philosophical theory of modality and related topics? And given that the instrumentalist does not deny us our *talk* of possible worlds (quantification included), don't we therefore have Quine's authority for rejecting the instrumentalist's claim that there are no such things? Doesn't the talk itself provide all the warrant we ever have for an existential claim?

However, it is important to appreciate that there are two ways to interpret this argument, resting on two quite different ways of interpreting Quine's views on ontology. On one reading, the Quinean doctrine is effectively a principle of ontological quietism—the principle that there is no separate second-order science of ontology, but simply the mundane business of existential quantification carried out by first-order specialists in the course of their working lives. I shall come back to this: I think it does provide an objection to instrumentalism, but not the objection that the metaphysical realist was hoping for. There seems to be a tendency to read the Quinean doctrine in quite a different way, however. Under this second reading, the activities of first-order specialists provide raw data to which the Quinean principle is then applied, yielding second-order ontological conclusions. In other words, the fact that first-order specialists quantify over the entities of a certain kind is held to constitute *evidence* that such entities actually exist. Far from dismissing the science of ontology, Quine's doctrine thus becomes the main instrument in the working ontologist's tool kit—a kind of "magic eye" for detecting otherwise invisible existents.

Had Quine provided us with such a magic eye, it would indeed provide a powerful weapon against instrumentalists (or at least those instrumentalists not prepared to take issue with Quine). "See for yourself," the realist would say, inviting the instrumentalist to peer at reality through Quine's lens. But I think that to make this explicit is to make it obvious that Quine intends no such thing. The right reading of Quine is the quietist one.[13] Now this reading too counts against the

13. This misinterpretation of Quine seems to me to parallel a misunderstanding concerning the role of best explanation of science. It is part of the practice of science to accept the best current explanations of observed phenomena. This is hardly more than a truism: to say that an explanation is the best we have is ipso facto to indicate that we give it more credence than anything else on offer. There is a tendency to make a second-order principle of inference out of this: to say that *because* they provide best explanations, the theories concerned are likely to be true, and therefore worthy of a further degree of credence. Another similar mistake is that of thinking that the principle that the best choice is the one that maximizes one's expected utility assigns a *further* value to the choice in question, over and above its expected utility.

instrumentalist. The instrumentalist requires that not all good theories involve ontological commitment (via their existential quantification); for it depends on whether the theory in question is genuinely descriptive or merely an instrument. As a quietist principle Quine's doctrine contends that there is no such further issue.

But does this favor realism? Yes, but only a realism of the discourse pluralist's minimal kind. For what the quietist principle denies us is something that is needed by additive monists, as well as by instrumentalists. Instrumentalism is a form of non-factualism. Like additive monism, though for a different reason, it thus depends on a substantial distinction between factual and non-factual uses of language. The monist needs an account of what keeps the domains of discourse together; the non-factualist an account of what sets them apart. The instrumentalist thus owes us an account of what is lacked by those domains of discourse that are judged "merely" instrumental, and hence of what is not lacked by those that pass the test. Without such an account, for one thing, there seems nothing to stop the above kind of argument for instrumentalism from going all the way down. All discourse would thus be construed as fictional discourse, and the contrast that gives point to instrumentalism would be lost. Modal and moral discourse would be on the same footing as discourse of any other kind, just as the pluralist and the additive monist both contend.

So the instrumentalist needs a substantial factual–non-factual distinction. Often this is supposed to be cashed in ontological terms. The instrumentalist is presented as denying the existence of a class of entities of a certain kind—possible worlds, or mathematical objects, for example. However, we have just encountered a reason for doubting that this can serve as the fundamental distinction. Construed à la Quine, ontological commitment is a more or less trivial consequence of serious theoretical commitment, even if there is always room for argument as to which ontology strikes the best ideological bargain. Hence instrumentalism cannot be primarily an ontological doctrine. The instrumentalist needs a prior distinction between full-blooded and merely fictional theoretical commitment. An ontological distinction would flow from such a distinction, but cannot provide it; not, at least, unless we are prepared to discard the Quinean principle that our only guide to ontology is the quantificational structure of accepted theory.

All of this applies equally to the additive monist. Quine's ontological quietism prevents the monist from casting the unifying principle that he or she requires in ontological terms.[14] However, there is nothing to prevent a discourse pluralist from embracing the Quinean doctrine; the pluralist too will be interested in the most advantageous theoretical formulation of any given level of discourse, and may well see the choice in Quinean terms. The pluralist thus

14. I argued in section 3 that the monist's unifying principle cannot be entirely ontological in any case, but must involve a semantic component. The present point is that Quinean quietism undercuts the ontological strategy at first base, as it were.

has an objection to instrumentalism that would be suicidal in the hands of an additive monist.

Discourse pluralism thus provides a particularly defensible form of realism—a position uniquely placed to exploit some of the hidden costs of irrealism. A corollary is that those who find themselves in the grip of realist intuitions about matters that are otherwise vulnerable to instrumentalist attack would do well to take pluralism seriously, for it may well be the only realism that they can have.

6. Conclusion

We began with two ways to respond to the moral inconsistency of a prosperous Franciscan. One response was simply to point out that he could well make do with less. I compared this to challenging the lapsed Humeans' case for particular metaphysical luxuries. This is what non-factualists do, in effect, in arguing that in order to make sense of, say, modal discourse, we don't need to assume a realm of modal facts; instead we may read the discourse non-descriptively, so that its interpretation does not require such facts. My main goal in this chapter has been to offer an alternative deflationary challenge to non-Humean metaphysics. This compares to granting that the Franciscan has the same range of human needs as anyone else, and the same right to reasonable satisfaction of those needs; but insisting that in granting this, we overturn the idea that there is any special virtue in self-imposed poverty.

Discourse pluralism thus allows the lapsed Humeans their talk of possible worlds, modal facts, or whatever, subject only to the modified Quinean requirement that such an ontology provides the most economical basis for the particular discourse in question (i.e., roughly, the basis that best enables that discourse to serve its intended function in human life). What it withholds is the concession that such talk maps the bare objective structure of a single independent reality. On the contrary, we pluralists maintain, the idea that there is such a mapping rests on a theoretical error about language, namely the view that there is a single substantial category of descriptive or fact-stating discourse.[15] It follows that the Humean conception of metaphysical virtue was always misguided. In granting the lapsed Humeans their metaphysical comforts, we thus deny them their Humean metaphysical virtue; for we say that there has never been any such thing.

Pluralism thus takes the heat out of contemporary metaphysical debates about a very wide range of topics: modality, mathematics, moral discourse, conditionals, and many others. As a final example, a well-motivated pluralism might allow one to endorse something like Dennett's account of the role and origins of intentional

15. We pluralists think that many of those who try to deflate the lapsed Humean in the first way also fall prey to this misconception.

psychology, without having to concern oneself as to whether the view amounts to instrumentalism about the mental.[16]

Some readers will see this supposed advantage as like that of theft over honest toil—or perhaps more accurately, of idleness over honest toil. I see it as rather the advantage of idleness over unnecessary and unproductive toil—the advantage of stopping work on a misconceived and unproductive philosophical seam. True, we cannot be certain that the seam will remain unproductive, but there is enough doubt about the matter for the wise course to be to consider some of the general issues on which its eventual productivity might depend. I have emphasized that these are naturalistic issues, in particular issues about language as a natural phenomenon. (Does it admit a significant descriptive–non-descriptive distinction, for example?) So they are hardly issues that the pluralist's likely opponents may justly ignore.

At the very least, we could then go back to work with a better idea of what we were looking for in the first place. Instead, however, we might want to explore other philosophical seams, other projects that would now seem more promising: perhaps the elaboration of the general descriptive/explanatory approach to truth; perhaps the broadly Kantian examination and classification of different domains of discourse, with reference to their role in human life;[17] perhaps the exploration of nice issues concerning the connections and disconnections between the various discourses—a different philosophy, certainly, but not an idle one.[18]

16. For Dennett's own response to this concern, see Dennett 1991.

17. Various work attempting to generalize the notion of a secondary quality might be seen as falling under this heading. See, for example, Wright 1993; Johnston 1993; Johnston 1989; Pettit 1991. For a critical view of this program, offering an alternative more in keeping with discourse pluralism, see chapter 4 of this volume.

18. I am grateful to audiences in Canberra, Brisbane, Sydney, and Wollongong, and particularly to John Burgess, John Campbell, John Hawthorne, Michaelis Michael, Philip Pettit, Michael Schepanski, and Mark Walker, for many comments on earlier versions.

3

Semantic Minimalism and the Frege Point

Speech act theory is one of the more lasting products of the linguistic movement in philosophy of the mid-twentieth century. Within philosophy itself, the movement's products did not in general prove so durable. Particularly striking in this respect is the perceived fate of what was one of the most characteristic applications of the linguistic turn in philosophy, namely the view that many traditional philosophical problems are such as to yield to an understanding of the distinctive function of a particular part of language. Most typically, the crucial insight was held to be that despite appearances, the function of the part of language in question is not assertoric, or descriptive, and that the traditional problems arose at least in part from a failure to appreciate this point. Thus problems in moral philosophy were thought to yield to an appreciation that moral discourse is expressive rather than descriptive, problems in the philosophy of mind to an understanding of the distinctive role of psychological ascriptions, and so on. The philosophical journals of the 1950s are rich with views like these. (No general term for this approach seems to have become widely accepted at the time. I shall call it "non-factualism," for what it denies, most characteristically, is the fact-stating role of language of a certain kind.)

At the time, many of these non-factualist endeavors drew on the new terminology of speech act theory, taking their lead at least in part from J. L. Austin. It is therefore somewhat ironic that when non-factualism came to be seen as discredited, one of the works responsible was John Searle's *Speech Acts* (1969).[1] Non-factualism was thus disowned by the movement from which, at least in part, it drew its inspiration. So it is that while speech act theory prospered outside philosophy, its early pretensions to application within philosophy were reviled or forgotten. Non-factualism was widely thought to have fallen victim to objections urged in the 1960s by Searle, and independently by Peter Geach (who took his inspiration from an argument of Frege's).

1. Searle had earlier presented the argument in question in Searle 1962.

Philosophical demise is rarely complete or permanent, however, and non-factualism has been receiving renewed attention more recently, particularly in a relatively new application to the problem of linguistic and psychological content (see, for example, Kripke 1982, Boghossian 1990). It would now be easy for a newcomer to fail to notice that for almost a generation the approach was commonly taken to be discredited. It therefore seems worth reexamining the supposedly fatal objection. After all, perhaps non-factualism really is dead, or as dead as a philosophical view can be, and its new devotees simply haven't noticed. If not, then it would be nice to know how it managed to recover from what many took to be a mortal blow.

This chapter thus begins with a brief reassessment of what I shall call "the Frege argument" (though I shall draw on the versions of the argument advanced by Geach and Searle). One possible outcome of this investigation would be a reaffirmation of the conclusions drawn by Geach and Searle, and thus a return to the status quo circa 1965—perhaps an unexciting result, but a useful one, if the Frege objection succeeds, given non-factualism's current reluctance to lie down. The actual outcome is rather more interesting, however. For one thing, the Frege argument turns out to be considerably less powerful than it has been taken to be, so that non-factualism remains a live option. Given the perceived importance of the Frege argument to the "overthrow" of linguistic philosophy, this conclusion suggests that contemporary philosophy might do well to reconsider. There are many contemporary metaphysical debates that would have looked sterile and misconceived to the linguistic philosophers of the 1950s. Without the Frege argument to fall back on, it would be a brave—or perhaps foolhardy—philosopher who would dismiss out of hand the linguistic point of view.[2]

In the present context, however, I want to emphasize a different benefit of reexamining the Frege argument. As we shall see, the issues thereby thrown open are ones of fundamental concern in the philosophy of language and the foundations of speech act theory. In hindsight, I think it is clear that when speech act theory detached itself from philosophy in the 1960s, a cluster of central issues concerning the nature of assertion, judgment, description, and the like were left largely unresolved. I hope to show that to reexamine the Frege argument is to reopen these issues in a particularly fruitful way.

This chapter is in three main parts. In the first (sections 1 to 4), I argue that the Frege argument is far from conclusive. It imposes certain constraints on the non-factualist, but fails to show that these constraints cannot be satisfied. I shall mention work by some prominent non-factualists that went some way toward showing how their view might meet these constraints. The upshot seems to be that the worst that the non-factualist can be convicted of is a degree of complexity in

2. For more on these themes see Price 1992.

linguistic theory that factualist views seem to avoid—and for all its unpleasantness, complexity is rarely a fatal complaint.

All the same, the desire to free non-factualism of this complexity motivates the second part of the paper (sections 5 to 7). This part draws on recent interest in what I here call minimal semantics, extending the terminology employed in discussions of so-called minimal theories of truth.[3] Briefly, I suggest that non-factualists might (i) concede that moral claims (or whatever) are statements in some minimal sense, and use this concession to meet the requirements identified by the Frege argument in the same direct and simple way that is available to a factualist; but (ii) reformulate their point about the character of moral claims in such a way that it does not conflict with the proposition that such claims are statements in the minimal sense. The move to a minimal semantics thus enables the non-factualist to sidestep the Frege argument.

I want to suggest that in the process we achieve a fresh and illuminating view of the relationship between truth-conditional semantics and the sort of pragmatic considerations about language often thought to be the proper concern of a theory of force, or speech act theory more generally. As reformulated, non-factualism directs our attention to the function of particular parts of discourse. (This functional side of non-factualism is not new, of course; what is new is that it should be clearly divorced from a claim about the *semantic* status of the utterances in question.) The recognition that non-factualism need not be a semantic doctrine then enables us to regard functional pragmatics not as an addition tacked on to deal with the problems of force and tone, but as a complement to the theory of sense whose task is to explain how there come to be uses of language with senses of a particular sort—how there come to be utterances with the sense of moral judgments, for example.

True, it is not clear that the reformulated doctrine should really be called non-factualism. As we shall see, it no longer involves the denial that the utterances of some disputed class are factual, or assertoric. Instead, it treats these as relatively superficial and uninteresting linguistic categories, overlying diversity of a different kind. It is this separation of semantic and functional categories that seems to me of most interest to speech act theory. It suggests, for example, that *assertion* is a very much less fundamental linguistic category than has usually been assumed.

3. I first heard the term "minimal truth" from Crispin Wright, who uses it in Wright 1993; it is used in a rather different sense by Horwich 1990. Roughly, Wright means by minimal truth the weakest notion of truth compatible with realism about an area of discourse. He takes this notion to encompass both the disquotational and normative aspects of truth, and argues that some but not all areas of discourse employ stronger notions of truth. Horwich, on the other hand, uses the term more or less as a synonym for the disquotational theory, and devotes his book to arguing that we don't need any stronger theory. For the purposes of this paper it won't matter whether the minimal theory is thought as embodying normativity as well as disquotation (though elsewhere I have sided with Wright in arguing that disquotation does not guarantee normativity, which therefore needs to be accounted for separately; see Price 1988, part II; 1998).

At best, it is a kind of higher-order category, grouping together some very diverse linguistic activities.

All the same, the question arises as to what these diverse activities have in common, in virtue of which they all come to be part of this single higher-order category. In the third part of the chapter (section 8), I conclude by drawing attention to this central issue, an issue that has tended to be overlooked in earlier work. I note that there is a sense in which the issue embodies some of the insights of the Frege argument, and hence that things are not quite so easy for my reconstituted non-factualist as they earlier appeared; but I also note that the issue is not one that the non-factualist's opponents can afford to shirk, so that the dialectical burden of the new issues is evenly spread.

1. The Frege-Geach-Searle Arguments and Searle's Unused Loophole

The Frege argument begins by observing that non-factualist accounts characteristically propose an interpretation of just those (*canonical*) sentences or utterances in which constructions of the relevant type—"It is probable that . . . ," "It is good that . . . ," "It is true that . . . ," or whatever—are not part of any clause other than a complete sentence. It is noted that there are many other (*subsidiary*) occurrences of such constructions, and argued that the proposed accounts are unable to deal with at least some of these new cases, though obliged to do so. As Geach says,

> Theories of non-descriptive performances regularly take into account only the use of a term "P" to call something "P"; the corroboration theory of truth, for example, considers only the use of "true" to call a statement true, and the condemnation theory of "bad" considers only the way it is used to call something bad; predications of "true" and "bad" in if or then clauses, or in the clauses of a disjunction, are just ignored.
>
> One could not write off such uses of the terms as calling for a different explanation from their use to call things true or bad; for that would mean that arguments of the pattern "if *x* is true (if *w* is bad), then *p*; but x is true (*w* is bad); ergo *p*" contained a fallacy of equivocation, whereas in fact they are clearly valid. (Geach 1960: 223)[4]

Searle's version of the argument is somewhat different, in that he admits a possibility which Geach's appeal to the validity of modus ponens would appear to exclude. Searle is objecting to what he calls "the speech act analysis" of words such

4. The argument is repeated in Geach 1965.

as "good," "true," "know," and "probably," the general form of which he takes to be: "The word W is used to perform the speech act A." Searle says that

> any analysis of the meaning of a word (or morpheme) must be consistent with the fact that the same word (or morpheme) can mean the same thing in all the grammatically different kinds of sentences in which it can occur. (Seale 1969: 137)

For example,

> the word "true" means or can mean the same thing in interrogatives, indicatives, conditionals, negations, disjunctions, optatives, etc. (Searle 1969: 137)

However, Searle recognizes that in order to meet this "condition of adequacy," speech act analysts are

> not committed to the view that every literal utterance of W is a performance of A, but rather [may claim] that utterances which are not performances of the act have to be explained in terms of utterances which are. (Searle 1969: 138)

Searle thus appears to acknowledge that it need not be said that the contribution the clause makes to the meaning of a conditional in which it occurs as antecedent is identical to the meaning it has when used canonically; but only that the former contribution depends in a rule-governed way (the rule being associated with the conditional form) on the meaning the clause has in the latter case. If Geach's appeal to validity were successful, this view would seem untenable. The validity of modus ponens would depend on the meaning of such a clause being invariant between the two contexts.

Having admitted this possibility, however, Searle fails to take advantage of it. He rightly points out that

> the speech act analysts . . . need to show . . . only . . . that literal utterances which are not performances of the act A stand in a relation to performances of A in a way which is purely a function of the way the sentences uttered stand in relation to the standard indicative sentences, in the utterance of which the act is performed. (Searle 1969: 138)

But he takes this to mean that if such sentences "are in the past tense, then the act is reported in the past; if they are hypothetical then the act is hypothesized, etc." He then notes the obvious, namely that

> the speech act analysis of the . . . words: "good," "true," "probable," etc. does not satisfy this condition. . . . "If this is good, then we ought to buy it" is not equivalent to "If I commend this, then we ought to buy it"; "This used to be good" is not equivalent to "I used to commend this"; and so on. (Searle 1969: 138–139)

Although Searle himself does not canvas other ways in which the meaning of clauses such as "It is good that P" in various contexts may be systematically related to their meaning when they stand alone, it is clear that if the general objection is to be answered, the solution will lie in this direction. However, the argument from modus ponens claims to bar the way. Let us test its strength.

2. The Appeal to Modus Ponens

As Geach notes, this argument is due originally to Frege (1960: 129–130), who uses it in arguing that a sentential negation operator cannot be construed as a sign of force: as an indication that a sentence, when uttered, has the force of a denial. Frege's argument is in two parts:

Fr1: He notes that a negated sentence may occur as the antecedent of a conditional, where it does not amount to a denial, and concludes that in such a case the negation contributes to the sense of (or thought expressed by) the antecedent.

Fr2: He infers from this that if we want to allow that a case of modus ponens involving such a conditional is valid, we shall have to allow that the negation does not mark a denial, even when the negated sentence concerned stands alone.

The general principle invoked in **Fr1** is something like this:

Embedded Force Exclusion (EFE): Force modifiers cannot occur in embedded contexts.

We shall come back to this, but let us first consider **Fr2**. Here the argument might seem to be that the validity of modus ponens depends on the meaning of the antecedent clause in the conditional premise being exactly the same as it is when the clause occurs alone (as in the categorical premise). It would follow that because (according to **Fr1**) the negative clause is not a denial in the former context, it is not a denial in the latter. But as Hare points out (Hare 1971: 87) the same argument would show that when the clause stands alone it does not have the force of an assertion; for it lacks this force when used as an antecedent.

A more charitable interpretation is therefore that the argument for **Fr2** depends on the following claim:

Sense Identity (SI): The inference

(1) If not-P then Q; not-P; therefore Q

is valid only if the second premise has the same sense (or expresses the same thought) as the antecedent of the conditional premise.

If we grant the conclusion of **Fr1**—that is, that the negation operator has a sense-modifying role in determining the meaning of the conditional premise in (1)—then **SI** implies that its role in the second premise must also be to modify sense. Thus as **Fr2** claims, the negation operator does not modify force, even in canonical cases.

The function of the appeal to modus ponens is therefore to extend the conclusion of **Fr1** to canonical uses of the negation operator (and similarly for such things as modal and ethical operators, in Geach's case). But how is **SI** to be justified? Not, on the face of it, by Geach's remark that otherwise the inference would contain a fallacy of equivocation. Of course, there are fallacious arguments of the syntactic form "if P then Q; P; therefore Q" in which the fallacy turns on the fact that P is used with different senses in each premise. However, to claim bluntly that any argument of this kind is fallacious is just to beg the question, given that both sides agree that (1) is valid. For both sides agree that this claim is incompatible with the view that the two occurrences of "Not-P" in (1) have different senses; but the disagreement is precisely as to which of these incompatible propositions must be given up.

In any case, the use that Frege and Geach make of **SI** depends on the principle **EFE**. It is **EFE** which underpins the claim that in the antecedent of a conditional, a negation operator modifies sense. But what are the grounds for accepting **EFE**? Apparently just the observation that in such a context no denial is being made. But this involves the very mistake we noted in the previous section, the loophole for avoiding which is recognized (if not adequately exploited) by Searle. In effect, Searle recognizes that in order to make sense of an occurrence of a denial operator in an embedded context, it is not necessary to say that such a subsidiary use has exactly the meaning it has when it stands alone. It is enough that its contribution to the meaning of the containing context should depend on the fact that it does signal a denial, when used canonically. For then there is a clear reason for including a force-indicator for denial in the subsidiary positions concerned: in order to show that the clause would have this force, if uttered alone.

We saw that Searle himself does not take advantage of this loophole. But so far we have found nothing in the argument from modus ponens that provides an obstacle to others doing so. On the contrary, the appeal to modus ponens has to this point depended on the assumption that no such loophole exists.

3. The Attractions of Uniformity

Frege and Geach do have another argument for **SI**, however, also appealing to modus ponens. Unlike the above argument, this one does not rely on the sub-argument **Fr1**. Indeed, it offers an independent argument for the conclusion of **Fr1** (i.e., that in the antecedent of a conditional, the negation operator modifies sense). This argument begins by noting that we evidently do have identity of sense in

(2) If P then Q; P; therefore Q (where P is not negated)

and moreover that this identity of sense is clearly crucial to the validity of the argument form. It then claims that if (1) is to exemplify the same form of inference—as in some sense it surely does—then identity of sense must play the same role. Uniformity seems to require that there be a common account of the conditional form, in the light of which identity of sense plays a constant role in guaranteeing validity. Thus this is an appeal not to a necessary condition for validity as such, but to the need for a uniform explanation of the validity of a class of inferences that evidently have a structural property in common.

Such theoretical uniformity is undoubtedly desirable, but is the only way to achieve it to treat (1) as a special case of (2)? Why not instead treat (1) and (2) as distinct sub-types of a single more general form of inference? It is not obvious that in that case the general criterion for validity would include the required identity of sense. There might rather be some more general condition, which reduced to identity of sense in the special case of (2). In the next section I outline an account of this kind.

4. Conditionals for Non-factualists

In summary then, the task of a non-factualist who wishes to evade the Frege argument seems to be twofold: first, to find a legitimate account of the significance of a force-modifying construction in a subsidiary clause; and second, to produce a general account of the linguistic function of the "if . . . then . . ." construction, such as to enable valid arguments to contain such force-modifiers in (at least) the antecedent position. The latter project is best tackled first, for the significance of a subsidiary force-modifier will inevitably depend on the nature of the subsidiary context in question. We shouldn't expect a single account, applicable to any and every subsidiary context. The individual accounts will, of course, have something in common, but this may be nothing more than a common reference to the meaning that the force-modifier in question has in a canonical context.

Now in arguing that the utterances of some disputed class are not genuine assertions, non-factualists commonly rely on a distinction between beliefs and other sorts of propositional attitude. With this psychological distinction assumed in place, the non-factualist argues, first, that we may characterize assertion as the linguistic expression of belief; and second, that the disputed utterances express some other sort of propositional attitude. Thus Frege's opponent might tell us that negated sentences express disbeliefs rather than beliefs; the emotivist tells us that moral judgments express evaluative attitudes; the probabilistic subjectivist tells us that utterances of the form "It is probable that P" express the speaker's high degree of confidence that P; and so on.

What concerns us here is not whether this is an adequate route to non-factualism in general, but the fact that by characterizing force in terms of an associated type of propositional attitude, it provides the means to escape the Frege objection. The strategy requires that indicative conditionals themselves be treated non-assertorically. A sincere utterance of "If P then Q" will be said to indicate that a speaker possesses what may be called an "inferential disposition"—a mental state such that if the speaker were to adopt the mental attitude associated with the utterance "P," she would be led to adopt the mental attitude associated with "Q." For example the utterance "If it is not snowing, then Boris has gone swimming" will be said to express a disposition to move from a state of disbelief that it is snowing, to a belief that Boris has gone swimming.

This suggestion provides a clear sense in which the force-modifying expression makes the same contribution to a canonical utterance, as to a conditional utterance in which it occurs in the antecedent or consequent. In each case it marks the association of the meaning of the whole utterance with a certain kind of propositional attitude: a disbelief, a degree of confidence, an evaluative attitude, or whatever. Other features of the particular occurrence of the expression in question determine first which particular propositional attitude of the given type is involved—its content, in other words—and second, how this propositional attitude stands in relation to the mental state associated with the utterance as a whole. For example, in the canonical case for negation (an utterance of the form "Not-P") the fact that negation is the outermost operator indicates that the mental state associated with the utterance as a whole is just disbelief itself. While in the conditional case, the occurrence of the expression in (say) the antecedent position indicates that possession of the state of disbelief in question is the antecedent condition of the inferential disposition associated with the conditional. (This process of determination may be iterated, if the conditional itself occurs as a component of some larger utterance.)

It is important to distinguish this suggestion from the claim that a conditional *reports* a speaker's possession of such an inferential disposition. If that were so, a conditional utterance would be an assertion *about* its speaker's state of mind, and would be true or false according to whether the speaker concerned actually had such an inferential disposition. However, the proposal is intended to explain the meaning of the conditional in terms not of its *truth conditions* but its *subjective assertibility conditions*—that is, in terms of the state of the speaker that normally licenses its correct use. (The term "subjective assertibility condition" is being used in the sense involved in saying that the normal condition for the correct use of a statement P is that one believe that P. To say this is not to say that in asserting P one asserts *that* one believes that P.)[5]

The above proposal is similar to, though perhaps a little more psychologically explicit than, one made by Hare in answer to the Frege objection. Hare puts the common central insight rather nicely, saying that we know the meaning of the conditional "if we know how to do modus ponens." In other words, the crucial thing is that we are in a position to affirm "If P then Q" "if we know that if we are in a position to affirm [P], we can go on to affirm [Q]" (Hare 1971: 87). Thus to say "If Not-P then Q" is to indicate (though not to *say*) that one's state of mind is such that if one were to deny that P, one would affirm (or be prepared to affirm) that Q. The correctness of the inference (1) thus amounts to the fact that (1) is the very inference a readiness to make which is signaled by the conditional premise; and of course the same may be said about (2). In both cases the correctness of the inference is thus analytic: the standard use of the conditional is just such as to license

5. For more on this important and often overlooked distinction see, for example, Hare 1976. On a related point, Michael Dummett once suggested that "If P then Q" could accommodate non-assertoric antecedents if interpreted along the lines of "If I were to assent (or commit myself) to P, I would commit myself to Q" (see Dummett 1973: 351–354; also Wright 1988: 31–33). However, precisely because it confuses a plausible subjective assertibility condition for a conditional with the *content* of the claim concerned, this is vulnerable to the objection that in saying "If P then Q" one is not (necessarily) speaking *about* oneself. In the context of a consideration of a non-factualist interpretation of probability, this objection to Dummett's proposal was raised by Cohen (1977: 29, n19), who notes that if Dummett's reading is to apply the probability case, there should be a use for a construction meaning "If I were to assert (agree) guardedly that A, then I should assert (agree) that B." But that would not be a use paraphrasable by "If it is probable that A, then B." For though it happens to be true that if I were to assert (agree) guardedly that it will be cloudy this afternoon I should also assert (agree) that I am excessively cautious in my weather predictions, it is not true that if clouds are probable then I am excessively cautious.

On the view described above, however, the conditional "If I were to assert guardedly that A, then I should assert that B" is associated with a disposition to infer from a belief that one has asserted guardedly that A, to a belief that one has asserted (or will assert) that B. There is nothing to prevent someone from holding this disposition, but not a disposition to infer from a belief that it is probable that A to a belief that B; and it is the latter disposition which this view associates with the conditional "If it is probable that A, then B." (Cohen makes the further point that on Dummett's reading there would be no obvious use for "If it is probable that A, then I should prefer not to assert guardedly that A"; whereas there is such a use, along the same lines as "Even if it is true that A, I would prefer not to say so." The present view handles this in much the same way.)

modus ponens. Moreover, the role of the force-modifying negation operator in the antecedent of the conditional is now clear. It helps to specify the nature of the circumstances in which the speaker indicates that she would be prepared to affirm the consequent—namely, those circumstances in which she would be prepared to deny that P.

In Hare's form or mine, this account is of course only a beginning. Much work would need to be done to show that the notion of an inferential disposition leads to a satisfactory account of ordinary language indicative conditionals, and of simple logical inferences in which they occur. And even if the account works for conditionals, it needs to be extended to the many other subsidiary contexts in which (what the non-factualist regards as) force-modifying operators may occur. For each such context we need a principle that links the general linguistic function of the context itself to the working hypothesis about operators in question, namely, that their independent use is to signal a non-assertoric force of some kind. Even as it stands, however, the suggested account of conditionals does serve to establish a crucial general point. To paraphrase Hare (who is concerned with the moral case, of course): The fact that sentences containing negation cannot be described without qualification as assertions, but have to be explained in terms of the more complex speech act of denial, is no bar to the appearance of negation in contexts where denial is not taking place, provided that the relation of these contexts to those in which it is taking place can be explained (Hare 1971: 93).

Hare's is not the only attempt in the literature to offer an account of conditionals with non-assertoric antecedents and consequents. I have already mentioned that of Michael Dummett (see note 5). Simon Blackburn also addresses the problem, again with the intention of defending a form of ethical non-factualism against the Frege argument. His suggestion is that

(3) If it is good that P then it is good that Q

is itself an evaluative remark: roughly, it expresses a speaker's approval of the disposition (or, as Blackburn calls it, the "moral sensibility") to approve of Q, given that one approves of P (see particularly Blackburn 1971, 1984). Like Hare's theory and mine, this account has the crucial feature that it makes the significance of an embedded force-modifier *dependent on* but not *identical to* the significance it has in a canonical context. That said, however, it seems to me that Blackburn's account is less plausible than the approach sketched above. It has the disadvantage that it does not give us a single unified account of conditional utterances, from which the required account of conditionals with embedded moral clauses falls out as a special case—conditionals in general are not expressions of moral sensibility. I suspect that Blackburn has confused two notions of endorsement, the first the semantic endorsement that we give to any proposition when we assent to it, and the second the peculiarly moral endorsement that we give to an act or state of affairs of which we approve. It is arguable that assent always involves an evaluative or normative element. To assent to a proposition is to take it to be right, correct, true. But this simply means that assent to an ethical proposition involves two sorts of evaluative attitude. To agree that war is evil is to take the proposition "War is evil" to be correct, to endorse it in that sense; and it is also to express one's disapproval of war. With these notions of endorsement kept distinct, however, there seems no reason to say that accepting a moral conditional necessarily involves anything more than semantic endorsement. It need not itself express a moral attitude, even though it may indicate a certain structure of dependencies between the speaker's moral and non-moral attitudes. "If all war is evil then the Gulf War was evil" is merely a logical truth.[6]

5. The Minimal Turn

Thus it seems that the Frege argument is less powerful than it appeared to be. It certainly isn't watertight, and considerable work has been done toward showing how its weaknesses may be exploited. All the same, there does seem to be at least one charge that will survive these ingenious attempts to evade the Frege argument. Even if they succeed, it will be at the cost of considerable theoretical complexity. It is doubtful whether this counts as an argument against the views that require this expenditure, but it is a valid expression of regret—regret that we cannot have the simplicity of the standard account. If only we could justly retain familiar platitudes about validity, truth-functional connectives, and the like, without cutting ourselves off from the insights of non-factualism.

Well, perhaps we may. An optimistic hint is to be found in recent interest in minimalist notions of truth. At one point in his recent book on minimal theories of truth, Paul Horwich notes that such a notion of truth is not incompatible with such meta-ethical positions as emotivism, provided of course that the emotivist doesn't insist on trying to characterize her view of moral judgments in terms of truth; for in this case the minimal notion won't bear the weight (Horwich 1990: 87–88).[7]

In the present case, this suggests that we might extend the minimalist notion of truth to a minimalist notion of statementhood. A (minimal) statement will

6. Blackburn returns to the issue of conditionals with moral antecedents in Blackburn 1988. He there distinguishes two possible approaches to the problem, one ("slow track quasi-realism") in keeping with his own earlier approach, and one ("fast-track quasi-realism") more similar to the approach suggested below. He argues that the two approaches are less dissimilar than they appear at first sight. I agree, but suspect that what the fast track yields when localized to the moral case is not Blackburn's version of the slow track but something closer to Hare's.

7. A similar train of thought has sometimes been used as an argument against non-factualism; see, for example, McDowell 1981 and Wiggins 1976.

simply be any utterance of which it makes sense to say that it is (minimally) true—in other words, in effect, any sentence that provides a well-formed substitution into the context "It is true that P." Now surely emotivists and other non-factualists cannot have been denying that certain classes of indicative sentences are statements in this minimal syntactic sense; they had some stronger thesis in mind (albeit perhaps a thesis they would have couched in terms of a stronger notion of truth). So there is evidently room for a simple compromise in response to the Frege argument. If the Fregean will concede that the ordinary platitudes about validity, truth-functional connectives, and the like may appeal to nothing more than a minimal notion of truth, then the non-factualist will be entitled to endorse these platitudes at face value, and won't have to embark on the evasive maneuvers whose complexity gave us cause for regret.

Both sides may resist this compromise on the grounds that they find the minimal notions of truth and statementhood unattractive. As noted, the non-factualist may want to characterize her position in terms of a stronger notion of truth, while the Fregean may feel that the minimal notion is inadequate for the purposes of logical and semantic theory, including that of accounting for the validity of inferences such as modus ponens. I don't want to try to address these concerns directly in this chapter.[8] Instead I want to sketch the form that non-factualism might take if it endorses this compromise, and thus to show indirectly that the compromise is one that it might happily live with. I also want to indicate some of the character of the minimalist semantic theory that would accompany the compromise—in particular, to indicate some respects in which it differs from orthodox Fregean semantics.

6. Facts and Linguistic Functions

Suppose that we accept that moral judgments are minimally descriptive, meaning by this that they can be said to be minimally true and false. How might we then formulate a non-factualist doctrine concerning such judgments?

We might appeal to psychology, saying that moral claims do not express beliefs, but rather evaluative attitudes. The immediate trouble with this is that our minimal notion of statementhood will bring with it a minimal notion of belief: a minimal belief will be simply the sort of propositional attitude expressed in a minimal statement. So we need a substantial belief–evaluative attitude distinction. It would be better to talk of a special kind of belief, here using "belief" in its minimal sense. The resulting position would then amount to the psychological equivalent of the following view.

8. In Price (1988: chapter 2), I argue at length that non-factualism cannot be satisfactorily grounded on a notion of truth; while Horwich 1990 responds to the claim that the minimal notion of truth is inadequate for various theoretical purposes.

Let us begin with the platitude that language serves many different functions. It is easy to agree on this, but more difficult to decide how to carve things up—what the various functions of language actually are, or indeed what is meant by a function in this context. It is very tempting to think that one of the main functions of language, perhaps indeed the primary one, is that of description, or the making of factual claims. I want to urge that we resist this temptation, and instead regard this particular functional category as an artificial one, imposed by the structure of language itself. I want to suggest that its apparent unity and cohesiveness is superficial, and overlies considerable diversity. To use an analogy that I have appealed to elsewhere, I want to suggest that the functional category of description is like that of manual tasks. What manual functions have in common is essentially that they are all performed or capable of being performed by hand—from a biological point of view, the right thing to say is not that the hand has evolved to perform tasks of a single functional category, but that the functional category consists of a diverse assortment of tasks which happen to be thrown together in virtue of the fact that all are or can be performed by that accident of evolution, the human hand.

I shall use the term "minimal description" for any utterance that is capable of being minimally true or false. The suggestion is thus that within the class of minimal descriptions, we may find sub-classes of utterances serving a range of different linguistic functions. (These sub-classes will overlap, of course, when sub-sentential constructions serving different functions are combined in a single utterance.)

Let us now suppose that one of the functions served by some minimal descriptions is that typified by ordinary and (perhaps more contentiously) scientific description of the physical world. Crudely, we might say that the function of this part of language is to signal the presence of certain conditions in the physical environment of a speaker. There would be a number of problems if we tried to make this more precise. For one thing, it would be hard to resist the slide into the semantic language of facts, states of affairs, and so on, which would soon lead us back to the very position from which we are attempting to distance ourselves, namely that the function concerned is that of minimal descriptions as a whole. For another thing, the limits of the "physical" are ill-defined in a number of relevant ways. Do we count such things as dispositions, for example, or does their modal character already exclude them?

Precision will not be critical, however. The important thing is that the nonfactualist should be able to mark some distinction between the function of (say) moral discourse, on the one hand, and the function or cluster of functions of at least a significant part of non-moral discourse, on the other. It will simplify things to assume that there is a single well-defined linguistic task with respect to which this contrast may be drawn—let us call it the task of physical signaling, or natural description—but the thesis could quite well be formulated in more general terms.

Given this simplifying assumption, we thus have a distinction between the semantic (or perhaps better, syntactic) notion of minimal description, and the functional notion of natural description (or physical signaling). My suggestion is then that the non-factualists' central thesis may be thought of as the claim that in certain cases we systematically confuse minimal descriptions for natural descriptions. Moral judgments (or whatever) are minimal descriptions, but are not natural descriptions. Rather they serve some quite distinct linguistic function.

To what extent is this suggestion compatible with the sorts of things that non-factualists typically say? In one sense, an emphasis on misconstrual of linguistic function is a core component of any non-factualist thesis. Before all else, non-factualism is the doctrine that utterances of a certain kind are systematically misconstrued (with significant philosophical consequences). However, the functional point is usually put in terms of semantic categories—a fact-stating–non-fact-stating distinction, or something of the kind. In other words the relevant functional divide is thought of in semantic terms. But on the present account the non-factualist's point becomes purely functional, the semantics on both sides of the distinction being agreed to be of the minimal sort. However, it seems to me that this shift makes surprisingly little difference to the philosophical force of the non-factualist move—the relevant philosophical consequences are much the same. A naturalistic reduction of moral properties is ruled inappropriate for the standard reason, for example (namely that it misconstrues the linguistic role of moral judgment).

Let us see how this goes in a little more detail. Consider emotivism. The emotivist typically says that moral claims express evaluative attitudes rather than beliefs. This is compatible with the suggested gloss so long as we make a distinction between minimal belief and natural belief, paralleling that between minimal description and natural description (physical signaling). For then the emotivist may be seen as making the point that moral claims express evaluative attitudes, and that although these are (of course) minimal beliefs, they are not natural beliefs. (Their function does not lie in matching a subject's mental state to states of the physical environment, as we might put it.) This claim will do the usual work of defusing philosophical concerns about the nature of moral facts. The question as to the real nature of a state of affairs referred to by a description is one that may properly be raised in naturalistic terms if the description concerned is a natural description—in this case it is a matter that may be investigated in scientific terms. But if all we have is a minimal description (or indeed if we are considering a natural description from the minimal semantic standpoint), then such a question involves a kind of category mistake. The only possible answers are the sorts of platitudes associated with the minimal notion of truth.

Let me mention two concerns to which this proposal might give rise. One is that on this view there would be seem to be no difference between non-factualism about moral discourse and a certain form of moral realism, namely the view that although there are moral facts and states of affairs, these are not part of the natural world, and are not reducible to natural or physical facts. (In a similar way, the objection would be that non-factualism about psychological ascriptions could not be distinguished from certain forms of dualism.) I think that this is a very important objection, requiring much more attention to do it justice than I can give it here. Briefly, my view is that the objection tends to backfire, in the sense that its effect is to undermine the credentials of such non-reductive realisms. Against a background of minimal semantics, I think that these positions become impossible to distinguish from the (Wittgensteinian?) form of pluralism that embraces the possibility that language comprises a multiplicity of different kinds of discourse. True, non-factualism is also drawn in this direction, but I think it fares rather better, being able to cash its concern with the different degrees of objectivity of different discourses in other terms (see Price 1992; Price 1988: part II; Wright 1988, 1993).

The second concern is more closely related to the issues with which we began. Non-factualism is often characterized in terms of the neo-Fregean conception of the structure of a theory of meaning. That is, the non-factualist can often be represented as claiming that a certain sentential construction is mistakenly thought to modify the sense of a sentence in which it appears, whereas in fact it modifies the force. The clearest example is again provided by the denial interpretation of sentential negation, which Frege himself was attacking in his original presentation of the Frege point.[9] What happens to this appealing characterization of non-factualism, if non-factualism is presented in the way I have suggested? This question deserves a section to itself.

7. Sense, Force, and Function in Minimal Semantics

The above concern may be focused by the following train of thought. Advocates of minimal truth have emphasized its affinity with Tarskian truth theories, and the truth-theoretic approach to a theory of meaning. (Conversely, the "minimalism" of the truth-theoretic notion of truth had already been emphasized by writers such as McDowell [see particularly McDowell 1981].) But doesn't this mean[10] that if non-factualists endorse minimal truth they become factualists? In the resulting theory of meaning, utterances of the form "Not-P" have assertoric force, for example.

9. It may seem odd to speak of the denial interpretation of negation as a example of non-factualism. As Lloyd Humberstone puts it, "there seems to be a striking discontinuity between the traditional fare of . . . non-factualism, and the force-based treatment of negation. No one has ever advanced a non-factualist thesis with respect to negative statements" (Humberstone, personal correspondence). It is true that some versions of non-factualism would have had trouble incorporating the denial view of negation. A position characterized in terms of possession of truth conditions will have its work cut out to maintain that Not-P is not simply true when P is false and false when P is true, for example. The grouping of the denial view with other forms of non-factualism looks much more natural if couched in terms of a Fregean force–sense distinction, however—the common claim being that certain utterances lack assertoric force. It seems to me that Humberstone's "discontinuity" is really a matter of degree, the relevant variable being the ease with which truth and falsity are extended to utterances having the non-assertoric force in question. In the case of negation, the bipolarity of truth and falsity guarantees that the extension is very easy indeed.

10. As in effect McDowell suggests (1981: 229, n9).

The non-factualist's response must be to accept the conclusion but to deny that it has the significance the objector is claiming for it. The crucial point is that on the minimal interpretation the conclusion is not incompatible with the non-factualist's positive theses about the significance of (here) negation. For the non-factualist about negation need not renounce the view that its primary role in language is to provide a universal means of indicating that one is dissenting from some particular proposition; or to put it psychologically, the view that negation is associated with the expression of disbelief. It is just that the non-factualist also now remarks that this activity of denial is the sort of linguistic activity which fruitfully comes to be couched in terms of the minimal notion of truth; and thus becomes an assertion, in the minimal semantic sense.

It is worth noting in passing that this opens the way to a considerably more plausible view of negation than is available to the opposition. In accepting Frege's criticism of the denial interpretation of negation, Geach appreciates that it commits him to the view that disbelief must be thought of as "belief that not." He says that

> believing, like seeing, has no polar opposite. . . . The distinction of "pro" and "contra," of favourable and unfavourable attitude, has its place only in the realm of appetite, will, and passion, not in that of belief; this shows the error in treating religious beliefs as some sort of favourable attitude toward something. (Geach 1965: 455)

Setting aside Geach's passing defense of religious factualism, let us consider the effect of this position on our understanding of the meaning of negation. All sides will agree that P and Not-P are not jointly acceptable, at least in the sense that there would normally be some serious mistake involved in assenting to both. How is the Fregean to account for this striking feature of negation? The obvious suggestion might seem to be that it results from the fact that in virtue of the truth-functional analysis of negation, P and Not-P cannot both be true: if P is true, then Not-P is not true, and vice versa. As it stands, this gets us no further, however, for the original issue simply reemerges with respect to the pair "P is true" and "P is not true" (or "Not(P is true)"). It might seem to be an improvement to note that if P is true then Not-P is *false*, but this simply avoids one difficulty at the expense of another. It now needs to be explained what it is about truth and *falsity* in virtue of which one would be ill advised to assent to a pair of propositions so related. It is no use saying simply that in virtue of their opposite truth values the two sentences in question are "incompatible" or "inconsistent," for then the question will be why incompatibility itself matters—why the rational speaker should take pains to avoid it, among the utterances to which she assents.

The moral of all this is that the notion of incompatibility involves an intrinsic bipolarity: it takes two to tango exactly out of step, so to speak, and these two must fail to hit it off in a very special way. At some point in the Mind-Language-World triangle, this incompatibility must make its appearance. Philosophers who are sufficiently thick-skinned may be inclined to accept a primitive bipolarity at some point on the Language-to-World side of the triangle; perhaps a primitive opposition between truth and falsity, or a primitive exclusion relation between negative and positive facts. In either case they then have the task of relating this piece of metaphysics to psychological and linguistic practice. In effect, they have to explain how speakers become aware of this relation of incompatibility that obtains in the world, link it to their understanding of negation, and hence display the appropriate caution in avoiding judgments of the form "P and Not-P."

Things are much simpler if we start at the psychological corner. We don't need negative facts or a mysterious primitive opposition between truth and falsity, but merely an appreciation of the situation that we face as creatures whose behavior is determined, in part, by what we may loosely call commitments—changeable behavioral dispositions of various kinds. The premise in the background here is a very simple one: if a creature is to meet the future with anything more than the tools it was born with, it needs the ability to prepare itself in the light of past experience. Plausibly, it is a feature of any reasonably complex system of behavioral dispositions of this kind that the states concerned may conflict, in the sense that they move their bearer in different behavioral directions. To avoid behavioral chaos, any creature capable of such commitments thus needs to be able to remove commitments from its current store, as well adding new ones. In particular, it needs to be able to spot conflicts before they are manifest in behavior, and to adjust its commitments accordingly. It needs to be able to *reject* one commitment in the light of another.

This act of rejection is functionally distinct from the simpler act of endorsement (the act of adding a commitment to one's current store). More importantly, its functional relationship to the simpler act embodies the incompatibility we were looking for. (The impossibility of simultaneously rejecting and endorsing a given commitment is much like that of entering and leaving a room at one and the same time.) It follows that if negation is explained as initially a sign of denial, and denial as the linguistic expression of rejection, then we shall have some prospect of explaining just what goes wrong with an attempt to endorse both P and Not-P.

In sum, we may say in answer to Geach that although strictly speaking he is right to say that belief is not bipolar, in that we can make sense of commitment without the possibility of its polar opposite, a consideration of the functional role of belief makes it plain that the ability to reject commitments is crucial to all but the simplest believers. In order to be useful, judgment must thus become bipolar—commitments must be rejected as well as endorsed—at a very early stage. And in this we have the beginnings of an explanation of a fact about language that otherwise remains primitive and mysterious, namely the incompatibility of an assertion and its negation—an explanation which turns on the hypothesis that the primary role of negation is to indicate denial, or to express disbelief.[11]

The suggestion is that negation thus begins life as a force modifier, indicating a linguistic move of a different pragmatic significance—a different functional role—from anything in the language so far. Once incorporated, however, utterances with this new significance are appropriately subject to the same operations as those of the old. If this suggestion seems puzzling, the following analogy may be helpful. Negative integers are initially introduced via a quite new operator, which is applied to positive integers to yield mathematical entities of a new kind—entities that are not numbers in the previously recognized sense. The existing operations (addition, etc.) extend in a natural way to these new entities, however, with the result that they too come to be thought of as numbers. Adopting the symbolic convention that symbols referring to numbers are of the form "[. . .]," the ordinary expression "-2" may therefore be parsed more explicitly either as "-[2]" or as "[-2]," depending on whether we have decided to treat the products of the operation denoted by the minus sign as themselves comprising numbers. There is no single correct parsing here, merely alternative ways of representing the same thing. The only substantial question is why it is that -[2] is the sort of thing that may be regarded as a number, in some natural extension of the previous usage—to which the answer lies in the availability of natural extensions of the arithmetical operations to the members of the broader class. (Is there a corresponding question in the semantic case? We shall see below that there is.)

In the case of negation the upshot is that we do not have to make a choice between the view that negation indicates denial (or expresses disbelief) and the view that it indicates an assertion with negative content (or expresses such a belief). We may say both things, so long as we are dealing with a suitably minimal notion of belief. Disbelief or dissent comes first, for it is such a notion, cashed in functional terms, that accounts for the presence and utility of negation in the first place. But given that this expression of disbelief takes the minimal assertoric form, we may think of it as the expression of belief.

Putting it in Fregean terms, we might say that the sense–force boundary is not unique—we may have two (or more) ways to parse a given utterance. "Not-P" may be thought of both as a denial of the proposition that P and as an assertion of the proposition that not-P. The pragmatic account of the function of denial is not a separate component of a theory of meaning from the theory of sense, but a subtheory, whose task is to explain how there come to be sentences with senses of a particular sort—how there come to be sentences with the sense of negative judgments, for example.

11. For more on the advantages and complexities of this, see Price 1990. However, the present account (in terms of the need for a procedure for rejecting commitments) now seems to me both simpler and more forceful than the corresponding argument in my earlier paper.

The two parsings engage with two different aspects of a theory of meaning. The platitude that to know the meaning of a sentence is to know the conditions for its correct use has two importantly different readings (not always properly distinguished). It may be taken to refer to what I earlier called subjective assertibility conditions, so that it amounts to the claim

(4) To know the meaning of "It is snowing" is to know that it is normally appropriate to say "It is snowing" only when one believes that it is snowing.

Or it may refer to truth conditions, so that the claim is that it is correct to say "It is snowing" if and only if it is snowing; or, in the more familiar form, that

(5) "It is snowing" is true if and only if it is snowing.

These claims are not incompatible, of course, and knowledge of meaning surely involves knowledge of both kinds. (5) has the form we expect of the theorems of a content-specifying truth theory—a systematic specification of the meanings of the sentences of an object language by means of sentences in the home language. As has often been emphasized, this enterprise needs only a thin notion of truth. It therefore applies uniformly to all minimally descriptive parts of the object language.

Principle (4), on the other hand, has the resources to cope with the functional perspective, which is crucial to the proposed reformulation of non-factualism. We may say for example that

(6) To know the correct use of "Not-P" is to know that it is normally appropriate to say "Not-P" only when one *disbelieves* that P.

Note that this is not incompatible with the following instance of (4):

(7) To know the meaning of "Not-P" is to know that it is normally appropriate to say "Not-P" only when one believes that not-P.

Interpreted in terms of minimal belief, (4) is true of all minimal descriptions. But it is (6) which captures what is distinctive about utterances of the form Not-P.

In summary, then, the proposed reformulation of non-factualism encounters no special problems with respect to the goals of a theory of meaning. To the extent that such goals are met by a content-specifying truth theory, the reformulated view coincides with the standard account; while to the extent that such a truth theory needs to be supplemented by theses of the form of (4), this form is flexible enough to accommodate the functional perspective adopted by the reformulated view.

8. Conclusion: Explaining Assertion

At the beginning of the chapter I suggested that the interest in a reexamination of the Frege argument lay not simply in its immediate bearing on the viability of non-factualist approaches to various philosophical topics, but also in the fresh perspective it promised to provide on some neglected issues in the philosophy of language and speech act theory. As we shall see, the latter benefit depends in part on an important qualification concerning the former. The path for non-factualism is not quite as smooth as the above account might suggest; and in its bumps lie the real nuggets for those interested more in language itself than in its philosophical applications.

To recap, I have suggested that non-factualism is best served by a strategic retreat, followed by an advance on new grounds. Non-factualists should concede that they put their view in the wrong way—namely, in semantic terms. What they should have said was that the mistake they opposed was that of reading substantial metaphysical conclusions into semantics. Conceding semantics is no significant loss, for the semantic ice is really too thin to support either party. While the non-factualists' intuitions concerning the distinctive role of (say) moral discourse are best cast in functional rather than semantic terms.

As noted earlier, there is an issue as to whether the resulting position should really be called "non-factualism." Non-factualists may be well advised to surrender their banner, as well as their untenable semantic position. In one sense this is a relatively insignificant change. The view retains the resources to combat many of the non-factualist's traditional opponents. In the moral case, for example, it remains opposed not only to the metaphysical realists who would populate the world with mysterious moral facts and properties, but also to those who, in fleeing this metaphysical nightmare, turn in preference to eliminativism or naturalistic reductionism. Non-factualists always stood opposed to all these choices, and may continue to do so under this new banner.

All the same, there are some respects in which orthodox non-factualists may be discomforted by the new arrangements. Non-factualists are accustomed to riding with anti-realists, even if in some cases uncomfortably so. Under the new scheme, their natural allies are realists, albeit of a non-metaphysical sort. Reconstituted non-factualists will find themselves sympathetic with the minimalist realism of writers such as Wittgenstein, Davidson, and Rorty (although as I point out elsewhere [Price 1992], the reconstituted view improves on these minimalist accounts in one crucial respect, namely that it directs our attention to the issue of what different parts of language are *for*).

The contemporary writer whose views are closest to those of my reconstituted non-factualist is perhaps Simon Blackburn. Blackburn begins with the Humean idea that we project our attitudes and prejudices onto the world, and so see it as populated by seeming facts of our own construction. He then goes on to argue that such a non-factualist can explain our conversing as if there really were such facts—in other words, that the Humean "projectivist" is entitled to a notion of truth, and to the other trappings of a realist linguistic practice. Thus projectivism supports "quasi-realism," as Blackburn calls it (see, in particular, Blackburn 1984). On this view, moral discourse (or whatever) is not *really* factual, but has—and is entitled to—the trappings of factuality.

One aspect of these trappings is the ability to be usefully embedded in conditional contexts, and as we noted in section 4, Blackburn has offered an account of what moral statements are doing in such contexts. We saw that in appealing to second-order evaluative judgments, Blackburn's account could be criticized for absorbing too much of the general character of the conditional form into peculiarities of the moral case. Viewed in the light of our appeal to minimal semantics in answer to the Frege point, Blackburn's approach may also seem unnecessarily complicated. In defense of Blackburn, however, it should be conceded that the quasi-realist program embodies an insight that is in danger of getting lost in the rush to embrace minimal semantics. Not all linguistic functions are such as to be usefully cast in terms of truth and falsity, however minimally these are conceived. Someone who wants to be pluralist about underlying linguistic functions thus owes us an account of what the truth-bearing form achieves in language, and hence an explanation, case-by-case, as to why various disparate functions should invoke it. Insofar as conditionals are associated with the truth-bearing form, for example, we need to be told how the general function of the conditional serves the specific purposes of moral discourse, modal discourse, or whatever.

This may sound like the difficult case-by-case work we tried to avoid in invoking minimal semantics. Have we therefore advanced at all by means of this long detour? It seems to me that from the non-factualist's point of view the situation has improved in one crucial respect: the question as to the general function of the truth-bearing form of language has now been raised as an issue that all sides need to address. Previously, in couching their views in semantic terms, the non-factualists effectively conceded to their opponent the latter's right to an unexamined notion of the genuinely factual (or truth-bearing) use of language. The explanatory onus thus lay almost entirely on the non-factualists' side. The new approach distributes the burden much more fairly. True, the non-factualists' opponents may not have *noticed* that there is a general question to be raised concerning the role of truth-bearing constructions in language; but this is hardly a point against non-factualism. In effect, the point is that the complexity which bothered us at the end of section 4 is not a burden for non-factualism alone. The appeal to semantic minimalism does not evade this complexity, for the difficult explanatory issues remain; but it does ensure that the burden is properly spread, and that all sides take their fair share of the load.

It is here that we find the promised theoretical dividend. In responding to the Frege point in the above terms, the non-factualist draws our attention to the existence of a degree of structural complexity in language that we otherwise might have little reason to notice. Our attention is drawn to the possibility that the apparent uniformity of assertoric or declarative discourse may well mask a multiplicity of different functions. More importantly still, this model of common form over diverse function raises the issue as to what the common form is *for*—what it *does* in the service of these diverse functions. Until the non-factualist pressed a case for diversity, we had little reason not to be satisfied with a very simplistic conception of assertoric discourse—roughly, the view that it serves to make descriptive claims, to "state the facts" as the speaker believes (or claims to believe) them to be. There are other formulations of this conception, of course, but they all take for granted that what is being at least gestured at is a single reasonably coherent linguistic function. The suggested defense of non-factualism gives us reason to question this assumption. The reconstituted non-factualist will argue that the usual formulations have little or no explanatory value, but simply rehash the same bundle of superficial idioms: "fact," "truth," "reference," "statement," "belief," and the rest. A genuinely illuminating account would be one that explained the existence of these concepts and idioms (or at least those which are in ordinary use) in terms of their contribution to the functions of language more basically construed. The new non-factualist points out that there is an important sense in which such an account need not be monistic—the same tool may do many jobs.

To conclude, the most central issue to which the above considerations direct our attention seems to me to be this one: *What does assertoric discourse do for us?* It is possible to distinguish a number of sub-issues here. What are the concepts of truth and falsity for? (What function do they serve in the lives of a linguistic community?) What is the significance of the linguistic constructions that apparently depend on truth—conditionals, for example? Again, how does it help us to have them? And is there a category of genuine judgments, as opposed to commitments more generally?[12]

In order to address these issues, it is necessary for us to take a detached explanatory stance toward our own linguistic practice. We need to step back from our familiar concepts and practices in order to be able to see the broader picture, and hence to discern the role that the concepts and practices concerned play in our lives. To a degree, this detached perspective comes easily to non-factualists, who are accustomed to arguing that language is misleading at close range. It should also come easily to speech act theorists, for they too are used to dissecting out the hidden functions of language. However, the main point I want to urge is that by and large, neither group has stepped back far enough. Both camps have tended to regard the linguistic categories of assertion, description, and the like as part of the bedrock—as a firm foundation on which other work may rest. Hence they

12. This last issue is central to the dispute between my view (see Price 1988, 1992) and that of Blackburn. In Blackburn's terms, I am someone who extends the quasi-realist project "all the way down." Blackburn's difficulty seems to me to be that non-global quasi-realism is in danger of being self-refuting: the better the quasi-realist does locally, the less reason there will be not to "go global."

have failed to see the importance of subjecting these categories themselves to explanatory scrutiny. In my view the great theoretical significance of the Frege point is that it directs our attention to these long neglected issues.

9. Postscript: Implications for Reductive Metaphysics

It seems to me that the above discussion sheds useful light on a range of debates in contemporary metaphysics. In particular, it highlights and clarifies an insufficiently recognized *linguistic* assumption that underlies a popular reductionist program. The program takes its lead from the arguments for a mind-brain identity theory advanced by Lewis and Armstrong in the 1960s. Lewis and Armstrong suggested independently that what is distinctive about mental states is their causal roles. Pain, for example, is simply the state apt to be caused in certain ways (by pins or heat, for example), and to have certain effects (wincing, crying out, desiring to avoid, and so on). Given this conceptual analysis, the physicalist principle that all such effects are explicable in physical terms then yields the conclusion that mental states are physical states. Which physical states? Simply those that occupy the relevant causal roles. As is well known, Lewis invokes Ramsey's technique for the elimination of theoretical terms in the service of this argument.

This approach has been taken to provide a general model for a reductionist materialism. The most explicit version of the general program I know is that spelled out by Frank Jackson (1994).[13] Jackson takes the path of conceptual analysis followed by "Ramseyfication" to be the appropriate general strategy for metaphysics. It was that paper, and a more recent one by Lewis himself (1994), that prompted me to try to formulate a concern I had already felt about the original argument for mind-body identity. It seemed to me that this reductionist program depended in any particular case on a crucial but usually unacknowledged assumption: roughly, the assumption that the reduced theory is doing the same linguistic job as the reducing theory. Unless this assumption is valid in the case in question, the proposed reduction would involve a kind of category mistake.

Thinking about how to make this point a vivid one, it seemed to me that a good strategy would be to point out that as it stood, the program could be applied in cases in which it seems quite clear that the concepts we start with are not in the same linguistic business as the physical descriptions the program would yield. By appealing to a case in which the relevant assumption would be quite implausible, I hoped to draw attention to the fact that it is also required in less contentious cases. Somewhat ironically, the case I had in mind was that of value.[14]

13. Jackson develops the program at greater length in Jackson (1998).
14. Frank Jackson and Philip Pettit (1995) defend just such an approach to value.

However, while I was wrong in thinking that no one would be tempted to apply Ramsey reduction to evaluative concepts, this actually makes very little difference to the relevance of the example. My argument is not a reductio, but simply requires a case in which it is easy to see that there is an issue as to whether the concepts whose reduction is contemplated belong to the same aspect of the linguistic enterprise as the physically kosher descriptions in terms of which the Ramsey program would cash them. Why is this obvious in the evaluative case? Simply because we are familiar with generations of evaluative non-factualists in philosophy, whose central thesis is that the role of evaluative judgments must be distinguished from that of ordinary descriptions.

Jackson and Pettit recognize the need for an assumption of this kind, and explicitly presuppose cognitivism. However, they appear to take for granted that this is an assumption to be cashed in semantic terms, as the thesis that evaluative judgments are genuinely "truth apt," or some such. The point I have emphasized above is that this seems to address the issue at the wrong level. A sophisticated non-factualist will simply deny that the interesting distinctions in language lie at this level. "Of course moral judgments are (minimally) truth apt," the cluey emotivist will say, "But this is quite compatible with my claim that such judgments are functionally distinct from natural descriptions."

Thus the reductionist program appears to be driven by what amounts to a substantial semantic thesis, namely that the various bits of language in question have a common purpose—that of describing the world, saying how things are, or some such. It is only when coupled with this semantic thesis that physicalism provides a motivation for reductionism. However, while the effect of semantic minimalism is to deflate this thesis somewhat, so that it is no longer clear what the different parts of language are being held to have in common, the initial result seems to be something of a stand-off. We might say that in minimalist terms it isn't clear why we should want to be Ramsey reductionists, but neither is there any explicit objection to the application of the algorithm. The charge that reductionism may be guilty of a category mistake cannot itself be formulated in semantic terms, minimally construed.

The charge of possible category mistake can be formulated from the functional standpoint, however. It simply depends on an appreciation that semantic minimalism and uniformity is compatible with the existence of substantial diversity at the functional level. (Minimal descriptions need not be natural descriptions, as we put it earlier.) More importantly still, the functional standpoint threatens to undercut the *motivation* for reductionism: once we have an adequate explanation for the fact that the folk *talk of* Xs and Ys and Zs, an explanation which distinguishes these activities from what the folk are doing when they do physics, why should we try to reduce the Xs and Ys and Zs to what is talked about in physics?

So it is the functional standpoint that matters in determining whether Ramsey reduction is appropriate. It is important to appreciate that the functional perspective is scientific, and naturalistic. Hence it can't be dismissed a priori—particularly by physicalists—and the reductionist program turns out to depend on an a posteriori theoretical thesis about language. Moreover, folk intuitions give us very little access to the matters addressed from this theoretical perspective. Such intuitions provide the explanandum—what we are after is a theory about the origins and functions of our folk intuitions—but not the explanans. So there really is no route into these issues other than the hard one of standing back from the concepts in question and asking how they arise, and what functions they serve in the lives of the creatures who employ them. Despite its naturalism, this seems to be a thoroughly Wittgensteinian stance.[15] In failing to notice the importance of the issues addressed from this stance, reductionist metaphysics has put its money by default on the assumption that indicative discourse is functionally univocal. It doesn't seem to me to be a very good bet, and it is certainly not a bet to be made with one's eyes closed. The moral is that if you want to do metaphysics in this way, you had better think first about language—and you had better think about it in Wittgensteinian terms![16]

15. There are two importantly different explanatory stances here: one which seeks to explain a use of language "from the inside," allowing the explanans to include a certain shared phenomenological basis on which the discourse in question may be held to rest; and one that is more detached, in seeking to explain the use in question in more-or-less biological terms. As Kevin Mulligan has helped me to see, it may be that the former stance is very much more Wittgensteinian than the latter. If so, then I part company with the Master at this point, in wanting to allow both.

16. I am very grateful for comments from Simon Blackburn, Daniel Stoljar, Lloyd Humberstone, and Michael McDermott, and also for the assistance of participants in seminars at Monash University and UNSW.

4

Two Paths to Pragmatism

1. Introduction

Particular topics of conversation seem to be inaccessible to speakers who lack an insider's view of the subject matter concerned. The familiar examples involve sensory deficiencies: discourse about music may be inaccessible to the tone deaf, wine talk to the anosmic, the finer points of interior decorating to the color blind, and so on. The traditional secondary qualities thus provide the obvious cases of concepts that seem to exhibit this form of subjectivity—this dependence on specific and quite contingent human capacities.

It is easy to think of further cases, resting on more specific perceptual and quasi-perceptual disabilities. (Could someone with no ball sense understand what it is like to be a batsman, for example?) But is this the end of the matter? How far does this phenomenon extend in language? How precisely should it be characterized? And what is its significance, if any, for the metaphysical status of the concepts concerned? Questions of this kind have been the focus of considerable attention in recent years. The original impetus for much of this work seems to have been the suggestion that there might be a useful analogy between moral concepts and the secondary qualities. This rather specific issue has then given rise to a more general interest in the nature and significance of the kind of subjectivity exhibited by the secondary qualities (and/or moral concepts). Writers such as Mark Johnston and Crispin Wright have sought to develop general formal frameworks within which to represent the dependence of concepts of a certain kind on particular human capacities (see, in particular, Wright 1993 and Johnston 1993; see also Johnston 1989 and Wright 1992).[1]

1. In keeping with the focus of the conference for which this piece was first prepared, I shall concentrate on Johnston's work. However, given that Wright's account invokes biconditional content conditions similar to those employed by Johnston, and that my main concern is to argue for a quite different means of explicating the significance of the relevant linguistic expressions, I think that much of what I say would equally stand opposed to Wright's approach.

As Johnston well appreciates, one excellent motive for seeking a general characterization of the kind of subjectivity in play in the case of the secondary qualities is to equip oneself for an assault on one of the most fascinating issues in philosophy: How much of the conceptual framework we apply to the world is simply taken over from the world itself, and how much of it "comes from us"? In a philosophical climate often dismissive of the sort of pragmatism that takes this question seriously, it is pleasing to see the attention it receives in Johnston's hands.

All the same, it seems to me that Johnston has done pragmatism a disservice. His advocacy of response dependence as the general species of subjectivity apparently exhibited by the secondary qualities has helped to obscure an attractive alternative path into the same territory. The effects of this are evident in Johnston's own position. In "Objectivity Refigured," Johnston argues tellingly that there is space for a species of pragmatism distinct from verificationism and Putnam's internal realism. He then assures us that the route to a pragmatism of this kind "goes by way of developing and applying the notion of response-dependence" (Johnston 1993: 103). So it comes as something of an anticlimax when he concludes that the notion of response dependence is of limited application, even in the hands of philosophers who are prepared to revise ordinary usage to put it on respectable metaphysical foundations. Though Johnston attempts to salvage some general consequences from a response-dependent treatment of theoretical "rightness," pragmatists hoping for historic victories on the field of metaphysics will feel a sense of anticlimax.

I want to show that the problem lies in the choice of response dependence as the path to the general issue of the extent of subjectivity in our representation of the world. There is an alternative route, and one that promises bigger dividends. Indeed, it suggests that the subjectivity in question is global, infecting all parts of language (though different parts to different extents). In endorsing a form of global pragmatism, I concur with Philip Pettit (1991). However, Pettit follows Johnston in regarding response dependence (or a closely related notion) as the proper path to such a pragmatism, and apparently in failing to appreciate that there is an alternative. (He disagrees with Johnston mainly in arguing that the resulting pragmatism is globally applicable.) But the global enterprise turns out to be particularly sensitive to the choice of route: the alternative path has advantages even in local cases, but becomes mandatory if the pragmatist's project is to be generalized in this way. So while I join Pettit in the quest for global pragmatism,[2] I want to argue that in setting a course in terms of response dependence, he is guiding our common ship by the wrong star.

2. Indeed, we both sail under the rule-following banner (see Pettit 1991: 588; and Price 1988: 192–195).

So the main task of this paper is philosophical cartography. I want to put the alternative path to pragmatism on the philosophical map, and draw attention to some of its advantages. The aim is to chart the least hazardous course for those of us who cannot resist the lure of a world whose conceptual joints all owe something to ourselves; and to present the complete picture for the benefit of less adventurous souls, so that at least they may see toward what monsters we set sail.

2. Two Ways of Explicating Meaning

The two paths to pragmatism are distinguished by the fact that they rely on different theoretical strategies for explicating the significance of a concept or linguistic expression. The first strategy—that employed by response theorists—is exemplified by the following simple version of Johnston's "basic equation":

> (1) X is C iff X is disposed to produce response R_c in normal subjects under suitable conditions.

I shall call this a *content condition*. Not much hangs on the terminology. Johnston, Pettit, and others warn us not to interpret such biconditionals as reductive *analyses* of the concepts referred to on the left-hand side (LHS). However, the term *content condition* will serve to mark a contrast with a second sort of explication of the significance of an expression, which is what I shall call a *usage condition*. The general form of such a condition is something like this:

> (2) The utterance S is prima facie appropriate when used by a speaker who has a psychological state ϕ_s.

The particular usage condition which contrasts to (1) will then be:

> (3) The utterance "X is C" is prima facie appropriate when used by a speaker who experiences response R_c in the presence of X.

A usage condition thus tells us something about the *subjective assertibility conditions* of an expression—about what condition must normally obtain *in the speaker* for the utterance of an expression to be appropriate. As such, it is of course only the very first step in a theoretical description of linguistic practice. It leaves out the Gricean hierarchy of intentional attitudes, to mention just one aspect of the larger picture. All the same, it may be an important first step, as a few familiar examples will illustrate.

> *Emotivism*: The utterance "X is good" is prima facie appropriate when used by a speaker who approves of (or desires) X.

Adam's Hypothesis: The utterance "If P then Q" is prima facie appropriate when used by a speaker who has a high conditional credence in Q given P.

Assertion and Belief: The assertion "A" is prima facie appropriate when used by a speaker who has the belief that A.

Again, these principles are only the most basic elements of a pragmatic account of the usage conditions of the utterances concerned. So it would be beside the point to object at this point that it is not always appropriate to say "X is good" when one approves of X. It is not always appropriate to say "P" when one believes that P, but there is still something important and informative in the principle that one should normally assert that P only if one does believe that P.

I shall be arguing that the insights of pragmatism are better served by usage conditions than by content conditions. However, I emphasize that I am not suggesting that content-specifying conditions have no role to play in the philosophical project of explicating meaning. In my view, a pragmatist is likely to find as much use as anybody else in a content-specifying truth theory of the Tarski-Davidson sort, and should have no more qualms about

(4) "X is good" is true iff X is good

than about

(5) "X is electrically charged" is true iff X is electrically charged.

My argument simply concerns the appropriate vehicle for the distinctive points that a pragmatist wants to make about the dependence of particular areas of discourse on human capacities or points of view. I want to urge that these points are better made in terms of usage conditions than in terms of the kind of biconditional content conditions that writers on response dependence have offered us.

I noted above that my description of these biconditionals as "content-specifying" might be thought contentious, given that Johnston and others take pains to point out that these principles are not to be read as straightforward reductive analyses. I don't want to become entangled in a discussion of the possible varieties of conceptual analysis. I simply want to show that even if we put these labels to one side, there is a clear distinction between response theorists and a usage pragmatist, in that usage conditions do not yield several of the key conclusions that Johnston and Pettit draw from their versions of response dependence. This will be enough to show that content conditions and usage conditions represent two incompatible paths to pragmatism. It will also give us some reasons for preferring the latter path.

One more terminological point: once it is appreciated that content conditions and usage conditions provide two distinct strategies for explicating the dependence of particular discourses on human abilities, responses and capacities, then a decision is needed as to whether we should take the term "response dependence" to be applicable to both, or only to the content-based approach. As my use of the term "response theorist" already indicates, I take the latter course. Given the central role of biconditional content conditions in the work of those who have introduced the term "response dependence," I think it would be misleading to apply it to an approach that rejects these biconditionals. I therefore refer to writers who rely on these content conditions as *response theorists*.

It should be emphasized that many of the general remarks that response theorists make in characterizing their pragmatic stance are quite compatible with a usage-based approach. In the first paragraph of his paper "Realism and Response-Dependence," for example, Pettit asks us to:

> Consider the concepts of smoothness, blandness and redness. They are tailor-made for creatures like us who are capable, as many intelligences may not be, of certain responses: capable of finding things smooth to the touch, bland to the taste, red to the eye. The concepts, as we may say, are response-dependent. (Pettit 1991: 587)

We may agree with Pettit that concepts such as these depend on particular human responses or capacities, and yet deny that this entails that they should be (let alone *need be*) seen as response-dependent, in the technical sense of the term that Johnston has introduced. The main point of this chapter is to show that there is an alternative to response dependence, providing a better way to explicate the relevant species of dependence on particular responses. It is perhaps a pity that the useful descriptive term "response dependent" has come to be associated with a less than general account of what the general phenomenon amounts to, but there it is. The crucial point to keep in mind is that the general pragmatic program is not at issue here. The dispute concerns the correct strategy for putting the program into effect.

Finally, it should be noted that Johnston himself distinguishes two sorts of conclusions that the pragmatist might aim for. The first is a descriptive doctrine about a discourse as it stands in ordinary use. The second is the revisionary proposal to replace an existing discourse with a discourse couched in acceptable pragmatic terms. My main interest is in the descriptive doctrine—in the question as to how to explicate actual linguistic practice. I want to show that the usage-based approach does better at this descriptive level than the response theorist's alternative. But we shall see that because it does better here, the usage approach avoids some difficulties that the response theorist might take to motivate the revisionary doctrine. As always, the linguistic revisionist bears an onus to justify the proposed change. For a response theorist the claimed justification might be that the (non–response-dependent) concepts presently employed in some area of discourse do not properly reflect their evident dependence on contingent human capacities; the proposed revision is intended to make this dependence explicit. However, the usage-based approach shows that this is a solution to a nonexistent problem. Usage conditions provide an alternative way to represent the dependence of particular discourses on human responses and capacities, and response theorists have simply looked in the wrong place. The discourses in question may adequately reflect their subjective origins as they stand, and hence be in no need of revision.

More later on the advantages of the usage approach. The first task is to show that the usage and content approaches are genuinely distinct. The best way to do this is to show that the usage approach does not have certain consequences that response theorists rightly draw from their content-based accounts.

3. Usage Conditions: Their Theoretical Austerity

If Johnston's biconditional is to be called the basic equation, then perhaps the alternative usage condition should be referred to as the *more* basic equation. For the usage condition embodies a very austere, general, and theoretically fundamental perspective on linguistic practice. Because it is so general and so austere, its philosophical consequences are correspondingly thin. It is committed to little, compatible with much. It is compatible with the most thoroughgoing realism, for example—realists about a particular subject matter will not deny that assertions about that subject matter are governed by a usage condition of the kind sketched above, under *Assertion and Belief*.

Similarly, the usage perspective does not of itself commit us to the view that speakers' responses or psychological states provide privileged access to the truth of the utterances concerned. This is clear in the case of *Assertion and Belief*, where the mistake of thinking otherwise is the Protagorean mistake of thinking that because we assert that P when we believe that P, to assert that P is to *say* that one believes that P (and is therefore true if one believes that P).

More interestingly, it seems that the usage perspective is not committed to privileged access to truth, even in the cases that will provide the direct alternative to the response theorist's biconditional, such as (3). For example, consider an explicitly fallibilist version of Moorean moral intuitionism. Here, the primary usage condition for "X is good" will be said to be whatever manifests the intuition that X is of moral worth. But this might be regarded as a fallible and defeasible condition, perhaps in such a way that normal speakers might be systematically mistaken about the moral status of certain kinds of entities. (Normal speakers might exhibit an irrational bias in favor of the so-called deserving poor, for example.) Normal consensus would thus be regarded as neither necessary nor sufficient to guarantee truth. Another example might be provided by realism in mathematics, coupled with a usage condition in terms of the belief that one has a proof. In this case, normal community consensus might be sufficient but not necessary for truth. So even in these cases, *the usage perspective is not necessarily response-privileging*. It is compatible with a more "cosmocentric" brand of realism, to use Pettit's term.

On the other hand, a usage-based approach is also compatible with a much less realist overlay than the response theorists offer us. In particular, it is compatible with the view that the area of discourse in question does not have truth conditions, or is non-factual in character. Examples are provided by the two principles headed *Emotivism* and *Adam's Hypothesis* above. Emotivism is usually associated with the view that moral judgments are non-factual and lack truth conditions; while Adam's Hypothesis is held by some to be the centerpiece of a non–truth-conditional view of indicative conditionals.

The fact that the usage-based theory is compatible with non-factualism perhaps marks the most striking and interesting contrast with content-based accounts. A response-dependent account is automatically truth-conditional. This is of course implicit in the biconditional form of the basic equation—there is nothing to stop us from adding ". . . is true" to the left-hand side, after all. Response theorists thus get their factualism for free, and therefore find it difficult to give serious consideration to alternative views. Johnston suggests that the fault lies with the opposition:

> An appropriate response-dependent account [of value] may thus threaten to make quasi-realism redundant. The quasi-realist programme is to *somehow* defend our right to employ the truth-conditional idiom in expressing evaluations.

However, the

> response-dependent account of value . . . implies that there is no need to *earn* the right to the truth-conditional form of expression. . . . [W]e have a natural conceptual right to this truth-conditional form. (Johnston 1989: 173–174)

Pettit simply passes over the point, noting that "there is no pressure from the traditional response-dependent thesis to go towards an instrumentalist . . . theory" (Pettit 1991: 607). Surely this is an indication that something has been missed. It is clear that philosophical attention to the dependence of particular concepts and discourses on human capacities has often found expression in non-factualist theories of one sort or another. Emotivism provides one familiar example, but there many others. Simon Blackburn's quasi-realist program provides a whole range of cases, for example—cases which, as Blackburn points out, may trace their ancestry to prominent themes in Hume (Blackburn 1993a).

These examples demonstrate that the pragmatist's concern to exhibit the dependence of language on human capacities and responses is not incompatible with non-factualism. So if the response theorist's reading of the pragmatist program cannot find room for non-factualism, so much the worse for that reading—or at least for the view that it is the sole available reading of what the pragmatist is up to.

At any rate, the usage approach provides a viewpoint from which the quasi-realist's concerns reemerge. It characterizes a pattern of usage using the very materials to which dispositional theories of value appeal, namely the existence on the part of speakers of dispositions to value certain things and states of affairs. But it does so in terms that don't prejudge the issue as to whether (and if so why) a pattern of usage meeting this characterization need take a truth-conditional form. On the face of it, speakers might display the relevant dispositions in language in a very minimal way, if at all. Humans might boo and cheer. Many animals successfully express their likes and dislikes in all sorts of pre-linguistic ways. So a lively disposition to value some things and disvalue other things need not sustain a *truth-conditional* linguistic practice, and it is entirely appropriate to inquire why, and with what justification, we ourselves do express certain evaluative dispositions in assertoric form. This is the quasi-realist's concern. It is a concern clearly addressable from the usage perspective, and hence the fact that a response-dependent account cannot make sense of it serves to emphasize the difference between the usage perspective and the content perspective. Both are pragmatic; both characterize evaluative discourse in terms of human responses. But content conditions and usage conditions engage with these responses in very different ways.

In trying to show that usage conditions provide the better path to pragmatism, I shall offer four main arguments. The first (section 6) turns on the consequences of the view that the species of pragmatism with which we are concerned is global in its application to language. I endorse this view, but argue that it leads to incoherence unless couched in terms of a usage pragmatism. Because it turns on globality, this first argument is not directly effective against a response theorist such as Johnston himself, who takes response dependence to be a local doctrine (and indeed potentially a revisionary doctrine). Against this position, my second argument (section 7) is in a sense a reversal of Johnston's above redundancy claim concerning quasi-realism. I argue that wherever there are the resources for a response-dependent reading (or re-reading) of a discourse, there are also the resources the quasi-realist needs for an adequate *explanation* of truth-conditional practice. So the response theorist's re-reading works only where it is unnecessary. But the relation is not symmetric: the usage-based approach often works where response dependence would not. In particular, it is entirely compatible with the minimalist metaphysical position that Johnston sees as the main rival to a response-dependent pragmatism with respect to many philosophically interesting topics.

In defense of a revisionary response-dependent reading, it might be claimed that, at least in certain cases, it alone enables us to *justify* judgments that play important roles in our lives. My third argument (sections 8–9) counters this claim, and in the process shows that the usage-based approach does a better job of explaining the characteristic role of judgments of various kinds. All parties agree that an account of evaluative judgments should explain why they motivate us (and *should* do so); an account of probabilistic judgment should explain its connection with decision under uncertainty, and so on. I want to show that the response theorists do rather poorly on this crucial task—a failure masked to some extent by a characteristic equivocation concerning the notion of rationality.

Finally (sections 10–13), I argue that the usage approach gives a more accurate explanation of some of the subtleties of ordinary language. In particular, it makes much better sense than its content-based rival of the peculiar mix of objectivity and subjectivity that we encounter in discourses subject to no-fault disagreements.[3] This should recommend the approach to those less sanguine than Johnston seems to be about the prospect of wholesale revision of linguistic practice.

The next two sections establish some of the groundwork for these arguments, particularly by drawing attention to useful analogies between response dependence and more familiar philosophical strategies.

4. *Assertion and Belief*: Some Protagorean Lessons

The principle *Assertion and Belief* embodies the uncontroversial idea that an account of the historical and psychological foundations of language will give a central explanatory role to the notion of belief; perhaps not to the full-blown propositional attitude, but at least to some weaker notion of behavioral commitment. For in an obvious sense, belief underlies and sustains the linguistic activity of *assertion*. Creatures who didn't have beliefs couldn't make assertions. Whatever else we say about assertion, we'll want to mark the fact that speakers typically assert that P only if they believe that P. Yet none of this entails that in saying that P a speaker asserts *that* he or she believes that P. True, it means that we can ordinarily infer that a speaker believes that P from the fact that she says that P. But there are several simple objections to identifying the content of an assertion with the belief that it normally expresses.

In particular, such an identification leads to analytic regresses, arguably vicious, of more than one kind. Suppose, for example, that our interest is in a general account of assertion. The view in question tells us to interpret the

3. All discourses have the potential to exhibit such disagreements, in my view; hence the global character of a usage-based pragmatism (see Price 1988: chapter 8).

assertion that P as the assertion that the speaker concerned believes that P. Here the target notion of assertion occurs again, central and yet unanalyzed.

Alternatively, let's focus on the content of the assertion that P. The view in question now leads us to the principle that this content is in some sense equivalent to that of the assertion that the speaker believes that P. The content of the latter assertion is then in the same sense equivalent to that of the assertion that the speaker believes that the speaker believes that P, and so on. The way is clear to a denumerable infinity of content sentences, whose related contents are all equivalent in the specified sense. So far what we have is not necessarily vicious. After all, it is a familiar idea that a denumerable infinity of logically equivalent sentences may all have the same content. But it teeters on the brink of viciousness: if the slightest analytic pressure is put on the right-hand side (RHS) of the relevant biconditionals, the whole structure collapses. For example, if we say on the psychological plane that to believe that P is to believe that "P" is true—that is, to believe that one believes that P—then immediately we are lost. Or if we say on the semantic plane that what *makes true* my assertion that P is the truth of the proposition that I believe that P, then again the regress carries us away. If not already incoherent, then, the position in question is at least highly unstable.[4]

One further point: if a reference to belief were a universal ingredient of the content of assertoric judgement in this way, then an obvious theoretical strategy would be to try to factor it out, and to concentrate on what varies from assertion to assertion, namely the content of this embedded belief—which would just take us back to where we started. This might well be the best practical strategy, as well. If *all* assertion were initially of the form "I believe that P," then the most advantageous strategy might be to let the qualification drop away; to invent a discourse of quasi-assertions, which pretended to talk about the world in an unqualified way. All the materials would be already at hand. The principle governing truth ascription would thus be that we should not worry about what *really* made one of these quasi-assertions true—they are, after all, only a game of our own devising—but simply that we should be prepared to *say* that one was true (or "quasi-true") when we had the relevant belief. Thus one should be prepared to quasi-assert that P, or ascribe quasi-truth to the quasi-assertion "P," when and only when one believes that P.

Thus the Protagorean's own materials allow us to construct a non-Protagorean practice. To close the trap, we need simply point to the possibility that the latter practice may be our actual practice. Later, this will be my strategy against content-based response theories.

4. Johnston suggests that circularity will be a problem for the Protagorean "only if it made the biconditionals and their associated identities empty"—i.e., if the Protagorean was aiming for a reductive definition, and the biconditional was too weak to supply it. (Johnston 1993: 106) But the infinite regress threatens because the biconditional is too strong, not because it is too weak.

5. Self-descriptivism

Thus in the familiar case of *Assertion and Belief*, it is easy to distinguish the role that belief properly plays in a usage-based account of the linguistic activity of making assertions, from a role that it might mistakenly be thought to play in a content-based theory of the content or truth conditions of assertoric utterances. In less commonplace places, however, it seems to have been less easy for philosophers to keep the distinction firmly in mind. Consider, for example, the familiar kind of non-cognitivist (or non-factualist) view that utterances of some disputed class do not express *beliefs*, but rather some other kind of propositional attitude. This is what a simple kind of emotivism says about moral judgments, or what a simple subjectivism says about probabilistic judgments. In these cases the relevant propositional attitudes are *approval* and *credence*, respectively: the emotivist says that "It is good that P" expresses a speaker's approval that P, not her belief that it is good that P; while the subjectivist says that "It is probable that P" expresses a speaker's high degree of credence that P, not his belief that it is probable that P.

These familiar expressivist positions are usage-based, not content-based: they give us usage conditions, not content conditions, for moral and probabilistic utterances. But they have often been confused with the following *self-descriptive* interpretations of moral and probabilistic claims: the view that in saying "It is good that P" a speaker *says that* she approves of the fact that P; and the view that in saying "It is probable that P" a speaker *says that* he has a high degree of credence that P. However, I hope it is clear, at least on reflection, that self-descriptivism is actually quite different from expressivism. The difference is just like that between the (correct) view that we typically say that P *when* we believe that P and the (incorrect) view that in saying P we say *that* we believe that P. In each case the difference rests on that between two distinct possible roles for the psychological state concerned: a usage-based role in an *explanation* of a linguistic practice, and a content-based role in an *analysis* or *explication* of the content of the utterances comprising that practice. Expressivism is usage-based; self-descriptivism is content-based.

However, while the self-descriptive interpretation is easily seen to be close to incoherency in the standard case of belief and assertion, it is not so obviously mistaken as an alternative to emotivism and probabilistic subjectivism. Indeed, it may seem to have some attractions, foremost of which might be thought to be that it doesn't leave us with any mystery as to what moral or probabilistic judgments actually mean, or as to why they look like regular assertions. They are regular assertions on this view, the only oddity being that their subject matter is not what it seems to be: they are about their utterer's state of mind, rather than about moral or probabilistic aspects of the world. (These views are not non-cognitivist, and are only non-factualist about their *apparent* factual referents.) A self-descriptivist might thus express puzzlement at the emotivist's concern with the issue as to why moral judgments take indicative form, and appear truth-conditional. "Once we explicate moral judgment in the way I suggest," the self-descriptivist might say, "We see that we have a natural conceptual right to the truth-conditional form of expression."

The response theorist's content conditions are not as implausible as those of these naive self-descriptivists, of course. All the same, I think that there is a valid comparison between the two kinds of position. In my view, the fallacy of interpreting expressivism as self-descriptivism involves simply a more graphic form of the same blindness that characterizes the response dependence program—that is, a blindness to the very possibility of a usage-based account built on the same psychological foundations. If nothing else, then, it will be helpful to have the self-descriptivist fallacy available as cautionary lesson, as I try to bring back into focus the possibility and advantages of a usage-based approach.

6. The Consequences of Global Pragmatism

As I noted in section 1, Philip Pettit argues that all concepts are response-dependent. His case turns on Wittgensteinian considerations about rule following: in virtue of the inability of any finite class of exemplars to constrain an intended concept to future cases in a unique way, the applicability of a concept F to a new potential instance X is always, in the last resort, dependent on the disposition of the members of a speech community to regard X as F. (The point is perhaps more evident if cast in terms of terms rather than concepts.) If endorsed, as I think it should be, Pettit's point has important ramifications for our present concerns. It invites a global generalization of the dispositional method of analysis. If

(6) X is good iff X is disposed to evoke (i.e., is such that it evokes) the "valuing" response in us.

then why not also

(7) X is F iff X is disposed to evoke (i.e., is such that it evokes) the "Seeing as relevantly similar to paradigm F's" response in us.

This suggestion cannot be rejected on the grounds that there is something illegitimate about the nature of the response referred to on the RHS. The point of Pettit's argument, and ultimately of the rule-following considerations themselves, is that language depends on responses or dispositions of this kind. Our use of the word "chair" ultimately depends on the fact that we have a certain ability to generalize to new cases on the basis of exposure to a small number of exemplars.[5]

5. Reductive definition of a term is a possibility, of course, but this simply delays the inevitable, as Kripke points out (1982).

What are the consequences of taking (7) seriously, however? In considering this question, let us pretend for the moment that the response theorist's biconditionals are to be taken as outright content specifications: if not as reductive analyses, then at least as indications of conceptual equivalence, or common content on both sides of the biconditional. Apparently, then, the consequence of (7) is that we cannot talk about the world as such, but only about its effect on us. All content becomes relational and anthropocentric in this way.

Recall that this is just what happens according to the Protagorean view that to assert that P is to assert that one believes that P. In section 4 I mentioned several objections to this view, turning mainly on the idea that it threatens a vicious regress. Similar problems would appear to afflict any attempt to take (7) as the general form of an analysis of concept ascription. The biconditional describes, if not an equivalence between contents, then at least an equivalence relation (namely, sameness of truth conditions). If the doctrine is to be universal, then the fact that the RHS is at the same time more complex and yet of the same basic logical form as the LHS—the form "X is G"—will guarantee us a denumerable infinity of content sentences, all specifying contents that stand to one another in the same equivalence relation. From here viciousness threatens in the same way as before: if the slightest weight is put on the RHS, the whole structure is liable to collapse.

Can a response theorist avoid this difficulty, by insisting that the relevant biconditionals have *no* analytic significance? It seems doubtful. As in the Protagorean case, even the suggestion that the RHS specifies what makes the LHS truth-apt will be enough to tip the balance, and it does seem that the response theorists are committed to this. As we have seen, Johnston relies on the biconditional to illustrate the response theorists "natural conceptual right" to truth conditions, for example, while Pettit apparently takes it as the basis of his suggestion that response dependence provides no pressure toward non-factualism.[6] But if the LHS has its truth value (or truth aptness) *in virtue* of that of the RHS, and the RHS has to acquire its own truth value (or truth aptness) in the same way, then the regress is certainly vicious. (By way of analogy, let's say that an object is well-grounded if it is standing on top of an object that is itself well-grounded. Now suppose that it's turtles all the way down. Can we show that the top turtle is well-grounded? No, for the same issue arises all over again at every level in the hierarchy of turtles.)

I think this is a decisive objection to a content-based global response theory. It is not a problem for local response theorists, of course, nor is it a problem for a theory which accepts that language is globally dependent on dispositions "to go on in the same way," but explains the role of these dispositions in usage conditions

6. Pettit also indicates (1991: 608) that the LHS of such a biconditional might be empirically falsified, in virtue of the lack of the various responses and conditions mentioned on the RHS.

rather than in content conditions. We can indeed be global pragmatists, then, but only if we abandon response dependence in favor of usage conditions.

7. The Redundancy Argument

In section 4, I mentioned another objection to the Protagorean view. It was that the Protagorean's own materials suffice to construct an alternative "language game," with respect to which the appropriate reference to belief takes the form of a usage condition rather than a content condition. In effect, then, the Protagorean's own resources provide a plausible alternative model of what might be going on in actual discourse. Unlike the regress point itself, this idea can be developed against local versions of content-based response theories.

Let's consider the raw materials required for a response-dependent account of, say, redness. What must be true of the members of a speech community in order for the dispositional account of color to yield truths of the form "Roses are red, violets are blue"? Simply that by and large, the members of the community share stable dispositions to experience similar responses in response to similar objects on similar occasions. The response theorist then tells us that when a member of the community says "Roses are red," what they say is true if and only if roses have the disposition to produce a particular psychological condition—the "redness" response—in normal members of the community under suitable conditions.

Suppose that a particular community have the appropriate responses, currently use the term "red" in accordance with this model, and are theoretically sophisticated enough to realize that this is what they are doing. It is open to them, in principle, to make the following linguistic policy decision. From now on, when they teach their children how to use the term "red," they will pretend that there is a response-independent property of redness in the world, and conform their practice to this pretence. I don't mean that they will explicitly say to their children that redness is response-independent; just that they will introduce "X is red" as the sort of claim that is capable of being true or false, independently of human dispositions to see things as red. Now it is a moot point just what is required to inculcate such an understanding. If our naive notion of color is already response-independent, as Johnston suggests it may be, then presumably these linguistic policy makers need only decide to follow the teaching practices actually followed by unsophisticated English-speaking folk. But if this is not enough, they could add explicit lessons in the fallibility of human access to color, taking care to pretend epistemological modesty with respect to color. The crucial point is that even this is not incompatible with a reliance on the usual means of indicating to novices the extension of these properties, namely the use of paradigm cases. (All it requires is the additional lesson that even the paradigms are defeasible.)

The policy makers thus set out to instill in the practice of novice speakers two main habits or principles. The first principle is the primary usage condition governing assertions of the form "X is red"—the relevant instance of (3), in effect. The second is the habit of taking redness to be something that falls under the objective mode of speech. Against the general background of assertoric practice, the way to combine these lessons will be to teach novices to describe their redness experiences in terms of the notions of perception and belief—ordinary, world-directed perception and belief, of course, not any introspective variety. In treating the distinctive redness response as defeasible perceptual grounds for a corresponding belief, we open the way to such comments as "You believe that it is red, but is it *really* red?" This in turn may call into play the standard methods of rational reassessment. In virtue of their acquaintance with the objective mode *in general*, speakers will be led into the practice of subjecting their color judgments to reflective scrutiny by themselves and others. The objective mode brings with it the methods and motives for rational inquiry. But notice the way rationality gets into the picture here. It is not a part of a content specification for the utterances in question, but a gift that comes for free with any choice to adopt the objective mode of speech, to use the indicative form, to speak of truth and belief. One of the attractions of usage-based rather than content-based pragmatism seems to me to be that it puts rationality in its proper place—extrinsic rather than intrinsic to the discourse. (More on this in the next section.)

Of course, we are not free to adopt the objective mode wherever we like; or rather, it won't get very far in some cases. It works in the color case because our color responses are sufficiently alike, across the community, for rational reassessment to get some grip. But notice that the requirements are extremely flexible. The practice is quite capable of tolerating a considerable degree of difference. For one thing, it may be quick to exploit pockets of similarity, small communities of like-minded responders. But it does this not by relativizing its claims to the standards of the community, but by exploiting the fact that the similarity within the community makes possible some degree of rational agreement on unrelativized claims.

Again, I'll come back to this. In section 11, I'll argue that this flexibility with respect to the scope of the speech community provides another advantage of the usage-based approach. For the moment, I simply want to emphasize the more basic point that where we have the resources in terms of which the content-based response theorists construct their accounts—that is, a sufficiently uniform pattern of responses across a community—these same resources provide sufficient foundation for a non–response-dependent discourse, characterized theoretically (and in effect to its novice speakers themselves) in terms of a usage condition. Thus it is the response theorist's account that now seems in danger of redundancy.

The response theorist might object that this so-called alternative will actually be equivalent to the content-based response-dependent account of the discourse in question. One way to see that this is not so is to observe that unlike the response-dependent account, the usage-based alternative is not committed to the a priori impossibility of global error. In principle the impossibility of such error might be accessible from one or both of two perspectives: to practitioners in the discourse in question, to theoreticians reflecting on the nature of the discourse, or to both. However, from the practitioners' point of view there is nothing in the usage-based account that rules out the possibility of global error. The discourse was explicitly designed not to exclude this (while the general possibility was illustrated in section 3 by the case of the fallible moral intuitionists). This leaves the theoreticians' point of view, and from here talk of error is simply a category mistake: because a usage-based theory is semantically austere, it tells us not when the utterances concerned are *true*, but how they are properly *used*.[7]

This point about theoretical perspective also provides the answer to a response theorist who asks what the truth conditions of the imagined discourse would be—hoping perhaps to show that there is no space for an alternative pragmatism at this point, between response-dependent truth conditions, on the one hand, and realist truth conditions, on the other. The answer is that *as theorists* we simply need not be in the business of providing truth conditions in the first place. As *speakers*, we may say with the crowd that "X is red" is true if and only if X is red. As *theorists*, we are simply interested in how discourse of this kind is *used*. (True, one important aspect of usage concerns the speakers' use of the terms "true" and "false," and this needs to be explained. However, there is no a priori argument in this for the kind of realism that would embarrass a usage pragmatist, at least as long as quasi-realism remains a viable alternative.)

The alternative is thus a genuine one. But could there be some reason for preferring the response-dependent practice; some reason for revising practice, if it is not already response-dependent? A possible suggestion is that only a response-dependent account enables us to *justify* the practice in question.[8] This would tie in

7. It is becoming a familiar point that semantic minimalism and metaphysical minimalism tend to go hand in hand. Here, semantic austerity accompanies metaphysical austerity. As I noted in section 3, the usage-based theory tells us very little about the metaphysical commitments of the community in question. But it is compatible with, and perhaps encourages, the minimalist metaphysical position that Johnston (1993: §4) regards as the most serious challenge to a revisionary response-dependent reading of several philosophically interesting topics. What Johnston fails to see is that in rejecting response dependence the metaphysical minimalist need not reject pragmatism. The usage path to pragmatism remains open.

8. The quest for justification or legitimation of linguistic practices is a prominent theme in Johnston's "Objectivity Reconfigured." In the opening paragraph he tells us that what "deserved the name of a progressive pragmatism" would be a critical philosophy which asked "whether the real explanations of our practices allow us to justify them" (Johnston 1993: 85). One possible answer to this question would of course be a negative one, in particular the view that it is hardly more appropriate to try to justify our linguistic practices than it is to try to legitimate (say) our digestive practices. In both cases we can describe the practices concerned, and perhaps say what function they serve in our lives, but little more than that. I suspect that Johnston would be unhappy with a pragmatism that yielded no more than this. At any rate, in the next section I shall try to show that someone who does want more won't find it in response dependence. True, they won't find it in a usage-based pragmatism, either. My point is that a content-based theory does not offer any advantage in this respect.

with the observation just made, namely that only the content-based approach yields talk of truth at the theoretical level. Only this approach provides a framework in which, with luck, it may turn out to be demonstrable that at least some of the claims we take to be true actually are true.

This is a tempting idea, but I think it is mistaken. In my view, response dependence tends to buy justification at the cost of devaluing the practice for which we wanted justification in the first place. This is bought out most starkly in cases in which the commitments typical of the original discourse have certain characteristic consequences for action, so that to justify the commitments concerned would be to justify the actions to which they give rise. The most important examples involve concepts of value and probability. I want to show that the response-dependent substitutes for these notions do not have the proper connections with action, and hence that justifying the substitute judgments does not serve to justify the associated behavior. As we shall see, the point has been obscured by some ambiguities in the use that response theorists make of the notion of rationality. When these ambiguities are resolved, response-dependent accounts of probability and value turn out to do rather worse than their usage-based rivals.

8. Justifying Choices

Moral cognitivists need to explain how moral beliefs can be genuine beliefs, on the one hand, and yet of an essentially motivating character, on the other. There seems to be an analytic connection between believing that X is good and desiring that X. Why should this be so? I call this the *Approval Problem*.[9]

There is an analogous problem on the other side of decision theory. Cognitivists about probability need to explain how beliefs about probability can be genuine beliefs, on the one hand, and yet have some non-contingent connection with particular degrees of belief (and hence with betting behavior), on the other. Someone who believes that it is probable that P tends to be confident that P, and to act accordingly. Again, why should this be so? I call this the *Confidence Problem* (see Price 1983a; 1988: chapter 4).

One of the great attractions of expressivist views of probability and morality is that they provide a very simple solution to these problems. If moral claims express evaluative attitudes, for example, then the Approval Problem vanishes: moral commitments simply *are* desires, in effect, and we don't need any further explanation of why they tend to be accompanied by desires. These are problems for cognitivists about value and probability, then—problems for people who think that there is a significant psychological distinction to be drawn between a belief

9. I use this terminology in Price 1988: chapter 4. Michael Smith (1989: 89) calls the same issue "the Moral Problem."

about probability and the corresponding degree of confidence, or between a belief about value and the corresponding affective disposition. If there are important psychological distinctions of this kind, it needs to be explained why the mental states so distinguished tend to occur together.

In both cases the problem can be given either a descriptive or a normative flavor. Why *do* people who believe X is good tend to desire that X? And why *should* they do so? In either flavor, however, these problems need to be distinguished from a more general problem of justifying our desires and credences (and hence the behavior that flows from them). The easiest way to see the more general problem is to suppose that we had solved the Approval and Confidence problems, in their normative versions. Suppose, in other words, we could show that our desires and credences were justified in the light of our beliefs about value and probability. It would still make sense, apparently, to wonder whether we had the right beliefs about value and probability, and hence the right desires and credences in this broader sense.

In effect, this broader problem is that of justifying the behavioral dispositions with which, as decision makers, we meet the world. I shall call this the "Behavioral Justification Problem," or "Behavioral Problem," for short. In order to solve it, cognitivists about value and probability need not only normative solutions to both the Approval and Confidence problems, but also a means of justifying our evaluative and probabilistic beliefs themselves.

What is involved in justifying our evaluative and probabilistic beliefs? It depends, obviously, on the content of these beliefs. One of the attractions of response dependence seems to be that it provides contents which make the task look manageable. After all, if moral and probabilistic claims are very general claims about human dispositions, then the knowledge required to justify them is a kind of self-knowledge. The subject matter of morality and probability becomes more accessible—as well as more palatable, metaphysically speaking, to those of a naturalistic frame of mind.

If the Approval and Confidence problems could be solved under their normative readings, then, the Behavioral Problem would reduce to that of justifying moral and probabilistic beliefs. And if that problem starts to look approachable from the response theorist's point of view—because these beliefs are about our own psychological dispositions, in some sense—an attractive vista opens up. A solution to the Behavioral Problem might seem to be in sight. I want to show that this prospect is quite illusory, however. In effect, response theorists can have one half of the solution or other, but not both together. Which half they get depends on what precisely goes into their biconditional content conditions, and the illusion rests on equivocation.

Let's think first about the Confidence Problem. I noted that the two-step solution to the Behavioral Problem requires a *normative* solution of the Confidence Problem—in other words, a demonstration that an agent who believes that it is probable that P is *justified* (and not merely *disposed*) to be confident that P. However, if the response theorist says that "It is probable that P" means that (or is true if and only if) normal people are disposed to be confident that P, then a normative solution to the Confidence Problem will not be forthcoming. After all, put yourself in the position of the agent concerned. You believe that normal people in your circumstances are disposed to be confident that P. But what have the habits of other people (normal or not!) got to do with whether *you* should be confident that P?

The usual approach at this point to put some normativity in by hand, so to speak, in the form of the notion of rationality. Roughly, the response theorist's suggestion is that "It is probable that P" means (or is true if and only if) a *rational* person would be confident that P. I want to show that this strategy is a dead end, or rather a whole neighborhood of dead ends, distinguished by a range of possible readings of the notion of rationality. I'll begin with the probabilistic case, and then apply the same lessons to the evaluative case.

The idea of analyzing probability in terms of rational partial belief has long seemed attractive. I call it the rationalist approach to probability. Roughly, it amounts to saying that P is probable if and only if a rational person would be confident that P, if properly acquainted with the relevant evidence.[10] How does a rationalist handle the Confidence Problem? In its normative version, the problem now comes to this: Why should a person who believes that it is *rational* to be confident that P, *actually* be confident that P?

There are a number of possible approaches, turning on different readings of the relevant notion of rationality. It would be almost impossible to be exhaustive at this point, of course, but the following alternatives will serve to illustrate the nature of the problem:

I. *Rationality cashed in terms of our own cognitive dispositions*. Either (a) the concept of the rational is the concept of what we are disposed to accept, or (b) the term "rational" is used to express a disposition to accept a claim to which it is applied.
II. *Rationality cashed in terms of practical utility*. Rational partial belief is useful partial belief.
III. *Objective rationality*. Rationality is an objective cognitive value, and our practice in the present case reflects our awareness of its presence and nature.

Option I(a) amounts to a response-dependent account of the relevant notion of rationality. Roughly, it says that a cognitive move is rational if and only if it is a

10. Among recent writers, Hugh Mellor has a theory of chance of this kind, for example, though in his case it is part of a hybrid theory including propensities, thought of as dispositions to produce arrangements of chances (see Mellor 1971). Mellor takes his theory to be in the spirit of F. P. Ramsey's view, developed in Ramsey 1978. Despite the apparent differences between Ramsey and Keynes on this topic, Keynes too might be thought of as an early exponent of the rationalist treatment of probability, given that his "logical" probability relations are characterized in terms of degrees of *rational* belief (see Keynes 1921).

move that we are disposed to make. To say that it is rational to be confident that P is thus to describe a disposition on our own part to be confident that P. (There are at least two readings of "our" here: it might be the speaker personally, it might be the community.) Option I(b) has a more expressive flavor: to say that it is rational to ϕ is to *express* (not *describe*) a disposition to ϕ. (In this case the bearer of the disposition is presumably just the speaker.) On either version of Option I, however, the idea that the response theorist's appeal to rationality leads to normative justifications for our behavioral dispositions turns out to be illusory: if rationality itself is cashed in descriptive or expressive terms, so too is whatever notion of justification rides on its back.

Option II may look more promising. It is world-directed, taking rational belief to be belief that works. But what is useful about a particular degree of credence? At best, only that it is (increasingly) *probable* to lead to success in the (increasingly) long run. Taken in this sense, then, the analysis of probability in terms of rationality is circular, at least in the sense that a rationalist account of probability is powerless to help with the Confidence Problem. The problem simply reemerges at the new level.

Option III is more interesting. It countenances an objective cognitive value, and interprets probability in terms of the value, in this objective sense, of certain degrees of partial belief. Why is it the case that people who believe that it is probable that P do, or should, also have a high degree of confidence that P? Because to say that P is probable is to say that it is valuable to have such a credence, in this objective sense of value. So if people believe that P is probable, then they believe that they *should* have a high credence that P, by their own evaluative lights.

So far so good, but this answer won't satisfy someone who has noticed the Approval Problem. For we now have what might be called the Rationality Problem: What is the connection between rationality and motivation? The question again has a descriptive and a normative aspect: Why does someone who believes that it is rational to F *actually* F (or at least typically have an inclination to F)? And why *should* they? Why does rationality matter, and why should it?

Just as in the case of the Approval Problem, the Rationality Problem might incline us to a response-dependent or expressive account of rationality. In the present context, however, these were the views we considered under Option I. So if Option III is to remain distinct we must reject this course—and yet the problem now seems intractable. Still, if one is prepared to live with this problem in the evaluative case, then there is no need to bite another bullet for the probabilistic case. Rationalism shows us how to use the same evaluative bullet for both cases.

In sum, then, does a rationalist account of probability succeed in providing a normative solution to the Confidence Problem? It depends on what we mean by rationality. There seem to be three possibilities, comprising two dead ends and one diversion:

(i) On a response-dependent or expressivist reading of the rationality claim, the connection between the probabilistic belief and credence is merely descriptive. At best, the disposition expressed or described by a probability judgment simply *gives rise to* the corresponding credence. It doesn't *justify* the adoption of that credence.

(ii) On a utilitarian reading of the rationality claim, the rationalist account of probability is circular.

(iii) On a normative reading of the rationality claim, the Confidence Problem is replaced by a version of the Approval Problem.

Rationalist response theorists thus do rather poorly on the normative aspect of the Confidence Problem. At best they succeed in shifting the issue to the evaluative case.

Perhaps not surprisingly, however, it turns out that much the same difficulties arise in the evaluative case (and here, of course, there is nowhere else to hide). To illustrate the nature of the problem, suppose we follow the response theorist in equating the good, or the valuable, with what substantial rationality leads us to value. In its normative aspect, the Approval Problem is now the question as to why we should actually value what we believe to be valuable in this sense. Why should we value what substantial rationality leads us to value? Once again, the structure of the answer turns on our understanding of the rationality claim. There seem to be three main possibilities, which roughly parallel those in the probabilistic case.

I*. *Response-dependent or expressive rationality*. These approaches cash rationality itself in terms of our own psychological dispositions. As in the probabilistic case, they provide descriptive but not normative solutions to the Approval Problem.

II*. *Rationality as a cognitive value*. This approach interprets rationality in terms of evaluative categories already in play. For example, it takes what it is rational to value to be what it is valuable to value. As in the probability case, the effect of this is to make rationality unhelpful in providing an account of value. The analysis leads in a circle.

III*. *Rationality as a sui generis cognitive value*. If rationality is an independent value, then the Rationality Problem is a distinct subspecies of the Approval Problem. Indeed, for rationalist response theorists it becomes the core species, to which other versions of the Approval Problem reduce.

Let's think about the normative aspect of the Rationality Problem in the light of III*. Given this sui generis notion of rationality, why should someone who believes that it is rational to ϕ, actually ϕ? One possible move is say that the solution is analytic, because "should" itself needs to be cashed in terms of this notion of rationality. If rationality itself is the core normative notion, there is no non-trivial normative issue to be raised at this point.

However, recall our reason for being interested in the normative versions of the Confidence, Approval, and Rationality problems in the first place: if successfully negotiated, they seemed likely to provide response theorists with the second half of a two-stage solution to the Behavioral Problem. The first stage of the solution required justification of our evaluative and probabilistic beliefs themselves. Here response theorists seemed well placed to make progress, in virtue of the fact that they take such beliefs to refer to our own psychological dispositions. However, if the notion of rationality invoked in the response theorist's content conditions is normative and irreducible, this easy progress is quite illusory. Justification now depends on access to the dispositions of *rational* agents, not merely those of *actual* agents. And the inquiry itself seems in danger of a problematic regress, if the notion of justification involved is to be cashed in terms of the same notion of rationality.

The underlying moral of this discussion is a simple one, which applies in both the probabilistic and evaluative cases. If the response theorist's content conditions invoke irreducibly normative notions, they leave unresolved all the old difficulties about normativity in a natural world. One issue left unresolved is the epistemological one: How could creatures like us have access to normative facts of the relevant kind? How could we be *justified* in holding particular beliefs about such facts?[11] On the other hand, if the response theorist's content conditions are not irreducibly normative, then the Confidence Problem and the Approval Problem loom large: Why should our behavior as agents be guided by what we believe about the psychological dispositions of our fellows? Only someone who equivocates about the normativity of the relevant notion of rationality could imagine that a response-dependent account of probability or value escapes both horns of this traditional dilemma.

9. Action as a Fixed Point

The previous section was motivated by the suggestion that a response theorist might answer the redundancy argument by claiming that a content-based account is better placed than its various rivals to justify our beliefs. In a sense this claim is true, of course. Because the effect of the response theorist's biconditionals is to read all our commitments in the relevant domains as partially self-descriptive, the commitments as interpreted are often easier to justify than they would be under other readings. However, opponents on both sides of the response theorist—more traditional realists on one side, and irrealists of various kinds on the other—are likely to feel that there is a trick involved. In effect, the response theory solves the problem by changing the subject.

11. There is a double problem here, of course, because what is being called for is *justification* for our beliefs about matters of *justification*.

The nice thing about the evaluative and probabilistic cases is that here the trick, if we may call it that, is blocked by the fact that the psychological states which play the role of the response in these cases—desire and credence—have direct connections with behavior. This means that they provide psychological fixed points, toward which the quest for justification is ultimately directed. When the response theorist tries to reconstrue evaluative or probabilistic belief, the necessary connections with credence and desire bring the issue of justification back to the same point. These connections are the core of the Confidence and Approval problems, respectively—problems which arise for any view that recognizes a gap between believing that X is valuable and desiring X, or between believing that P is probable and being confident that P. As I noted earlier, one of the great attractions of expressivist views is that they minimize these gaps.

In the case of the traditional secondary qualities, however, there are no psychological fixed points of this kind. There is no distinctive behavioral manifestation of "seeing red," for example, such that an account of the content of the belief that X is red has to explain why people who have this belief typically do (or should) display this behavior. "Seeing red" simply doesn't play that sort of a role in our mental lives. This might explain why the response-dependence strategy has long seemed so attractive in these cases. When it came to seem that there was no place for the folk properties of color in a scientific account of the objective contents of the world, the strategy of revising in favor of the Lockean dispositional account did not have to confront anything analogous to the Confidence and Approval problems. So the attractions of the Lockean account—for example, the fact that by sacrificing their observer-independent status, colors retain a respectable place in the scientific world—are not offset by difficulties elsewhere.

With color properties so construed, of course, the scientific view *can* justify our color ascriptions. As always, response dependence interprets our commitments in a way that makes them more accessible. Whatever the merits of this move in the color case, I have argued that it doesn't work in the probabilistic and evaluative cases. Here, the justification we want is justification for our credences and desires, and the dispositional revision doesn't give it to us.

As long as the secondary qualities constitute an isolated case, there is an evident attraction in keeping them within the scientific fold by reading them dispositionally. This advantage would be undermined by the acceptance that whatever the nature of the subjectivity in play here, it is a global feature of language. For in this case it infects our scientific discourse as well, and hence cannot be quarantined where it occurs in other discourses by means of the revisionary dispositional reading. True, we may see an advantage in reducing multiple sources of infection to one, taking the view that the scientific discourse is the most hygienic we have. But if it is acknowledged that we live (and have no choice but to live) with the infection in this case, an obvious thought is that we might just as well do so in other cases as well. This would be to defend our right to the old unsterilized naive discourse about color, relying on our internal systems of cognitive quarantine to avoid serious conflict with our scientific beliefs. This would in a sense be quasi-realism about color, but a quasi-realism defended by the claim that in virtue of the global nature of the relevant kind of subjectivity, the same quasi-realist attitude is appropriate everywhere. There is no embarrassing divide between "real" realism and quasi-realism, on this view—a divide that several of the quasi-realist's critics[12] have identified as a weak spot.

10. Making Sense of Usage

I have argued that globality is incompatible with a thoroughly content-based approach to explicating the sort of subjectivity with which we are here concerned; that wherever a content-based account may be given, the materials also exist for a usage-based account; and that in the moral and probabilistic cases there is no advantage for the content-based account—quite the contrary, if anything—concerning the justification of the relevant action-guiding psychological states. To finish, I want to exhibit a further advantage of the usage-based approach. Like the redundancy point, this turns on the fact that the usage-based theory is more austere and less demanding than its rival. Here the effect is not simply that the usage-based theory works wherever the content-based theory claims to work, but a stronger point: in accounting for folk linguistic practice, the usage approach often works smoothly where the content-based approach does not. As we shall see, this advantage is most evident in the case of discourses whose patterns of usage exhibit a subtle combination of objective and subjective aspects.

11. Truth Conditions: The Objective–Subjective Dilemma

Let's return to the self-descriptivist misreading of emotivism. It has often been noted that self-descriptivism is unable to make sense of ordinary intuitions about moral objectivity, and in particular about the possibility of moral error and moral ignorance. For example, there is nothing particularly counterintuitive about

(8) I believe that X is good but I may be wrong

or about

(9) There are many good things of whose existence I am quite unaware.

12. Including me: see Price 1988: chapter 4; 1992.

Apparently, however, the self-descriptivist is required to parse these propositions as something like

> (10) I believe that I approve of X, but it may be the case that I do not approve of X

and

> (11) There are many things of which I approve without being aware that they exist,

respectively. But (11) is clearly counterintuitive, and (10) mislocates the source of moral error, taking it to involve a mistake about oneself. (In folk moral practice it simply isn't true that self-knowledge excludes moral error.) In this respect, then, the self-descriptivist's paraphrases do not do justice to a degree of moral objectivity that is claimed by ordinary usage.

The problem becomes even more acute in cases of moral disagreement. Folk intuition regards the utterances "X is good" and "X is bad" as prima facie incompatible, even if said by different speakers. In response to the assertion "Discipline is good," for example, the utterance "Discipline is bad" would normally be taken to amount to a clear (if rather stilted) expression of dissent. Yet the self-descriptivist should see no more conflict between these propositions, expressed by different speakers, than between "I approve of discipline" and "You disapprove of discipline."

These are familiar objections to self-descriptivism, of course. They turn on the fact that the self-descriptivist's truth conditions for moral claims are too subjective to account for the apparent objectivity of ordinary moral discourse, and a promising response is therefore to "objectify" in one or both of two respects: (a) by taking moral claims to refer not to the evaluative dispositions of the individual speaker, but to those *normal* in the speech community as a whole; or (b) by appealing not to *actual* responses, but to possibly counterfactual responses under *ideal* conditions. Taken together, these moves give the self-descriptivist something like this:

> (12) X is good iff a normal person would approve of X, if acquainted with it under ideal conditions.

In other words, the effect of these moves is to bridge the gap between naive self-descriptivism and response-dependence. As response theorists recognize, of course, this opens the way for moral error and ignorance. To the extent that an individual speaker is abnormal, or less than ideally situated, his or her evaluations may be out of step with the objective standard. It also makes possible moral disagreement: two speakers may simply disagree about how the normal speaker would react to some state of affairs under ideal conditions.

So much for capturing the objectivity of moral usage. But moral usage is also notoriously subjective, in the sense that it appears to leave room for speaker-relativity, for no-fault disagreements: cases of moral difference in which usage appears to allow that neither speaker need be at fault. Can the modified self-descriptivist theory make sense of these? On the face of it not, for surely it is a perfectly objective matter whether a given X is such as to evoke a given response in normal people under specified conditions.

Response theorists have an answer to this challenge, whose adequacy I'll consider in a moment. First note that the problem cannot be avoided by denying moral relativity, or in some other way appealing to the special features of the moral case. For the problem turns on the possibility of no-fault disagreements, and these are not simply a feature of the moral case. Indeed, they are potentially global, in virtue of the same rule-following considerations that lead Pettit to conclude that response dependence is global: because the application of any general term is finitely based, it is always conceivable that a speech community will divide on the issue of a future application. If it turns out that such a division underlies an apparent disagreement, that disagreement will be held to involve no fault (see Price 1988: chapter 8). In general, wherever language depends on a response that might vary from speaker to speaker, we have a potential source of no-fault disagreements.[13] So our present concern is not peculiar to the moral case.

Insofar as it acknowledges the possibility of no-fault disagreement, the solution that the response theory proposes is to invoke an indexical specification of the relevant "response community"—for example, to suggest:

(13) X is good iff *I* would approve of X, if I were acquainted with X under ideal conditions.

Roughly speaking, the strategy is thus to dispense with (or at least water down) the notion of normality, but to retain a reference to ideal conditions (thereby, hopefully, retaining the ability to deal with the objectivity problem).

The revised account can certainly make some sense of moral error: I might simply be mistaken as to how I would respond under ideal conditions. But can it make sense of moral disagreements? We noted earlier that a naive self-descriptivist should see no more prima facie conflict between "X is good" and "X is bad," said by different speakers, than between "I approve of X" and "He disapproves of X." Clearly, the same applies to this indexical version of the content-based theory. Normality was thus doing important work, and the problem reemerges if it is omitted.

13. Are there other potential sources? Yes, in various kinds of context-dependencies (see Price 1988: chapter 8).

Response theorists thus face the following dilemma. If they leave out the notion of normality, the resulting account is insufficiently objective to make sense of ordinary prima facie disagreements about the matters in question. If they put in normality, on the other hand, the account cannot make sense of the very real possibility of no-fault disagreements, arising in cases in which there is statistically significant divergence in patterns of response.

In practice, response theorists may choose a different horn of this dilemma in different cases. They may favor subjectivity where no-fault disagreements are most obvious, such as in the moral case, and objectivity ("normal response") elsewhere. This is mere damage control, however. Both choices are unsatisfactory, and in any case, any such division is bound to be arbitrary. No-fault disagreement is a global phenomenon in language, and its incidence varies only by degree from one discourse to another.

Let's focus on a case in which response theorists do invoke normal conditions, and consider the sensitivity this engenders to the issue as to whether there are statistical norms in the community in question in the given respect. Pettit recognizes (1991: 608) that it is a consequence of the content-based theory that if there is no normal response, the relevant property ascription should be regarded as false. A related conclusion is that as long as the bounds of the community are indeterminate, so too is the content of the property ascription concerned. But consider the consequences of this in perfectly ordinary cases. Canberra is a small city, with a lot of open space. By Sydney standards, it is a quiet place. But if I were to deny that Canberra is a bustling place, would I be speaking to the rather refined bustle-sensitivities of Canberra residents themselves, to those of my own Sydney community, or to some other "normal" class? A disadvantage of the content-based approach is that until the issue is resolved, the significance of what I have said is simply not determinate.

A great advantage of the usage-based approach is that it avoid these ambiguities *at the level of the meaning specification*. Roughly, Canberra residents and Sydney residents learn to use the term "bustle" in accordance with the same usage condition: the assertion "This place is bustling" is prima facie appropriate when one experiences the "Oh, it's so busy!" response. This provides the sense in which the two communities speak the same language in using the term. But it leaves room for divergence later, if it turns out that Canberra residents and Sydney residents are differently sensitive to experiencing this response. The response theorist has to try to account for this divergence in terms of a difference in meaning which—perhaps unknown to the participants—has been present in their linguistic practice all along. (The term "bustle" simply latched onto different concepts in Canberra and Sydney.) By specifying meaning in terms of usage, in contrast, my kind of pragmatist is able to explain the fact that in one important sense, the term does mean the same to the members of the two speech communities—and to explain the divergence in its application by differences between the speakers which lie in the background, as preconditions for the practice in question.

There are two main arguments for leaving these differences in the background, rather than incorporating them into the content of the assertions concerned. First, it makes much better sense of ordinary usage. Naive Canberra and Sydney folk need have no sense that their notion of bustle is not universal, and to insist on such gross indeterminacies in content unreasonably detaches meaning from speakers' understanding. (There is a theoretical redundancy point lurking here. Even if initially we thought there were such content indeterminacies, an obvious and appealing theoretical move would be to factor them out, thus concentrating on what would have better claim to be thought of as speaker-accessible meanings.) Second, and ultimately even more telling, not all the preconditions of language can be made explicit, in the sense of figuring in the content of the linguistic expressions for which they are preconditions. This is a familiar point, related to what the Tortoise said to Achilles. Something must stay in the background, crucial and yet unsaid. Whatever it is, it might vary from speaker to speaker, or from community to community. In this way, we'll get precisely what we have in the case of "bustle": a divergence in application that rests not on any difference in content, and not on any mistake by either party, but simply on a difference in the background.

Many discourses handle these no-fault disagreements surprisingly smoothly. We are able to "switch off" the objective mode sufficiently to accommodate such irreconcilable differences, without seriously undermining its useful application in ordinary cases. We thus combine objectivity with a certain tolerance of subjectivity (or relativity). (In *Facts and the Function of Truth* [Price 1988] I tried to explain this in terms of an account of what in general the objective mode is *for*.) A usage-based account can readily make sense of this feature of language, but a content-based theory is bound to be torn between the objective and subjective aspects of practice.

In particular, a usage-based account puts normality in its proper place. There is a direct comparison here with a coherence theory of truth. Opponents of such a theory can agree, of course, that in the long run what we *take to be true* is what we converge on believing—roughly, what normal people come to believe in in the ideal limit of rational discussion. But this is simply a consequence of the more basic usage condition for truth, namely, that it is prima facie appropriate to assert that "P" is true only if one believes that P. Against a background of communal reassessment of belief, this basic condition guarantees, more or less, that what normal people *take to be true* in the long run will be what the community converges on. Since this fact about usage can be explained by any theory of truth which accepts the minimal usage condition, it provides no argument for the coherence account's attempt to explain it analytically, by analyzing truth in terms of normal rational convergence. On the other hand, the coherence theory does violence to usage at other points. (With respect to the phenomenology of truth, for example: as correspondence theorists like to point out, what we seem to care about in rational inquiry is not whether we'll all come to agree that P, but whether P is in fact the case.)

As for the coherence theory, so for the content-based approach in general: the right place for the notions of normality, rationality, and the like is in an account of the consequences, after the fact, of the adoption of a usage rule that makes no mention of these things.

12. Pragmatics to the Rescue?

We have been considering the objection that content-based theories do a poor job of accounting for certain features of ordinary usage. In various respects, for example, the ordinary use of the notions of truth and falsity is not what it should be, if the response theorist's biconditionals captured the content of the utterances concerned.

In reply, response theorists may well try to invoke various "pragmatic" factors about language use, to explain the apparent mismatch. Depending on the version of the response theory on offer, the task may be to explain apparent objectivity or apparent subjectivity. If (13) is the preferred reading of moral judgments, for example, then the problem will be to explain the possibility of moral disagreement: to explain why "X is good" and "X is bad" are normally taken to be incompatible, even when uttered by different speakers.[14] A number of suggestions might be made at this point. For example, it might be suggested that the benefits of social cohesion provide a reason for attempting to "align" the evaluative attitudes of the different members of a speech community, and that this is encouraged by treating such cases as if they embody a genuine disagreement.

There are other possibilities—linguistic pragmatics is fertile territory—but I think they are uniformly misguided. However, the fault lies not with the pragmatic considerations themselves, but with the ailing program they are called on to patch up. For the irony is that the content-based theory has now taken on the quasi-realist's project, but with the added handicap of having to explain not only why usage bestows "apparent" truth conditions, but also why it does not accord with real truth conditions. Initially it might have seemed that the content-based theory provided an attractive way to bypass the quasi-realist's rather tedious concern with this business of explaining usage: invoke one's natural conceptual rights, and get on with something more interesting. Tripped up on the awkward tendency of usage to combine objectivity in some respects with subjectivity in others, however, the content-based theory now finds itself bogged in the same

14. Alternatively, if the preferred content-based response theory errs toward the objective side, the task will be to account for the apparent subjectivity of no-fault disagreements. One possibility, to which Johnston seems attracted, at least as a last resort, is to simply deny that the parties concerned are speaking the same language (see Johnston 1989: 170).

messy territory. And it is burdened, as the quasi-realist is not, with a doctrine about the "real" truth-conditions of the utterances in question.[15]

True, a disdain for the painstaking work of pragmatism may not have been the only factor that led the content-based theory to reject the quasi-realist path in the first place. Another motive might have been the feeling that it is the quasi-realist who does violence to ordinary usage by suggesting that folk truth is not univocal—by distinguishing between genuine truth (where realism is appropriate attitude to discourse) and constructed truth (where quasi-realism is as close as we get). I want to emphasize that in this respect the usage-based theory I recommend sides with the content-based theory. It takes the view that there is no sharp divide in language where real truth conditions cease and ersatz ones take over. Rather, throughout language the explanatory task is the same: to account for the fact that dispositions to respond to the world in certain ways come to be expressed in the objective assertoric mode.

Finally, it might be felt that there is a powerful argument for the content-based theory in the intuition that truth conditions play a crucial role in a theory of meaning (or theory of linguistic competence). Certainly this intuition seems to have been influential in underpinning resistance to non–truth-conditional treatments of various topics, such as conditionals. The point might well be linked to the previous one: it will be at least inelegant if a theory of meaning has to offer one sort of account of the meaning of those indicative sentences that do have genuine truth conditions, and another sort of account of those that do not.

This suggestion calls for three responses. First, there is another conception of knowledge of meaning, apart from that of knowledge of truth conditions—namely, knowledge of (subjective) usage conditions. The usage-based theory is tailor-made for a role in such a theory. Roughly, knowledge of the meaning of a descriptive term will amount to knowledge as to which response that term expresses. Second, we have just seen that the content-based theory cannot fully account for the ordinary use, and hence the meaning, of the relevant utterances in terms of the truth conditions it provides for them. An appeal to pragmatic features is also necessary. This concession deflates any general appeal to the idea that

15. One consequence of this burden will be that the content-based response theorist will be bound to admit that there are some circumstances in which a speaker's own judgments of truth and assertibility may part company: either she grants that P is true but declines to assert that P (or disagrees with the assertion that P); or she asserts that P, but declines to claim that P is true. Moreover, note that the content-based response theorist should really now explain why usage accords with underlying truth conditions when it does do so, as well as why it sometimes parts company. In effect, this means that the content-based response theorist needs a complete pragmatic account of the usage conditions of the utterances in question, not merely a patch for a few exceptional cases.

meaning is simply a matter of truth conditions.[16] And third, the role of truth in a general theory of meaning is in any case widely acknowledged to be fulfilled by a very thin disquotational notion. Such a truth predicate can easily be added to a language by stipulation, if need be; and ipso facto, cannot be of any relevance to the issues at stake between the content-based theory, the usage-based theory, and quasi-realism.[17]

13. Conclusion

In sum, the usage path to pragmatism has the following four main advantages. It avoids a vicious regress that threatens a global version of the content-based approach. In any local case, it makes more economical use than the content-based approach of the same raw materials—the same facts about shared human responses. It gives a much better account of some of the subtleties of ordinary usage, particularly of the peculiar mix of objectivity and subjectivity that we find in discourses prone to no-fault disagreements. And it avoids the Approval Problem and the Confidence Problem, while doing no worse than its rivals at *justifying* our credences and evaluative attitudes.

Let me finish by mentioning what may seem the most unattractive feature of a usage-based pragmatism. Such an approach requires us to distance ourselves from our own linguistic practices, to such an extent that we are able to ask not *what* we are saying (what its content is) but *why* we are saying it—why we use those words and concepts in the first place. Many philosophers seem to be deeply troubled by this detached perspective, feeling that it threatens our right or ability to continue to engage in these practices in a meaningful way. The attempt to regard one's practices "from the outside" thus engenders something akin to agoraphobia—a fear that one is losing touch with one's values and community. I don't know what to do about this problem, beyond pointing out that the

16. Perhaps there is tendency to underestimate the necessary role of a pragmatic element in a theory of meaning, even where truth conditions are well behaved. It is easy to overlook the need for a truth-conditional theory of content to be supplemented by a theory of assertion—a pragmatic theory that relates the truth conditions of an asserted sentence to the *point* of asserting it. In my view this project is of doubtful coherency, since it assumes in effect that the notion of truth is prior to that of assertion (and hence *correct* assertion). But even if it is coherent, the existence of this project inevitably undermines the apparent theoretical advantages of the truth-conditional approach. For one thing, it will presumably be an ingredient of the required pragmatic account that (canonically) it is appropriate to assert that P when one believes that P. This takes us back to the usage-based theory's subjective assertibility conditions, with the difference that we now lack a suitably general account of belief (or judgment). The usage-based theory has this built in: beliefs (or judgments) are just what we come to call our responses of the relevant kinds, when these responses come to be expressed in the objective truth-conditional mode.

17. For more on this point see Price 1988: chapter 9.

viewpoint involved is only a small aspect of the perspective on ourselves that human biology already offers us. It *is* sometimes unsettling to take this detached view of practices so central to our lives. At least since Darwin, however, there has been no honest escape from this kind of problem. We cannot avoid the source of the discomfort, except by self-deception. The best treatment seems to be to try to alleviate the symptoms.[18] Lasting relief requires the ability to be untroubled by a certain cognitive distance between one's theoretical standpoint and everyday linguistic activity.[19]

18. If there are any lasting symptoms, at any rate. In other areas of life we seem to be able to accommodate the two perspectives quite painlessly. Are our appetites less urgent, their satisfaction less enjoyable, in the light of what we know about their biological basis? Is pain itself less unpleasant because we know what it's for? Unless there is something special about our linguistic behavior, these cases suggest that the objection may be too precious—that most of the time, at any rate, it is quite easy to combine the two perspectives in one cognitive life.

19. Australians might thus be expected to make good usage pragmatists. The ability to be untroubled by distance is a national characteristic, and Australians are used to contemplating matters of interest from great remove. This view from the middle of nowhere is not without its advantages—those of critical distance, of seeing the big picture. Often it is important to step backward, to move off Broadway in order to contemplate its activities objectively. Ignoring the pessimistic thought that it is quite possible to have too much of a good thing, it is thus an engaging speculation that an aptitude for a detached, skeptical, and explanatory stance might yet prove a more enduring characteristic of Australian philosophy than the famous local brand of naive realism.

The usual naturalistic explanation of Australian naive realism attributes it to the bright Australian light. As David Armstrong puts it, reality forces itself upon one in these conditions. There are rival hypotheses, of course, including the mischievous suggestion that Australian philosophers only became naive realists when they stopped wearing hats. A more plausible hypothesis is that naive realism is itself a response to isolation—a straw-clutching attempt to steady oneself against the vertigo induced by distance.

These chauvinistic comments are prompted by a footnote in early versions of Mark Johnston's "Objectivity Refigured" (1993)—sadly, it is missing from the published version—in which Johnston notes the possible emergence of a distinctively Australian pragmatism. As I have indicated, this worthy project seems to rest on sound geographical foundations. All the same, it may be that those Australian pragmatists whose hearts are too close to Broadway have yet to achieve the cognitive distance required to cast such a pragmatism in its most desirable form.

5

How to Stand Up for Non-cognitivists

Is non-cognitivism compatible with minimalism about truth? A contemporary argument claims not, and therefore that moral realists, for example, should take heart from the popularity of semantic minimalism. The same is said to apply to non-cognitivism about other topics—conditionals, for example—for the argument depends only on the fact that ordinary usage applies the notions of truth and falsity to utterances of the kind in question. Given this much, minimalism about truth is said to leave no room for the view that the utterances concerned are non-cognitive in nature.[1]

In this chapter we want to derail this fast-track route to cognitivism. We want to show that with a proper understanding of what is essential to non-cognitivism, the position turns out to be largely untouched by the adoption of any of a range of minimalist views about truth. The issue as to the nature of non-cognitivism is crucial, however, and we begin in section 1 below by defending a broader characterization of the position than is common in contemporary literature. The nature of minimalism also calls for clarification, and in section 2 we distinguish two importantly different strands that are both prominent in contemporary debates. Against this background, we go on to explore two possible strategies for standing up for non-cognitivism in the face of minimalism.

One of these strategies has been propounded in a recent paper by Frank Jackson, Graham Oppy, and Michael Smith (1994). It turns on the idea that minimalism about truth is quite compatible with a non-minimalism about *truth-aptness*, and that the latter can be used to ground non-cognitivism. In section 3 we discuss this strategy in some detail. We argue that it is less general and more vulnerable to a minimalist counterattack than Jackson, Oppy, and Smith suppose; and, worse, that one of its central planks seems constitutionally unsuited to the weight it is required to bear.

1. The argument may be found, for example, in Boghossian 1990, Wright 1992, Horwich 1993, Humberstone 1991. For an early use of a similar point, see McDowell 1981: 229, n9.

Our own strategy, which we introduce in section 1 and go on to elaborate in section 4, depends on our broader than usual conception of the essential character of non-cognitivism. In section 5 we illustrate this broader conception with a number of examples from the contemporary literature. We show that it makes non-cognitivism—or a doctrine recognizably descended from non-cognitivism—a very tenacious position, though one which does the same sort of philosophical work as its more traditional ancestors.

In the last two sections of the chapter we turn to some important ramifications of this broader conception of non-cognitivism. Section 5 is concerned with some important questions about language—about truth, in particular—that seem especially salient from the theoretical perspective associated with the second strategy. We argue that some minimalists and many non-cognitivists are at fault in ignoring these questions. And in section 6, finally, we turn to an issue that provides a broader motivation for the present discussion. We think that our second strategy for defending non-cognitivism points to a serious difficulty for an increasingly popular reductionist strategy in metaphysics—an approach based on the Ramsey-Lewis approach to theoretical terms—of which Frank Jackson is one of the leading contemporary proponents. Briefly, the preconditions for an application of the Ramsey-Lewis reductionist program are much harder to establish with non-cognitivism understood from our theoretical perspective than under more conventional characterizations. The linguistic issues raised in this chapter thus turn out to be of considerable importance to contemporary metaphysics.

1. What Is Non-cognitivism?

Non-cognitivism about a particular family of terms presupposes a more general distinction: that between cognitive and non-cognitive discourse in general. In effect, the standard literature offers two possible answers to the question as to how this distinction is to be characterized. One view is that it is primarily a semantic distinction, to be defined in terms of possession of truth conditions, or some such. The other view is that it is primarily a psychological distinction, to be defined in terms of the nature of associated psychological states—whether they are genuine beliefs, for example. Either view might well hold that the characterization offered by the other is correct, although derivative or secondary. Indeed, a possible third view is that the relevant semantic and psychological notions are tied together in such a way that neither can really claim precedence. In practice, writers tend to slide from semantic to psychological characterizations and back again, without saying where, if anywhere, they think the priority lies.

Let us call these two varieties of non-cognitivism the semantically defined form and the psychologically defined form, respectively. What do they have in common? Indeed, by what right do we treat these two positions as different forms of the same basic view? Most basically, we suggest, what these positions have in common is that they characterize a linguistic *function*, or *category*, in terms of which the non-cognitivist may claim that the disputed sentences *serve a different function from*, or *belong to a different category from*, other parts of language (and in particular, to paradigmatic causal–explanatory parts of language). In one case the category is characterized in terms of truth, in the other case in terms of belief, but the common factor is the functional or categorial distinction itself. In support of this diagnosis, note that it is a categorial distinction of this sort that underpins the philosophical impact of non-cognitivism, particularly in opposition to reductionist or eliminativist moves. Non-cognitivists argue that these programs, and the philosophical concerns from which they arise, rest on a distinctive kind of mistake about language—on a misidentification of the linguistic category within which particular families of concepts have their home (more on this in section 6 below).

Once we see that in principle there might be a number of different ways to characterize the relevant distinctions in language—we cannot be sure in advance that the only possibilities are those provided by the familiar semantic and psychological notions—it is easy to see that non-cognitivism is really a collection or genus of possible positions, sharing the thesis that philosophy is prone to category mistakes of these kinds, but differing in how the categories should be characterized. The familiar semantic and psychological forms are two of the species of this common genus, but there might well be others.

Thus we want to suggest that non-cognitivism is best construed in more general terms than is usual in the literature—as the *genus*, rather than as either or both of its common sub-species. Nothing hangs on the terminology, of course. We could quite well use another name for the genus, if anyone preferred to reserve "non-cognitivism" for the semantically or psychologically defined versions. What matters is that it is the functional characterization of the genus as a whole that captures what is philosophically most interesting here, and that to fail to notice the genus is to fail to see the potential strength of the general philosophical strategy.

Once we notice the genus, moreover, it is easy to appreciate the possibility of a powerful strategy for defending non-cognitivism against minimalism: simply find some third way of characterizing the cognitive–non-cognitive distinction, which will be capable of bearing the weight the non-cognitivist wants to place on it, even if notions such as truth and belief are conceded to the minimalist. In the ethical case, for example, the non-cognitivist will be immune, prima facie, from the objections raised by minimalists about truth or belief, provided that she characterizes the distinctive function of ethical judgments in other terms.

We might call this way of defending non-cognitivism the "third leg" strategy, for it rests on the idea that non-cognitivism itself might be defined in neither of the two ways common in the contemporary literature. The third leg strategy is easy to appreciate, at least in abstract, once the general functional characterization of non-cognitivism is in view, but is almost invisible otherwise. All the same, there are many proposals in the contemporary literature that illustrate how the strategy might operate in practice, and we shall describe some of these in section 4. The strategy itself has been clearly identified by Paul Horwich. Responding to the charge that semantic minimalism would trivialize "a substantive issue in meta-ethics," Horwich says

> the moral here is not that minimalism and emotivism are incompatible, but that emotivism should be re-formulated. For a minimalist could quite easily accept the correctness and philosophical importance of the emotivists' central insights: namely, that the function and assertibility conditions of certain ethical claims are fundamentally different from those of empirical, explanatory descriptions, and that an appreciation of the difference will help to resolve philosophical problems surrounding the notion of an ethical fact. My point is that this position need not, and should not, be formulated in such a way as to preclude the minimalist conception of truth. (Horwich 1990: 87–88)[2]

We shall come back to the third leg strategy in section 4. Before that, however, in order to display the comparative strength of this approach, we want to consider the nature of minimalism, as it figures in these debates; and we want to criticize a rival approach suggested by Jackson, Oppy, and Smith.

2. What Is Minimalism?

Semantic minimalists reject traditional philosophical concerns with the nature of truth, arguing that the traditional project rests on a misconception. This rejection comes in two importantly different forms, however. On one view, the traditional mistake is to assume that there is a "thick" or "substantial" property of truth, the understanding of the nature of which is the main goal of a philosophical theory of truth. This view does not deny that there is a place for philosophy in understanding the function of the truth predicate in sociolinguistic practice—it merely denies that this function is a matter of making reference to a substantial property, whose nature is therefore a matter for philosophical concern.

What is it for a property to be "substantial," or "thick"? The following gloss fits a number of minimalist sources: a substantial property is one that enjoys a causal–explanatory role in mature scientific theory. Thus the minimalist's thought is

2. Horwich makes it clear that he is not merely proposing to fall back on the idea that ethical judgements do not express beliefs, saying that "the essential character of emotivism might be captured without having to question the existence of ethical propositions, beliefs, assertions, etc."

something like this: serious science puts the category *tree* in explanations of sundry phenomena, including indeed our use of the term "tree"; whereas serious science doesn't need to refer to any real property of truth, either to explain our ordinary use of the term "true," or for any other causal–explanatory purpose. Instead, for example, it might be suggested that the primary function of the truth predicate is as a grammatical device that facilitates a kind of generality in language which would otherwise be difficult to express.

Views of this kind might be developed in a number of ways. For present purposes, however, we want to draw attention to a distinction between this general strand of minimalism, and a second strand, which is in some ways more radical. Often called "quietism," this second strand rests on the view that philosophy really has nothing to say about certain of its traditional concerns. In particular, it asserts that philosophy cannot be revisionary of folk usage about the matters in question, taken at face value.

In contemporary philosophy this quietist view is often associated (perhaps wrongly [see Blackburn 1990, 1993c]) with the work of the later Wittgenstein. It is easy to see how it is thought to challenge non-cognitivism. After all, one of the standard characteristics of traditional non-cognitivism is the claim that ordinary usage is not to be taken at face value, on pain of category mistakes. So if we are to defend the possibility of a non-trivial non-cognitivism against contemporary challenges, quietism should be one of the views we consider.

These two forms of minimalism really are distinct. Quietists might well reject the idea that there is anything insubstantial about truth, finding no basis for this view in ordinary usage itself. For their part, minimalists of the first kind—"insubstantialists," we might call them—need hardly be quietist, since the view that truth is not a deep explanatory property entails nothing about the priority of ordinary practice. Indeed, some theories of this kind are radically anti-quietist. Hartry Field has recently suggested that in opting for an insubstantial conception of truth, we may have to overturn our ordinary conceptions of meaning and synonymy, for example (1994).

In effect, then, we have characterized three views of the project of a philosophical theory of truth—*quietism*, *insubstantialism*, and the non-minimalist position we may call *substantialism*. Moreover, it is easy to see how there can be an analogous range of positions about belief. An insubstantialist about belief will deny that beliefs need play a causal–explanatory role—whether of folk belief-talk or of anything else—in mature scientific theory.[3] And a quietist about belief will refuse to countenance any philosophical perspective on belief that might overturn folk practice, taken at face value. We thus have six possible positions before us (see table 5.1).

3. The claim isn't merely that mature science needn't have recourse to the term "belief," of course, but that the explanatory needs of science won't require a category that deserves the title "belief"—that there is no such natural kind, as we might put it.

Table 5.1. **Minimalism and non-minimalism: Six options**

	Substantialism	*Insubstantialism*	*Quietism*
About truth	A	B	C
About belief	D	E	F

In light of table 5.1, we can make some preliminary points about the prospects for non-cognitivism, given minimalism. We have already indicated how quietism makes trouble for non-cognitivism, since one of the key tenets of traditional non-cognitivism is that folk usage should not be taken at face value. Hence semantically defined non-cognitivism seems incompatible with position C above, while psychologically defined non-cognitivism appears to be incompatible with position F.

In the face of minimalism at positions B or E, however, the problems for non-cognitivism are more subtle. The basic tension seems to be something like this: if there is an important distinction in language whose defining characteristic concerns the possession of truth conditions (or something similar), then the notion of a truth condition thereby plays an important role in linguistic theory—which seems incompatible with the insubstantialist's claim that truth itself plays no significant causal–explanatory role. In other words, a semantically defined non-cognitivism seems bound to reject the central claim of insubstantialism about truth; and similarly, *mutatis mutandis*, for psychologically defined non-cognitivism and insubstantialism about belief.

Quietism and insubstantialism thus lead to rather different kinds of problems for non-cognitivism. However, it is easy to see that the third leg strategy avoids both kinds of problem. If the cognitive–non-cognitive distinction is drawn in terms of linguistic functions that are not themselves couched in terms of truth or belief, then the non-cognitivist will not be relying on substantial notions of truth or belief, and will have no immediate need to challenge the quietist's claim that philosophy has nothing interesting to say about the folk use of these notions.

We shall illustrate these virtues of the third leg strategy in section 4. We turn first to a rival strategy for defending non-cognitivism in the face of semantic minimalism, recently suggested by Jackson, Oppy, and Smith (hereafter, JOS).

3. Aptitude and Platitude: The JOS Strategy

JOS take non-cognitivism to be the view that the sentences of a disputed class are "not truth apt"—"not in the business of being either true or false" (JOS 1994: 287). Thus they operate, at least initially, with what we have called a semantic definition of non-cognitivism. With this characterization of non-cognitivism in place, JOS argue for four main points:

(i) To claim (as semantic minimalists do) that truth ascriptions are not ascriptions of a substantial property, does not commit one to the *truth-aptness* of any disputed class of sentences;
(ii) Only an appropriate minimalism about *truth-aptness* would provide a blanket resolution of these disputes in favor of cognitivism;
(iii) Considerations about "folk platitudes" serve to defeat minimalism about truth-aptness, and thus show that there is no cheap victory for cognitivists on the score of the truth-aptness of any disputed class; and hence
(iv) Non-cognitivist proposals do indeed need to be settled case by case—minimalism provides no blanket victory.

JOS's argument for point (iii) depends on the claim that at least in central cases, a sentence is truth-apt just in case its normal use would be to express a belief.[4] Once this is granted, it follows that so long as there is no cheap victory for the cognitivist concerning which sentences express belief, there can be no cheap victory concerning which discourses are truth-apt—"in the business of being either true or false."

In other words, JOS's point is that a non-cognitivist may accept that truth is an insubstantial property, but define non-cognitivism in terms of *truth-aptness*, and ground a substantial notion of truth-aptness on a substantial notion of belief. Though defined semantically, the resulting non-cognitivism will actually be defended on psychological territory: in the ethical case, for example, the non-cognitivist will need to show that moral claims or sentences do not normally express beliefs. Thus the non-cognitivism whose possibility JOS defend is close to the variety that simply defines non-cognitivism in psychological terms to begin with. In terms of table 5.1, JOS's strategy amounts to pointing out that it is possible to be a non-cognitivist while endorsing position B (insubstantialism about truth) so long as one also endorses position D (substantialism about belief).

It is possible to meet the challenge to non-cognitivism from quietism about truth in a similar way. That is, one might endorse position C and yet base a non-trivial non-cognitivism on position D. The trick is simply to operate with a psychologically defined version of non-cognitivism, immune from the enervating effects

4. JOS recognize that the connection between belief and truth-aptness is not so tight as to entitle us to say in general that a sentence is truth-apt if and only if it would normally express a belief. Unusably long truth-apt sentences might violate the "only if" clause, for example, and paradoxical claims that are believed true might violate the "if" clause. Nevertheless, JOS take it that in all the central areas of dispute between cognitivism and non-cognitivism—ethics, conditionals, and so on—the central issue for cognitivism is whether the sentences concerned are normally used to express beliefs.

of quietism about semantic notions. It is doubtful whether this option is available to JOS themselves, however. Given that they define non-cognitivism in terms of truth-aptness, rather than explicitly in terms of belief, a quietist about the notion of truth is likely to balk at the sort of refusal to take things at face value that comes with such claims as that ethics is not truth-apt. As it stands, then, JOS's argument does not show that non-cognitivism is compatible with the quietist form of minimalism about truth, but at best that it is compatible with the insubstantialist version.[5]

Note also that JOS do not argue that non-cognitivism is compatible with the conjunction of positions B and E, let alone with that of C and F. Their defense of the compatibility of non-cognitivism and B depends on position D, since it turns on considerations about the sort of causal–explanatory role proper to the notion of belief. So their conclusion that non-cognitivism is not excluded by minimalism is a rather limited one. It does not apply to the more radical of the two main forms of minimalism about truth in the current literature, and does not apply to either of the two corresponding forms of minimalism about belief. At the psychological level they rely more on *rebutting* minimalism than on trying to show that it is compatible with non-cognitivism.

These points might be of little significance, of course. Quietism about any subject matter might be held to be an independently implausible philosophical position,[6] in which case if JOS's case for position D is successful, it does all we need ask of a defense of the possibility of non-cognitivism. All the same, we think there is more to be said. For one thing, with a clearer view of the conceptual landscape now before us, it is at least worth asking whether a more general response to contemporary minimalism is possible—whether there is a version of non-cognitivism that is compatible with positions C, E, and F, as well as B. As we noted at the end of section 2, our broader functionalist conception of non-cognitivism has this desirable generality. So long as the non-cognitivist relies on a functional distinction that is not itself cashed in terms of truth or belief, non-cognitivism seems compatible with either form of minimalism about these notions.

The issue of generality aside, however, we think that JOS's strategy is unsatisfactory even in its own terms. In the remainder of this section, we want to show that there is an internal tension in the strategy, to which JOS fail to attend sufficiently.[7] The tension arises from the fact that JOS's own methodology is in some

5. This is not a failing in JOS's own terms, it should be noted, for they understand minimalism as something close to what we have called insubstantialism. Our point is that there are others in contemporary philosophy who call themselves minimalists, and reject non-cognitivism, whose motivation is closer to quietism.

6. Is it correct to call quietism a *philosophical* position? Certainly, for ordinary practice hardly takes it as non-negotiable that the lover of wisdom cannot overturn ordinary practice. Indeed, isn't it common sense that the wise person knows a whole lot more than common sense?

7. We shall also be raising a further worry about JOS's approach in section 5.

respects very close to quietism. JOS share with quietists a great respect for ordinary usage, taking it that the prime task of a philosophical account of truth is to collate and present what ordinary folk take to be platitudinous about truth. This provides a very questionable basis for a defense of non-cognitivism in the face of semantic minimalism, however. As we shall show, it is doubtful whether the platitudes-based approach can sustain the distinction between belief-expressing discourse and other discourse in such a way as to give non-cognitivism a fighting chance.

The platitude-based approach to philosophy has an evident appeal. As JOS put it:

> The beauty of this approach to analysis is that it is hard to see how anyone could object to it. An objection to an analysis consists in pointing to something intuitively evident that conflicts with it. But if we have included everything platitudinous, there is no such intuition to be found. (JOS 1994: 295)

All the same, this very quality of the approach seems likely to alarm any thoughtful non-cognitivist. By its very nature, non-cognitivism is a view that challenges first appearances and prima facie intuitions. Non-cognitivists hold that things are not as they seem, and that philosophers, let alone ordinary folk, are easily misled by linguistic appearances.

In JOS's terms, for example, the non-cognitivist needs to argue that moral and conditional claims are not truth-apt—not "in the business of being either true or false." At first blush, however, it doesn't seem questionable that the folk take them as being so. Isn't it a platitude—if anything is—that some ethical claims are true and some false? Or that it is appropriate to wonder whether it is true that if the prime minister loses the next election then his party will dump him? And similarly with belief, so that there is no advantage to the non-cognitivist in moving to the psychological level. Commonplace references to the moral beliefs of others are hardly marginal features of folk practice. If we allow ourselves to be guided by what ordinary folk take to be uncontroversial, then, it seems that non-cognitivism of either the semantic or psychological kind will simply be ruled out of court.

JOS recognize this danger, of course, but their attempt to meet it seems to us to be unsatisfactory. It depends on a crucial qualification to the platitude-based program of analysis, which they introduce in the following passage:

> The right view is that there is no natural stopping point in analysing a concept short of finding an analysis that captures the whole network of the central, equally appealing platitudes surrounding the concept we are trying to analyse—provided, of course, that they really are central and that they can all be satisfied. (JOS 1994: 297)

This sentence embodies what we see as the central tension of JOS's platitude-based approach. On the one hand the sentence emphasizes the all-inclusive nature of the approach. (It occurs in a paragraph in which JOS criticize Crispin Wright for failing to take sufficient account of platitudes linking truth and belief.) But it also introduces the qualifications whose function is to prevent the approach from being *so* all-inclusive that it necessarily embraces cognitivism. JOS seek to exploit these qualifications in the following passage:

> The issue is not one about common parlance, but rather about the centrality of platitudes and their robustness under scrutiny. In common parlance we . . . apply the words "true" and "false" to ethical sentences and to conditionals. This does not mean that we should conclude straight away that given the platitude preserving approach to analysis, ethical and conditional sentences are truth apt. On that approach the issue does not turn on the prevalence of the words "belief" and "true" and "false" in everyday talk about ethics and conditional. The issue turns rather on the appeal of the claim that ethical sentences and conditionals are truth apt and give the content of beliefs *after reflection and explanation of the issues in the light of all the relevant platitudes*. After all, the word "valid" is often enough used to describe statements rather than arguments in everyday talk, and the words "thinking" and "memory" are used to describe what is going on inside an electronic calculator. But that does not mean that statements are valid and that calculators think and remember, and what reveals this is what we say after considered reflection and explanation of the issues. (JOS 1994: 297)

The analogies at the end of this passage are surely red herrings, however. "Valid" is a term of art in philosophical discourse, and we don't pretend to be using a folk concept when we talk about logical validity. Logicians would hardly be embarrassed to discover that in ordinary discourse "valid" was interchangeable with, say, "reasonable." But non-cognitivists of the kind JOS are discussing would certainly be embarrassed to discover that the literal meaning of "true" in ordinary discourse was such that it applied to moral judgments.

The case of thinking calculators is different but no more decisive. It doesn't take "considered reflection and explanation of the issues" to see that calculators don't literally think—we know that it is intended as a metaphor all along. (Perhaps some people don't know this, but they are people who are mistaken about whether calculators literally think. This is not analogous to non-cognitivism, however. The non-cognitivist is not someone who thinks that folk practice is mistaken, but someone who says that folk practice isn't doing what it seems to be doing.) Ordinary folk find it odd if we suggest that there is something non-standard about the use of "believe" in a sentence such as "Most of us believe that torture is wrong." They don't find it odd if we suggest that calculators don't literally think.

Turning to the more general issues raised by the quoted passage, JOS's suggestion is that the platitudes that seem problematic for the ethical non-cognitivist may turn out to conflict with other central platitudes. As philosophers we might notice this conflict, and see that some central folk platitudes need to be sacrificed in the interests of consistency. Hence we might vindicate non-cognitivism as the theory that does best after "'due reflection and explanation of the issues in the light of all the relevant platitudes." We might discover, say, that on pain of contradiction, one cannot hold that what the folk call "moral beliefs" really are beliefs.

Such a discovery of contradiction among the folk platitudes seems to be the only way that a platitude-based approach could possibly lend any weight to a denial of truth-aptness in any of the disputed domains. But is it a real threat to the cognitivist? In JOS's terms, the problem is to show that after "due reflection," we might have good reason to reject the following platitude (and thereby to avoid cognitivism "on the cheap"):

(1) There are moral beliefs.

JOS suggest (1994: 298) that a non-cognitivist might argue as follows:

(2) The states we call "moral beliefs" are essentially motivating.
(3) Real beliefs are not essentially motivating, and can only produce action by combining with desires.

Therefore

(4) The states we call "moral beliefs" are not real beliefs (so that (1) is not a "central platitude," or at least is not to be taken literally).

But where are premises (2) and (3) supposed to come from, according to the platitude-based analysis? Ordinary folk do not explicitly endorse these principles, and so presumably the idea must be that they are implicit in folk practice. But given that (2) and (3) together contradict a literal reading of (1), then the fact that the folk regard (1) as a platitude means that they are implicitly committed to the *denial* of the conjunction of (2) and (3). After all, implicit commitment is simply what consistency demands. As Moore pointed out long ago, a claim to have discovered a contradiction in common sense provides good evidence that one has mis-characterized common sense. The upshot seems to be that the technique of extracting implicit platitudes can never yield the kind of conflicts that JOS's proposed defense of non-cognitivism requires. Given consistency at the level of explicit platitudes, the quietist always has the upper hand, for what lies on the surface does not need to be unearthed as an implicit commitment.

Hence it seems to us that there is a fatal flaw in the particular strategy that JOS suggest for defending non-cognitivism. We emphasize that the problem does not lie in the argument for the claim that non-cognitivism is compatible with semantic minimalism—that follows immediately, once we appreciate that non-cognitivism can be framed in psychological terms, and that minimalism about truth need not imply minimalism about belief. The problem concerns JOS's own argument for a non-minimalist position about belief. The methodology of a platitude-based approach seems to require that explicit platitudes always take precedence over claimed implicit platitudes, where the two threaten to conflict.[8] If so, then the cognitivist is always on secure grounds in appealing to the fact that the folk say there are moral beliefs, as well as moral truths.

4. Non-cognitivism as Functional Pluralism

Despite our reservations about JOS's argument, we agree with their main conclusion, at least in spirit: we too endorse a conception of non-cognitivism according to which non-cognitivist proposals do indeed need to be settled case by case, and according to which minimalism provides no blanket victory. We have argued that so long as non-cognitivism is correctly construed in the first place, this conclusion falls out in a simple and general form. The third leg strategy shows that non-cognitivism is compatible with a broad range of minimalist positions: in the notation of table 5.1, with positions C, E, and F, as well as position B.

The key to the third leg strategy is the observation that most generally construed, non-cognitivism is a doctrine about the functions of parts of language. In ethics, for example, the non-cognitivist's essential claim is that the function of ethical discourse is different from that of, say, scientific discourse, in some philosophically significant respect—in such a way as to make attempts to reduce ethical talk to scientific talk inappropriate, for example. Once our attention is drawn to the possibility, it is not difficult to see that the functional distinctions that do this sort of philosophical work might be neither the semantic nor the psychological distinctions of folk usage. After all, this is little more than the possibility that not everything of interest about the functions of language lies in view on the surface, where the ordinary folk can see it.

In practice, however, we find that this is a sticking point. Our opponents claim to have difficulty in seeing what kinds of things these linguistic functions could be, and hence how there could be a non-cognitivist position that was not cast in the usual semantic or psychological terms. Part of the difficulty may lie in the terminological problem we mentioned earlier: because the term "non-cognitivism" has direct links to the semantic and psychological vocabulary, it is in one sense an

8. Note that the problem would not arise if (2) and (3) were offered as products of speculative psychology theory, for then there would be some basis for the claim that the folk are simply wrong about (1). It only arises if (2) and (3) are themselves said to be platitudinous.

inappropriate label for a position that renounces these links. We have chosen to let this be outweighed by the fact that the new position represents a genus of which traditional forms of non-cognitivism were the early species, but nothing really hangs on this choice. The genus is the philosophically more interesting position, and it is this position whose clear compatibility with minimalism we want to defend, whatever one wants to call it.

As an aid to the visibility of this position, we want to show that it is already well exemplified in the philosophical literature. In this section we describe three well-known views which are naturally read in these terms. Each case involves a claim about the distinctive function of a particular part of language—a claim that the author of the view in question takes to do the philosophical work of traditional non-cognitivism, such as blocking reductionist moves. The functions concerned are not described in the non-cognitivist's usual semantic or psychological terms, however, and hence the resulting views are thoroughly compatible with minimalism about both truth and belief. (Our use of these examples does not require that we endorse the particular functional claims concerned, of course. We present them simply as an aid to those who have trouble visualizing the possibility of our functional brand of non-cognitivism, unless it is couched in the usual semantic or psychological terms.)

We turn first to Robert Brandom's seminal paper, "Reference Explained Away" (1984). Brandom argues that "refers" is primarily a device for constructing complex anaphoric pronouns. The notion of anaphora is familiar: when we say "Jones went to the shop and he bought a leek," the pronoun "he" depends anaphorically on the term "Jones." Brandom contends that the primary use of "refers" is to be found in such linguistic episodes as this:

> Evans to Williams: "Jones is fond of leeks."
>
> Williams, later: "The person to whom Evans referred is fond of leeks."

Here "The person to whom Evans referred" is anaphorically dependent upon "Jones" in a manner analogous to that of "he" on "Jones" in the first example.

This is an account of the linguistic *function* of the term "refers," then, and Brandom is explicit about its relevance for certain more traditional approaches:

> The anaphoric approach will not tell us how to understand sentences such as
>
> Reference is a physical, causal relation.
>
> The reason is clear. On the anaphoric account although ". . . refers to . . ." plays a syntactically relational role, its semantic role is anaphoric and pronominal rather than relational. Philosophers have misconstrued the plain man's use of "refers" . . . Such a mistake is of a piece with the search for the objects corresponding to each expression that syntactically plays the role of a term. (Brandom 1984: 487–488)

We emphasize that Brandom doesn't deny that we have *beliefs* about what refers to what, or that claims about what refers to what are sometimes *true*. All the same, however, he claims to identify a crucial functional difference between "reference talk" and ordinary descriptive discourse—a difference in virtue of which there would be a sort of category mistake involved in seeking to reduce one to the other. Since the functional difference that he is interested in is not couched in terms of the distinction between having and lacking truth conditions, or between expressing and failing to express a belief, he is certainly not relying in a covert way on a substantialist conception of belief or truth. Nor is he offering the sort of challenge to folk practice that the quietist is likely to baulk at. His imputation of a category mistake in attempting to understand "refers" on the model of causal–relational predicates thus appears perfectly compatible with the sundry varieties of minimalism we have looked at.

Now to our second example: In *Wise Choices, Apt Feelings* (1990), Allan Gibbard takes over from emotivism the view that the basic function of normative claims is that of expressing attitudes of approval and disapproval on the part of the speaker. He argues that naturalistic analyses of normative claims miss "a general element of endorsement—an element an expressivist analysis can capture" (1990: 10). But Gibbard is quite happy to say that we have normative beliefs, so long as we recognize that normative beliefs and empirical beliefs are not the same sort of thing. And he takes it for granted that distinctive function of normative discourse is to be characterized from the standpoint of theoretical psychology (in alliance with human evolutionary biology), not in terms of the folk notion of belief.

Gibbard himself goes on to defend a semantically characterized version of this kind of non-cognitivism about normative discourse: he argues that "normative judgments are not pure judgments of fact" (1990: 105). But he is more sensitive than many non-cognitivists to the question as to what this claim amounts to: "On the account as I am now giving it, after all, normative terms act much like other terms. What are we denying if we claim that normative judgments are not strictly factual?" (1990: 105). The answer he goes on to suggest is reminiscent of the terms in which we have characterized the issue between substantialists and insubstantialists: he sees the crucial point as the claim that "our normative capacities can be explained without supposing that there is a special kind of normative fact to which they typically respond" (1990: 107).

In effect, then, Gibbard addresses the issue as to whether normative judgments are factual in terms of a substantialist account of factuality. The point we wish to emphasize is that this move is not a necessary condition of the claim that normative judgments have a distinctive functional role. Gibbard could quite well have taken the same deflationary attitude to factuality as he takes to belief, and accepted that there are normative facts—and yet continued to insist that in virtue of the fact that normative judgments express motivational states, there can be no reduction of normative claims to naturalistic claims.[9] (As our page references indicate, indeed, Gibbard presents his anti-reductionist view of normative discourse long before he addresses the issue as to whether normative claims are factual. The functional point stands on its own, and does not depend on the later gloss.) Once again, the general point is that the philosophically interesting work of non-cognitivism—the work of blocking reductionist moves, in particular—is done by the functional characterization. With this in place, a non-cognitivist has no need to insist on a distinction in terms of the folk semantic and psychological notions.

For our third example we turn to the insubstantialist theory of truth itself. An insubstantialist theory of truth is typically grounded in a story about the function of the truth predicate. Let us focus briefly on Paul Horwich's version of the view, for example (1990). According to Horwich,

> the truth predicate exists solely for the sake of a certain logical need. On occasion we wish to adopt some attitude towards a proposition—for example, believing it, assuming it for the sake of argument, or desiring that it be the case—but find ourselves thwarted by ignorance of what exactly the proposition is. . . . In such situations the concept of truth is invaluable. For it enables the construction of another proposition, intimately related to the one we can't identity, which is perfectly appropriate as the alternative object of our attitude. (1990: 2–3)

Horwich does not conclude that we do not have beliefs about truth, or that claims about what is true cannot be true. But he does deploy his account of the distinctive functional role of the truth predicate to the same sorts of philosophical ends as classical non-cognitivism: on the one hand, we get a story about the continuing need for the truth predicate in our practice; on the other, an insistence that any attempt to reduce truth to some naturalistic property involves a kind of category mistake. The latter moral is particularly clear in the following passage:

> What the minimalist wishes to emphasize . . . is that truth is not a *complex* or *naturalistic* property but a property of some other kind. (Hartry Field suggests the term "*logical* property.") The point behind this jargon is that different kinds of property correspond to different roles that predicates play in our language, and that unless these differences are appreciated we will be tempted to raise questions regarding one sort that can legitimately arise only in connection with another sort. (1990: 38–39)

9. Horwich makes this point in Horwich 1993.

Hence Horwich himself is a non-cognitivist, in our generalized sense of the term, and a live exemplar of the fact that non-cognitivism of this kind is compatible with minimalism about truth.[10] Indeed, insubstantialism about truth is almost automatically a non-cognitivist position, in claiming that the function of the truth predicate is not—as it seems—to refer to some substantial property. To understand the general character of non-cognitivism is to see that at least in this special case, it cannot be incompatible with this common form of minimalism about truth.

The special case aside, the three examples above provide ample illustration of the main points we want to make. It is quite possible to be a non-cognitivist, in a philosophically well-motivated sense of that term, without characterizing one's position in terms of either truth or belief. As a result, non-cognitivism is compatible not only with insubstantialism about truth or belief, but also, at least in general,[11] with quietism.

5. The Functions of Truth

Insubstantialist theories of truth raise a range of questions concerning the functions of the folk concept of truth, questions not often given their due prominence. What is the truth predicate for? Why do its limits fall where they do in language; that is, why are there large classes of sentences with respect to which the construction "P is true" is disallowed? If the truth predicate is applied to discourses which themselves perform different linguistic tasks, does it have a common function in relation to the various tasks concerned?

Questions of this kind ought to have been addressed by traditional non-cognitivists, who often characterized their position in terms of truth, and yet wanted to draw a deep ("cognitive–non-cognitive") distinction within the class of sentences to which ordinary usage applies the truth predicate. In some respects, however, we think that the lack of the broader functional perspective we have advocated has prevented these issues from being given their due prominence. In this section we want to identify some of the proper concerns of philosophy in this area, bringing out along the way the merits of the functional perspective, and some of the errors of traditional non-cognitivism. JOS's discussion again provides a useful foil. Given that folk practice is the explanandum here, we might expect their platitude-based methodology to be sensitive to questions of this kind. In some respects, however, we think that they perpetuate some of the errors and oversights of traditional non-cognitivists, whom they themselves criticize on

10. We noted earlier that Horwich himself endorses this compatibility, as well as exemplifying it.

11. The qualification is needed because, as Horwich's case illustrates, insubstantialism about truth is a non-cognitivist position that is doubtfully compatible with quietism about truth.

similar grounds. By calling attention to what is missing in JOS's account, we hope to highlight the general *desiderata* for work in this area.

Non-cognitivists who characterize their position in terms of truth often seem curiously immune to the thought that there must be some foundation for the fact that ordinary usage applies "true" and "false" to the sentences for which they advocate a non-cognitivist interpretation. After all, unless non-cognitivism is willing to ascribe some deep mistake to the folk—a move out of keeping with the view's typically conservative tendencies—it will have to allow that there is some legitimate basis for folk usage in this respect. A natural suggestion is that the use of truth in these cases is somehow idiomatic or non-standard, but any serious attempt to make good this assumption would lead to the sort of reflection on the role of truth envisaged above. After all, it is implausible to tell us that truth does something different in, say, ethical discourse, without telling us just what it does there, and what it does elsewhere, in supposedly cognitive discourses.

Prima facie, these questions are difficult for an insubstantialist about truth: insofar as the concept of truth is thin, there seems little room for a distinction between the two kinds of cases. As long as non-cognitivism is characterized in terms of truth, insubstantialism about truth leaves little room for the non-cognitivist to maneuver. Indeed, this is the basis of the claim that insubstantialism about truth excludes non-cognitivism.

Our third leg strategy avoids the problem by characterizing non-cognitivism in completely different terms. In a more limited way, the same is true of an orthodox psychologically defined non-cognitivism. But does JOS's brand of non-cognitivism escape the problem? If so, only because it too is psychologically grounded, though semantically defined. Unless JOS are prepared to be more explicit about the psychological foundation than they actually are in their paper, however, the problem seems bound to reemerge. The non-cognitivist they envisage would be claiming that ethical utterances are not truth-apt, while conceding that ordinary usage applies truth and falsity to ethical claims (and not seeking to revise this aspect of folk usage). But what is the concept of truth supposed to be doing in these cases, if the claims concerned are not truth-apt? And whatever the answer, how does it relate to what the concept of truth does with respect to claims that are truth-apt?

Presumably, JOS envisage that the non-cognitivist will claim that the ordinary application of "true" to ethical claims is somehow idiomatic, or less than full-blooded. But if truth is insubstantial to start with—a logical device for expressing generality, for example, as many insubstantialists have suggested—then it is easy for its use to be full-blooded, and this response seems implausible. As a device for generality, truth seems just as at home in ethical discourse as it is elsewhere: after all, what difference does it make to the logical function of "true" in "What the Pope said is true" whether the Pope was giving voice to a moral opinion? The same goes for any brand of insubstantialism: if truth is insubstantial, there is very little room to deny that the use of the truth predicate is full-blooded, in any discourse in which it normally appears—in other words, very little room to deny that the sentences of the discourse in question really are truth-apt.[12] JOS's strategy for combining semantically defined non-cognitivism with insubstantialism about truth thus seems unstable—in contrast, note, to its close relative, the position which defines non-cognitivism psychologically from the start.[13]

If non-cognitivism is characterized in the functional terms we recommend, the questions about the functions of truth with which we began this section still need to be addressed, of course. The non-cognitivist still needs to confront the fact that truth applies in a uniform way to parts of language that are being claimed to have different functions. Here the non-cognitivist's interests coincide with those of insubstantialists about truth, however. Both sides are interested in the functions of parts of language, and they have a common interest in producing a coherent account—an account in which the function of truth talk can be seen to mesh with that of other parts of language, in such a way as to explain the data of ordinary language. We take it to be an advantage of the more general functional perspective we advocate, and in terms of which we have suggested that non-cognitivism is best formulated, that it does give these questions about truth their due prominence.[14] Finally, we emphasize that there is no reason to think that the issues raised from this perspective can be addressed by a platitude-based strategy. The linguistic functions to which such accounts appeal might be no part of the folk repertoire, and hence be unmentioned in any platitude, explicit or otherwise.[15]

12. A referee for the original version of this chapter suggested that the non-cognitivist might say that the folk application of the truth predicate to ethical claims is full-blooded, but relies on a deep error: the error the folk make of thinking that ethical claims have cognitive meaning. Granted, this move is in keeping with the sort of non-cognitivism that we find, for example, among the Positivists. Nevertheless, the main point is untouched: If having cognitive meaning is a matter of being truth-apt, and truth is insubstantial, then there is very little room for the folk to be in error about the cognitive status of any discourse to which folk usage applies the truth predicate, assuming that the truth predicate plays its insubstantial function perfectly well in sentences of that discourse.

13. At this point JOS themselves rely on the claim that there is "a platitudinous connection between . . . truth aptness and belief" (1994: 294). This claimed platitude ought to seem questionable, however, by their own lights. Why? Simply because they themselves maintain that it is questionable whether moral "beliefs" are real beliefs—whether "There are moral beliefs" turns out to be a central platitude, robust under scrutiny—and yet the folk maintain that moral claims can be true and false (and are hence truth-apt). One way to maintain consistency here is to allow that moral claims really are truth-apt, and to reject the analytic tie between (real) belief and truth-aptness. JOS's own methodology seems ill equipped to reject this possibility a priori. All parties concede that there is some loose sense of "belief" in which moral claims do express beliefs. Why not say that it is this liberal use of "belief" which is deployed when the folk recognize a connection between belief and truth-aptness? Our point above is that insubstantialism about truth makes any other course implausible. An insubstantial truth predicate is likely to be at home in any discourse to which "belief" applies, strictly or loosely—if truth is insubstantial, truth-aptness comes cheaply.

14. For more on these issues see Price 1988, 1994.

15. Our examples in the previous section all illustrate this point. In seeking to explicate the function of reference talk, normative talk, and truth talk, respectively, Brandom, Gibbard, and Horwich are not systematizing snippets of folk wisdom, but addressing deep issues in sociolinguistic theory.

6. Non-cognitivism and Reductive Metaphysics

We close with a note about the wider significance of the issue as to how non-cognitivist positions should be formulated. There has been considerable recent interest in a reductionist program in metaphysics that takes its lead from an argument for the mind–brain identity theory advanced by David Lewis in the 1960s. In outline, the general proposal is that we treat folk platitudes about particular topics in the way that Ramsey suggested we treat scientific theories: we replace problematic terms with existentially quantified bound variables, and take the folk to be talking about whatever makes the resulting "Ramsey sentence" true. As their interest in folk platitudes might suggest, the JOS team includes some of the proponents of this program.[16] (Some of the program's advocates have taken up an ironic suggestion we made in an earlier version of the present chapter, and now call it "the Canberra Plan."[17])

The program depends in any particular case on a crucial linguistic assumption—roughly, the assumption that the reduced theory is doing the same linguistic job as the reducing theory. Unless this assumption is valid in the case in question, the proposed reduction involves a kind of category mistake. (This is just the point that non-cognitivism is antithetical to reductionism.) Jackson himself recognizes the need for this assumption, of course. In a recent paper in which he and Philip Pettit seek to apply the strategy to the case of value, for example, they explicitly presuppose cognitivism (Jackson and Pettit 1995). However, they take for granted that this is an assumption to be cashed in the standard terms. (As it turns out, they employ the psychological version of the standard story, saying that "cognitivists . . . maintain that practical evaluations . . . are expressions of judgement and belief" [Jackson and Pettit 1995: 20]). The point we have emphasized above is that this may well address the issue at the wrong level. A sophisticated non-cognitivist may simply deny that the relevant distinctions in language and linguistic psychology lie at this accessible level.)

Our examples in section 4 illustrate this point. It is quite clear that Brandom, Gibbard, and Horwich would deny that reference, rationality, and truth are fit topics for the Ramsey-Lewis-Jackson program. In each case, they would say that to apply the program would be to make a mistake about the linguistic category of the target discourse, the kind of mistake that traditional non-cognitivists urged philosophy to avoid. The linguistic categories are not now drawn in terms of truth, but the continuity with traditional truth-grounded non-cognitivism is quite clear. What survives unchanged is the idea that a reductionist program is

16. There is a very clear exposition of the program in Jackson 1998. See also Lewis 1994.

17. The intended metaphor will be lost on readers unfamiliar with Canberra. Canberra's detractors often charge that as a planned city, and a government town, it lacks the rich diversity of "real" cities. Our thought was that in missing the functional diversity of ordinary linguistic usage, the Canberra Plan makes the same kind of mistake about language.

liable to category mistakes, to avoid which we need to reflect on the linguistic function of the parts of language concerned. We conclude that to miss the functional standpoint is to fail to notice the true character of the assumption on which the Canberra Plan depends. Indeed, the functional standpoint threatens to undercut the *motivation* for reductionism of this sort. Once we have an adequate explanation for the fact that the folk *talk* of Xs and Ys and Zs, an explanation which distinguishes these activities from what the folk are doing when they do physics, why should we try to reduce the Xs and Ys and Zs to what is talked about in physics?[18]

Finally, it is important to appreciate that the functional perspective is itself scientific, and naturalistic. Hence it can't be dismissed a priori—particularly by physicalists—and the reductionist program turns out to depend on an a posteriori theoretical thesis about language. As noted above, moreover, folk intuitions may give us very little access to the matters addressed from this theoretical perspective. Such intuitions provide the *explanandum*—what we want is an account of the origins and functions of our folk intuitions, in effect—but not the *explanans*. In particular, therefore, these are not issues that can be addressed by the platitude-based methodology of the Canberra Plan itself—even setting aside the obvious concern about circularity—for almost certainly they concern things that the folk have simply not thought about. So there really is no route into these issues other than the hard one of standing back from the concepts in question and asking how they arise, what functions they serve in the lives of the creatures who employ them, and so on. Despite their importance, however, these are issues whose visibility in contemporary philosophy is tenuous at best, a fact well illustrated by the terms in which JOS's discussion of the possibility of non-cognitivism is couched. In drawing attention to a more general perspective on the same problem—in showing in particular that a functionally grounded non-cognitivist is a much more sure-footed opponent—we hope to have bestowed on these issues some of the visibility they deserve.[19]

18. This line of thought is pursued at length in connection with talk about meaning in Lance and O'Leary-Hawthorne 1997, and more generally in Price 1992.

19. We are grateful to Michaelis Michael, Graham Oppy, Philip Pettit, Daniel Stoljar, and an anonymous referee for *The Australasian Journal of Philosophy* for helpful comments and discussion.

6

Naturalism and the Fate of the M-Worlds

Like coastal cities in the third millennium, important areas of human discourse seem threatened by the rise of modern science. The problem isn't new, of course, or wholly unwelcome. The tide of naturalism has been rising since the seventeenth century, and the rise owes more to clarity than to pollution in the intellectual atmosphere. All the same, the regions under threat are some of the most central in human life—the four Ms, for example: Morality, Modality, Meaning, and the Mental. Some of the key issues in contemporary metaphysics concern the place and fate of such concepts in a naturalistic worldview.[1]

True, some philosophers hold that at least some of these topics are not worth saving, and that the tide of science does us a favor by sweeping them away. Others hold that they do not need saving, being already out of reach of the waters of science—no part of scientific landscape, in effect, but no less respectable for that. To many contemporary philosophers, however, neither view seems appealing. The first—"eliminativism"—seems to underestimate the value of what would be lost. The second—"non-naturalism"—sometimes seems to rely on a Canute-like faith in the limits of science, and to offer no satisfactory account of how there could be a region of the world both out of reach of science, and yet of relevance in human life.[2] While affirming the vulnerability of the "M-concepts," then, most philosophical naturalists look for some sort of rescue strategy—some legitimate place for the M-concepts, *within* a naturalistic framework.

In my view, however, contemporary naturalists have overlooked the most promising rescue strategy. The two main strategies currently on offer are

1. What is naturalism? For the moment I take it to be the view that the project of metaphysics can properly be conducted from the standpoint of natural science. One reason for not being more specific is that the issue depends on the main project of this paper, which is to show that there is a recognizably naturalistic program in metaphysics that is largely ignored by contemporary "naturalists."

2. There are important arguments for non-naturalist views, of course, among them those of Frank Jackson (1982) concerning the status of qualia. As I think Jackson would be the first to acknowledge, however, these arguments do not remove the element of mystery in non-naturalism.

non-cognitivism and reductionism. I want to argue that the contemporary debate is incomplete, at the very least, in failing to recognize a third approach. As I'll explain, this third strategy rests on two main premises, each of which, while controversial, is of some plausibility in its own terms. I won't try to defend these premises in any detail here: I simply want to show that if both are granted, there is an attractive alternative to non-cognitivism and reductionism.

The new approach has much in common with non-cognitivism, however, so I'll begin below with non-cognitivism, and explain how the new strategy differs. I'll then contrast it briefly to Frank Jackson's reductionist program. I'll also show that although it is naturalist in spirit, the new strategy offers an olive branch to non-naturalists. In effect, it explains in the naturalists' own terms how topics such as morality and meaning might remain high and dry, untouched and unthreatened by the rise of the scientific tide—it offers the benefits of non-naturalism, without the metaphysical downside.

1. Non-cognitivism and the Carnap Thesis

Non-cognitivism is often a response to the kind of philosophical concern just described. Some topic of human discourse—morality, say—seems difficult to accommodate in a naturalistic worldview. The choices seem to be to accept the existence of moral aspects of reality distinct from the aspects of reality described by science, or to conclude that science has shown that moral talk is in error, in failing to connect with anything in the external world. Non-cognitivism offers an escape from this dilemma. If moral talk isn't in the business of describing reality—if its linguistic *function* is quite different—then we can leave it in place, without conflict with the ontological lessons of the naturalistic view.

This solution is pleasing to a naturalist in two respects. First, as noted, it entails that there are no moral facts or properties to be accommodated within the natural world. Second, the price of this escape—the notion of a linguistic function—is itself acceptable, in naturalistic terms. A naturalist need find nothing objectionable in the hypothesis that human languages serve a number of different functions.[3]

Non-cognitivism appeals most in the moral case, but even here some feel that it devalues the talk it claims to save. If this is rescue, moral realists think, we do better to take our chances against the tide of naturalism on our own terms. This response is more common with respect to topics that metaphysicians are inclined to take more seriously, such as modality, meaning, and mind. In these

3. So long as the functions concerned can be characterized in naturalistically acceptable terms, of course. It isn't obvious that orthodox non-cognitivism passes this test. If the functions concerned are characterized in intentional terms, and intentionality itself is naturalistically suspect, non-cognitivists may well have a problem.

cases, few people think that non-cognitivism provides any sort of rescue worth having.[4]

Recently, non-cognitivism has been under attack from a different direction. Non-cognitivists need an account of the nature of the distinction they claim to find in language, between cognitive and non-cognitive discourse. In practice this distinction gets cashed in a number of ways, some semantic and some psychological. On the semantic side, non-cognitive discourse is said to be non-assertoric, non-descriptive, non-truth-conditional, non-truth-apt, or non-fact-stating, among other things. On the psychological side, the distinction is normally drawn in terms of a belief–non-belief distinction: cognitive utterances are said to be those that express genuine beliefs, rather than other psychological attitudes, such as desires.

However, it not clear that these distinctions can be drawn in the way the non-cognitivist requires. One source of doubt has been minimalism about truth: roughly, the view that the linguistic function of the truth predicate is not to refer to a substantial property, but to do something else—perhaps to provide a mere grammatical convenience, for example. This view shares with non-cognitivism a concern with the functions of particular parts of language, but seems to leave little room for the claim that moral discourse, say, is not genuinely truth conditional (or truth-apt). If truth is merely a grammatical device of "disquotation," for example, isn't it immediate that *any* indicative utterance is truth-apt?[5] What is the non-cognitivist denying, when she denies that there are moral truths?[6]

This point is familiar with respect to non-cognitivism and truth. There is an analogous but less familiar point about non-cognitivism and ontology, stemming from the work of Quine and especially Carnap in mid-century. Carnap (1950) argues that there is no absolute, theory-independent ontological viewpoint available to metaphysics. Ontological questions about the entities mentioned in a particular theory or linguistic framework can properly be raised as what Carnap calls "internal questions"—questions posed within the framework or theory in question—but not as "external questions," posed from a stance outside that framework. (Carnap follows Quine in taking it that the kinds of entities to which a theory is ontologically committed are those over which the theory quantifies, when cast in canonical form.)

Carnap himself applies this conclusion to argue that the traditional debate between platonists and nominalists about the existence of abstract entities is

4. In the case of meaning, it is not clear that non-cognitivism is even coherent, for reason mentioned in the previous note; cf. Boghossian (1990).

5. Jackson, Oppy, and Smith (1994) answer "no" to this question, arguing that one might be a minimalist about truth but not about truth-aptness, or the belief–non-belief distinction. This is quite true, but no help in defending non-cognitivism against some of the more thoroughgoing forms of contemporary minimalism, which do extend to these notions (see O'Leary-Hawthorne and Price 1996).

6. There is a clear statement of this argument in Wright (1992: chapter 1).

misconceived, except to the extent that it can be construed in one of the following two ways. First, Carnap allows that there are legitimate (internal) issues as to what abstract entities, if any, are quantified over in the most satisfactory representation of the framework concerned—some nominalists might be construed as arguing that such quantification is always eliminable—and as to what particular entities there are of the recognized kinds.[7] Second, Carnap also recognizes a legitimate pragmatic issue that may be raised from the external standpoint: roughly, an issue concerning the utility of the framework concerned. What is disallowed, according to what I shall call the Carnap thesis, is the external ontological question as to whether there are "really" sets, numbers, or whatever.

This thesis seems to make things difficult for a non-cognitivist. If there is nothing more to the issue of the existence of moral properties, or possible worlds, or meanings, than is settled by the fact that these things need to be quantified over in the relevant parts of language—and the non-cognitivist grants this, and does not want to say that these parts of language are in error—then how can it be denied that such things exist (and hence that the relevant parts of language do describe them)?[8] Again, reflection on the function of existence claims leads to trouble for the very view that stakes its living on the thesis that linguistic functions may not be what they seem.

In my view, the difficulty stems from the fact that non-cognitivism took a wrong turn early in its history. Non-cognitivists were right in thinking that the notion of linguistic function provides a naturalistic solution to metaphysical concerns, but wrong to try to characterize the functions concerned in the terms normally used. To get things right, we need to retain the insight that different bits of language may serve different functions in a way that isn't obvious at first sight, but set aside the usual attempts to characterize the functions concerned in terms of truth, factuality, belief, and the like.

I want to show that the resulting position actually derives great strength from minimalism about semantics and ontology. In particular, the Carnap thesis plays a crucial role in what follows. At various points the thesis blocks natural objections to my proposal. Often the block seems counterintuitive, but in a sense this was Carnap's point: he thought that various "natural" moves in philosophy turn out to be inadmissible, in presupposing an illegitimate externalist viewpoint. This suggestion has considerable plausibility, in my view, but I shall not attempt to

7. In extreme cases the recognized categories might even be held to be empty, as in the view of the atheist, who accepts the conceptual framework of theism, but argues from within it that, in fact, there are no deities. Contrast this with the view of the person who regards the entire framework as meaningless or pragmatically irrelevant. Both views seem legitimate in Carnap's terms, but they shouldn't be confused.

8. True, the non-cognitivist might say that the Carnap thesis applies only to cognitive uses of language, and that the cognitive character of moral discourse is precisely what non-cognitivism denies. But the point is that this denial seems implausible, if a moral ontology is so close at hand.

defend Carnap's thesis here. I simply want to show that if Carnap is right, the issue of the fate of the M-worlds takes on a surprising new form.

2. Functional Pluralism

I'll call the new approach *functional pluralism*.[9] A functional pluralist accepts that moral, modal, and meaning utterances are descriptive, fact-stating, truth-apt, cognitive, belief-expressing, or whatever—and full-bloodedly so, not merely in some ersatz or "quasi" sense. Nevertheless, the pluralist insists that these descriptive utterances are functionally distinct from scientific descriptions of the natural world: they do a different job in language. They are descriptive, but their job is not to describe what science describes.

Of course, as my phrasing is meant to emphasize, this makes a functional pluralist sound like a Moorean non-naturalist, who asserts that the world contains moral properties, in addition to the things talked about by science. The difference is that pluralism rejects the idea of a single world, containing both moral and natural entities. I don't mean that it replaces this single world with a bare multiplicity of worlds, which would be equally unappealing. The point is that the judgment of unity or plurality could only be made from the framework-independent external stance, which the Carnap thesis disallows. Without that stance, functional pluralism is neither monist nor pluralist, in a primarily ontological sense—for there is no such sense.

The multiplicity that the pluralist does recognize is one of linguistic function, and therefore naturalistically respectable.[10] The multiplicity of worlds, such as it is, is merely what follows from the fact that more than one linguistic function may be exercised at the same time. From the evaluative stance it is correct (let us suppose) to say that there are values and evaluative properties. From the scientific stance it is correct to say that there are electrons. If I say that electrons are terrific little particles, I occupy both stances—employ both frameworks, in Carnap's terminology—but no metaphysical spooks are thereby required.[11]

9. In O'Leary-Hawthorne and Price (1996), John O'Leary-Hawthorne and I use this term, but refer to the view as a version of non-cognitivism. There is no significant inconsistency with my present terminology, however. O'Leary-Hawthorne and I note that while the view in question is not standard non-cognitivism, it is a product of the same intuition about the functions of language, and hence that a terminological decision must be made as to whether to call it a non-cognitivist view. Here, in order to highlight the contrast with orthodox non-cognitivism, I am using a different label. In Price (1992) I called the same view "vertical pluralism," to distinguish it from the ("horizontal") kind of pluralism, which merely allows a plurality of theories within a given area of discourse—a plurality of theories of electromagnetism, for example.

10. Subject to the earlier caution—see n3.

11. Obviously a functional pluralist will have to allow frameworks, or linguistic functions, to "mix" in this way. The task of making sense of this seems considerably less severe than that facing non-cognitivists, however, who are required to account for the same mixed examples in the standard semantic terms.

The possibility of a functional pluralism has been obscured by a tendency to read into the notion of description an ontological monism for which the Carnap thesis implies there is no justification. When philosophers think of description, or representation, they often have in mind a familiar picture: on one side, the World; on the other side, Mind, or Language (the medium of representation). Once this picture is in place, the path I want to take is practically invisible. Either the World in the picture is the natural world, in which case moral discourse must either be understood in naturalistic terms, or be treated as somehow less than full-blooded, successful, description; or it is the non-naturalist's world, which contains moral facts, say, in addition to the kind of facts described by science.

Innocent as this picture may seem, I think it embodies two mistakes. The first is the mistake that the Carnap thesis corrects, of imagining that there is an extra-linguistic stance available to metaphysics—a stance external to every linguistic framework or viewpoint, from which we may survey the World. The second is the mistake of failing to notice the plurality of linguistic functions, or frameworks, within descriptive discourse as a whole. Once we recognize that there is more than one framework in use in ordinary language, and that there is no framework-independent stance for metaphysics, it follows immediately that the naive picture is misleading, unless explicitly confined to one framework (in which case it can be thought of harmlessly, as a metaphorical picture of what can be said in internal terms).

In a limited way this conclusion is already drawn by Carnap himself. Carnap's treatment of a fifth M-world, Mathematics, is the treatment a functional pluralist seeks to extend to the other four. So why has this avenue not been explored? Mainly, I think, due to the grip of the non-cognitivists' idea that their functional distinction needed to be drawn elsewhere, in terms of a divide between descriptive and non-descriptive uses of language.[12]

I'll come back to the Carnap thesis, for the picture I'm using it to oppose is very tenacious, and will try to reassert itself at several points. For the moment I want to turn to the aspect of functional pluralism that may seem especially puzzling: the suggestion that in some philosophically interesting sense, description might serve more than one function in language.

3. Description as a Multipurpose Tool

In one sense, the claim that descriptive discourse serves more than one function in language is entirely trivial. Even if we set aside the fact that we use descriptions for a wide variety of secondary purposes—to persuade, to shock, to entertain, for

12. This idea was already firmly established when Carnap was writing, of course. Carnap himself refers to the "non-cognitive character" of the external issue as to the acceptability of frameworks.

example—there is still a huge range of functional differences associated simply with differences of content. Descriptive utterances about aardvarks serve different purposes from descriptive utterances about zygotes, simply in virtue of the differences between (our relationship to) aardvarks and (our relationship to) zygotes. However, this kind of functional variety is no threat to the assumption that description itself constitutes the basic functional category—in effect, the assumption that a functional taxonomy of these uses of language would have description itself (or some cognate notion, such as assertion) as the core linguistic notion. Whatever else the various uses might be, they are all instances of this core descriptive use of language.

Not all human instruments wear their essential properties on the surface, however. Think of string, or cord, which also has many different uses: tethering animals, hanging washing, securing parcels, binding splints, producing musical notes, and so on. If we were interested in a functional taxonomy of the uses of human artifacts, how would we represent what these uses have in common? A proper theory would have to recognize that string has certain core properties—length, thinness, strength, and flexibility, for example—all or most of which are exploited in each of these uses. A theory that didn't identify these core properties would be inadequate in at least two ways. First, it would be unable properly to characterize the difference between a multipurpose artifact, such as string, and a single-purpose artifact, such as a Phillips-head screwdriver. A screwdriver may be used on many different screws, but this isn't the same as the functional diversity we find in the case of string.[13] Second, such a theory would fail to exclude various uses of string which don't rely on any of the core properties: the use of a ball of string as a paperweight, for example.[14]

Hence if we were interested in a functional taxonomy of human artifacts, the naive category "uses of string" would not play a significant role in our final theory. On the contrary, the theory would appeal to the core properties themselves, and classify applications accordingly, as different ways of making use of these core properties.

Analogously, my functional pluralist suggests that notions such as "description" and "assertion" may be nothing more than relatively superficial labels for a linguistic category whose core properties remain to be discovered—a category that may turn out to have a multifunctional role in language, in the sense that its core properties serve a range of very different functions. One of these functions, perhaps, is that served by assertion in scientific discourse. (Actually, I think it is much more plausible that scientific discourse is already multifunctional. More on this below.) But if we fail to notice that there are other uses of the same linguistic

13. The difference may be a matter of degree, of course.

14. The test here is replaceability: the function served by the ball of string could be served by many objects with none of the core properties of string. The use of a screwdriver as a lever provides another example.

instrument, we are likely to make the kind of mistakes that would be made by someone whose acquaintance with string was biased toward just one of its many uses. Imagine someone whose main acquaintance with strings has been in an orchestra pit, for example. He encounters a tethered goat, recognizes that what connects the goat to the post is a string, and wonders how it is possible to make music on such an erratic instrument. He is right about the string, but wrong about what its use entails.

Thus the functional pluralist needs to answer two questions: What are the core properties of the descriptive or assertoric use of language? And what are (some of) the various uses to which a linguistic form with these core properties may be put? For the purposes this paper I shall simply suggest one possible answer to the former question, which I have defended in detail elsewhere.[15] The suggestion is that the core function of assertoric language is to give voice to speakers' mental states and behavioral dispositions, *in a way which invites criticism by speakers who hold conflicting mental states*. The key thing about assertoric discourse is thus that it embodies a normative idea of answerability to an external standard, the effect of which is to place an onus on speakers to be prepared to defend their views in the case of disagreements. The notions of truth and falsity play a key role, being the most pure expression of the relevant norms.

Again, I emphasize that what matters for present purposes is not whether this is the right characterization of the core function of assertoric discourse, but simply that it provides an hypothesis about what the core function might be, in terms of which we can see that the same core function might have many different applications. However, I call attention to one feature of this proposal that would need to be shared by any satisfactory alternative: it avoids the kind of circularity that would be involved if we tried to characterize the core functions of assertoric discourse in terms of the very group of concepts whose functional significance is at issue.[16] It isn't helpful to be told that the key function of descriptive discourse is to "make statements," or "express beliefs," if these notions are simply part of the package whose deep significance we are trying to understand. It would be like being told that a string is a light rope, or a heavy thread. We would be no closer to an understanding of the underlying nature of the tool in question.

Let's turn to the second question: For what range of purposes might a linguistic device with this core property be employed? What different functions might description serve, in different cases? The striking thing is that these functions may be just those to which non-cognitivists also appeal. They might include the function of giving voice to a range of psychological states with distinctive functional

15. Price (1988). For a related account of assertion that might also be used for these purposes, see Brandom (1983, 1994).

16. At least, it avoids this kind of circularity if notions such as conflict between mental states can be explicated in sufficiently basic terms, so that they don't themselves depend on notions such as truth and falsity. I address this kind of concern in Price (1988: chapter 7).

roles of their own, or distinctive dependencies on contingent human capacities and responses: motivational states ("desires"), say, or states that play distinctive roles in reasoning ("conditional beliefs"), or perceptual states of various kinds. Of course, non-cognitivists appeal to these psychological distinctions in order to argue that the attitudes concerned are not beliefs, and a functional pluralist thinks that this step is misguided. Concerning the psychological distinctions themselves, however, the two views might well agree.

4. Belief and Ontology

Why do non-cognitivists feel bound to say that psychological states distinguished in these ways are not beliefs? An important factor, I think, is the thought that because genuine beliefs have genuine truth conditions, someone who allows that moral beliefs (say) are genuine beliefs is committed to genuine moral facts or states of affairs (or to an error theory, of course). If reductionism is disallowed, so that these moral states of affairs are not simply natural states of affairs in disguise, then we seem to be left with the metaphysical mystery that non-cognitivism seeks to avoid: non-natural facts, floating free of the physical world.

Again, however, the Carnap thesis tells us that this relies on an illegitimate conception of belief: roughly, the idea that beliefs are the mind's attempt to stand in correspondence with a preexisting World—"preexisting" in the sense that it is thought of from an external stance which supposedly we occupy as semanticists and ontologists, asking to what our beliefs *refer*, and what makes them *true*. But there is no such stance, according to the Carnap thesis. We construct our semantics after the fact, relying on the theories to which we already subscribe.[17] As users of moral language, holders of moral beliefs, we can describe their semantics, and may discover that when our beliefs are expressed in canonical form, they refer to moral properties. We thus find ourselves committed to the existence of moral properties, in the only sense of ontological commitment recognized by the Carnap view.

The key insight, shared by non-cognitivists and my functional pluralists, is that at this point the remaining puzzle is merely sociolinguistic, and not metaphysical. It is the issue as to why creatures like us should find ourselves engaged in this

17. I think it is important not to confuse the pseudo-externality provided by what Quine calls "semantic ascent" with the genuine externality with which Carnap is concerned. Semantic ascent is available to us from within a linguistic framework: it allows us to pose what are really internal questions by talking about the framework itself. Instead of asking "Is there a prime number greater than 100" we can ask "Is the sentence 'There is a prime number greater than 100' true?" Questions of this kind are only sensible if the sentences in question retain their interpretation: otherwise, it would be like asking "Is the sentence '!@#$%^&*' true?" Carnap's external standpoint must be more remote: the issue as to whether to adopt a framework is like the issue as to whether to interpret in the first place.

particular linguistic practice, not the issue as to what these moral properties *are*. But whereas the non-cognitivist thinks that the metaphysical issue is only deflected by a concession about language—a concession which entails that moral language does not involve genuine ontological claims—the functional pluralist sees that this concession may be unnecessary. If Carnap and Quine are correct about the nature of ontological claims, and the minimalists correct about truth, then the metaphysical issue is already empty, and the linguistic concession is unnecessary.

Doesn't the metaphysical issue emerge again, from *within* the sociolinguistic perspective? This perspective is naturalistic, at least in initial orientation: it simply inquires into an aspect of the behavior of natural creatures (ourselves). But when we ask for the function of moral discourse, aren't there two possibilities? The first is that we need to appeal to moral properties or states of affairs, to which the speakers of moral discourse can be construed as responding. In this case we are in the same position as before—that is, still faced with the problem of the nature of such things. Alternatively, if we don't need to appeal to moral properties or states of affairs, then the sociolinguistic perspective seems to have shown us that moral talk is in error—unless, as the non-cognitivist claims, it is not intended to be descriptive in the first place.

But the second outcome is misrepresented, and the source of the mistake is the same as before. The fact that there are no moral properties in the natural world does not entail that moral talk is in error, if its function is not to describe such properties. Inquiring into its function, we find (let's suppose) that it is to give voice to certain mental states, distinguished by their motivational role in human psychology. Suppose—this is where the pluralist parts company with non-cognitivism—that this function is one of those appropriately served by the core properties of the descriptive language. This would explain why moral discourse takes descriptive form, and hence why it involves truth claims, and existence claims. We would thus have a naturalistic understanding of what speakers are doing when they engage in moral discourse, and hence a reason to deny that such speakers are guilty of some global error, *without any concession about the descriptive function of moral discourse*. On the contrary, the account explains why such discourse does take (genuinely) descriptive form, in terms of an account of what core properties are genuinely distinctive of descriptive language.

5. The Primacy of Science

There is another factor that may have helped to favor non-cognitivism at the expense of functional pluralism. Won't any view that focuses on the role of (apparently) descriptive language in different areas of discourse want to say that science is special, or primary, in some way? Indeed, what would commitment to naturalism amount to, within this picture, if not something like this? And it is easy to take this as the thought that science (or perhaps some subset of it, such as its observational part) involves *genuine* descriptions, in contrast to the quasi-description of the other discourses. If we say this, we are committed to a form of non-cognitivism, at the expense of functional pluralism. So a functional pluralist needs to resist this move, and yet to deal with the intuition that there is something primary about science.

In my view, the explanation lies in the fact that as functional pluralists, we speak from *within* the scientific framework, but *about* other frameworks. This gives the scientific framework a kind of perspectival primacy. Our viewpoint is internal to science, but external to morality, for example. It is a viewpoint which allows us to refer directly to the objects and properties countenanced by science, but not—given the Carnap thesis—to the objects countenanced by the moral stance. It is tempting to think that it thus makes the moral reality somehow ersatz, fictional, or second-rate, but I think this is a mistake. The apparent difference is explained as one of perspective, an artifact of the viewpoint. To mistake it for an absolute ontological difference is again to lose sight of the Carnap thesis, and to fall for the mirage of a framework-neutral stance: to think that science gives us that stance, in effect.

For a functional pluralist, then, the question "What is the distinguishing function of scientific discourse?" is as important and non-trivial as the question "What is the distinctive function of moral discourse?" The circularity involved in the fact that the former question is itself posed from a scientific standpoint is not vicious, of course—it is no more problematic than the use of human language in the study of the deep structure of human language, for example. However, scientific discourse may appear distinctive in that when we address this sort of question with respect to science, our answer will refer to the entities countenanced by the discourse in question—science itself—in a way that isn't true of other discourses.

Even if we discount the perspectival factor just mentioned, it might seem that an important insight remains. In the case of science, or at least folk science, it seems that we need to appeal to the existence of ordinary-sized physical objects to explain folk talk about such things, in a way in which we don't need to appeal to moral properties to explain folk talk of moral properties. This might encourage the thought that genuinely descriptive discourse is whatever discourse needs to be explained as a response to a preexisting world—a world which itself needs to be described in terms of the discourse in question.

This is an appealing idea, closely related to a familiar suggestion as to how we should settle claims between realists and antirealists in metaphysics: roughly, the suggestion that realism is appropriate when the putative entities do causal–explanatory work. However, if this were our criterion for genuinely descriptive language, it is far from clear that science, or even folk science, would count as genuinely descriptive. For example, science seems irreducibly modal at various points, and perhaps irreducibly committed to the notion of causation. Yet there might well be a naturalistic explanation of our use of our causal and modal discourse which didn't presuppose the existence of modal facts—an explanation in which the existence of such facts played no causal role. (This isn't as controversial as it might sound. A modal realist such as David Lewis is committed to the view that the origin of human modal talk is a causal product of nothing but the actual world; being causally isolated from the actual world, other possible worlds play no causal role. More generally, it is far from clear that causal relations themselves are among the causes of our talk of causal relations.) Even the use of kind terms and general concepts would be suspect, given that our causal contact is always with tokens. So the category of genuine description might be considerably narrower than that of (even) folk science. Indeed, it might turn out that there is no language explicable purely in these terms—no useful residue from this attempt to distill pure representation from functional reflection on human thought and language.[18]

To put the point slightly differently, we cannot take it for granted that all the conceptual tools used by science are themselves to be explained as bare responses to proper objects of scientific study. It might be a mistake to think that science could or should study causation in the same way that it studies gravitation, even if talk of causation turns out to be ineliminable from science. The appropriate scientific course might be to study *talk* of causation—to ask why we have it, what it does for us. As I've emphasized, this reflection on the functions of language need in no way devalue its original uses. Science has no more reason to be wary of a functional account of the concept of causation than it has to be wary of the deflationists' functional account of truth, for example.

Some philosophical positions may have reason to be wary of a functional account of causation, of course. For example, some reductionist programs rely on the principle that all causation is at base physical causation. In the classic Armstrong-Lewis arguments for materialism about the mental, for example, this principle supports the ontological claim that mental states are identical with certain physical states. However, a study of the origins and functions of causal concepts might reveal that there is no more justification for this kind of bare physicalist monism about causation than—according to the Carnap thesis—there is for a bare physicalist monism about ontological claims themselves.

6. Jackson's Program

Mind–body reductionism of the kind just mentioned illustrates the second major contemporary strategy for rescuing the M-worlds from the rising waters of science. Contemporary reductionism is perhaps best exemplified in Frank Jackson's

18. For an insightful discussion of related objections to the causal–explanatory criterion of reality, see Rosen (1994: 309–313).

elegant program, which relies on generalizing Lewis's treatment of the mental case, using the Ramsey-Carnap-Lewis approach to theoretical terms.[19]

In order to contrast functional pluralism with Jackson's approach, it will be helpful to have a toy example. I'll use the concept *cool*, as employed by speakers of English dialect (foreign, I suspect, to most of my readers) called "Street Cred." When members of the Street community say that something is cool, they do not mean that its constituent molecules have low mean kinetic energy. They mean that it is good, in a particular way. In what particular way? The available answers depend in part on where we stand. Among themselves, Street speakers might explain it in terms of near synonyms: "Cool things are, like, wicked," they might say, using another positive evaluative term. But I'll assume that this kind of answer either isn't accessible to us, or isn't what we were after, because the deeper theoretical issue we had in mind arises again with respect to the synonyms. If we want a naturalistic understanding of this aspect of Street usage it may be some help to be told that "cool" and "wicked" are near synonyms, but it doesn't get us very far.

Let's assume that the Street use of "That's cool" is descriptive. With this assumption in place, Jackson's strategy is to assemble the various statements Street folk take to be true of the property of being cool, to form these by conjunction into a single statement of Street "Cool Theory," and then to apply Ramsey's technique, replacing all occurrences of the term "cool" with a variable bound by an existential quantifier. The result is something of this form:

> There is a property F such that CT(F).

Cool is whatever property makes this true—in other words, whatever property best realizes the role of cool in the theory CT.

Up to this point, Jackson's program involves nothing with which a functional pluralist need disagree. From the pluralist's standpoint, there is no objection to marshaling the commitments of those who subscribe to the CT framework in this way. In effect, the marshaling shows us that those who employ this framework are committed to the existence of a property with certain properties, specified within the theory.

The difference comes at the next step. For the functional pluralist, the appropriate questions concern the function of the CT framework in the lives of Street speakers. There need be no further significant issue about what property cool is, and no mystery in the lack of such an issue. From inside the framework the issue does arise, of course, but has a trivial answer (once the marshaling has been done). What property is cool? Why, simply that property F such that CT(F). From outside the framework, the issue does not arise, as the Carnap thesis tells us. What does

19. There is a clear exposition of the program in Jackson (1998).

arise from outside is the issue as to why such a framework is in use in Street, and here the functionalist standpoint is the appropriate one to take up. (It may not provide a complete explanation, of course. To some extent, the framework may be simply an historical accident, maintained by linguistic convention.)

Jackson's view is that there is a further ontological issue, however: the issue as to what *physical* (or *natural*) property F is such that CT(F).[20] The view that this issue is legitimate—not simply a category mistake—seems to rest on two lines of argument.[21] The first is one we have already encountered. If we fail to recognize that description may be a multipurpose linguistic device, and reject the non-naturalists' ontological pluralism, then if ascriptions of cool are agreed to be descriptive, it seems that there is nothing for them to describe but the natural world. (We are also rejecting an error theory of cool, of course, but the "whatever fits" character of Jackson's program makes an error theory more than usually unappealing.) What else could cool be but a natural property?

A functional pluralist meets this argument by denying that description is univocal in the right sort of way. There is a core function that descriptive uses of language share, according to the functional pluralist, but it may be one that permits a range of quite different applications. And as I've explained, the pluralist appeals to the Carnap thesis to prevent this view from degenerating into non-naturalism of the metaphysical kind.

However, this leaves untouched Jackson's second line of argument, which relies on the fact (agreed on all sides, let's assume), that coolness supervenes on natural properties. If two things are the same in all physical respects, then either both are cool or neither is. In effect, then, coolness covaries with physical properties in some regular way. There is some (perhaps highly disjunctive) physical property that is simply what it takes for an object to be cool—a property that objects have if and only if they are cool. Supervenience requires that there be such a property. Given that there is, the fact that it covaries with coolness ensures that it occupies the role described by CT: the various things that CT takes to be true of cool are true of this physical property.

The easiest way to see where the functional pluralist parts company with this argument is to see where a non-cognitivist would part company, and then transpose into pluralist terms. Non-cognitivists can allow that the use of evaluative terms such as "cool" is supervenient on natural properties in at least two different senses. First, we may be able to say if two objects are physically identical, then normally functioning Street speakers will judge both to be cool or neither to be

20. Here, as elsewhere in this paper, nothing is meant to rest on the physical–natural distinction.

21. Perhaps there are three lines of argument, the third being the kind of appeal to a physicalist view of causation mentioned at the end of the previous section. If this appeal were invoked in the present case, on the basis that Street speakers take coolness to be a causally efficacious property, I think the pluralist's response should be to ask whether the function of causal talk in Street usage provides support for the thesis that all causation is physical causation.

cool. In other words, our study of the practices of Street speakers may show that their use of the concept *cool* is sufficiently regular and rule-governed to ensure that this is the case. This shows that in principle there's a naturalistic specification of the class of things normal Street speakers take to be cool. It doesn't show that to *be* cool is to have the natural property that marks this class. These are quite different propositions, as shown by the fact that the latter one uses the term "cool," whereas the former only mentions it—and just as well, for if the non-cognitivist were to accept the latter proposition, it would undermine the claim that "That's cool" is non-descriptive, by providing this utterance with a descriptive content.

The second sort of supervenience that a non-cognitivist might recognize is stronger. It might turn out that Street speakers themselves acknowledge that coolness supervenes on the physical, in the sense that they themselves will assent to the suggestion that if two things are physically indistinguishable, then either both are cool or neither is. Does this mean that in ascribing cool, Street speakers are ascribing a physical property? Of course not, says the non-cognitivist, for consider this analogy: We can easily imagine a group of rather insightful spectators (at a tennis match, say) who recognize that if two moves in the game are physically indistinguishable, then either it is appropriate to applaud both, or appropriate to applaud neither. This provides a sense in which applause supervenes on the physical, but obviously it doesn't entail that to applaud is to ascribe a physical property—similarly with "That's cool," according to the non-cognitivist. Its function is more like that of applause than that of a property ascription, and the fact that it supervenes on the physical in the sense described does not show otherwise. It does not show that ascriptions of cool are ascriptions of a physical property.

The key idea here is that the attempt to extract reduction from supervenience is blocked by functional difference: the reduction does not go through, despite supervenience in the acknowledged sense, because the function of the supervening discourse is different from that of science (the subvening discourse). And this implies that the point works equally well for a functional pluralist, even if he affirms that the supervening discourse is descriptive, so long as there is a deeper sense in which the supervening and subvening discourses differ in function.

So I think a pluralist can account for the supervenience intuitions, without allowing the identity claim. It might be said that this doesn't show that the identity claim is false, merely that it is unmotivated. However, is falsity what the pluralist requires? A better approach seems to be to argue that identity claims are simply not well-formed, unless they respect the lessons of the Carnap thesis. To ask whether an entity referred to in one framework is identical to an entity referred to in another framework seems to presuppose a framework-independent stance, from which the question can be raised. If we reject the idea of such a stance, the upshot seems to be that identity claims such as "Karl Marx is the father of Groucho Marx" and "Karl Marx is the number 3" go wrong in quite different ways. The first is false, from within the framework in which we talk about persons. The second is "not even false": it simply involves a category mistake.

But where does the boundary between these two kinds of cases lie? What constitutes a framework? A functional pluralist needs an answer to these questions which admits as meaningful not only such identity claims as "Karl Marx is the father of Groucho Marx" and "The morning star is the evening star," but also, apparently, certain acceptable reductionist claims in science: aqua fortis *is* HNO_3, for example. There are various important issues here. How are frameworks individuated? How do they combine in language, so that we may employ more than one in a single judgment? Can there be nested structures of frameworks, so that natural science might be unified by some overarching framework (which licenses reduction within science)?

I don't have developed answers to these questions, or space here to try to present some. My aim has been much more modest: to point out that the reductionist approach to the problem of the M-worlds assumes that language is homogeneous in a way in which it may well not be, and that non-cognitivism (as usually conceived) is not the only way to challenge this assumption.

The new challenge, that of functional pluralism, depends on the Carnap thesis. Without the Carnap thesis, naturalism seems to require ontological monism. This imposes homogeneity on descriptive language by default, as it were, by providing it with a single target—a single World to be described. In blocking this move, the Carnap thesis has radical implications for the project of saving the M-worlds from the tide of naturalism. It seems to permit a naturalistic alternative to non-cognitivism and reductionism—a path with the attractions of non-naturalism, in allowing talk of the M-worlds to be taken at face value, but without the metaphysical spooks.

The view that naturalism requires ontological monism is deeply entrenched, of course, and the suggestion that there might be a middle path of this kind is one that contemporary philosophical naturalists find hard to take seriously. However, I have argued that taking it seriously turns out to demand very little: simply the Carnap thesis, and a willingness to entertain the possibility that descriptive judgment might be a multipurpose tool. I conclude that advocates of any of the more familiar positions—eliminativists and non-naturalists, as well as non-cognitivists and reductionists—should think about which of these moves they reject, and why. If both are admitted, then contemporary metaphysical debates seem to be seriously incomplete, at the very least, in failing to engage with the possibility of a functional pluralism.[22]

22. I am grateful to Chris Daly, Max Kölbel, Michaelis Michael, John Hawthorne, Graham Oppy, Nick Smith, Daniel Stoljar, and Ed Zalta for many helpful comments on this material.

7

Ramsey on Saying and Whistling: A Discordant Note

1. Introduction

In his 1929 paper "General Propositions and Causality" (Ramsey 1990a), Frank Ramsey argues that unrestricted universal generalizations such as "All men are mortal" are not genuine propositions. About this, as about much else in that paper, Ramsey had recently changed his mind. A few years earlier, both in "Facts and Propositions" and in "Mathematical Logic," he had argued that such generalizations are equivalent to infinite conjunctions (see Ramsey 1990b: 48–51; 1990c: 236ff). But by 1929 his ideas about infinity had changed, and it was concerns about the infinite character of unrestricted generalizations which led him to his new view.

In our view, Ramsey's late position is highly unstable, in a way that is interesting both philosophically and historically. For the issues about infinity are essentially those underlying Wittgenstein's "rule-following considerations." On the face of it, if they show that generalizations are not genuine propositions, they show that none of our claims is a genuine proposition. This connection between Ramsey's view of generalizations and the rule-following considerations is certainly causal, as well as logical. In 1929 Wittgenstein had just returned to Cambridge, and it is well known that this year marked a turning point—indeed, a U-turning point—in his philosophical development. It is well known, too, that lengthy philosophical discussions with Ramsey formed a major part of Wittgenstein's intellectual life at this stage. It is also clear that Wittgenstein's preoccupations at that time had a lot to do with the recent influence of Brouwer on his thinking, especially his thinking about infinity. Finally, it is well known that Ramsey, too, enjoyed at least a partial conversion to such ideas—"General Propositions and Causality" is very much a product of that conversion.

But some things remain unclear about these influences and interactions. For one thing, what was the direction of influence between Ramsey and Wittgenstein?

Was it perhaps Ramsey who first saw the significance of what became the rule-following considerations, for example? In our view, the fact that Ramsey didn't appreciate the instability to which we here draw attention suggests that it was not. Had Ramsey been aware of the rule-following considerations, we think, the position advocated in "General Propositions and Causality" could hardly have seemed satisfactory.

Another thing that has been unclear is the nature of Ramsey's late conversion, and this too we hope to clarify. As it turns out, the influence of Hilbert seems greater than that of Brouwer—Ramsey's view is more formalist than intuitionist. And the instability of his position reflects an interesting general problem for formalist views, and their analogues elsewhere in philosophy.

Thus we suggest that "General Propositions and Causality" is an unstable product of a partial conversion, completion of which would have required a grasp of what we now call the rule-following considerations. While one can only speculate about what Ramsey would have made of a fuller conversion, such speculation is neither uninteresting nor necessarily uninformed. Among other things, some of what Ramsey does say about how we might live with the conclusion that generalizations are not propositions provides an indication as to how he might have presented the more radical conclusion that nothing is a proposition (in the assumed sense). In other words, they give us some indication as to how Ramsey's eminently practical pragmatism might have glossed what we now think of as Wittgensteinian or Kripkensteinian conclusions.

Our first aim is to demonstrate the instability of Ramsey's distinction between universal generalizations and (what he thinks of as) genuinely propositional claims. Our case involves two strands (which we take up separately).

First, we argue that the same considerations concerning infinity come up everywhere, due to the "infinite" character of our grasp of concepts (though strictly speaking, we contend, the crucial point in both cases is not a matter of infinity, but of something like open-endedness or unsurveyability, which we characterize further below). So the pressure to treat universal generalizations as non-propositional generalizes to all cases. Thus Ramsey's "skeptical problem" turns out to be global, and not (as he himself thought) confined to the case of generalizations.

Second, we argue that Ramsey's positive account of what universal judgments are—namely, that they are dispositional—is also applicable to other judgments, in virtue, ultimately, of the dispositional character of grasp of a concept (i.e., acquisition of a habit to apply a term in certain cases). In a sense, then, Ramsey's "skeptical solution" also turns out to be universal. At any rate, his positive account of the nature of universal generalizations doesn't provide a basis for distinguishing them from other propositions, once the skeptical problem itself is seen to be global.

The first task is therefore to understand Ramsey's reasons for denying that universally quantified sentences are equivalent to conjunctions.

2. Ramsey on Why Generalizations Are Not Propositions

The first argument Ramsey gives in "General Propositions and Causality" is the consideration that a universally quantified sentence can be written out, whereas an infinite conjunction cannot. If we treat universally quantified sentences as expressing propositions, we will be forced to see them as equivalent to conjunctions which, since they are infinite, "we cannot express for lack of symbolic power." But that is no good: "what we can't say we can't say, and we can't whistle it either" (Ramsey 1990a: 146).

Is this argument convincing? At first sight, apparently not, for consider an analogy. What do you get if you divide one by three? If you try saying the result as a decimal expansion, you will never stop: 0.33333 . . . However, that doesn't mean that you can't say it, only that you need to express it in a different way: as the fraction 1/3. Or consider a slightly more complicated example. What is the ratio of the circumference of a circle to its diameter? If you try saying that as a decimal expansion you will never stop; and any ratio of finite numbers will be inaccurate. But we can still say it, because we have a term purpose-built for the job, namely "π".

So the fact that you can't write out an infinite conjunction but can write out a universal generalization doesn't show that the two are not equivalent. It could be that the universal generalization is the way that you express an infinite conjunction, just as π is the way of expressing a certain irrational number. As we might put it: What we can't say in one form of words we can sometimes whistle in another. Or again, in the King James version: Whereof one cannot speak, thereof one should investigate the possibility of other modes of expression.[1]

These are fairly elementary points, which should make us wonder whether we have understood what Ramsey was getting at. One possibility is this. Sometimes when Ramsey talked about the use of words, he seemed to mean not simply the utterances themselves but also the whole mental state that is involved in accepting them.[2] Perhaps then Ramsey's point should be understood as the contention that we cannot ever come to accept infinite conjunctions, since we cannot ever grasp them. In contrast, we can grasp universal generalizations. This makes the

1. We shouldn't be distracted here by finitist worries about the existence of infinite expansions. Ramsey isn't arguing that there could be no infinite conjunctions; his argument is that even if they exist they cannot be equivalent to finite expressions, since, unlike finite expressions they cannot be written out. If his claim had simply been that there could be no infinite conjunctions, this argument about what could be written out would have been redundant.

2. Thus in "Facts and Propositions" Ramsey speaks of the mental factors in belief as consisting in "words, spoken aloud or to oneself or merely imagined" (Ramsey 1990b: 40). We follow Loar (1980: 55) in thinking that the best way to understand this is not just as the words themselves, but as "the whole state of affairs of one's accepting such and such a sentence."

point very similar to the two other arguments that Ramsey marshals against the idea that universals are conjunctions.[3] So let us turn to them.

The first argument is initially presented as an argument about *use:* an infinite conjunction is never used in its entirety. Ramsey then glosses the idea by saying that an infinite conjunction "goes beyond what we know or want":

> A belief of the primary sort is a map of neighbouring space by which we steer. It remains such a map however much we complicate it or fill in details. But if we professedly extend it to infinity, it is no longer a map. We cannot take it in or steer by it. Our journey is over before we need its remoter parts. (Ramsey 1990a: 146)

At first glance this seems to run together two quite different points. On the one hand, there is the claim that infinite conjunctions would not be useful to us, that we would have no need of them. On the other, there is the claim that we could not take them in. Moreover, the first of these claims might appear to fall well short of the conclusion that it is supposed to support. The world is sadly full of useless objects, so we can't in general move from (a) the claim that, on a certain conception of its nature, an object wouldn't be useful to us, to (b) the conclusion that it doesn't have such a nature. However, on Ramsey's pragmatic account of belief, there is no fallacy here, and no equivocation. In "Facts and Propositions" he holds in general that "the meaning of a sentence is to be defined by reference to the actions to which asserting it would lead" (1990b: 51). More specifically: "any set of actions for whose utility *p* is a necessary and sufficient condition might be called a belief that *p*" (1990b: 40).[4] So there could not be a belief that could not be used,

3. Note that Ramsey still does not endorse Russell's argument for thinking that universals cannot be conjunctions, namely that the former do, while the latter do not, contain the information that the objects listed are *all* the objects. Ramsey had dismissed this argument in "Facts and Propositions" on the grounds that this information is logically true, and hence does not add anything to the proposition expressed. There is a real question whether Ramsey's argument is valid: it rests on some modal principles which it is doubtful that his opponents would have accepted (for discussion see Hazen 1986: 496–498). But even if it is valid, it raises a number of difficult questions about the identity criteria for propositions, in particular whether propositions should be individuated by necessary equivalence or by a priori equivalence. But we shall not pursue these questions here.

4. The latter quotation comes from a passage in which Ramsey is discussing beliefs that are not expressed in language. However, the same dispositional account applies in essence to beliefs which are expressed in language; it is simply that there the account needs to be complicated in various ways to accommodate the role of the words in the mind of the speaker. Note, for instance, these comments of Ramsey's on the attitude of linguistic belief: "To say that feeling belief towards a sentence expresses such an attitude is to say that it has certain properties which vary with the attitude, i.e. with which possibilities are knocked out and which, so to speak, are left in. Very roughly the thinker will act in disregard of the possibilities rejected, but how to explain this accurately I do not know" (Ramsey 1990b: 46). In saying this, we seem to be in disagreement with John Skorupski (1980), who takes Ramsey to be proposing a picture theory of belief in these sections.

a belief that would never issue in any action. Moreover, and for the same reasons, there could be nothing that would constitute understanding a belief that could not be used.

Ramsey's second argument concerns the grounds on which we can come to believe universal generalizations, and hence the degree of confidence that we can have in them. How could we have grounds for believing an infinite conjunction?

> The relevant degree of certainty is the certainty of the particular case, or of a finite set of particular cases; not of an infinite number which we never use, and of which we couldn't be at all certain. (Ramsey 1990a: 146)

We make two observations about these two arguments. The first is that strictly speaking, they depend on a feature of language which is much more modest and ubiquitous than infinity itself. Both arguments apply equally well in a finite domain, so long as that domain is large enough to extend beyond the cases actually "encountered" by a speaker or group of speakers. At a first pass, the crucial point is simply that the set of true instances of a generalization normally extends well beyond the set of those instances with which any speaker or group of speakers are or will be acquainted. This notion—let us call it the Extension-Transcends-Acquaintance Principle, or E-TRAP, for short—is usefully refined in various ways, as we shall see. Even as it stands, however, it seems enough to support Ramsey's two arguments. True infinity appears to do no significant work.

Second, it is interesting to compare these two arguments with Michael Dummett's "manifestation" and "acquisition" arguments, which Dummett takes to provide the main case for his species of verificationism. Dummett's arguments concern the meaning of terms, rather than the status of universal judgments, but their basic character is very similar to the above arguments of Ramsey. Dummett argues that the meaning of a word cannot go beyond what could be manifested in its use, on pain of indeterminacy, redundancy, and inaccessibility. Differences of meaning beyond the limits of use would be both ineffectual, in the sense that they would make no difference in our linguistic practices, and inaccessible, in the sense that they couldn't be conveyed from speaker to speaker. Given then that novices can acquire a grasp of the meaning of a new term, meaning cannot transcend use.

Famously, Dummett is influenced in these arguments by intuitionistic concerns (see especially Dummett 1978: 216–217).[5] Was Ramsey similarly influenced by intuitionism? Russell, for one, thought that he was, arguing that Ramsey's last papers "show a tendency towards the views of Brouwer" (Russell 1931: 481). However, our suggestion here will be that the primary influence was not intuitionism

5. To say that Dummett is influenced by intuitionists is not to deny that he also departs from them in many ways. See the brief discussion of this in Moore (1990: 141–142).

but formalism. Intuitionism represents one possible answer to the worry that we cannot understand universal quantifiers as classically conceived: the answer that comes from reconstruing their content in a form which we can understand. Formalism provides an alternative answer: don't try to give them a meaning at all, but treat them as meaningless methods of manipulating that which does have a meaning. A useful comparison here is with reductionist and instrumentalist forms of phenomenalism about theoretical terms. Reductionists are comparable to intuitionists, in reconstruing the content of such terms in phenomenal language. Instrumentalists are like formalists, in seeking a non-descriptive function for theoretical discourse. As we shall see, Ramsey's approach had more in common with the latter approach than the former.

We'll come back to these issues in a moment. Before that, we want to say some more about why Ramsey's position is unstable—why nothing should really count as a proposition, by the standards that Ramsey applies to generalizations.

3. Why Nothing Is a Proposition, by These Lights

As we noted, Dummett takes the manifestation and acquisition arguments to apply to the meaning of all terms, rather than simply to that of universal quantifiers (and related logical machinery). Dummett's basic thought is something like this. Take the predicate ". . . is red," for example. If meaning were a matter of truth conditions, the meaning of ". . . is red" would depend on the extension of the class of red things. Essentially, the meaning of ". . . is red" would be given by a list of all the red things—perhaps a list extending to non-actual red things. Even if restricted to actual red things, this list would extend well beyond the class of red things encountered by a speaker or group of speakers. This fact—the E-TRAP, as we called it earlier—ensures that the view that a grasp of the meaning of ". . . is red" is fixed by grasp of such a list is incompatible with the manifestation and acquisition requirements. Therefore, Dummett concludes, meaning cannot be a matter of truth conditions.

Our present interest is not in Dummett's alternative proposal about meaning, but in the observation that the problem stems from a very basic feature of language use. Plausibly, no term at all escapes the E-TRAP—grasping any term involves an open-ended skill, an ability to use it in previously unencountered cases. Proper names might seem to be an exception, but these too surely have an open-ended range of possible applications, as an extension of Goodman's (1983) considerations about "Grue" makes clear. *So for no normal term at all can a grasp of its meaning amount to grasp of a list.* The required list always transcends at least our current acquaintance.

We want to emphasize two points about this conclusion. First, it does seem to amount simply to extending to linguistic terms at large the kind of concerns Ramsey has about universal generalizations. In both cases, the concern is precisely that a set of instances (in one case of conjuncts, in the other of true instances of the application of a term) goes beyond what human language users could use or survey. Second, the issue concerned is that at the heart of the so-called rule-following considerations. Indeed, the rule-following considerations seem to expose the real teeth of the E-TRAP. On the one hand, they confront us with the fact that the application of terms to novel cases is essential to language (and hence that in a very strong sense, grasp of meaning necessarily precedes acquaintance with the totality of relevant cases). On the other, they point out that no finite basis of acquaintance logically determines a unique extrapolation to new cases (and hence that there is no unique way to cantilever ourselves out of the E-TRAP).

Given this connection, it seems reasonable to infer that the rule-following considerations had not occurred to Ramsey, at least when he wrote "General Propositions and Causality" in 1929. It may seem uncharitable to Ramsey to suggest that his position in that paper is highly unstable. But it would be far more uncharitable to suggest that Ramsey was aware of what makes it unstable (namely, the rule-following considerations) and simply failed to draw the obvious conclusion.

In any case, we haven't yet ruled out the possibility that Ramsey has alternative grounds for a distinction between generalizations and other kinds of statements, in terms related to his positive account of what we do with generalizations. Perhaps the real work takes place on the positive side of the account. It is to that side that we now turn.

4. Ramsey's Positive Story, and a Scholarly Digression

How should we understand universal generalisations, if not as propositions? Ramsey says that they are "variable hypotheticals," and that these "are not judgements but rules for judging 'If I meet a ϕ, I shall regard it as a ψ'" (1990a: 149). In other words, in committing ourselves to a universal generalization we adopt a habit of forming beliefs in a certain way. As Ramsey puts it:

> To believe that all men are mortal—what is it? Partly to say so, partly to believe in regard to any x that turns up that if he is a man he is mortal.
>
> The general belief consists in
>
> (a) A general enunciation
>
> (b) A habit of singular belief
>
> These are, of course, connected, the habit resulting from the enunciation according to a psychological law which makes the meaning of "all." (1990a: 148–149)

In contemporary jargon, we may say that Ramsey's view is thus that to accept a generalization is to acquire a double disposition—to become disposed to adopt a belief of one sort, whenever one adopts a belief of another sort, and to enunciate a certain sentence.[6] He goes on to say that, since they are not judgments, universal sentences cannot be negated. They can, however, be disagreed with, in the sense that one can fail to have the disposition concerned.

Where does Ramsey get these views from? Both Majer (1989, 1991) and Sahlin (1997) have pointed to the influence of the Swiss mathematician Hermann Weyl. In his 1920 lectures "Über die neue Grundlagenkrise der Mathematik" (Weyl 1921), with which Ramsey was very familiar,[7] Weyl gives a account of universal quantifiers that is very close to that later given by Ramsey. After characterizing existential statements as "abstracts of judgments" rather than judgments proper, he says:

> Neither is the generalization "Every number has a value E"—for example "For every number m, m + 1 = 1 + m"—a real judgement, but rather an instruction for judgement. (Weyl 1921: 157)

Weyl goes on to say that since they are not judgments, neither existentials nor universals can be negated. This is his rationale for rejecting excluded middle for quantified judgments, since its instances cannot be meaningfully formulated (Weyl 1921: 158).

In this paper Weyl represents himself as a follower of Brouwer; and when describing intuitionism in his later *Philosophie der Mathematik und Naturwissenschaft*, this is the position he gives (Weyl 1927: section 9).[8] So it is tempting to think that in apparently following Weyl, Ramsey was taking a step toward intuitionism. But in giving this account of the quantifiers, Weyl is in fact far from the intuitionist mainstream. Brouwer and his followers didn't deny that quantified statements, as intuitionistically construed, expressed propositions; nor did they deny that they could be negated. Of course they rejected the classical construal of the quantifiers; but this they thought should be abandoned. The intuitionists thus had no place for Weyl's halfway house of quantified sentences that had a useful role but did not express propositions.[9] In contrast, the

6. Why does Ramsey add the requirement that one must be prepared to make the general enunciation? Presumably he is worried that one may in fact treat every man one meets as mortal without believing that every man is mortal; perhaps because one thinks that an immortal one may turn up. Ramsey's solution to this worry is not very satisfactory: after all, the assertion must be sincere, which brings us back to the requirement that it must be believed. But the fact that he is worried suggests that he was sensitive to some of the problems with purely dispositional accounts that would surface later in Kripke's discussion of rule-following. (We are grateful here to the comments of a referee for *Noûs*.)

7. Apparently Ramsey copied out the relevant passages of Weyl's lectures, in a manuscript that is now in the Ramsey collection in Pittsburgh (see Sahlin 1997: 73). Ramsey discusses Weyl's position in some length (1990c: 228–233).

8. Ramsey had read this work, as the Pittsburgh notes make clear.

9. In addition, Weyl's reasons for rejecting excluded middle were quite different from Brouwer's. Weyl seems to have accepted it for the propositional calculus. His reason for rejecting it for the predicate calculus, as we have seen, was that quantified sentences, not being meaningful, cannot be

kind of approach favored by Weyl in 1920, and later by Ramsey, is very much in line with formalist thinking. Quantified sentences are thought of as devices, strictly meaningless in themselves, that allow for the manipulation of meaningful sentences.[10] (Again, compare reductionism and instrumentalism about theoretical terms.)

Ramsey (e.g., at 1990c: 233) was well aware that Weyl's view of quantifiers differed from Brouwer's and was in fact much closer to Hilbert's. He was well aware, too, that Weyl's commitment to intuitionism was short-lived, and that by 1928 Weyl was describing himself as a follower of Hilbert (see Weyl 1928).[11] Moreover, in some notes made in August 1929 under the heading "The Infinite in Theories," Ramsey writes:

> Taken formally an infinite theory asserts whatever may follow from it; this has, however, no clear meaning unless we know how to decide whether a given primary proposition does or does not follow . . .
>
> . . . if the principle is unbounded, the theory must have the status of a general prop, which is perhaps not a judgement but a fount of judgements, or rule for judging.
>
> The essential thing about the theory is that it is a way of saying something in the primary system, and it must be simple and agreeable. These can both be secured by representing the primary system as part of a wider structure, but this is not essential and if the wider structure is infinite it is not really conceivable but only a way of talking? . . .
>
> It is obvious that mathematics does not require the existence of an infinite number of things. We say at once that imaginary things will do,

---

meaningfully negated; and hence that no instance of excluded middle is meaningful. Now it is not even clear that this should be regarded as a rejection of excluded middle, which is surely only meant to apply to meaningful sentences. We do not count as rejecting it if we merely refuse to accept "Either og ur blig or not og ur blig" on the grounds that "Og ur blig" is meaningless.

10. See the useful discussion of Hilbert's position in Dummett (1993). Here Dummett attributes to Hilbert the view that universally quantified sentences do not express propositions since, making implicit reference as they do to the "cognitive position" of the speaker, they cannot be embedded under the extensional sentential operators as these are classically conceived. In contrast, the intuitionists sought to generalize this view of universal quantifiers to embrace the operators too. There is an interesting parallel between this generalization and that which we are suggesting is forced upon Ramsey.

11. Ramsey's notes (1991: 235) show that he had read this lecture. Ramsey there complains that "Weyl always seems to confuse method with interpretation e.g. he says in last paper in Hamburg that if Hilbert triumphs this will be a decisive blow to phenomenalism. But only to the phenomenalist method which no one now believes in; Hilbert is altogether on the side of a phenomenalist interpretation." We take it that in Ramsey's eyes Hilbert maintained the phenomenalist view that the only thing that is meaningful is the phenomenally given (this is what it is to accept the phenomenalist *interpretation*), while denying that in manipulating it one must restrict oneself to the phenomenally given (that is what it is to reject the phenomenalist *method*).

> i.e. theoretical secondary terms. But there are no imaginary things, they are just words, and mathematicians and physicists who use the infinite are just manipulating symbols with some analogy to propositions. (Ramsey 1991: 235–236).

Clearly, these passages are of a very formalist tenor, and in them Ramsey gives the same account of universal judgments that he gives in "General Propositions and Causality." We take this as good evidence that Ramsey was motivated primarily by formalist rather than intuitionist concerns.

That said, the point should not be exaggerated. Despite the controversy between Brouwer and Hilbert, the distinction between formalism and intuitionism was not altogether clear in 1929; indeed, the formal differences only really became clear in the light of subsequent work by Heyting (1930a, 1930b), Gödel (1933), and Gentzen (1933). There are, moreover, a few passages in which Ramsey sounds a distinctly intuitionist note: in "General Propositions and Causality," for example, he says that the use of excluded middle in mathematical proofs "is now recognised as fallacious" (Ramsey 1990a: 147). What we should rather say is that, given our contemporary understanding of the difference between formalism and intuitionism, Ramsey's position was primarily formalist.

5. Why the Positive Story Doesn't Stabilize Ramsey's View

We have seen that Ramsey takes universal beliefs to be dispositions to form other beliefs. But according to Ramsey, *all* beliefs are dispositions. Where, then, is his basis for a distinction between those dispositions which are genuine judgments, and those which are not? He tells us that "a belief of the primary sort is a map of neighbouring space by which we steer," but surely the use of maps is itself dispositional. To adopt a map as a guide is simply to become disposed to respond in certain ways to certain stimuli: "If that's the Post Office, I'll turn left." (More precisely, we can think of a map as providing a kind of complex disposition. In combination with other maps and our desires, it generates a set of dispositions. And they needn't be dispositions to action: "If that's the Post Office, then the yellow building is the Town Hall.")

So what is the distinction between universal beliefs and beliefs of the primary sort? It is hard to see that there is any radical difference in functional terms, by Ramsey's own lights. It might perhaps be suggested that there is a distinction of level: Beliefs of the primary sort are dispositions to act on desires, while universal beliefs are dispositions to act on other beliefs (to act by forming further beliefs). But why should this distinction make all the difference as to what should be counted as a belief? Moreover, even this distinction will not really stand up.

Beliefs of the primary sort can themselves be dispositions to form new beliefs on the basis of other beliefs: the belief that Martha is dangerous will itself amount to a disposition to form the belief that a dangerous person is approaching, given the belief that this is Martha approaching.

Indeed, dispositionality applies at an even more basic level, that of concepts. Our grasp of a concept surely manifests itself as a disposition—the disposition to apply the term in certain circumstances. Indeed, the complex disposition corresponding to holding a belief ("using a map," in Ramsey's account) depends on simpler dispositions of this kind. Grasp of concepts is like grasp of the map's key. To use a map we need to know what its symbols signify—we need to have adopted a practice that takes us from things in the world to symbols on the map and back again. And these are dispositions. So it seems that here, too, there is no boundary between universal judgments and others.

Earlier we noted that the grasp of an ordinary concept involves the same kind of exposure to unencountered cases that Ramsey takes to show that generalizations are not propositions. We can now see that the grasp of ordinary concepts also has the dispositionality that Ramsey appeals to in telling us what generalizations *are*. On both the negative and positive sides then, Ramsey's distinction between universal generalizations and other propositions seems impossible to sustain.

At times, Ramsey himself seems perfectly happy to acknowledge that habit or disposition goes all the way down, in this sense. "[A]ll belief involves habit," he says at one point (1990a: 150).[12] So does he himself think that there is the material here for a distinction between genuine judgments and others? Or is it rather that he thinks the distinction is drawn somewhere else, and that the story about the psychological role of universal judgments just meets an obligation incurred elsewhere (namely, to explain how such things function, given that they are not genuine judgments, and hence can't be dealt with under the wing of a more general account)?

The most charitable story seems to be the latter. Not having noticed what became the rule-following considerations, Ramsey thought that the problems he characterized in terms of infinity were confined to unrestricted generalizations. Against that background, he took it that he had a basis for a deep distinction between such generalizations and other judgments—a basis invulnerable to the observation that in some ways generalizations are like real judgments, given that the latter, too, are dispositional. Thinking that there was a clear distinction on the negative side, he had no reason (or at least no immediate reason) to insist that there be one on the positive side.

12. See also pp. 159–160, where Ramsey says that "variable hypotheticals involve causality no more and no less then ordinary beliefs; for it belongs to the essence of any belief that we deduce from it, and act on it in a certain way, and this notion involves causality just as much as does the variable hypothetical."

However, it is interesting to note Ramsey's own earlier sensitivity to the question as to whether there is a genuine distinction. This is from "Mathematical Logic," in 1926:

> It is possible that the whole assertion that general and existential propositions cannot express genuine judgements or knowledge is purely verbal; that it is merely being decided to emphasise the difference between individual and general propositions by refusing to use the words judgement or knowledge in connection with the latter. This, however, would be a pity, for all our natural associations to the words judgement and knowledge fit general and existential propositions as well as they do individual ones; for in either case we can feel greater or lesser degrees of conviction about the matter; and in either case we can be in some sense right or wrong. And the suggestion which is implied, that general and existential knowledge exists simply for the sake of individual knowledge, seems to me entirely false. In theorising what we principally admire is generality, and in ordinary life it may be quite sufficient to know the existential proposition that there is a bull somewhere in a certain field, and there may be no further advantage in knowing that it is this bull and here in the field, instead of a bull somewhere. (Ramsey 1990c: 235–236)

Ramsey here rejects the idea that what is at stake is merely a verbal matter, and appeals to the way in which we use generalizations (treat them as true, etc.) both against the idea that it is a matter of choice and in favor of the view that they are genuine propositions. Three years later he has changed his mind on the status of generalizations, and (as we shall see below) has interesting things to say about how to explain what he earlier took to be evidence to the contrary. He has not changed his mind about whether there is a substantial issue at stake, but this passage makes it clear that this was not because he had never contemplated the possibility that there might not be such an issue.

It is hard to believe that Ramsey himself would not have soon been struck by the lack of any substantial distinction in functional terms. The appropriate conclusion seems to be that formalism (understood as the doctrine that the infinite part of the theory is strictly meaningless, but nonetheless useful) gets no grip, once we move to a functionalist account of belief. And isn't this what we should expect? Analogously, what scope is there for the view that theories are mere instruments, if all judgment is to be understood in utilitarian terms—if belief in general is nothing more than a tool for getting us around a hostile environment?

In effect, this amounts to the point that the inability to draw a distinction on the positive side applies as much to formalism in mathematics as it does to formalism in other spheres. Even more interestingly, the same seems to apply on the negative side. In other words, if the rule-following considerations show that Ramsey's concerns about the infinitary character of quantified sentences extend to all of language, then they seem to suggest equally that the considerations in favor of finitism cannot be met merely by a finitistic account of universal quantification, but will need to apply to all of arithmetic.[13] And after all, shouldn't Kripke's (1982) Wittgenstein, who takes addition as his central example, already have taught us this much?

6. Contemporary Comparisons

Given the importance that Ramsey had earlier attached to the fact that we treat general judgments as if they were propositional (e.g., in taking them to be right and wrong), it is not surprising that when he does change his mind, he devotes some effort to *explaining* such features of ordinary usage. He now says:

> Many sentences express cognitive attitudes without being propositions; and the difference between saying yes and no to them is not the difference between saying yes or no to a proposition. . . . In order therefore to understand the variable hypothetical and its rightness or wrongness we must consider the different possible attitudes to it; if we know what these are and involve we can proceed easily to explain the meaning of saying that such an attitude is right or wrong, for this is simply having such an attitude oneself and thinking that one's neighbour has the same or a different one. (Ramsey 1990a: 146)

We might compare Ramsey to a quasi-realist, in Blackburn's (1993a) sense. He wants to be non-cognitivist about generalizations, but recognizes the importance of explaining why, for at least some purposes, such claims do avail themselves of the machinery available to genuine judgments—why they are described as true and false, for example.

What would an older Ramsey have made of the realization that the considerations which led him to deny that generalizations were genuine propositions are actually global in character—that his position in "General Propositions and Causality" is unstable in the way we have urged? One possibility is that he would have retreated to his former position. However, a more interesting and we think more plausible possibility is that his developing pragmatism would have led him forward—led him to acknowledge that there are no genuine propositions, *in the sense that he had earlier taken for granted*. Had he taken this path, he would certainly have asked globally the kind of questions he does ask with respect to generalizations: Why do we treat the judgments concerned as propositional in character? Why do we take them to be true and false, for example? What does agreement and disagreement amount to?

13. Thanks to Michael Potter for discussion here.

In one sense, this might be characterized as global quasi-realism—the position of someone who begins with quasi-realism, and then concludes that there is no significant declarative use of language which should not be understood in a quasi-realist way. In another sense, the term "quasi-realism" is now misleading. It suggests that the view allows that there is still a "non-quasi" species of realist or cognitive speech act, which, even though absent in practice, *might* have been found in language. Presumably, however, the globalizer will want to say that what was previously characterized as *quasi*-realism is the only kind of realism available. The distinction between realism and quasi-realism makes good sense if both sides make sense; but if the contention is that one doesn't, we start to lose our grip on the distinction.

A converse note of caution would be needed if we characterized the position simply as a more relaxed and inclusive realism, or cognitivism. This characterization is acceptable, provided we note the reconstruction that has taken place behind it. By assumption, it does not amount to Ramsey's earlier view, that generalizations are propositions *in the sense of the term he then took for granted*. Rather, it results from the recognition that that notion of proposition needs to be abandoned.[14]

We close with two remarks about the relevance of this imagined older Ramsey—"Ramsey*," let's call him—to recent debates. First, the questions posed by Ramsey* seem to be just those questions that need to be addressed to defend a dispositionalist approach to rule-following. As Kripke (1982) makes clear, there is a puzzle as to how dispositions can give rise to norms. Ramsey*'s approach would presumably have been to explain the phenomenology—to explain what normative notions such as truth and falsity are doing in conjunction with a practice founded on such dispositions. After all, this is just what Ramsey himself does for the case of generalizations. As the passage just quoted indicates, his approach is distinctly deflationary. The notions of rightness and wrongness simply express agreement or disagreement with "one's neighbour," as Ramsey puts it—in other words, with another speaker.[15]

It is far from clear that such an account is adequate. After all, how could it explain the difference between attitudes with respect to which we do apply the notions right and wrong and those with respect to which we don't. (There are many attitudes with respect to which I may differ from my neighbor, without

14. The reconstruction amounts to something like this. In the old version, there is a class of speech acts (or, more basically, mental states) which have their representational character essentially—they *are* "propositions," or "thoughts." In the new version, however, the essential characteristics are all merely functional—speech acts and associated attitudes are described in terms of what we do with them. Hence there is *always* room for the question Ramsey asks about generalizations: Why does something with that functional role get treated as representational (or "truth-apt")?

15. The account thus seems to anticipate the performative account of truth, propounded in an early article by P. F. Strawson (1949).

regarding him as wrong.) However, what interests us for the present is not the adequacy of Ramsey's account, but the philosophical stance it embodies. Clearly, Ramsey thinks the task of philosophy in this case is simply to explain the use of the notions concerned—he thinks that that's what explaining their meaning amounts to, in this case.

Second, it seems unlikely that Ramsey* would have had much time for Kripkenstein's own "skeptical solution," read as a local non-cognitivism about content.[16] Having been led to his own global view by the recognition that the problems first identified in generalizations infect every bit of language via meaning, it is hardly likely that Ramsey* would find it plausible that they could then be quarantined again, by Kripkenstein's local non-cognitivism about meaning ascriptions. More likely, surely, he would have recognized that there is no sterile field to be had, and that the mistake is to hang on to a view of language which makes the features first identified in the case of generalizations seem deviant or abnormal. More likely, then, Ramsey* would have come to endorse with increasing confidence this modest suggestion first made by Ramsey himself: "I think perhaps it is true that the theory of general and existential judgments is the clue to everything" (Ramsey 1990d: 138).[17]

16. This reading is controversial; see Boghossian (1989: 518–519).

17. We are grateful to audiences in Sydney, Canberra, Edinburgh, and Cambridge, and to Allen Hazen, Lloyd Humberstone, and a referee for *Noûs*, for helpful comments on this material.

8

Truth as Convenient Friction

1. Introduction

In a recent paper, Richard Rorty begins by telling us why pragmatists such as himself are inclined to identify truth with justification:

> Pragmatists think that if something makes no difference to practice, it should make no difference to philosophy. This conviction makes them suspicious of the distinction between justification and truth, for that distinction makes no difference to my decisions about what to do. (Rorty 1998: 19)

Rorty goes on to discuss the claim, defended by Crispin Wright, that truth is a normative constraint on assertion. He argues that this claim runs foul of this principle of no difference without a practical difference:

> The need to justify our beliefs to ourselves and our fellow agents subjects us to norms, and obedience to these norms produces a behavioral pattern that we must detect in others before confidently attributing beliefs to them. But there seems to be no occasion to look for obedience to an *additional* norm—the commandment to seek the truth. For—to return to the pragmatist doubt with which I began—obedience to that commandment will produce no behavior not produced by the need to offer justification. (Rorty 1998: 26)

Again, then, Rorty appeals to the claim that a commitment to a norm of truth rather than a norm of justification makes no behavioral difference.

This is an empirical claim, testable in principle by comparing the behavior of a community of realists (in Rorty's sense) to that of a community of pragmatists.

In my view, the experiment would show that the claim is unjustified, indeed false. I think that there is an important and widespread behavioral pattern that depends on the fact that speakers do take themselves to be subject to such an additional norm. Moreover, it is a behavioral pattern so central to what we presently regard as a worthwhile human life that no reasonable person would knowingly condone the experiment. Ironically, it is also a pattern that Rorty of all people cannot afford to dismiss as a pathological and dispensable by-product of bad philosophy. For it is conversation itself, or at any rate a central and indispensable part of conversation as we know it—roughly, interpersonal dialogue about "factual" matters.[1]

In other words, I want to maintain that in order to account for a core part of ordinary conversational practice, we must allow that speakers take themselves and their fellows to be governed by a norm stronger than that of justification. Not only is this a norm which speakers acknowledge they may fail to meet, even if their claims are well-justified—this much is true of what Rorty calls the cautionary use of truth (1991: 128)—but also, more significantly, it is a norm which speakers immediately assume to be breached by someone with whom they disagree, *independently of any diagnosis of the source of the disagreement*. Indeed, this is the very essence of the norm of truth, in my view. It gives disagreement its immediate normative character, a character on which dialogue depends, and a character which no lesser norm could provide.

This fact about truth has been overlooked, I think, because the norm in question is *so* familiar, so much a given of ordinary linguistic practice, that it is very hard to see. Ordinarily we look through it, rather than at it. In order to make it visible, we need a sense of how things would be different without it—hence, in part, my reason for beginning with Rorty. Though I disagree with Rorty about the behavioral consequences of a commitment to "a distinction between justification and truth," I think that the issue of the behavioral consequences of such a commitment embodies precisely the perspective we need, in order to bring into focus this fundamental aspect of the normative structure of dialogue.

In sharing Rorty's concern with the role of truth in linguistic practice, I share one key element of his pragmatism. But my kind of pragmatism about truth is not well marked on contemporary maps, and hence my second reason for

1. Irony aside, nothing here turns on whether by "conversation" I mean the same as Rorty. For me, what matters is the role of truth in the kind of interpersonal linguistic interaction I'll call factual or assertoric dialogue, or simply dialogue. I don't claim that dialogue exhausts conversation, in Rorty's sense or any other. I used scare quotes on "factual" above in anticipation of the suggestion that the notion of factuality in play might depend on that of truth, in a way that would create problems for my own account of the role of truth in dialogue. There is no such difficulty, in my view. On the contrary, I take the perceived "factuality" or "truth-aptness" of the utterances in question to be part of the explanandum of the kind of account here proposed; cf. n17.

beginning with Rorty. Rorty has explored the landscape of pragmatist approaches to truth more extensively than most pragmatist writers, past or present, and at different times has been inclined to settle in different parts of it. By locating my own kind of pragmatism with respect to views that Rorty has visited or canvassed, I hope to show that there is a promising position that he and others pragmatists have overlooked.

As noted, my view rests on the claim that a norm of truth plays an essential and little-recognized role in assertoric dialogue. In pursuit of this conclusion, it will turn out to be helpful to distinguish three norms, in order of increasing strength: roughly, sincerity, justification, and truth itself. Though somewhat crudely drawn, these distinctions will suffice to throw into relief the crucial role of the third norm in linguistic practice. My strategy will be to contrast assertion as we know it with some non-assertoric uses of language. In these latter cases, I'll argue, the two weaker norms still apply. Moreover, it turns out that some of the basic functions of assertoric discourse could be fulfilled in an analogous way, by a practice that lacked the third norm. But it will be clear, I hope, that this practice would not support dialogue as we know it. What is missing—what the third norm provides—is the automatic and quite unconscious sense of engagement in common purpose that distinguishes assertoric dialogue from a mere roll call of individual opinion. Truth is the grit that makes our individual opinions engage with one another. Truth puts the cogs in cognition, at least in its public manifestations.[2]

To use a Rylean metaphor, my view is thus that truth supplies factual dialogue with its essential esprit de corps. As the metaphor is meant to suggest, what matters is that speakers think that there is such a norm—that they take themselves to be governed by it—not that their view be somehow confirmed by science or metaphysics. Science has already done its work, in pointing out the function of the thought in the lives of creatures like us. This may suggest that a commitment to truth is like a commitment to theism, an analogy which Rorty himself draws, against Wright, in the paper with which I began. In effect, Rorty's point is that it is one thing to establish that we do employ a realist notion of truth, a normative notion stronger than justification; quite another to establish that we ought to do so. As in the case of theism, we might do better to wean ourselves of bad realist habits.

However, there are several important differences between the two cases. First, the behavioral consequences of giving up theism are significant but hardly devastating.[3] But if I am right about the behavioral role of truth, the consequences of

2. If private cognition depends on the norms of public dialogue, then truth plays the same role, at second hand, in the private sphere. This is a plausible extension of the present claim, in my view, but I won't try to defend it here.

3. At least compared to the alternative.

giving up truth would be very serious indeed, reducing the conversation of mankind to a chatter of disengaged monologues.[4]

Second, it is doubtful whether giving up truth is really an option open to us. I suspect that people who think it is an option haven't realized how deeply embedded the idea of truth is in linguistic practice, and therefore underestimate the extent of the required change, in two ways. They fail to see how radically different from current practice a linguistic practice without truth would have to be, and they overestimate our capacity to change our practices in general to move from here to there (underestimating the practical inflexibility of admittedly contingent practices).[5]

Third, and most interestingly of all, the issue of the status of truth is enmeshed with the terms of the problem, in a way that is quite uncharacteristic of the theism case. Metaphysical conclusions tend to be cast in semantic vocabulary. Theism is said to be in error in virtue of the fact that its claims are not *true*, that its terms fail to *refer*. For this reason, it is uniquely difficult to formulate a meaningful anti-realism about the semantic terms themselves. In my view, the right response to this is not to think (with Paul Boghossian [see Boghossian 1990]) that we thereby have a transcendental argument for semantic realism. Without an intelligible denial, realism is no more intelligible than anti-realism. The right response—as Rorty himself in any case urges—is to be suspicious of the realist–anti-realist debate itself.[6] However, Rorty ties rejection of the realist–anti-realist debate to rejection of a notion of truth distinct from justification, and of the idea of representation. I think this is the wrong path to the right conclusion. We should reject the metaphysical stance not by rejecting truth and representation, but by recognizing that in virtue of the most plausible story about the function and origins of these notions, they simply don't sustain that sort of metaphysical weight.

Concerning his own view of truth, Rorty describes himself as oscillating between Jamesian pragmatism, on the one hand, and deflationism, on the other: "swing[ing] back and forth between trying to reduce truth to justification and propounding some sort of minimalism about truth" (1998: 21). My own view is neither of these alternatives, but has something in common with each. On the one hand, it is certainly some sort of minimalism about truth, but not the familiar sort that Rorty has in mind—not "Tarski's breezy disquotationalism," as he calls it (1998: 21). I agree with familiar disquotationalist minimalists such as Quine (1970)

4. "Global *Waiting for Godot*," as a member of an audience in Dundee suggested I put it. Even more seriously, as noted above, giving up truth might silence our own "internal" rational dialogues.

5. Jonathan Rée makes a point of this kind against Rorty: "[C]ontingencies can last a very long time. Our preoccupations with love and death may not be absolute necessities, but they are not a passing fad either, and it is a safe bet that they will last as long as we do" (Rée 1998: 11).

6. A realist could object that a commitment to the third norm might be useful and yet in error, but Rorty can't. It is fair for him to object against Wright that this commitment might be like theism, because Wright takes metaphysics seriously. By Wright's professed standards, then, the theism objection poses a real threat.

and Paul Horwich (1990) that truth is not a substantial property, about the nature of which there is an interesting philosophical issue. Like them, I think that the right approach to truth is to investigate its function in human discourse—to ask what difference it makes to us to have such a concept. Unlike such minimalists, however, I don't think the right answer to this question is that truth is merely a grammatical device for disquotation. I think that it has a far more important function, which requires that it be the expression of a norm. But like other minimalists, again, I think that there is no further question of interest to philosophy, once the question about function has been answered.

On the other hand, my view of truth is also pragmatist, for it explicates truth in terms of its role in practice. (This is also true of standard disquotational views, of course, although they ascribe the truth predicate a different role in practice.) In another sense, it conflicts with pragmatism, for it opposes the proposal that we identify truth with justification. This contrast reflects a deep tension within pragmatism. From Peirce and James on, pragmatists have often been unable to resist the urge to join their opponents in asking "What is truth?" (Indeed, the pragmatist position as a whole is often characterized in terms of its answer to this question.) Pragmatism thus turns its back on alternative paths to philosophical illumination about truth, even though these alternative paths—explanatory and genealogical approaches—are at least compatible with, if not mandated by, the pragmatist doctrine that we understand problematic notions in terms of their practical significance.

Rorty himself is well aware of this tension within pragmatism. In "Pragmatism, Davidson and Truth," for example, he notes that James is less prone than Peirce to try to answer the "ontological" or reductive question about truth, and suggests that Davidson may be thought of as a pragmatist in the preferable non-reductive sense (Rorty 1991).[7] As he swings between pragmatism and deflationism, then, Rorty himself is at worst only intermittently subject to this craving for an *analysis* of truth. All the same, it seems to me that he is never properly aware of the range of possibilities for non-reductive pragmatism about truth. In particular, he is not properly aware of the possibility that such a pragmatism might find itself explaining the fact that the notion of truth in ordinary use is (and perhaps ought to be, in whatever sense we might make of this) one that conflicts with the identification of truth with justification: a normative goal of inquiry, stronger than any norm of justification, of the very kind that realists about truth—opponents both of pragmatism and of minimalism—mistakenly sought to analyze. In other words, Rorty seems to miss the possibility that the right thing for the explanatory pragmatist to say might be that truth is a goal of inquiry distinct from norms of justification, and that the realist's mistake is to try to *analyze* this normative notion, rather than simply to investigate its function and genealogy. It is this latter possibility that I want to defend.

7. Robert Brandom makes a similar point (1988).

2. Falsity and Lesser Evils

As I have said, I want to argue that truth plays a crucial role as a norm of assertoric discourse. It is not the only such norm, however, and a good way to highlight the distinctive role of truth is to distinguish certain weaker norms, and to imagine a linguistic practice which had those norms but not truth.[8] By seeing what such a practice lacks, we see what truth adds.

There are at least two weaker norms of assertion, in addition to any distinctive norm of truth.[9] The weakest relevant norm seems to be that embodied in the principle that it is prima facie appropriate to assert that P only when one believes that P—prima facie, because of course many other factors may come into play, in determining the appropriateness of a particular assertion in a particular context. Let's call this the norm of *subjective assertibility*.[10] The norm is perhaps best characterized in negative form—that is, in terms of the conditions under which a speaker may be censured for failing to meet it:

> *Subjective assertibility*: A speaker is incorrect to assert that P if she does not believe that P; to assert that P in these circumstances provides prima facie grounds for censure, or disapprobation.

The easiest way to see that this norm has very little to do with truth is to note that it is analogous to norms which operate with respect to utterances that we don't take to be truth-apt. Prima facie, it is inappropriate to request a cup of coffee when one doesn't want a cup of coffee, but this doesn't show that requests or expressions of desires are subject to a norm of truth. In effect, this norm is simply that of sincerity, and some such norm seems to govern much conventional behavior. Conventions often depend on the fact that communities censure those who break them in this specific sense, by acting in bad faith.

The second norm is that of (personal) *warranted assertibility*. Roughly, "P" is warrantedly assertible by a speaker who not only believes that P, but is *justified* in doing so. The qualification "personal" recognizes the fact that there are different kinds and degrees of warrant or justification, some of them more subjective than others. For example, is justification to be assessed with reference to a speaker's actual evidence as she (presently?) sees it, or by some less subjective lights? For

8. For present purposes I can remain open-minded on the question as to whether such a practice is really possible. Perhaps a truth-like norm is essential to any practice that deserves to be called linguistic. At any rate, my use of the following linguistic thought experiment does not depend on denying this possibility.

9. In what sense "weaker"? In the sense, at least, that they apply to a wider range of linguistic behaviors. "Less specialized" might be a better term.

10. This corresponds to a common use of the term "assertibility condition," as for example when it is said that the subjective assertibility condition for the indicative conditional "If P then Q" is a high conditional credence in Q given P.

the moment, for a degree of definiteness, let us think of it in terms of subjective coherence—a belief is justified if supported by a speaker's other current beliefs. This is what I shall mean by *personal* warranted assertibility.

Again, this second norm is usefully characterized in negative or censure form:

> *Personal warranted assertibility:* A speaker is incorrect to assert that P if she does not have adequate (personal) grounds for believing that P; to assert that P in these circumstances provides prima facie grounds for censure.

A person who meets both the norms just identified may be said to have done as much as possible, *by her own current lights*, to ensure that her assertion that P is in order. Obviously, realists will say that her assertion may nevertheless be incorrect. Subjective assertibility and (personal) warranted assertibility do not guarantee truth. To an extent, moreover, most pragmatists are likely to agree. Few people who advocate reducing truth to (or replacing truth by) a notion of warranted assertibility have personal warranted assertibility in mind. Rather, they imagine some more objective, community-based variant, according to which a belief is justified if it coheres appropriately with the other beliefs of one's community. If we call this *communal* warranted assertibility, then the point is that we can make sense of a gap between the personal and communal notions. A belief may be justified in one sense but not the other.

Pragmatists and realists may thus agree that there is a normative dimension distinct from subjective assertibility and personal warranted assertibility—an assertion may be *wrong*, despite meeting these norms. This does not yet establish that the normative standard in question need be marked in ordinary discourse. In principle, it might be a privileged or theoretical notion, useful in expert second-order reflection on linguistic practice but unnecessary in folk talk about other matters. In practice, however, there seems a very good reason why it should not remain restricted in this way. Unless individual speakers recognize such a norm, the idea that they might *improve* their views by consultation with the wider community is simply incoherent to them. (It would be as if we gave a student full marks in an exam, and then told him that he would have done better if his answers had agreed with those of other students.)

It may seem that as yet, this argument doesn't favor realism over pragmatism. If the normative standard an individual speaker needs to acknowledge is that of the community as a whole, there is as yet no pressure to a notion of truth beyond community-wide warranted assertibility. But what constitutes the relevant community? At any given stage, isn't the relation of a given community to its possible present and future extensions just like that of the individual to her community? If so, then the same argument applies at this level. At each stage, the actual community needs to recognize that it may be wrong by the standards of some broader community.[11]

11. Compare Rorty's remark that "[f]or any audience, one can imagine a better-informed audience" (1998: 22).

The pragmatist might now seem obliged to follow Peirce, in identifying truth with warranted assertibility in the ideal limit of inquiry. The useful thing about this limit, in this context, is that it transcends any actual community. But in my view, as I'll explain below (and as Rorty in some moods already agrees), a better move for a pragmatist is to resist the pressure to *identify* truth with anything—in other words, simply to reject the assumption that an adequate philosophical account of truth needs to answer the question "What is truth?" Better questions for a pragmatist to ask are the explanatory ones: Why do we have such a notion? What job does it do in language? What features does it need to have to play this role? And how would things be different if we didn't have it?

For the moment, we have the beginnings of an answer to the last question. If we didn't have a normative notion in addition to the norms of subjective assertibility and personal warranted assertibility, the idea that we might improve our commitments by seeking to align them with those of our community would be simply incoherent. I'll call this the passive account of the role of the third norm—passive, because it doesn't yet provide an active or causal role for a commitment to truth. Later, I'll argue that the third norm not only creates the conceptual space for argument, in this passive sense, but actively encourages speakers to participate.[12]

3. The Third Norm in Focus

The best way to bring the third norm into focus is again to consider its negative or censure form:

> *Truth:* If Not-P, then it is *incorrect* to assert that P; if Not-P, there are prima facie grounds for censure of an assertion that P.

The important point is that this provides a norm of assertion which we take it that a speaker may fail to meet, even if she does meet the norms of subjective assertibility and (personal) warranted assertibility. We are prepared to make the judgment that a speaker is *incorrect*, or *mistaken*, in this sense, simply on the basis that we are prepared to make a contrary assertion; in advance, in other words, of any judgment that she fails to meet one or other of the two weaker norms.[13]

12. This account has prescriptive and non-prescriptive readings. The former uses the notion of improvement full-voice, saying that if speakers are to improve their commitments, they need the idea of the third norm. But as N. J. J. Smith pointed out to me, it could well be objected that the relevant notion of improvement simply presupposes the third norm, and therefore can't provide any independent rationale for adopting it. However, no such circularity undermines the non-prescriptive reading, whose point is that because our existing conversational practice does take for granted such a notion of improvement, it thereby reveals its commitment to a third norm.

13. Note the contrast with Rorty's cautionary use of true. In that use we say of a claim that we take to be well-justified that it might not be true. In the present use we say of a claim that we might even allow to be well-justified by its speaker's own lights that it is not true. It is the difference between mere caution and actual censure.

One of the reasons that this third norm is hard to distinguish from the two weaker norms of assertibility is that when we apply it in judging a fellow speaker right or wrong, the basis for our judgment lies in our own beliefs and evidence. It is not as though we are in a position to make the judgment from the stance of reality itself, as it were. I think this can make it seem as if application of this norm involves nothing more than reassertion of the original claim (in the case in which we judge it correct), or assertion of the negation of the original claim (in the case in which we judge it incorrect). Construed in these terms, our response contains nothing problematic for orthodox disquotational versions of the deflationary view, of course. Reassertion of this sort is precisely one of the linguistic activities that disquotational truth facilitates. Construed in these terms, then, there is no need for truth to be a distinct *norm*.

However, our response is not merely reassertion, or assertion of the negation of the original claim. If it were, it would involve no commendation or criticism of the original utterance. This non-normative alternative is hard to see, I think, because the norm in question is so familiar and so basic. As a result, it is difficult to see the immense difference the norm makes to the character of disagreements. But it comes into focus, I think, if we allow ourselves to imagine a linguistic practice which allowed reassertion and contrary assertion, but without this third normative dimension. What we need to imagine, in other words, is a linguistic community who use sentences to express their beliefs, and have a purely disquotational truth predicate, but for whom disagreements have no normative significance, except insofar as it is related to the weaker norms of assertibility.

This imaginative project is not straightforward, of course. Indeed, it isn't clear that it is entirely coherent. If there is a third norm of the kind in question, isn't it likely to be constitutive of the very notions of assertion and belief? If so, what sense is there in trying to imagine an assertoric practice that lacked this norm?

Well, let's see. What we need is the idea of a community who take an assertion—or rather the closest thing they have to what we call an assertion—to be *merely* an expression of the speaker's opinion. The relevant idea is familiar in the case of expressions of desires and preferences. It is easy to imagine a community—we are at least close to it ourselves—who have a language in which they give voice to psychological states of these kinds, not by *reporting* that they hold them (which would depend on assertion), but directly, in conventional linguistic forms tailored specifically for this purpose.

Think of a community who use language primarily for expressing preferences in restaurants, for example. (Perhaps the development of such a restricted language from scratch is incoherent, but surely we might approach it from the other direction. Imagine a community of dedicated lunchers, whose language atrophies to the bare essentials.) In this community we would expect a norm analogous to subjective assertibility: essentially, a normative requirement that speakers use these conventional expressions sincerely. Less obviously, such a practice might also involve a norm analogous to personal warranted assertibility.

In other words, expressed preferences might be censured on the grounds that they were not well-founded, by the speaker's own lights (for example, on the grounds that they did not cohere with the speaker's other preferences and desires). However, in this practice there need be no place for a norm analogous to truth—no idea of an objective standard, over and above personal warranted assertibility, which preferences properly aim to meet.

At least to a first approximation, we can imagine a community who treat expressions of beliefs in the same way. They express their beliefs—that is, let us say, the kind of behavioral dispositions that we would characterize as beliefs—by means of a speech act we might call the *merely-opinionated assertion* (*MOA*, for short). These speakers—"Mo'ans," as I called them in another piece (see Price 1998)[14]—criticize each other for insincerity and for lack of coherence, or personal warranted assertibility. But they go no further than this. In particular, they do not treat a disagreement between two speakers as an indication that, necessarily, one speaker or other is mistaken—in violation of some norm. On the contrary, they allow that in such a case it may turn out that both speakers have spoken correctly, by the only two standards the community takes to be operable. Both may be sincere, and both, in their own terms, may have good grounds for their assertion.[15]

A speech community of this imagined kind could make use of a disquotational truth predicate, as a device to facilitate agreement with an expression of opinion made by another speaker. "That's true" would function much like "Same again," or "Ditto," used in a bar or restaurant. Just as "Same again" serves to indicate that one has the same preference as a previous speaker, "That's true" would serve to indicate that one holds the same opinion as the previous speaker. The crucial point is that if the only norms in play are subjective assertibility and personal warranted assertibility, introducing disquotational truth leaves everything as it is. It doesn't import a third norm.

The difficulty we have in holding on to the idea of such a community stems from our almost irresistible urge to see the situation in terms of our own normative standards. There really is a third norm, we are inclined to think, even if these simple creatures don't know it. If two of them make incompatible assertions, then one of them must be objectively incorrect, even if by their lights they both meet the only norms they themselves recognize. (I think even pragmatists will be inclined to say this, even though they want to equate the relevant kind of incorrectness not

14. The present section and the next draw significantly on that paper.

15. As I noted earlier, my use of this example does not depend on the claim that such a linguistic practice be possible. It is doubtful whether notions such as belief, assertion, and opinion are really load-bearing, in the imagined context. However, much of the effect of the example could be achieved in another way, by imposing suitable restrictions on real linguistic practices—by imagining self-imposed restrictions on what we are allowed to say. One way to approach the Mo'an predicament from our own current practice would be to adopt the convention that whenever we would ordinarily assert "P," we express ourselves instead by saying "My own opinion is that P."

with falsity but with lack of some kind of justification more objective than that of personal warrant.) But the point of the story is precisely to bring this third norm into sharp relief, and hence I am quite happy to allow challenges to the story on these grounds, which rely on the very conclusion I want to draw. *For us*, there is a third norm. But why is that so? Where does the third norm come from? What job does it do—what difference does it make to our lives? And what features must it have in order to do this job?

4. What Difference Does the Third Norm Make?

Let's return to the Mo'ans, and their merely opinionated assertions. Recall that Mo'ans use linguistic utterances to express their "beliefs," as well as other psychological states, such as preferences and desires. Where they differ from us is in the fact that they do not take a disagreement between two speakers in this belief-expressing linguistic dimension to indicate that one or other speaker must be at fault. They recognize the possibility of fault consisting in failure to observe one of the two norms of subjective assertibility or personal warranted assertibility, but lack the idea of the third norm, that of truth itself. This shows up in the fact that by default, disagreements are of a no-fault kind, in the way that expression of different preferences often are for us.

What does it take to add the third norm to such a practice? Do the Mo'ans need to come to believe that there is a substantial property that the attitudes they use MOAs to express may have or lack—perhaps the property of corresponding to how things are in the world, perhaps that of being what their opinions are fated to converge on in the long run? Does adoption of the third norm depend on a piece of folk metaphysics of this kind? Not at all, in my view. The practice the Mo'ans need to adopt is simply that whenever they are prepared to assert (in the old MOA sense) that P, they also be prepared to ascribe fault to anyone who asserts Not-P, independently of any grounds for thinking that that person fails one of the first two norms of assertibility. Perhaps they also need to be prepared to commend anyone who asserts that P, or perhaps failure-to-find-fault is motivation enough in this case. At any rate, what matters is that disagreement itself be treated as grounds for disapproval, as grounds for thinking that one's interlocutor has fallen short of some normative standard.

At this point it is worth noting what may seem a serious difficulty. If the Mo'ans don't *already* care about disagreements, why should they care about disagreements about normative matters? Suppose that we two are Mo'ans, that you assert that P, and that I assert that Not-P. If this initial disagreement doesn't bother me, why should it bother me when—trying to implement the third norm—you go on to assert that I am "at fault," or "incorrect"? Again, I simply disagree; and if the former disagreement doesn't bite, neither will the latter. And if what was needed to motivate me to resolve our disagreement was *my* acceptance that I am "at fault," then motivation would always come too late. If I accept this at all, it is only after the fact—after the disagreement has been resolved in your favor.

To get the sequence right, then, I must be motivated by your disapproval itself. This is an important point. It shows that if there could be an assertoric practice that lacked the third norm, we couldn't add that norm simply by adding a normative predicate. Insofar—so very far, in my view—as terms such as "true" and "false" carry this normative force in natural languages, they must be giving voice to something more basic: a fundamental practice of expressions of attitudes of approval and disapproval, in response to perceptions of agreement and disagreement between expressed commitments. I'll return to this point, for it is the basis of an important objection to certain other accounts of truth.

Imagine for the moment that the Mo'ans could add the third norm by adding a normative predicate, or pair of predicates ("correct" and "incorrect," say). What would be the usage rule for these predicates? Simply that one be prepared to assert that P is correct if and only if one is prepared to assert that P; and to assert that P is incorrect if and only if one is prepared to assert that Not-P. In other words, the usage rule is something very close to the disquotational schema ("P" is true if and only if P). As a result, the present proposal, that the truth predicate is an explicit expression of the third norm, already seems well on the way to an explanation of the disquotational functions of truth. We have already noted that the converse argument does not go through. A practice that lacked the third norm could still make use of a disquotational truth predicate.[16]

For the moment, we are interested in the function of the third norm. Why might the invention of such a norm be useful? What distinctive job does it do? We already have one answer to the latter question, and hence possibly to the former, in the passive account. Without a norm stronger than that of warranted assertibility *for me*, or *for us*, the idea of improving *my*, or *our*, current commitments would be incoherent. The third norm functions to create the conceptual space for the idea of further improvement. To do this job, we need a norm stronger than that of warranted assertibility for any *actual* community. (Of course, this doesn't yet show that we need something more than Peircean ideal assertibility, but one thing at a time.)

However, we can do better than the passive account. The third norm doesn't just hold open the conceptual space for the idea of improvement. It positively

16. A defender of the disquotational view might argue that although there is a third norm, it is not the function of the truth predicate to express it. This will be a difficult position to defend, however. If any predicate—"correct," for example—expresses the third norm, then that predicate will function as a disquotational predicate, for the reason just mentioned. Hence it will have been pointless to maintain that true itself is not normative. So the disquotationalist needs to claim that the third norm is not expressed at all in this predicative form, and that seems implausible.

encourages such improvement, by motivating speakers who disagree to try to resolve their disagreement. Without the third norm, differences of opinion would simply slide past one another. Differences of opinion would seem as inconsequential as differences of preference. With the third norm, however, disagreement automatically becomes normatively loaded. The third norm makes what would otherwise be no-fault disagreements into unstable social situations, whose instability is resolved only by argument and consequent agreement—and it provides an immediate incentive for argument, in that it holds out to the successful arguer the reward consisting in her community's positive evaluation of her dialectical position. If reasoned argument is generally beneficial—beneficial in some long-run sense—then a community of Mo'ans who adopt this practice will tend to prosper, compared to a community who do not.

I'll call this the active account of the role of the third norm. In effect, it contends that the fact that speakers take their belief-expressing utterances to be subject to the third norm plays a causal, carrot-and-stick role in encouraging them to settle their differences, in cases in which initially they disagree. The force of these carrots and sticks should not be overstated, however. In any given case, we are free not to give voice to our third-norm-grounded disapproval. If we do express it, the speakers with whom we disagree are free not to rise to the bait. Many factors may determine what happens in any particular case. My claim is simply that the third norm adds something new to the preferential mix. In particular, it gives rise to a new preferential pressure toward resolution of the disagreement in question—a pressure which would not exist in its absence, which does not exist for the Mo'ans, and which could not exist for us, if we did not care in general about the approval and disapproval of our fellows. The third norm depends on the fact that (to varying extents in varying circumstances) we do care about these things. It exploits this fact about us to make disagreements matter, in a way in which they would not otherwise matter. But the third norm does not come for free, with a general disposition to seek the approval of our fellows. What we have but the Mo'ans lack is an additional, special purpose, disposition: the disposition to disapprove of speakers with whom we disagree. This disposition is the mark of the third norm.

As in the case of the passive account of the role of the third norm, we need to be careful that this active account does not viciously presuppose the very notions for which it seeks to account. The notion of disagreement requires particular care. For one thing, recognition that one differs from a previous speaker must take some form more basic than the belief that he or she has said something "false," for otherwise there could not be a convention of applying this normative predicate when one perceives that one differs. For another, there is an important sense in which on the proposed account, it is the practice of applying the third norm which creates the disagreement, where initially there was mere difference. Properly developed, the view seems likely to be something like this. There is a primitive incompatibility between certain behavioral commitments[17] of a single individual, which turns on the impossibility of both doing and not doing any given action A—both having and not having a cup of coffee, for example. All else—both the public perceived incompatibility of "conflicting" assertions by different speakers, and the private perceived incompatibility essential to reasoning—is by convention, and depends on the third norm.

Obviously, much more needs to be said about this. At another level, much also needs to be said about possible advantages of such a mechanism for resolving differences—about its long-run advantages, for example, both compared to the case in which there is no such mechanism and compared to the case in which there is some different mechanism, such as deference to social rank. For immediate purposes, however, my claim does not depend on this latter work. For the present, my claim is simply that truth does play the role of this third norm, in providing the friction characteristic of factual dialogue as we know it. (I also claim, roughly, that this is perhaps the most interesting fact about truth, from a philosophical perspective.) In principle, this claim could be true, even though the practice in question was not advantageous. In principle, truth, and with it dialogue, could turn out to be a bad thing for the species, biologically considered.[18] No matter. It would still be true that we wouldn't have understood truth until we understood its role in this debilitating practice.

Is talk of dialogue really essential here? Couldn't we say simply that the third norm is what distinguishes a genuinely assertoric linguistic practice from the "merely opinionated" assertoric practice of the Mo'ans? The distinguishing mark of genuine assertion is thus that by default, difference is taken as a sign of *fault*, of breach of a normative standard.

It would not strictly be incorrect to say this, in my view, but it ought to seem unsatisfying, by pragmatist lights. A pragmatist is interested in the practical significance of the notions of truth and falsity, in the issue of what difference the possession of these notions makes to our lives. According to the view just

17. This is another place where circularity threatens. We need to be sure that the psychological states mentioned at this point are not thought of as already "factual" or "representational" in character, in a way that presupposes truth. Insofar as it is truth-involving, the "factual" character of the domain in question needs to be part of the explanandum—something that emerges from, rather than being presupposed by, the pragmatic account of the origins and consequences of "truth talk." In my view, one of the attractive features of this approach is that it offers the prospect that the uniformity of "factual," truth-involving talk might be compatible with considerable plurality in the nature and functions of the underlying psychological states. It thus offers an attractive new form for expressivist intuitions (compare Price 1988: chapter 8; 1992: §IV; 2004b).

18. Even if not dangerous on its own, the third norm might become so in combination with some particularly deadly source of intractable disagreements, such as religion commitment. More generally, the thought that argument is sometimes dangerous suggests a link between the concerns of this paper and the motivations of the Pyrrhonian sceptics. On the present view of truth, the question whether we could get by without truth seems closely related to that as to whether we could live as thoroughgoing Pyrrhonian sceptics.

suggested, the answer will be something like this. The difference that truth and falsity make is that they make our linguistic practice genuinely assertoric, rather than Mo'an. "I see that," the pragmatist will then say, "But what practical difference does *that* difference make, over and above the obvious difference—that is, over and above the fact that we approve and disapprove of some of our fellow speakers on occasions on which we wouldn't otherwise do so?"

My own answer to the new question is that these habits of approval and disapproval tend to encourage dialogue, by providing speakers with an incentive to resolve disagreements. It is true that at this point the pragmatist's question—"What difference does *that* make?"—can be (indeed, should be) asked all over again. The importance I have here attached to dialogue rests in part on the gamble that this question will turn out to have an interesting answer, in terms of the long-run advantages of pooled cognitive resources, agreement on shared projects, and so on. But not entirely. Dialogue seems such a central part of our linguistic and social lives, that the difference between a world without dialogue and our world is much greater than *merely* the difference between MOAs and genuine assertions. So even if it were to turn out that the development of dialogue had been an historical accident, of no great value to the species biologically considered, it would still be true that the most interesting behavioral consequence of the third norm would be dialogue, and not merely the more-than-merely-Mo'an assertion that makes dialogue possible.[19]

Recall that I began by challenging Rorty's claim that no behavioral consequences flow from a distinction between justification and truth. In one sense, my challenge does indeed amount to pointing out that the third norm—a notion of truth stronger than justification—brings with it the following behavioral difference: a disposition to criticize, or at least disapprove of, those with whom one disagrees. But if this were all the challenge amounted to, Rorty would be entitled to reply that of course there is this difference, but that this difference makes no interesting further difference—hence the importance of dialogue, in my view, which turns a small difference in normative practice into a big difference in the way in which speakers engage with one another (and thereby ensures that Rorty's claim fails in an interesting rather than an insignificant way).

5. Peirce Regained?

Now to the question deferred above. Does the third norm need to be other than a more-than-merely-personal notion of justification? In particular, couldn't it be a Peircean flavor of ideal warranted assertibility? I have several responses to this suggestion.

19. This point would acquire new and even stronger force, if it were to be established that private cognition rests on the norms of public dialogue, in the way suggested in n2.

First, I think that the proposal is mistakenly motivated. As I said in the introduction, I think it stems from the tendency, still too strong in Peirce, to ask the wrong question about truth. If we think that the philosophical issue is "What is truth?," then naturally we'll want to find an answer—something with which we may identify truth. Then, given standard objections to metaphysical answers, it is understandable that Peirce's alternative should seem attractive. But the attraction is that of methadone compared to heroin. Far better, surely, from a pragmatist's point of view, to rid ourselves of the craving for analysis altogether. To do this, we need to see that the basic philosophical needs that analysis seemed to serve can be met in another mode altogether: by explanation of the practices, rather than reduction of their objects. (Moreover, the explanatory project has the potential to allow us realist truth without the metaphysical disadvantages. The apparent disadvantages of realist truth emerge in the light of the reductive project, for it is from this perspective that it seems mysterious what truth could be. If we no longer feel obliged to ask the question, we won't be troubled by the fact that it is so hard to answer. We lose the motivation for seeking something else—something less "mysterious" than correspondence—with which to identify truth.)

"I accept all that," the pragmatist might say. "Nevertheless, perhaps it is true of the notion of truth (as we find it in practice), that it is identical (in some interesting sense) to ideal warranted assertibility. Shouldn't you therefore allow, at least, the possibility that a Peircean account is the correct one?"

Two points in response to this. The first, an old objection, is that it is very unclear what the notion of the ideal limit might amount to, or even that it is coherent. For example, couldn't actual practice be improved or idealized in several dimensions, not necessarily consistent with one another? In this sense, then, the Peircean pragmatist seems a long way from offering us a concrete proposal.[20]

The second point—also an old point, for as Putnam observes, it is essentially the naturalistic fallacy (1978: 108)—concerns the nature of the proposed identification of truth with ideal warranted assertibility. Truth is essentially a normative notion. Its role in making disagreements matter depends on its immediate motivational character. Why should ideal warranted assertibility have this character? If someone tells me that my beliefs are not those of our infinitely refined future inquirers, why should that bother me? My manners are not those of the palace, but so what? In other words, it is hard to see how such an identification could generate the immediate normativity of truth.[21] (It seems more plausible

20. As Rorty notes (1998: 130), Michael Williams makes a point of this kind: "[W]e have no idea what it would be for a theory to be ideally complete and comprehensive . . . or of what it would be for inquiry to have an end" (1980: 269).

21. It may seem that this argument begs the question against the pragmatist, by assuming that there is an epistemologically relevant gap between ideal warranted assertibility and truth. (I am grateful to a referee at this point.) But the issue is not whether we need some norm in addition to ideal warranted assertibility, but whether ideal warranted assertibility itself could be immediately normative, in

that we begin with truth and define the notion of the ideal limit in terms of it: what makes the limit ideal is that is reaches truth. This doesn't tell us how and why we get into this particular normative circle in the first place.)

I haven't yet mentioned what seems to me to be the most telling argument against the pragmatist identification of truth with warranted assertibility (in Peircean form or otherwise). It often seems to be suggested (by Rorty himself, among others—see the quotes with which I began), that instead of arguing about truth, we could argue about warranted assertibility. This seems to me to miss a crucial point. Without truth, the wheels of argument do not engage; disagreements slide past one another. This is true of disagreements about any matter whatsoever. In particular, it is true of disagreements about warranted assertibility. If we didn't already have truth, in other words, we simply couldn't argue about warranted assertibility. For we could be aware that we have different opinions about what is warrantedly assertible, without that difference of opinion seeming to matter. What makes it matter is the fact that we subscribe to a practice according to which disagreement is an indication of culpable error, on one side or other; in another words, that we already take ourselves to be subject to the norms of truth and falsity.[22]

The crucial point is thus that assertoric dialogue requires an intolerance of disagreement. This needs to be present already in the background, a pragmatic presupposition of judgment itself. I am not a maker of assertions, a judger, at all, unless I am already playing the game to win, in the sense defined by the third norm. Since winning is already characterized in terms of truth, the idea of a conversational game with some alternative point is incoherent. It is like the idea of a game in which the primary aim is to compete—this idea is incoherent, because the notion of competition already presupposes a different goal.[23]

---

the way in which truth is. No one disputes that the manners of the palace are normative for those who live there—that's what it is to be manners—but it is an open question whether they are or should be normative for the rest of us. Similarly for ideal assertibility, except that in this case no one lives at the limit, so that there is no one for whom the question is not open.

22. I noted above that the same point applies to the normative predicates themselves. If we weren't already disposed to take disagreement to matter, we couldn't do so simply by adding normative predicates, for disagreement about the application of those predicates would be as frictionless as disagreement about anything else. My claim is thus that the notions of truth and falsity give voice to more primitive implicit norms, which themselves underpin the very possibility of "giving voice" at all. In effect, the above argument rests on the observation that this genealogy cannot be reversed: if we start with a predicate—warrantedly assertible or any other—then we have started too late. (I suspect that by "giving voice," I mean something close to "making explicit," in Brandom's sense.)

23. Here, incidentally, we see the essential flaw in the pious sentiments of Grantland Rice:

> For when the One Great Scorer comes,
> To write against your name,
> He marks—not that you won or lost—
> But how you played the game.

The One Great Scorer might assign marks on this basis, for divine purposes. *Pace* Rice, however, we couldn't play with such marks as our primary goal, for then it would be a different game altogether.

There is a connection here with an old objection to relativism, which tries to corner the relativist by asking her whether she takes her own relativistic doctrine to be true, and if so in what sense. The best option for the relativist is to say that she takes the doctrine to be true in the only sense she allows, namely, the relativistic one. When her opponent replies, "Well, in that case you shouldn't be troubled by the fact that I disagree, because you recognize that what is true for me need not be true for you, and vice versa," the relativist has a reply. She can argue that truth is relative to communities, not to individual speakers, and hence that disagreements don't necessarily dissolve in this way.

My pragmatist opponents fare less well against an analogous argument, I think. The basic objection to their position is that in engaging with me in argument about the nature of truth (as about anything else), they reveal that they take themselves to be subject to the norm whose existence they are denying. If they didn't take themselves to be subject to it, they would be in the same boat as the Mo'ans, with no reason to treat the disagreement between us as a cause for concern. They affirm P, I affirm Not-P; but by their lights, this should be like the case in which they say "Yes" and I say "No," in answer to the question "Would you like coffee?" (This is what it should be like even if P is of the form "Q is warrantedly assertible.") The disagreement simply wouldn't bite.

6. Truth as Convenient Fiction?

The third norm thus requires a notion of truth that differs from justification, even of a Peircean ideal variety. In this sense, then, the present account is realist rather than pragmatist about truth. In another sense, however, the view surely seems anti-realist. After all, I have argued that what matters is that speakers take there to be a norm of truth, not that there actually be such a norm, in some speaker-independent sense. Isn't this anti-realism, or more precisely, in the current jargon, a form of *fictionalism* about truth?

If so, could this be a satisfactory outcome? If truth does play the role I have claimed for it in dialogue, wouldn't the realization that it is a fiction undermine that linguistic practice, by making it the case that we could no longer consistently feel bound by the relevant norms?

Let's call this objection the threat of dialogical nihilism. In my view, it isn't a practical threat. I think that in practice we find it impossible to stop caring about truth. This isn't an argument for realism, of course. The discovery that our biological appetites are not driven by perception of preexisting properties—the properties of being tasty, sexually attractive, or whatever—does not lessen the force of those appetites, but no one thinks that this requires a realist view of the properties concerned. Even if nihilism were a practical threat, this wouldn't be reason for thinking that the claim that truth is a fiction is *false*, by the lights of the game as currently played. It might be a pragmatic reason for keeping the conclusion quiet, but that is a different matter altogether (especially according to my realist opponents).

So even if the present view is correctly characterized as a form of fictionalism about truth, the nihilism objection is far from conclusive. But are the labels "fictionalism" or "anti-realism" really appropriate? The need for caution stems from the fact that this approach to truth threatens to deprive both sides of the realism–anti-realism debate of conceptual resources on which the debate seems to depend. As I noted earlier, the relevant metaphysical issues tend themselves to be framed in terms of truth, and related notions. A theory is said to be in error if its claims are not *true*, or if its terms fail to *refer*, for example. So the issue of the status of truth is here enmeshed with the terms of the problem, in a way that is quite uncharacteristic of metaphysical issues about other notions. As a result, it may be impossible to formulate a meaningful anti-realism or fictionalism about the semantic terms themselves. This doesn't mean that we have to be realists about semantic notions, but only that if we are not realists we should be cautious about calling ourselves anti-realists (or fictionalists), if these categories presuppose the very notions we want to avoid being realist about.

This may sound like an impossible trick, but in fact the kind of distinction we need is familiar elsewhere. It is the distinction between someone who "talks god talk" and espouses atheism, and someone who rejects the theological language game altogether (on Carnapian pragmatic grounds, say). These are two very different ways of rejecting theism. In the present case, the point is that we may consistently reject semantically grounded realism about the semantic notions themselves, so long as we do so by avoiding theoretical use of semantic notions altogether, rather than by relying on those notions to characterize our departure from realism. (Why "theoretical use"? Because there is nothing to stop us from continuing to use these semantic notions in a deflationary or disquotational sense.)

It might be suggested that we can sidestep this difficulty altogether by casting the relevant metaphysical issues in ontological rather than semantic terms. On this view, the relevant issue is whether truth exists, not whether (some) truth-ascriptions are true. Against this suggestion, however, it is arguable that the relevant metaphysical issues arise initially from data concerning human linguistic usage, and only become metaphysical in the light of substantial semantic assumptions about the functions of the language concerned—for example, that it is truth-conditional, or referential, in function. If so, then truth is once again enmeshed with the terms of the problem. And even if we concede the possibility of the ontological shift, the authority of Quine, Carnap, and others may perhaps be invoked in support of a deflationary attitude to ontology, with the result that the realist–anti-realist issue still dissolves.[24]

24. I defend the first of these two options in chapter 9 and the second in chapter 13.

These issues are complex, and deserve a much more detailed examination than I can give them here. For present purposes, I simply flag the following as a possible outcome (of considerable plausibility, in my view). In common with other deflationary approaches to truth, the present account not only rejects the idea that there is a substantial metaphysical issue about truth (a substantial issue about the truthmakers of claims about truth, for example). Because it is about truth, it also positively prevents "reinflation." In other words, it seems to support a general deflationary attitude to issues of realism and anti-realism. If so, then deflationism about truth is not only not to be equated with fictionalism, but tends to undermine the fictional–non-fictional distinction, as applied in the metaphysical realm.[25]

As I noted at the beginning, the present account of truth is hard to find on contemporary maps. In part, as should now be clear, this is because it combines elements not normally thought to be compatible. In one sense it is impeccably pragmatist, for example, for it appeals to nothing more than the role of truth in linguistic practice. Yet it rejects the pragmatist's *ur*-urge, to try to identify truth with justification. Again, it defends a kind of truth commonly seen as realist, but does so from a pragmatist starting point, without the metaphysics that typically accompanies such a realist view of truth. So in thinking about how to characterize this account of truth, we should be sensitive to the possibility that our existing categories—fictionalism, realism, and perhaps pragmatism itself—may need to be reconfigured. If so, then putting the position on the map is not like noticing a small country (Liechtenstein, perhaps) that previously we'd overlooked. It is more like discovering a geographical analogue of the platypus, a region that our preexisting cartographical conventions seemed a priori to disallow.

I began with Rorty's claim that the distinction between justification and truth makes no difference in practical life, no difference to our "decisions about what to do." Rorty regards a commitment to a notion of truth stronger than justification as a relic of a kind of religious deference to external authority. He recommends that just as we have begun to rid ourselves of theism, we should rid ourselves of the "representationalist" dogma that our beliefs are answerable to standards beyond ourselves. For Rorty, then, realist truth is a quasi-religious myth, which we'd do better without.

Despite my reservations about the fictionalist label, I have agreed that truth is in some sense a myth, or at least a human creation.[26] But I have denied that in providing a norm stronger than justification, a commitment to truth makes no

25. Rorty often says that he wants to walk away from realist–anti-realist disputes. In other words, he doesn't think that there is an interesting philosophical question as to whether our commitments "mirror" reality. The above argument suggests that, like other deflationists about truth, I have reason to follow Rorty in walking away from these issues. (In particular, my defense of truth over justification does not force me to stay.)

26. In the light of the argument above, this is a point more about the genealogy than about the reality of truth.

behavioral difference. On the contrary, I've argued, it plays an essential role in a linguistic practice of great importance to us, *as we currently are*. It is not clear whether we could coherently be otherwise, whether we could get by without the third norm. If so, however, then the result would be a very different language game. My main claim is that we haven't understood truth until we understand its role in the game we currently play.[27]

27. I am grateful to participants at a conference in honor of Richard Rorty at ANU in 1999, and to many subsequent audiences, for much insightful discussion of these ideas; and also to an anonymous referee for *The Journal of Philosophy* for helpful comments on an earlier version.

9

Naturalism Without Representationalism

1. The Relevance of Science to Philosophy

What is philosophical naturalism? Most fundamentally, presumably, it is the view that natural science constrains philosophy, in the following sense. The concerns of the two disciplines are not simply disjoint, and science takes the lead where the two overlap. At the very least, then, to be a philosophical naturalist is to believe that philosophy is not simply a different enterprise from science, and that philosophy properly defers to science, where the concerns of the two disciplines coincide.

Naturalism as spare as this is by no means platitudinous. However, most opposition to naturalism in contemporary philosophy is not opposition to naturalism in this basic sense, but to a more specific view of the relevance of science to philosophy. Similarly on the pro-naturalistic side: What most self-styled naturalists have in mind is the more specific view. As a result, I think, both sides of the contemporary debate pay insufficient attention to a different kind of philosophical naturalism—a different view of the impact of science on philosophy. This different view is certainly not new—it has been with us at least since Hume—nor is it prominent in many contemporary debates.

In this paper I try to do something to remedy this deficit. I begin by making good the claim that the position commonly called naturalism is not a necessary corollary of naturalism in the basic sense outlined above. There are two very different ways of taking science to be relevant to philosophy. And contrary, perhaps, to first appearances, the major implications of these two views for philosophy arise from a common starting point. There is a single kind of core problem, to which the two kinds of naturalism recommend very different sorts of answer.

I'll argue that the less well-known view is more fundamental than its rival, in a sense to be explained; and that in calling attention to the difference between the two, we call attention to a deep structural difficulty for the latter. I'll thus be defending philosophical naturalism in what I take to be its more fundamental form, while criticizing its popular contemporary manifestation.

Both the difficulty for the popular view and the conceptual priority of its unpopular rival turn on the foundational role of certain "semantic" or "representationalist" presuppositions in naturalism of the popular sort. This role is not well understood, in my view, but of considerable interest in its own right. (It deserves a more detailed examination than I can give it in this chapter.) For present purposes, its importance lies in four facts. First, the presuppositions concerned are non-compulsory, and represent a crucial choice point for naturalism—reject them, and one thereby rejects naturalism of the popular variety. Second, the standpoint from which the choice is properly made is that of naturalism of the unpopular variety—this is the sense in which this kind of naturalism is conceptually prior to its more popular cousin. Third, the possibility of rejection of these suppositions is no mere idle threat; it is a corollary of some mainstream views in contemporary philosophy. And fourth, and potentially worst of all, the presuppositions concerned turn out to be doubtfully acceptable, by the standards of the kind of naturalism they themselves are supposed to underpin.

Concerning naturalism itself, then, my argument is something like this. To assess the prospects for philosophical naturalism, we need a clear sense of the task of philosophy, in the areas in which science might conceivably be relevant. Clarity about this matter reveals not only that the approach commonly called naturalism is not the only science-sensitive option for philosophy in these areas, but also that a different approach is the preeminent approach, in the various senses just outlined. As bad news for contemporary naturalists of the orthodox sort, this may sound like good news for contemporary non-naturalists. But I hope it will be clear that my intentions are much more even-handed. Many non-naturalists share the representationalist presuppositions of their naturalist opponents, and in questioning those presuppositions, we question both sides of the debate they underpin. So I oppose both naturalism and non-naturalism as popularly understood, and favor a different kind of naturalism—a naturalism without representationalism.

2. Two Kinds of Naturalism

The popular kind of naturalism—the view often called simply "naturalism"—exists in both ontological and epistemological keys. As an ontological doctrine, it is the view that in some important sense, all there *is* is the world studied by science. As an epistemological doctrine, it is the view that all genuine knowledge is scientific knowledge.[1]

I'll call this view *object naturalism*. Though it is widely endorsed in contemporary philosophy, many of its supporters agree with some of its critics, in thinking

1. It is a nice issue whether there is any deep difference between these two versions of the view, but an issue I'll ignore for present purposes.

that it leads to some profound difficulties. The view implies that insofar as philosophy is concerned with the nature of objects and properties of various kinds, its concern is with something in the natural world, or with nothing at all. For there simply is nothing else. Perhaps there are very different ways of talking about the world-as-studied-by-science—different "modes of presentation" of aspects the same natural reality. But the object of each kind of talk is an aspect of the world-as-studied-by-science, or else nothing at all. The difficulties stem from the fact that in many interesting cases it is hard to see what natural facts we could be talking about. Different people will offer different lists of these "hard problems"—common candidates include meaning, value, mathematical truth, causation and physical modality, and various aspects of mentality, for example—but it is almost an orthodoxy of contemporary philosophy, on both sides of the issue between naturalists and their opponents, that the list is non-empty.

More in a moment on these issues—*placement problems*, as I'll call them. Before we turn to such issues, I want to distinguish object naturalism from a second view of the relevance of science to philosophy. According to this second view, philosophy needs to begin with what science tells us *about ourselves*. Science tells us that we humans are natural creatures, and if the claims and ambitions of philosophy conflict with this view, then philosophy needs to give way. This is naturalism in the sense of Hume, then, and arguably Nietzsche.[2] I'll call it *subject naturalism*.

What is the relationship between object naturalism and subject naturalism? At first sight, the latter may seem no more than an obvious corollary of the former. Contemporary "naturalists"—object naturalists, in my terms—would surely insist that they are also subject naturalists. After all, if all real entities are natural entities, we humans are surely natural entities. But in my view, the relationship between the two approaches is much more interesting than this. Subject naturalism comes first, in a very important sense.

I want to defend the following claim:

> *Priority Thesis:* Subject naturalism is theoretically prior to object naturalism, because the latter depends on validation from a subject naturalist perspective.

What do "priority" and "validation" mean in this context? As I noted earlier, subject naturalism directs our attention to the issue of the scientific "respectability" of the claims and presuppositions of philosophy—in particular, their compatibility with the recognition that we humans are natural creatures. If the presuppositions of object naturalism turn out to be suspect, from this self-reflective scientific standpoint, then subject naturalism gives us reason to reject object naturalism. Subject naturalism thus comes first, and could conceivably "invalidate" object naturalism.

2. Both attributions call for some qualification. As a parent of empiricism, for one thing, Hume certainly bears some responsibility for the object naturalist's conception of the nature of knowledge.

In my view, this threat to object naturalism is very real. I'll also defend this claim:

> *Invalidity Thesis:* There are strong reasons for doubting whether object naturalism deserves to be "validated"—whether its presuppositions do survive subject naturalist scrutiny.

As advertised, my case for this claim will depend on the role of certain "semantic" or "representationalist" presuppositions in the foundations of object naturalism. The crucial role of such presuppositions is far from obvious, however. To make it visible, we need to examine the structure of the well-recognized hard cases for object naturalism, the cases I've termed placement problems.

3. The Placement Issue

If all reality is ultimately natural reality, how are we to "place" moral facts, mathematical facts, meaning facts, and so on? How are we to locate topics of these kinds within a naturalistic framework, thus conceived? In cases of this kind, we seemed to be faced with a choice between forcing the topic concerned into a category which for one reason or another seems ill-shaped to contain it, or regarding it as at best second-rate—not a genuine area of fact or knowledge.

One way to escape this dilemma is to reject the naturalism that produces it. If genuine knowledge need not be scientific knowledge, genuine facts not scientific facts, there is no need to try to squeeze the problem cases into naturalistic clothing. Thus placement problems provide the motivation for much contemporary opposition to naturalism in philosophy. However, there are two very different ways to reject the kind of naturalism that gives rise to these problems. One way is to be non-naturalistic in the same ontological or epistemic keys—to be an object non-naturalist, so to speak. The other way is to be naturalistic in a different key—to reject *object* naturalism, in favor of a subject naturalist approach to the same theoretical problems.

At first sight, there seems to be no conceptual space for the latter view, at least in general, and at least if we want to avoid a universal subjectivism about all the hard cases. For subject naturalism rests on the fact that we humans are natural creatures, whereas the placement problems arise for topics that are at least not obviously human in nature. This is too quick, however. The possibility of a distinctive subject naturalist approach to the placement issues turns on the fact that, at least arguably, these problems *originate* as problems about human linguistic usage.

In fact, it turns out that there are two possible conceptions of the origins of placement problems—two conceptions of the "raw data" with which philosophy begins in such cases. On one conception, the problem begins with linguistic (or perhaps psychological) data; on the other, it begins with the objects themselves.

These two conceptions are not often clearly distinguished, but the distinction turns out to be very important. As I'll explain, the priority of subject naturalism, and hence the vulnerability of object naturalism, rest on the thesis that the linguistic conception is the right one.

4. Where Do Placement Problems Begin?

On the face of it, a typical placement problem seeks to understand how some object, property, or fact can be a *natural* object, property, or fact. Ignoring for present purposes the distinction between objects, properties, and facts, the issue is thus how some thing, X, can be a *natural* thing—the sort of thing revealed by science (at least in principle).

How do such issues arise in philosophy? On one possible view, the starting point is the object itself. We are simply acquainted with X, and hence—in the light of a commitment to object naturalism—come to wonder how this thing-with-which-we-are-acquainted could be the kind of thing studied by science. On the other possible view, the starting point lies in human linguistic practices, broadly construed. Roughly, we note that humans (ourselves or others) employ the term "X" in language, or the concept *X*, in thought. In the light of a commitment to object naturalism, again, we come to wonder how what these speakers are thereby talking or thinking *about* could be the kind of thing studied by science.

Let us call these two views of the origin of the placement problem the *material conception* and the *linguistic conception*, respectively. In favor of the material conception, it might be argued that the placement problem for X is a problem about the *thing* X, not a problem about the *term* "X." In other words, it is the problem as to how to locate X itself in the natural world, not the problem about how to locate the term "X."

In favor of the linguistic conception, on the other hand, note that some familiar moves in the philosophical debates to which placement problems give rise simply don't make sense, if we assume a material construal of the problem. Consider non-cognitivism, which tries to avoid the placement problem by arguing that *talk* of Xs—that is, standard *use* of the term "X"—does not have a referential or descriptive function. Here, the claim is that in the light of a correct understanding of the *language* concerned, there is no *material* problem. Of course, non-cognitivism might be mistaken in any particular case, but if the material view of the placement problem is right, it is not so much wrong as completely wrongheaded—a view which simply starts in the wrong place. Perhaps non-cognitivism is wrongheaded in this way. But the fact that this is not a common view reveals widespread implicit acceptance of a linguistic conception of the placement issue.

This appeal to philosophical practice isn't meant to be conclusive, of course. Instead, I'm going to proceed as follows. For the moment, I'll simply assume that the linguistic conception is correct, and explore its consequences for object naturalism. (I'll remind readers at several points that my conclusions depend on this assumption.) At the end of the chapter I'll come back to the question of whether the assumption is compulsory—whether object naturalism can evade my critical conclusions by adopting the material conception. I'll argue, albeit somewhat tentatively, that this is not a live option, and hence that my earlier conclusions cannot be sidestepped in this way.

5. The Semantic Ladder

If the linguistic conception is correct, then placement problems are initially problems about human linguistic behavior (or perhaps about human thought). What turns such a concern into an issue about something else—about value, mathematical reality, causation, or whatever? The answer to this question was implicit above, when our attention shifted from the *term* to what it is *about*. The shift relies on what we may call the *representationalist* assumption. Roughly, this is the assumption that the *linguistic* items in question "stand for" or "represent" something *non-linguistic* (at least in general—let's leave aside for present purposes the special case in which the subject matter is also linguistic). This assumption grounds our shift in focus from the *term* "X" or *concept X*, to its assumed *object*, X.

At first sight, however, the required assumption may seem trivial. Isn't it a truism that "X" refers to X? Isn't this merely the referential analogue of the fact that "Snow is white" is true if and only if snow is white?

The familiarity of these principles masks a serious confusion, in my view. True, the move in question is in one sense a familiar semantic descent. A semantic relation—reference, if we are dealing with terms, or truth, if we are dealing with sentences—is providing the "ladder" that leads us from an issue about language to an issue about non-linguistic reality. But it is vital to see that in the present case, the move involves a real shift of theoretical focus, a real change of subject matter. So this is a *genuine* logical descent, then, and not a mere reversal of Quine's deflationary "semantic ascent." Quine's semantic ascent never really leaves the ground. Quine himself puts it like this: "By calling the sentence 'Snow is white' true, we call snow white. The truth predicate is a device of disquotation" (1970: 12). So Quine's deflationary semantic ladder never really takes us "up," whereas the present semantic ladder does need to take us "down."

If we begin with Quine's deflationary semantic notions, in other words, then talking about the *referent* of the term "X," or the *truth* of the sentence "X is F," is just another way of talking about the *object* X. So if our original question was really about language, and we rephrase the issue in these semantic terms, we've simply changed the subject. We haven't traversed the semantic ladder, but simply taken up *a different issue*, talking in what Carnap called the formal mode about objects, rather than talking about language. On this deflationary view, then, object naturalism commits a fallacy of equivocation—a kind of mention–use fallacy, in fact[3]—on the way to its formulation of what it takes to be the central issue.

This point is easy to overlook, because we run up and down these semantic ladders so easily. But if Quine is right, the reason the climbs are so effortless is that the ladders lead us nowhere. In the present case, we do need to get somewhere. If we begin with a linguistic conception of the origins of the placement issues—if we see these issues as initially questions about linguistic usage—then it takes a genuine shift of theoretical focus to get us to an issue about the nature of non-linguistic objects. If the shift is to be mediated by semantic properties or relations of some kind, they must be substantial properties, in the following sense. They must be such that in ascribing such properties to a term or sentence we are making some theoretical claim about the linguistic items concerned, rather than simply using those items to make a claim about something else.

True, these properties must also be such as to allow us to make the transition to an issue about objects. Our theoretical focus must be led from the issue about the terms and sentences to an issue about their assumed semantic objects or values. For the object naturalist's conception of the resulting program, moreover, it is vital that this transition track the disquotational schema. (How else could a concern with the use of the term "X" lead us to an interest in X itself?) My point is that unless there is more to the semantic notions than simply disquotation, the starting point is not genuinely linguistic, and so there is no transition at all. (One might argue that this is good news, because the placement issue begins at the material level in any case. But for the moment we are assuming the linguistic conception of the origin of the problem, and this response is therefore excluded.)

Given a linguistic view of the placement issue, then, substantial, non-deflationary semantic notions turn out to play a critical theoretical role in the foundations of object naturalism. Without such notions, there can be no subsequent issue about the natural "place" of entities such as meanings, causes, values, and the like. Object naturalism thus rests on substantial theoretical assumptions about what we humans do with language—roughly, the assumption that substantial "word–world" semantic relations are a part of the best scientific account of our use of the relevant terms.

However, these assumptions lie in the domain of subject naturalism. Moreover, as the conceptual possibility of deflationism already illustrates, they are non-compulsory; more on this in a moment. Hence my Priority Thesis: given a linguistic conception of the origin of placement problems, subject naturalism is theoretically prior to object naturalism, and object naturalism depends on validation from a subject naturalist perspective.

3. The fallacy turns on the fact that on the disquotational view, an expression of the form "'Snow is white' is true" contains a use masquerading as a mention. If it were a genuine mention, to call "Snow is white" true would not be "to call snow white," as Quine puts it. If we term this disquotational mention a *formal* mention, then formal mention is effective use, and the fallacy here involves a confusion between genuine and formal mention, or true mention and effective use.

6. Should Object Naturalism Be Validated? Three Reasons for Pessimism

It is one thing to establish a need, another to show that there are serious grounds for doubting whether that need can be met. However, it seems to me that there are actually strong grounds for doubting whether object naturalism can be satisfactorily validated, in the above sense. These grounds are of three kinds.

A. The Threat of Semantic Deflationism

I have already noted that deflationism about truth and reference blocks an object naturalist's access to the kind of semantic ladder needed to transform a theoretical question about terms into a question about their assumed objects. Given the attractions of deflationism, this is clearly grounds for concern, from an object naturalist's point of view.

It is worth emphasizing two further points. First, deflationism itself is clearly of a subject naturalist character. It offers a broadly scientific hypothesis about what linguistic creatures like us "do" with terms such as "true" and "refers"—what role these terms play in our linguistic lives. Of course, the use of these terms itself comprises the basis of one particularly interesting placement problem. So semantic deflationism *exemplifies* a subject naturalist approach to a particular placement problem—an approach that seeks to explain the *use* of the semantic terms in question—as well as providing a general obstacle to an object naturalist construal of placement problems at large.

Second, it is worth noting in passing how the distinctions in play at this point enable semantic deflationism to avoid Paul Boghossian's charge that any such view is inconsistent (1990, 1989). Boghossian argues that irrealism about semantic notions is incoherent, because irrealism involves, precisely, a *denial* that the term or sentence in question has semantic properties (a referent, or truth-conditions). If this characterization of irrealism is indeed mandatory, then Boghossian seems right. Irrealism *presupposes* semantic notions, and hence the denial in question is incoherent in the case of the semantic terms themselves.

However, the point turns on the fact that so construed, irrealism relies on the kind of theoretical framework provided by the representational view of language. So long as a semantic deflationist simply *rejects* this theoretical framework, her position is not incoherent. Of course, one might insist that the resulting position no longer deserves to be called irrealism, but this is merely a terminological issue. The important point is that it is indisputably deflationary. A deflationist can consistently offer a use-explanatory account of semantic terms, while saying nothing of theoretical weight about whether these terms "refer," or "have truth-conditions."

The answer to Boghossian's challenge to deflationism thus depends on a distinction between *denying in one's theoretical voice* that these terms refer or have truth-conditions (which Boghossian is right to point out that a deflationist cannot do); and *being silent in one's theoretical voice* about whether these terms refer or have truth-conditions. A deflationist can, indeed must, do the latter, having couched her theoretical claims about the terms concerned in other terms entirely—and having insisted, *qua* deflationist, that the semantic notions do no interesting causal–explanatory work.

I'll return to Boghossian's argument in a moment, for in my view it does comprise a problem for my object naturalist opponents. For the moment, what matters is that it does not provide an obstacle to a well-formulated deflationism.

B. Stich's Problem

We have seen that in the light of a linguistic conception of the origins of the placement problem, semantic deflationism is incompatible with object naturalism. Insofar as deflationism is an attractive view, in other words, the "validation" of object naturalism must remain in doubt.

But rejecting deflationism does not necessarily solve the object naturalist's problems. One way to appreciate this is to adapt the considerations discussed by Stephen Stich in chapter 1 of *Deconstructing the Mind* (1996). In effect, Stich argues that even a non-deflationary scientific account of reference is unlikely to be determinate enough to do the work that object naturalism requires. Stich's own immediate concern is with eliminativism, and thus (in linguistic mode) with issues as to whether terms such as "belief" refer at all. He argues that so long as we retain a linguistic conception of our starting point in metaphysics, these questions inevitably become hostage to indeterminacies in our theory of reference. Evidently, if Stich is right, then the problem is not confined to eliminativism. It affects the issue "What is belief?," for example, as much as it affects the issue "Are there any beliefs?" So realist as well as anti-realist responses to the placement problem are equally afflicted.

Stich himself responds by disavowing the linguistic conception of the explanandum. We'll return below to the question as to whether this is really an option. For the moment, I simply help myself to Stich's useful discussion of these issues, in support of the following tentative conclusion. Even setting aside the threat of deflationism, it is very far from clear that a "scientific" account of semantic relations is going to provide what we need, in order to turn an interesting theoretical issue about *terms* ("causation," "belief," "good," and so on) into an interesting issue about *objects*.

C. Is Object Naturalism Coherent?

We have seen that if placement problems originate at the linguistic level, substantial semantic notions are needed to transform a question about linguistic usage into a question about non-linguistic objects. Object naturalism thus presupposes substantial semantic properties or relations of some kind. The two previous reasons for doubting whether object naturalism is entitled to this presupposition turned first, on the possibility of deflationism, which denies that semantic properties are load-bearing in the appropriate sense; and second, on the possibility that even a non-deflationary scientific account of reference might be too loosely constrained to be useful as the required semantic ladder.

Now to an even more serious difficulty: In view of the fact that object naturalism presupposes the semantic notions in this way, it is doubtful whether these notions themselves can consistently be investigated in an object naturalist spirit. Naturalism of this kind seems committed to the empirical contingency of semantic relations. For any given term or sentence, it must be to some extent an empirical matter whether, and if so to what, that term refers; whether, and if so where, it has a truthmaker. However, it seems impossible to make sense of this empirical attitude with respect to the semantic terms themselves.

Part of the difficulty turns on Boghossian's objection to semantic irrealism. In that context, the problem was that if semantic notions are presupposed in the issue between realists and irrealists—for example, if the realist–irrealist issue is taken to *be* that as to whether the terms and sentences of some domain refer, or have truth-conditions—then irrealism about these notions themselves is incoherent. Here, the problem is as follows. The object naturalist's project requires in general that irrealism be treated as live empirical possibility; but Boghossian's point shows that the object naturalist cannot adopt this attitude to the semantic terms themselves.

Boghossian takes the point to amount to a transcendental argument for a non-naturalist realism about semantic content. In my view, however, it is better seen as a pro-naturalist—pro-*subject* naturalist—point, in that it exposes what is inevitably a non-naturalistic presupposition in the leading contemporary conception of what is involved in taking science seriously in philosophy. Of course, the possibility of this interpretation depends on the fact that there is a consistent alternative naturalism, which walks away from the usual semantically grounded conception of issue. (In a different way, it also depends on a linguistic conception of the starting point, a conception we are assuming at this point, and a conception to which Boghossian himself is obviously committed.)

It might seem implausible that there could be a problem here that is specific to object naturalism. After all, I have suggested that it is an empirical possibility that the subject naturalist standpoint might not yield the kind of substantial semantic relations required for object naturalism. Isn't this same possibility all that object naturalism needs to make sense of the possibility of irrealism about semantics, in its sense?

No. The empirical possibility we have discussed is not that subject naturalism will discover that there are no semantic properties of the right sort, but simply that it will find no reason to say that there are. This is the distinction I appealed to above, in explaining how deflationism escapes Boghossian's trap. The subject naturalist's basic task is to account for the use of various terms—among them, the semantic terms themselves—in the lives of natural creatures in a natural environment. The distinction just mentioned turns on the possibility that in completing this task, the subject naturalist might simply find no need for an explanatory category of semantic properties and relations. (At no point would she need to say that the term "refer" does or does not refer to anything, for example, except in the deflationary, non-theoretical sense.) Of course, from the object naturalist's perspective this looks like an investigation as to whether there are semantic properties, but the subject naturalist has no reason to construe it that way. Indeed, she has a very good reason *not* to construe it that way, if, as Boghossian has argued, that construal is simply incoherent.

The issue of the coherence of the object naturalist approach to the semantic terms is subtle and difficult, and I don't pretend to have made a case that the difficulty is conclusive. What I hope to have established is something weaker. A naturalist has neither need nor automatic entitlement to a substantial account of semantic relations between words or thoughts and the rest of the natural world—no automatic entitlement, because by naturalism's own lights, it is at best an empirical matter; and no need, because there are ways of being naturalist which don't depend on any such assumption. Nevertheless, the stronger thesis, the incoherency thesis, seems to me both fascinating and plausible, and I want briefly to mention another way of fleshing out the difficulty.

If there is a coherent object naturalist account of the semantic relations, then as we noted earlier, the object naturalist will want to say that the right account is not a priori—there is more than one coherent possibility, and the issue is in part an empirical matter. Let's consider just two of the coherent possibilities—two rival accounts of what reference is, for example. Account one says that reference is the natural relation R*, account two that it is the natural relation R**. Thus, apparently, we have two incompatible views as to what reference actually is.

But do we? Let's think a little more closely about what each of these views claims. The first account claims that the ordinary term "Reference" picks out, or refers to, the relation R*—in other words, by its own lights, that

> "Reference" stands in the relation R* to the relation R*.

The second account claims that the ordinary term "Reference" picks out, or refers to, the relation R**—in other words, by its own lights, that

> "Reference" stands in the relation R** to the relation R**.

Are these claims incompatible? Not at all. The term "Reference" might very well stand in these two different relations to two different things, even if we allow (as proponents of both views will want to insist), that in the case of each relation singly, no term could stand in that relation to both.

Again, the problem stems from the fact that the object naturalist is trying to ask a question that renders its own presuppositions fluid. There is no fixed question, with a range of answers, but, so to speak, a different question for each answer. I leave as an exercise another puzzle of this kind. It is multiple choice:

The option selected below is:
A. Option A ☐
B. Option B ☐
C. Option C ☐
D. None of the above ☐

The problem is not that there is no right answer, but that there are too many right answers.[4] Again, the upshot seems to be that in the light of the role of semantic notions in the object naturalist's conception of the task of philosophy, that task does not make sense with respect to the semantic terms themselves.

7. Does the Problem Lie with the Linguistic Conception of the Explanandum?

As I have emphasized, the above discussion has assumed a linguistic conception of the origins of the placement problem. Is this an optional assumption? Can a material conception get object naturalism off the hook? I close with two reasons for skepticism on this point.

A. The Cat Is Out of the Bag

It is clear that the linguistic conception of the placement issue is already in play. I noted earlier that to treat non-cognitivism as an option in these debates is to commit oneself to a linguistic conception of the origin of the problem. The threat to object naturalism takes off from this point, noting that the representationalist assumption is non-compulsory—that there are other possible theoretical approaches to language, in which semantic notions play no significant role. We have thus been offered the prospect of a (subject) naturalistic account of the relevant aspects of human talk and thought, from the perspective of which the material question ("What are Xs?") simply doesn't arise.[5] At this stage, the

4. In a more detailed examination of these issues, it would be interesting to consider the connection between this kind of consideration (and indeed Boghossian's argument) and Putnam's "just more theory" concerns about the metaphysical use of a theory of reference (Putnam 1978; 1981).

5. That is to say, it doesn't arise as a question driven by naturalism. Such questions arise in many other contexts, of course —"What is justice?," "What is irony?," "What is choux pastry?," for example. If more or less commonplace questions of these kinds do give rise to puzzles of an object naturalist sort, the subject naturalist recommends a dose of linguistic therapy: Think carefully about what you are assuming about language, before you allow yourself to be convinced that there's a genuine ontological puzzle.

only way for object naturalists to regain control of the ball is to *defend* the representationalist assumption (a project fraught with difficulty, for the reasons noted above).

Couldn't an object naturalism challenge the current conception of the starting point? What is wrong with Stich's proposal, that we simply begin at the material level, and do metaphysics without semantic crutches? What is wrong with it, I think, is that it amounts to the proposal that we should simply *ignore* the possibility that philosophy might have something to learn from naturalistic—*subject* naturalistic—reflection on the things that we humans do with language. (If this seems controversial, note that it would be to ignore the possibility of non-cognitivism.) So it is a radically anti-naturalistic move. For someone who takes science seriously, the only route to object naturalism is the hard one: to concede that the problem begins at the linguistic level, and to defend the representationalist view.

B. Semantic Notions Are Part of the Tool Kit of Modern Metaphysics

The second consideration deserves a much more detailed discussion than I can give it here. Briefly, however, it seems that semantic notions such as reference and truth have become instruments in the investigative program of contemporary metaphysics. It has become common practice to identify one's objects of interest in semantic ways—as truthmakers or referents, say, or more generally as "realizers" of semantic roles.

However, the relevance of this observation about philosophical practice is far from straightforward. One of the difficulties is to decide which of the many uses of such semantic notions are "substantial" theoretical uses, and which can be regarded in a merely Quinean fashion—convenient but theoretically uncommitted uses of deflationary semantic terms. For the reasons discussed earlier, the use of deflationary semantic notions in metaphysics is not incompatible with a material conception of the origins of the placement issue. But if more substantial notions are in play, then the linguistic domain seems to play a correspondingly more significant role. Claims about language come to play a role analogous to that of observational data in science, with the semantic relations supporting inferences to an unobserved reality. The enterprise thus becomes committed to a linguistic conception of its starting point.

There are many strands in this linguistic retooling of contemporary metaphysics—the Linguistic Return, as we might call it. One significant strand runs as follows, I think. In David Lewis's influential conception of theoretical identification in science (1970a, 1972), objects of interest are identified as occupiers of causal roles. If the theoretical term "X" is defined in this way, we know what to do to answer the question "What is X?" We experiment in the laboratory of the world, adjusting this, twiddling that, until we discover just what it is that does the causal job our theory assigns to X.

In the view of many, however, Lewis's program is fit not just for science but metaphysics as well (see especially Jackson 1998). Indeed, some who think this would reject the suggestion, implicit in my formulation, that metaphysics is something different from science. But there is one difference at least. In metaphysics, there is no guarantee that our objects of interest will be the kinds of things that have *causal* roles. We might be interested in numbers, or values, or indeed in causation itself, and for all of these things it is at least controversial whether they can be identified as the cause of this, the effect of that.[6]

So in the global program, the place of causation must be taken by something else. What else could it be? It seems to me that there are two possibilities. One is that causal roles get replaced by semantic roles. In this case, the procedure for answering a question of the form "What is X?" is analogous to the one described above, except that the aim of our fiddling and twiddling—conceptual, now, rather than experimental—is to discover, say, to what the term "X" *refers*, or what *makes true* the claim that X is F.

That's the first possibility—that semantic relations play the same substantial role in the general program as causal relations played in the original program. If so, then the upshot is as we have seen. Language has become the starting point for metaphysics, and the resulting position is vulnerable in the ways described above.

The second possibility is that *nothing* specific replaces causation. It simply depends on the particular case, on what the Ramsey-Lewis method turns out to tell us about the X in question. Semantic terms may figure in the description of the task, but on this view they are no more than deflationary. We say, "X is the thing that makes this Ramsey-sentence true," but this is just a convenient way of doing what we could do by saying "X is the thing such that . . ." and then going on to *use* the Ramsey-sentence in question.

I think that this second version does avoid essential use of non-deflationary semantic notions, and is hence compatible with a material conception of our starting point in metaphysics. The problem is that it thereby cuts itself off from any general argument for (object) naturalism, of a kind that would parallel Lewis's argument for physicalism about the mental (1966). Lewis's argument relies on a premise to the effect that all causation is physical causation—the assumption of "the explanatory adequacy of physics," as Lewis puts it. Without such a premise, clearly, there is nothing to take us from the conclusion that a mental state M has

6. The claim that metaphysics extends beyond the causal realm is perhaps more controversial than I here allow. Someone who rejects it will be inclined to say that where causation stops, non-metaphysical modes of philosophy begin: formalism, perhaps, in the case of mathematics; non-cognitivism in the case of value; and so on. For present purposes, it is enough to point out that such a view is thereby committed to a linguistic conception of the placement issue, for the latter views are linguistic in nature. However, it is worth noting that in a causally grounded metaphysics of this kind, the notion of causation is likely to be problematic, in a way analogous to the semantic notions in a linguistically grounded object naturalism. It will be a primitive notion, inaccessible to the program's own professed methods.

a particular causal role to the conclusion that M is a physical state. The problem for the second of the two versions of the generalized Lewisean program is that without any single thing to play the role that causation plays in the restricted program, there can be no analogue of this crucial premise in support of a generalized argument for physicalism.

Thus it seems to me that object naturalists face a dilemma. If they appeal to substantial semantic relations, they have some prospect of an argument for naturalism, couched in terms of those relations—for example, an argument that all truths have natural truthmakers. In this case, however, they are implicitly committed to a linguistic conception of the "raw data" for these investigations, and face the problems identified earlier. If they don't appeal to substantial semantic relations, they avoid these difficulties, but lose the theoretical resources with which to formulate a general argument for naturalism, conceived on the object naturalist model.

Without the protection of such an argument, the difficult opponent is not someone who agrees to play the game in material mode but bats for non-naturalism, defending a primitive plurality of ontological realms. The difficult opponent is the naturalist who takes advantage of a non-representationalist theoretical perspective to avoid the material mode altogether. If such an opponent can explain why natural creatures in a natural environment come to *talk* in these plural ways—of "truth," "value," "meaning," "causation," and all the rest—what puzzle remains? What debt does philosophy now owe to science?

Summing up, it is doubtful whether an object naturalist can avoid a linguistic conception of the placement issue, and thereby escape the difficulties identified earlier. Some versions of object naturalism help themselves to the linguistic conception in any case, in order to put semantic relations to work in the service of metaphysics. In other cases, the inescapability of the linguistic conception turns on the fact that it is always available to the object naturalist's subject naturalist opponent, as the basis of an alternative view of the task of philosophy in these cases. The object naturalist's instinct is always to appeal to the representational character of language to bring the issue back to the material level; but this, as we have seen, is a recipe for grave discomfort.

8. Natural Plurality

Linguistically construed, the placement problem stems from a striking multiplicity in ordinary language, a puzzling plurality of topics of talk. Given a naturalistic conception of speakers, the addition of a representationalist conception of speech makes the object naturalist's ontological interpretation of the placement problem almost irresistible. Term by term, sentence by sentence, topic by topic, the representationalist's semantic ladder leads us from language to the world, from words to their worldly objects. Somehow, the resulting multiplicity of kinds of entities—values, modalities, meanings, and the rest—needs to be accommodated within the natural realm. To what else, after all, could natural speakers be related by natural semantic relations?

Without a representationalist conception of the talk, however, the puzzle takes a very different form. It remains in the linguistic realm, a puzzle about a plurality of *ways of talking*, of forms of human linguistic behavior. The challenge is now simply to explain in naturalistic terms how creatures like us come to talk in these various ways. This is a matter of explaining what role the different language games play in our lives—what differences there are between the functions of talk of value and the functions of talk of electrons, for example.[7] This certainly requires plurality in the world, but of a familiar kind, in a familiar place. Nobody expects human behavior to be anything other than highly complex. Without representationalism, the joints between topics remain joints between kinds of behavior, and don't need to be mirrored in ontology of any other kind.

For present purposes, what matters is on the one hand, that this is a recognizably naturalistic project; and on the other, that it is a very different project from that of most contemporary philosophical naturalists. I have argued that the popular view (object naturalism) is in trouble by its own lights, in virtue of its semantic presuppositions. The availability of the subject naturalist alternative makes clear that the problems of object naturalism are not problems for naturalism per se—not a challenge to the view that in some areas, philosophy properly defers to science.

We began with the relevance of science to philosophy. Let's finish with the relevance of science to science itself. Object naturalism gives science not just center-stage but the whole stage, taking scientific knowledge to be the only knowledge there is (at least in some sense). Subject naturalism suggests that science might properly take a more modest view of its own importance. It imagines a scientific discovery that science is not all there is—that science is just one thing among many[8] that we do with "representational" discourse. If so, then the semantic presuppositions of object naturalism are bad science, a legacy of an insufficiently naturalistic philosophy. The story then has the following satisfying moral. If we do science better in philosophy, we'll be less inclined to think that science is all there is to do.

7. This kind of linguistic pluralism is very Wittgensteinian in spirit, of course. One of Wittgenstein's main themes in the early sections of the *Investigations* is that philosophy misses important distinctions about the uses of language, distinctions that are hidden from us by "the uniform appearances of words" (1968: #11). The view proposed here may be too naturalistic for some contemporary Wittgensteinians, but would Wittgenstein himself have objected to it? (He might have thought that it is science, not philosophy, but that's a different matter.)

8. Or more likely, I think, "several things among many," in the sense that scientific language itself is not monofunctional. I think that causal and modal talk has distinct functions in this sense, and, while essential to any interesting science, is not the whole of it. If so, this is enough to show that there is functional plurality within scientific language, as well as outside it. For more on this theme, and the program here envisaged, see Price (2007a) and chapters 2 and 13 in the present volume.

10

Immodesty Without Mirrors: Making Sense of Wittgenstein's Linguistic Pluralism

1. Is Assertion a Natural Kind?

Wittgenstein is often thought to have challenged the view that assertion is an important theoretical category in a philosophical view of language. One of Wittgenstein's main themes in the early sections of the *Investigations* is that philosophy misses important distinctions about the uses of language, distinctions hidden from us by "the uniform appearances of words" (1968: #11). As Wittgenstein goes on to say:

> It is like looking into the cabin of a locomotive. We see handles all looking more or less alike. (Naturally, since they are all supposed to be handled.) But one is the handle of a crank which can be moved continuously (it regulates the opening of a valve); another is the handle of a switch, which has only two effective positions, it is either off or on; a third is the handle of a brake-lever, the harder one pulls on it, the harder it brakes; a fourth, the handle of a pump: it has an effect only so long as it is moved to and fro. (1968: #12)

Few contemporary philosophers share Wittgenstein's evident familiarity with the cabin of a steam locomotive, and in general, most of us are increasingly remote from all but the most superficial understanding of the underlying functions of the tools on which we rely. So we are perhaps even more prone to the mistake that Wittgenstein thinks that philosophy makes with respect to language, that of regarding it as one tool rather than many: "Think of the tools in a tool-box: there is a hammer, pliers, a saw, a screw-driver, a rule, a glue-pot, glue, nails and screws.—The functions of words are as diverse as the functions of these objects"[1] (Wittgenstein 1968: #11).

1. It is worth noting that in these passages Wittgenstein offers us two significantly different metaphors. The handle metaphor compares uses of language to a single kind of tool—a handle—that

Like the steam locomotive, this aspect of Wittgenstein's philosophy is apt to seem a relic of a quaint but happily bygone age, in which philosophy showed an excessive interest in ordinary language. But whatever one's view of ordinary language philosophy, it would be a mistake to dismiss Wittgenstein's view of language by association. For Wittgenstein's view is a view about language itself—a contribution to philosophy of language, not a linguistic approach to other philosophical topics. True, if Wittgenstein is right, then the view may have applications of the latter kind. But distaste for these applications is not an argument against the view of language on which they rest.

To assess Wittgenstein's view we should try to connect it with mainstream ideas in the philosophy of language—to ask what it amounts to, if couched in such terms. Perhaps it involves rejection of mainstream views, but we ought to be able to say what is being rejected. However, there seems to have been little serious attempt to connect Wittgenstein's view to more conventional philosophy of language in this way. The present chapter is a contribution to this project.

One of few prominent writers who does discuss Wittgenstein's view is Michael Dummett. In the chapter on "Assertion" in *Frege: Philosophy of Language*, Dummett raises the question as to "whether there is . . . any genuine point in grouping together all those utterances which we class as assertions." He goes on:

> This question is answered negatively by Wittgenstein in the *Investigations* #25: "But how many kinds of sentence are there? Say assertion, question and command?—There are countless kinds: countless different kinds of use of what we call . . . 'sentences.'" (Dummett 1973: 356)

Dummett is interested in contrasting Wittgenstein's view to Frege's. However, he thinks that it isn't entirely clear what Wittgenstein's view is. He suggests two interpretations of what he calls Wittgenstein's "repudiation of the notion of assertion" (Dummett 1973: 360), but argues that both are unattractive.

For my part, I have considerable sympathy with what I take to be two important ingredients of Wittgenstein's view, on any adequate interpretation. One of these ingredients plays down the theoretical significance of the idea that a function of (a large part of) language is to "describe" or "represent" reality. The other plays up the idea that the language concerned has many different functions, in a way that is not evident "on the surface." I'll call these ingredients *non-representationalism* and *functional pluralism*, respectively.

It isn't controversial that these two ingredients are present in Wittgenstein's later thinking in some form, or that they comprise important parts of what is new

---

does different jobs in different applications. The toolbox metaphor compares uses of language to the diverse kinds of tools to be found in a toolbox. I shall be proposing that the former metaphor is the more useful one, in the case of assertions.

in the shift from the early to the later Wittgenstein. But it is far from clear how to make these rather vague ideas precise, and connect them with other projects and frameworks in the philosophy of language.

In this respect, Dummett's discussion provides a useful anchor. While I think there is a more promising version of Wittgenstein's view than Dummett allows, it depends on a different conception from Dummett's of the task of a philosophical theory of language. In the relevant respects, moreover, Dummett's is the orthodox view. The possibility of making sense of Wittgenstein's view has thus been hidden by some deep-seated presuppositions of modern philosophy of language, I think, and the interest of the view coincides in large part with the interest of the landscape revealed if those presuppositions are given up.

As I'll explain, the resulting position is a kind of generalized or global expressivism. Its expressivism consists in theorizing about language in a non-representational key, its generality in prescribing this key universally (in contrast to a local expressivism, say about ethical discourse). A useful comparison is therefore with Robert Brandom, who is one of the very few contemporary writers to endorse a non-representationalist, expressivist starting point for a theory of meaning. I think that although my version of Wittgenstein's view diverges from Brandom's project in an important way—Brandom is ultimately less non-representationalist than my Wittgenstein—they start at the same point. Because the starting point is unorthodox, a large part of the dialectical task is simply to make it visible—to show that it is possible to begin the relevant inquiry *there*. Brandom is therefore a useful ally, from my point of view.

I don't claim that the view outlined here is exactly Wittgenstein's. But I do think that in making interesting sense of non-representationalism and functional pluralism, it is Wittgensteinian in spirit. It is an underappreciated position, which provides one interesting way of filling out the intuition that assertion is a less homogeneous linguistic category than tends to be assumed, especially in the tradition stemming from Frege—a tradition to which the early Wittgenstein belonged, and against which his later linguistic pluralism is evidently directed.

2. Themes from Frege

According to Dummett, the first way of understanding Wittgenstein's view "would be [as] a denial of the idea, common to most philosophers who have written about meaning, that the theory of meaning has some one key concept" (1973: 360). As Dummett notes, the idea thus denied is due in particular to Frege: "Frege viewed the key concept of the theory of meaning as being the notion of truth: to grasp the sense of a sentence is to grasp its truth-conditions" (1973: 360). Moreover, although some philosophers (including Dummett himself) have proposed replacing truth with some other central notion, such as method of verification, the basic Fregean structure has been thought to survive this modification. As Dummett says:

> Other candidates for the role of key concept have been put forward: but it has been common to philosophers to suppose that there is some one feature of a sentence which may be identified as determining its meaning. (1973: 360)

Dummett goes on to explain the standard view of connection between this Fregean "key concept" conception of meaning and the explanation of linguistic *use*:

> [T]he implicit assumption underlying the idea that there is some one key concept in terms of which we can give a general characterisation of the meaning of a sentence is that there must be some uniform pattern of derivation of all the other features of the use of an arbitrary sentence, given its meaning as characterized in terms of the key concept. It is precisely to subserve such a schema of derivation that the [Fregean] distinction between sense and force was introduced: corresponding to each different kind of force will be a different uniform pattern of derivation of the use of a sentence from its sense, considered as determining its truth-conditions. (1973: 361)

In using the phrase "each different kind of force," Dummett reflects the orthodox but not incontestable view that there is more than one kind of force. On this orthodox view, sense and force comprise what we might think of as orthogonal dimensions of variations of meaning. The resulting two-dimensional structure is illustrated by the examples in table 10.1. Within each column of the table, the utterances listed have the same *sense* (or *descriptive content)*, but differ in *force*. Within each row, the various utterances have the same *force*, but differ in *sense* (or *descriptive content)*.

A virtue of the Fregean approach is that it does capture the powerful intuition that meaning is (at least) two-dimensional in this sense—that is, that there is something that the meanings of the utterances across each row have in common, in respect of which they differ from the utterances in the other rows; and also something that the meanings of the utterances in each column have in common, in respect of which they differ from the utterances in the other columns. But it is worth noting that the apparent two-dimensionality alone does not show that the variation of meaning in one dimension is of a fundamentally different kind from that in the other. After all, we get a similar two-dimensionality from the most basic two-place relational expression *Fxy*, if we consider the two kinds of variations of meaning that result from (i) substituting a fixed name for *x* and then a range of names for *y*, and (ii) substituting a fixed name for *y* and then a range of names for *x*. In principle, it might be maintained—as it is by David Lewis (1970b), for example—that all the utterances in table 10.1 have assertoric force, and that what distinguishes the rows is a particular kind of variation of sense.

Table 10.1. **The Fregean sense–force distinction**

	The door is shut	*Grass is green*	*The art of conversation is dead*	. . .	(Sense)
Assertoric	"The door is shut"	"Grass is green"	"The art of conversation is dead"	. . .	
Imperative	"Shut the door!"	"Make it the case that grass is green!"	"Make it the case that the art of conversation is dead!"	. . .	
Interrogative	"Is the door shut?"	"Is it the case that grass is green?"	"Is the art of conversation dead?"	. . .	
Optative	"Would that the door were shut!"	"Would it were the case that grass is green!"	"Would that the art of conversation were dead!"	. . .	
. . .	. . .	. . .	. . .		
(Force)					

However best explained, the particular kind of two-dimensionality provided by the Fregean sense–force distinction seems to deserve prominence in a theoretical account of meaning. One of Dummett's interpretations of Wittgenstein takes him to be challenging the sense–force framework. On the face of it, any such challenge is going to be hard-pressed to explain the intuitions about meaning reflected in the structure of table 10.1. (Dummett himself objects to the proposed view in similar terms.) I take it to be an advantage of my version of the Wittgensteinian view that it does retain the sense–force framework, or something recognizably related to it.

Dummett makes a converse point about the apparent necessity of the sense–force distinction:

> It is difficult to see how, on any theory of meaning which takes meaning as to be characterized in terms of some one key concept, whether that of truth or that of verification or some other, some such distinction between sense and force could be dispensed with. (1973: 361)

The thought behind this is the one Dummett expresses in the earlier passage: one of the tasks of a theory of meaning is to explain the *use* of an arbitrary utterance, in terms of its meaning. If the "key concept" invoked by the theory in question is not immediately a specification of use, then the task is to show how use is determined by something not characterized in terms of use. For each variety of Fregean force, this requires a function whose input is specified in terms of the "one key concept," and whose output is a use prescription. In other words, it requires, as

Dummett says, "some uniform pattern of derivation of all the other features of the use of an arbitrary sentence, given its meaning as characterized in terms of the key concept" (1973: 361).

Such functions are therefore use-determining or "pragmatic" rules, and the sense–force distinction is commonly characterized as a "semantic–pragmatic" distinction. Across each row in table 10.1, the difference in meaning between the utterances concerned is a *semantic* difference—a difference of truth conditions, for example, if this is the central semantic notion in play, in terms of which sense is characterized. Down each column, the difference in meaning is a *pragmatic* difference—a difference in the use of the utterances in question, in virtue of their different forces.

We now have sufficient terminology for a rough characterization of the view for which I'm aiming. We've seen that for Frege and Dummett, the project is to generate the pragmatic from the semantic—to explain *use* in terms of *content*—by appealing to a set of principles, one for each variety of force. Each such principle needs to stipulate how the use of an utterance with the force in question depends on the descriptive content of the utterance concerned. My goal is to identify a second and more fundamental role for pragmatic considerations. Roughly, I want to give a pragmatic account of *how there come to be* descriptive contents, or thoughts, of particular kinds—in effect, we might say, a pragmatic account of the origins of the semantic.[2]

Consider a familiar example. On a Fregean view, specification of the meaning of a typical utterance of "Snow is white" involves two components. The first component specifies the sense of the utterance, typically by telling us something of this form: "Snow is white" is true iff P. (There are two importantly different conceptions of what is involved in such a "telling," but let's ignore this for the present.) The second component invokes some general principle governing the assertoric force, to describe the use of an utterance with the specified truth conditions—for example, the principle that when making assertions, speakers aim to utter true sentences.

On my view, this Fregean specification is not misconceived—at least under one of the two possible conceptions of "telling" of truth conditions—but it is seriously incomplete. Roughly, what it leaves out is an account of *how there comes to be* a thought to the effect that snow is white. One component of this thought is the concept *white*, for example. My proposal looks for a pragmatic account of the origins and "possession conditions" of this concept, for creatures like us—natural creatures, in a natural environment. It asks, in effect, how does such a creature have to *be*, and what does it have to *do*, to count as possessing and employing the concept?[3]

2. More precisely, what I'm after is a pragmatic account of the linguistic practices that we'd ordinarily describe as application of particular concepts, or expression of particular thoughts. The distinction is important because I am interested in the possibility that the semantic notions—content, truth, and the like—are not among the theoretical ontology of the view in question. More on this below.

3. As we'll see, this project has two importantly distinct parts to it. We want a general pragmatic account of the origins of judgment or assertion in general, and specific accounts of the origins of particular concepts.

It is far from obvious how an answer to this question could amount to what Wittgenstein thought he'd found—a position in tension with much orthodox philosophy of language. After all, doesn't everybody need an account of concept possession? In order to reveal the tension, we'll need to be more explicit about the tasks of a theoretical account of language. For one thing, it turns out that in the orthodox approach there are actually already two distinct roles for pragmatic considerations in such a theoretical enterprise (one of them commonly elided). My proposal is therefore to add a third role, and it will be important not to confuse it with a mere rediscovery of the second. For another thing, the proposal needs to be distinguished from two other possible views, one more radical and one less so. Finally, there are several distinct conceptions of the goals and methodology of a "theory of meaning," and the proposal is at home in some but not in others. I address these various distinctions in the following four sections.

3. Three Roles for Pragmatism in Linguistic Theory

Science often proceeds by formulating abstract or idealized models, models that are thought to "fit" reality more or less well. In the case of the science of language, these models may be more or less inclusive in scope. They may be models simply of languages, or of languages-in-a-world, or—perhaps most usefully of all—of languages-and-language-users-in-a-world. As linguistic theorists, then, we are likely to have an abstract or idealized conception of a language, or language-plus-world, or language-plus-world-and-speakers, and face the question as to what counts as fitting reality—what it takes for such a model to "fit" a given community of (real) speakers.[4] (Notice that this is a different question from one that may arise *within* the model, as to whether a given sentence "fits" or is "true of" the world.)

By thus distinguishing the model—the abstract, formal, idealized conception of a language—from the issue of what it takes for that model to fit sociological reality, we give ourselves two locations where pragmatic considerations may play a part. In the latter location, indeed, it seems that nothing but pragmatic considerations can be relevant. In some sense, whether our model correctly represents the linguistic activity of the community in question can depend on nothing but the *use* of linguistic items in the day-to-day practice of that community.

In the former location—that is, *within* the formal model—the obvious example of a pragmatic factor is Fregean force. In a model language conceived in Fregean terms, the basic items are something like possible speech acts—at any rate, sentences considered as possessing force, as well as sense. As we have already noted, it is usual to say that force needs to be explicated in terms of pragmatic or use-determining rules.

It is a nice question to what extent this formal use of pragmatic considerations can be detached from the considerations that bear on the correctness of the ascription of a given model language to a particular community. There seem to be

4. A classic description of the task in these terms is that of David Lewis (1975).

different theoretical strategies possible at this point. As I noted, one attractive option is to model language users, as well as languages themselves. According to this approach, a typical item within the model is a particular speech act, by a particular speaker. The pragmatic or use-related distinctions between speech acts with different Fregean forces will then be represented explicitly within the model. But we'll still need to appeal to *real* use, in order to justify the claim that a particular such model fits the linguistic practice of a given real community. So use will be relevant in two places: theoretically, within the model, and practically, concerning the fit of the model to sociological reality.

In this orthodox approach, the models in question ascribe semantic properties to certain linguistic items, such as sentences. The semantic properties themselves are part of the model. In effect, my proposal is to model languages in different terms, replacing semantic properties with (additional) pragmatic or usage-grounded properties.

The proposal is most easily visualized if users and usage patterns are themselves an explicit component of our linguistic models. In this case, as we noted, the model itself embodies the full two-dimensional structure associated with the Fregean sense–force distinction. On the orthodox view, sense differences correspond to differences in semantic properties (e.g., differences in truth conditions), while force differences correspond to differences in usage rules. In my proposal, both kinds of differences correspond to differences in usage properties—differences of different kinds, of course—and semantic properties are absent from the model altogether. As we'll see, this doesn't imply (absurdly) that the theory says nothing about language–world relations, but only that the theoretically significant such relations are not the familiar semantic relations.

The possibility and character of such a model will become clearer as we go along. For the moment, the point I want to stress is that this approach will provide a crucial role for pragmatic or usage-grounded factors, which is different both from the roles associated with Fregean force distinctions, and from those associated with the issue as to whether a given linguistic model fits a given body of sociological data—that is, as to whether the model fits the linguistic community in question.

4. Idealism, "Mere Presentationalism," and Semantic Deflationism

In presenting this proposal, one important task is to show that it differs from two other proposals with which it is liable to be confused. Earlier I characterized the view as offering a pragmatic account of how there comes to be a thought to the effect that snow is white—how the possibility of such a thought depends on contingent features of the thinker. On one side, it is important that this is not the ("idealist") view that the *fact* that snow is white is "mind-dependent," or a product of human linguistic practices. I want to say that the fact that we have the conceptual machinery to judge that snow is white depends on broadly pragmatic (and broadly contingent) factors concerning ourselves.[5] But the whiteness of snow does not depend on these factors.

Why is the proposed view not idealism? Simply because *it doesn't say anything* about snow, or whiteness. It is a view about our use of the terms "snow" and "white," or the concepts *snow* and *white*, not about snow itself, or about the color white. It holds that the use of the terms (or possession of the concepts) depends on contingent features of us, but it would be a category mistake to interpret this as the view that snow, whiteness, or the fact that snow is white depend on these features of us.[6]

On the other side, it is important to distinguish the proposed view from the familiar and uncontroversial claim that what depends on contingent pragmatic factors is merely our "mode of presentation" of the fact that snow is white—the particular way in which we humans think that thought. This more familiar view admits contingency at the level of concepts, but finds reassurance in the idea that these contingently different concepts will in many cases "pick out," or refer to, the same worldly objects or facts. (The term "mode of presentation" conveys this idea.) For example, suppose we thought that colors were physical properties, complex attributes involving the wavelength of electromagnetic radiation. A familiar view is that these physical properties are actually presented to us under a description something like this: that which produces certain visual effects in normal human subjects under normal conditions. On such a view, it is a contingent fact about us that we pick out the colors under a description, or mode of presentation, of this kind. Martians might pick out the same properties under a different mode of presentation, involving normally sighted Martians. Nevertheless, according to this view, we and the Martians are talking *about—referring to*—the same things.

In principle, there are two ways in which someone who agrees about the contingency of the concepts might distance himself from this familiar view—"mere presentationalism," as I'll call it. One way would be to extend contingency to the referents, as well as to the concepts. That would lead to idealism—that is, to the conclusion that the fact that snow is white depends on contingent facts about ourselves. The other way is to leave reference out of the picture altogether, *for theoretical purposes*. This is the approach that I favor, and that I want to propose as a way of making sense of Wittgenstein's remarks about assertion.

5. Again, this conceptual machinery has two levels to it: roughly, the general machinery that supports assertoric judgements, and the specific machinery associated with the particular concepts in question.

6. Another way to put this: the idealist reading thus involves a use–mention confusion, because the proposed view *mentions* the terms, but doesn't *use* them.

The conceptual space for this view thus turns on the possibility that reference—and related "word–world" semantic notions, such as truth itself—might play no significant explanatory role in a mature scientific theory about language use. As noted earlier, the interesting possibility is not that a mature theory might simply have nothing to say about the relations between language, on one side, and the world, or environment inhabited by language users, on the other. It is rather that the theoretical notions important in describing these relations might not be the semantic notions, such as reference, truth, and content itself—a mature scientific view of language might not treat *representation* as a significant theoretical relation between language and the world.[7]

This possibility is almost invisible to many contemporary philosophical audiences, in my experience. It is odd that this should be so. For one thing, non-representationalism is a major theme of twentieth-century pragmatism.[8] For another, to take seriously the idea that linguistic theory is a matter for empirical science is surely to acknowledge, inter alia, that it is an empirical possibility that mature linguistic theory will not turn out to require the folk semantic notions, such as reference and truth.[9] But perhaps most importantly, such a view of the theoretical significance of reference, truth, and the like is an immediate consequence of views familiar under the labels *deflationism* or *minimalism*. Deflationism has a number of aspects, but one central element is the thesis that truth or reference are not "substantial" notions—in particular, not such as to play a significant role in mature scientific theory.

Wittgenstein himself is well-known as an early advocate of a deflationist or redundancy theory of truth. Dummett notes Wittgenstein's view of truth, and says that it is incompatible with a Fregean approach to meaning, which characterizes sense in terms of truth conditions. I think that Dummett is only half right at this point. Roughly, there are two conceptions of the role of truth conditions in a

7. Two notes: First, this view should not be confused with the view that does treat representation as a significant theoretical relation, but argues that it is less widespread in language than we tend to assume. That view is (or is close to) orthodox non-cognitivism, or non-factualism, whereas the view envisaged here is more radical. It lacks the theoretical vocabulary in which to say that some part of language is or is not, cognitive, factual, or genuinely representational. (More on this contrast in section 7 below.) Second, the view that reference, truth, and the like are not significant theoretical notions is compatible with acknowledging that there is a legitimate non-theoretical role for these notions—e.g., a "merely disquotational" use, in the case of truth.

8. Menand (2001: 361) quotes Dewey as writing in 1905 that pragmatism will "give the *coup de grace* to *representationalism*." More recent pragmatist writing in the same vein includes Rorty's *Philosophy and the Mirror of Nature* (Rorty 1981), and—with some significant qualifications, as we'll see below—that of Robert Brandom. In contrast, a striking aspect of Dummett's work is that despite pragmatist elements—especially a focus on assertibility in preference to truth—it fails to provide a sympathetic bridge between the non-representationalist strand in pragmatism and the Fregean tradition.

9. I develop this theme in Price (2004a).

Fregean theory of meaning, depending on two conceptions of the task of such a theory. On one conception—the one he himself evidently has in mind—Dummett is right, for the use of truth conditions depends on a non-deflationary conception of truth. But on the other conception, a theory of meaning needs only a deflationary truth predicate. This suggests that it may be possible to combine a version of the Fregean project with the non-Fregean view that I want to advocate—a view that points to pragmatic contingency in the domain of concepts, without ameliorating that contingency by appeal to further semantic facts.

In order to make this possibility clear, we'll thus need two distinctions: first, a distinction between two versions of the Fregean project, only one of which requires non-deflationary truth; and second, a distinction between the Fregean project in either form, and a different theoretical perspective concerning language. I'll discuss these distinctions in the following two sections.

For the moment, the point to emphasize is that semantic deflationism supports the following response to the suggestion that the proposed version of Wittgenstein's view reduces to mere presentationalism—that is, to the familiar contingency of "modes of presentation." In one sense, the view *is* just the familiar contingency. Where it differs from the orthodoxy is in not ameliorating that familiar contingency by anchoring the contingent concepts via reference to items in a non-contingent world. Because the view *says nothing* of a theoretical nature about the referents of terms, it doesn't provide such anchors. For the same reason, it is in no position to say that two different terms or concepts have the same referents. It doesn't say that they have different referents, either. It simply remains silent on the matter. Insofar as it is committed to deflationism about the semantic relations, it denies that there is anything of theoretical interest to be said, *in these semantic terms*.[10]

5. Two Conceptions of the Task of a Fregean Theory of Meaning

The first distinction we need is between two versions of the Fregean meaning-specifying project. Let's approach this distinction by looking at why Dummett thinks that Wittgenstein's deflationary view of truth is incompatible with the Fregean project:

> The ideas about meaning which are contained in Wittgenstein's later writings in effect oppose the view that the distinction between the sense

10. This attitude of "principled theoretical silence" is the key to non-representationalism, in my view, and plays a crucial role in what follows. Again, it needs to be emphasized that such an attitude is quite compatible with acceptance of ordinary, non-theoretical uses of notions such as truth and reference, so long as these can be read in a deflationary spirit.

> of a sentence, as given by a stipulation of its truth-conditions, and the force attached to it is fruitful for an account of the use of sentences. In particular, whereas for Frege the notions of truth and falsity play a crucial role in the characterisation of the sense of a sentence, for the later Wittgenstein they do not. He expressly avowed what I have elsewhere called the "redundancy theory" of truth, namely that the principle that "It is true that A" is equivalent to "A" and "It is false that A" is equivalent to "Not A" contains the whole meaning of the words "true" and "false". . . . *If this is* all *that can be said about the meaning of "true," then learning the sense of a sentence "A" cannot in general be explained as learning under what conditions "A" is true: since to know what it means to say that "A" was true under certain conditions would involve already knowing the meaning of "A."* For Wittgenstein "meaning is use," and this involves among other things, that we must describe the use of each particular form of sentence directly, instead of trying to specify the use of an arbitrary sentence of some large class, such as assertoric or imperative sentences, in terms of its truth-conditions, presupposed known. (1973: 359, emphasis added)

At first sight, the highlighted claim is puzzling. Suppose we accept with the redundancy theory that "N is prime" and "'N is prime' is true" are equivalent in meaning. Does this imply that it cannot be informative about the meaning of "N is prime" to be told that "N is prime" is true if and only if the natural number N has no divisors other than one and itself? Surely the most it implies is that this can be *no more informative* than being told that N is prime if and only if N has no divisors other than one and itself. But isn't that informative? Isn't it precisely the kind of thing we would say to explain the meaning of "N is prime," to someone who did not know it?

In defense of Dummett, however, it might be said that we can't explain the meaning of primitive concepts in this way, and that Dummett's point is therefore valid in such cases. More generally, we can make sense of Dummett's argument by means of a distinction that he himself draws between two conceptions of a Fregean theory of meaning.

The distinction turns on the issue as to whether a theory of meaning is allowed to help itself to the full expressive power of the theorist's home language, and to specify the meaning of expressions of the object language by (in effect) offering paraphrases of those expressions in the home language. The alternative theoretical perspective is more austere. To use an image that Dummett employs in making a related point, we might think of it as the perspective of an alien and not necessarily linguistic intelligence, who encounters human language as a phenomenon to be explained and described in the natural world—as Dummett puts it, "a Martian, say, who communicated by means so different from our own that he would not for a long time recognise human language as a medium of communication" (1979: 133–134).

Dummett calls these two conceptions of the task of a theory of meaning *modest* and *full-blooded*, respectively. As he says, a modest theory aims to "give the interpretation of the language to someone who already has the concepts required," while a full-blooded theory "seeks actually to explain the concepts expressed by primitive terms of the language" (1975: 102).

It is a familiar idea that a modest theory of meaning needs only a deflationary notion of truth. In particular, Davidson's truth-theoretic approach is widely interpreted both as modest,[11] and as requiring only a disquotational notion of truth. In the heyday of Oxford Davidsonianism, for example, John McDowell described what he called "the best version" of the Davidsonian proposal "along these lines":

> We may reasonably set ourselves the ideal of constructing, as a component of a complete theory of meaning for a language, a sub-theory which is to serve to specify the contents of (for instance, and surely centrally) assertions which could be made by uttering the language's indicative sentences. . . . [A] direct assault on that task would be to look for a sub-theory which generates, on the basis of structure in the object-language sentences, a theorem, for every appropriate sentence, of this form: "s can be used to assert that p." Now there is a truistic connection between the content of an assertion and a familiar notion of truth . . . ; the connection guarantees, as the merest platitude, that a correct specification of what can be asserted, by the assertoric utterance of a sentence, cannot but be a specification of a condition under which the sentence is true. A radical proposal at this point would be as follows: as long as the ends of the theorems (think of them as having the form "s . . . p") are so related that, whatever the theorems actually say, we can use them as if they said something of the form "s can be used to assert that p," it does not actually matter if we write, between those ends, something else which yields a truth in the same circumstances; our platitude guarantees that "is true if and only" if fits that bill, and this gives a more tractable target than that of the direct assault. (1981: 228–229)

So conceived, the task of a theory of meaning is modest. Given a target sentence S of the object language, the task is to produce a sentence P of the metalanguage such that by *using* P, we show what it is that S itself may be used to say. McDowell points out that for indicative sentences, "S can be used to say that P" is true in the same circumstances as "S is true iff P," so that producing a biconditional sentence

11. As Dummett himself says, "a Davidsonian theory of meaning is a modest theory" (1975: 103). Later in the same paper Dummett withdraws this interpretation, however.

of the latter form achieves our goals just as well. The "truistic connection" on which this depends is just the disquotational schema, so the move calls for nothing more than a deflationary truth predicate.[12]

Indeed, the connection between deflationism and the modest–full-blooded distinction may need to be even closer than this. For the distinction can easily appear tendentious. What can a full-blooded theory employ *except* the conceptual resources of the metalanguage, after all? Yet if it does the content-specifying job using these materials, why does it not count as modest?

The issue of the theoretical role of the semantic notions comes to the rescue here. We've just seen that a modest theory doesn't need substantial semantic notions. In effect, content (as a substantial theoretical notion) simply drops out of such a theory.[13] It is open to us to make the converse a matter of definition—to say that the distinguishing characteristic of a full-blooded theory is precisely that it does employ the semantic notions in a substantial way.

In favor of this proposal is the following argument. A full-blooded theory takes the specification of the truth conditions of a sentence to amount to more than a mere paraphrase. But this requires that the semantic notions bear theoretical weight somewhere other than in the clauses specifying truth conditions. Why? Because we know that in that place—in those clauses—the disquotational aspect of truth is all we need. If truth wasn't doing some theoretical work somewhere else, in other words—in a theory of judgment, for example, or a substantial account of the representational function of the relevant part of language—there would be nothing to stop us from reading the proposed theory in modest terms. To prevent this "slide into modesty," there must be something that the theory does that couldn't be done with a deflationary notion of truth; and this can't be done in the clauses specifying truth conditions, because in that place, disquotation is all we need.

The connection between semantic deflationism and the possibility of a full-blooded theory of meaning thus seems to be a close one: to be precise, the two views appear to be mutually exclusive. This makes immediate sense of Dummett's view of the consequences of Wittgenstein's redundancy theory of truth. Dummett has a full-blooded theory of meaning in mind, and in the full-blooded theory,

12. It might be maintained that the resulting theory amounts in the end to a more substantial theory of truth. If so, so much the worse for deflationism. However, it will still be true that the individual theorems of a McDowellian theory do not rely on the "substance" of a thicker notion of truth, but only on the disquotational property.

13. One manifestation of this is that the modest approach works equally well for parts of language not thought to be descriptive. If we are simply *showing* the meaning of a sentence of the object language by *using* a sentence of the metalanguage, then we are doing something which can be done equally with non-indicative as well as indicative sentences. Indeed, as I noted in Price 1988: chapter 2, McDowell's schema "S can be used to say that P," interpreted in terms of Davidson's paratactic analysis, yields "S can be used to say this: 'P'"—which allows straightforward substitution of non-indicative sentences for P, without violating any grammatical rules.

truth does substantial theoretical work. To accept Wittgenstein's redundancy theory would thus be to abandon the Fregean approach, as Dummett sees it.

However, there is a less drastic alternative, which at the same time makes more interesting sense of Wittgenstein's remarks about the plurality of things we do with language. This alternative view takes the lesson of deflationism to be that the Fregean content-specifying project is necessarily modest, but notes that the resulting theoretical "thinness" on the side of semantics may be compensated by "thickness" in a different theoretical vocabulary for linguistic theory. This brings us to the second of the two distinctions foreshadowed at the end of section 4, a distinction between the Fregean content-specifying project in either its modest or full-blooded form, and a different, non–content-specifying conception of linguistic theory.

6. Two Conceptions of the Task of Linguistic Theory

We've seen that a modest theory of meaning needs no distinctively linguistic theoretical vocabulary. If a linguistic concept occurs in some target sentence S of our object language, then a "corresponding" concept will be need in our metalanguage, in order to express a content specification of the form:

S may be used to say that P.

But this requirement doesn't distinguish linguistic concepts from any other concepts in the object language. Such a theory has no *new* need for linguistic concepts.

Let's use the term *immodest* for linguistic theories of which this is not true—that is, for theories with a distinctively linguistic theoretical vocabulary, the need for which is independent of the existence of corresponding linguistic concepts in the object language. A full-blooded theory in Dummett's sense thus counts as immodest. It requires substantial semantic notions—truth, reference, content, and the like—regardless of whether the object language in question is sophisticated enough to contain these notions itself. But as we're about to see, the converse is not true. Not all immodest linguistic theories count as full-blooded theories of meaning, in Dummett's sense.

Why not? Because there are possible immodest theories that are simply not in the business of ascribing *contents*, or *meanings*, in the sense that Dummett has in mind. One way to see this is to note an ambiguity in the term "explain," in the Dummett's remark above that a full-blooded theory "seeks actually to explain the concepts expressed by primitive terms of the language." According to one possible reading—the one that Dummett has in mind—to explain a concept is to put oneself in a position to use that concept. According to the other possible reading, explanation of a concept need confer no such ability. We might come to understand the role of a concept in the lives of a community to which we ourselves could not belong—come to understand the relation of a concept to a perceptual sense we do not ourselves possess, for example. If use of the concept requires possession of the perceptual sense in question, our new knowledge of the concept does not enable us to use it. Nevertheless, we certainly know something about the concept that we did not know before. It has been *explained* to us, in one reasonable use of that term.

The crucial distinction at work here is that between *content-specifying* and *use-specifying* theories. A content-specifying theory tells us what is said *in*, or *by*, saying an object language sentence S—in other words, as we have seen, it tells us something of the form "S may be used to say *that*. . . ." (This is what puts us in a position to say the same thing ourselves.) A use-specifying theory tells us something about an object language expression by telling us *when* it is typically or properly *used*. The above example shows that knowledge of normal or proper use need not enable us to use the expression in question ourselves. Its use conditions may be conditions that we ourselves cannot satisfy.

In a use-specifying linguistic theory, *use* itself functions as a theoretical concept. (We could easily imagine applying such theoretical approach to an object language that lacks the concept *use*.) Hence a use-specifying theory is automatically immodest, according to the above criterion. In contrast, we have seen that a content-specifying theory may be either modest or immodest—only full-blooded content-specifying theories are immodest.

Thus we have the three possibilities shown in table 10.2. Dummett's preferred full-blooded approach occupies position 2. My Wittgensteinian alternative occupies position 3, and exploits the fact that position 3 and position 1 are not incompatible options. A modest Fregean content-specifying theory is compatible with the view that the interesting *theoretical* vocabulary for linguistic theory is pragmatic or use-theoretic, rather than semantic as required in position 2. In the next section I want to illustrate this possibility by thinking about how the modest and immodest views come apart, in a familiar kind of philosophical example.

7. Expressivism: Immodesty Without Mirrors

Consider a familiar kind of expressivism, say about evaluative judgements—the view that what is distinctive about evaluative judgements is that they express psychological states with a motivational character. This view is often characterized, in

Table 10.2. **Three species of linguistic theory**

	Modest theories	*Immodest theories*
Content-specifying theories	1	2
Use-specifying theories		3

part, as the view that evaluative judgements lack truth conditions. However, a modest truth-conditional approach of the kind described by McDowell is blind to what the expressivist takes to be distinctive about evaluative judgements, namely, their distinctive psychological "history." The sentences

> "Le bonheur c'est bien" is true iff happiness is good

or

> "Le bonheur c'est bien" can be used to assert that happiness is good

tell us nothing about the expressive origins of such evaluative remarks, but are none the less useful for that, in the context of a modest theory of meaning.[14]

Many writers—McDowell himself is an early example—have been inclined to take this as an objection to expressivism.[15] If truth is minimal, it is easy to be truth-conditional, and implausible to claim that evaluative claims are not truth-conditional. However, this is not an objection to the central expressivist claim that evaluative judgments are to be understood as expressions of motivational states, but only to the additional claim that such judgments are not truth-conditional—and even then, only if the additional claim is understood in a deflationary way. So it is simply a mistake to think that minimal truth rules out expressivism.

In fact, I think, the boot is on the other foot. If we take it that the expressivist's core claim is that the linguistic role of the judgments in question is non-representational, then deflationism about the key semantic notions is at least close to a *global* motivation for expressivism—a global reason for thinking that whatever the interesting theoretical conclusion about a class of judgments turns out to be, it cannot be that they are "referential," or "truth-conditional." For deflationism amounts to a denial that these notions *have* an interesting theoretical role![16]

Note that in contrast to a McDowellian theory of meaning grounded on deflationary truth, expressivism about evaluative judgements is *essentially* immodest.[17] Whatever else it does, expressivism tells us something of a theoretical nature

14. Indeed, we've already noted that McDowell's version of a theory of meaning is blind even to the indicative–non-indicative distinction.

15. The argument may be found for example in Boghossian (1990), Wright (1992), and Humberstone (1991). For McDowell's early version of a similar point, see his 1981: 229.

16. The objectors are right to think that minimalism poses a problem for "local" varieties of non-factualism—views that are non-factualist about some topics but not about others. Minimalism does indeed make that position unstable, but it does so because it implies global expressivism, in my view, not because it implies global factualism. See also O'Leary-Hawthorne and Price (1996) and Price (2004a).

17. We noted above that the same is true of any use-specifying theory.

about evaluative judgments—something that may be both inaccessible to ordinary speakers who make those judgments, and accessible to theorists who don't or can't make such judgments themselves (because they lack the relevant motivational psychology, for example). Moreover, what it tells us is not couched in representationalist terms.

Expressivism about evaluative judgements thus illustrates the possibility of the following combination of views:

(i) An immodest explication of the linguistic role of a particular class of judgments, in non-semantic or non-representational terms.[18]
(ii) A modest specification of meaning of a truth-conditional sort, along the lines suggested by McDowell.

Stage (i) of such an approach would provide a pragmatic account of how there come to be the kind of judgments whose contents may be specified by the modest theory of stage (ii).

As I have noted, such a pragmatic account must itself combine two components. For a start, we need to be told what is distinctive about evaluative judgments, as opposed to other sorts of judgments. This part of the theory might appeal to the distinctive motivational role of associated psychological states, for example, along familiar lines. By itself, however, this part of the theory cannot explain why the expressions of motivational attitudes come to have the character of assertoric judgments. To do that, we need some general theory of what judgment or assertion is "for"—of what is at stake in treating something as an assertion.

The program might come unstuck at this point. It might turn out that an adequate account of what is involved in treating something as a judgment needs to invoke a substantial notion of truth. In effect, the notion of assertion would then be dependent on that of representational content.[19] (The same might apply to the non-assertoric forces.) So there is a general onus on the kind of account I am recommending to show that this is not the case. And one large part of this task is to provide an account of what the assertoric or declarative part of linguistic practice is "for," without *presupposing* representational content.

This is very a large project, of course, and although I'll provide a slightly more detailed sketch in a moment (see section 9), my present aims are necessarily limited. I want to show simply that there is a intelligible theoretical program in the offing here—an unorthodox but apparently coherent approach to a philosophical theory of language which does embody the key ingredients of Wittgenstein's

18. Immodesty without mirrors, in other words. As we've noted above, such a theory will not be a theory of meaning at all, in Dummett's sense.

19. And expressivism would be ruled out, unless it could be combined with the view that despite their expressive origins, evaluative judgements achieve a genuinely representational status.

view of assertion, namely, non-representationalism and functional pluralism. In the hope of enhancing the visibility of this unusual approach, I want now to compare it with Robert Brandom's pragmatist approach to meaning. Although I think that my proposal diverges from Brandom's in significant ways, it starts at a similar point. Since a large part of the battle is to establish that it is possible to start one's theory of language at this unconventional location, Brandom is certainly an ally, from my point of view.

8. Brandom on Platonism versus Pragmatism

Earlier I characterized my approach as seeking to explain in pragmatic terms how there come to be contents, concepts, or thoughts of particular kinds. I contrasted this to the orthodox Fregean approach, which takes a semantic notion as fundamental, and goes on to explain the pragmatic in terms of the semantic. Here is Brandom's description of what I take to be a closely related contrast between these two orders of explanation:

> Here is another strategic methodological issue. An account of the conceptual might explain the use of concepts in terms of a priori understanding of conceptual *content*. Or it might pursue a complementary explanatory strategy, beginning with a story about the practice or activity of applying concepts, and elaborating on that basis an understanding of conceptual content. The first can be called a *platonist* strategy, and the second a *pragmatist* (in this usage, a species of functionalist) strategy. One variety of semantic or conceptual platonism in this sense would identify the content typically expressed by declarative sentences and possessed by beliefs with sets of possible worlds, or with truth conditions otherwise specified. At some point it must then explain how associating such a content with sentences and beliefs contributes to our understanding of how it is proper to use sentences in making claims, and to deploy beliefs in reasoning and guiding action. The pragmatist direction of explanation, by contrast, seeks to explain how the use of linguistic expressions, or the functional role of intentional states, confers conceptual content on them. (2000: 4)

Brandom goes on to say that his own view is "a kind of conceptual pragmatism":

> It offers an account of knowing (or believing, or saying) *that* such and such is the case in terms of knowing *how* (being able) to do something. . . . The sort of pragmatism adopted here seeks to explain what is assert*ed* by appeal to features of assert*ings*, what is claim*ed* in terms of claim*ings*, what is judg*ed* by judg*ings*, and what is believ*ed* by the role of

> believ*ings* . . . —in general, the content by the act, rather than the other way around. (2000: 4)

Later, Brandom distinguishes between views which understand the conceptual "in representational terms" (2000: 7), and his own view, which seeks "to develop an expressivist alternative" to this "representational paradigm" (2000: 10).

In some respects, then, Brandom's project seems close to mine. In endorsing expressivism and rejecting platonism, Brandom aligns himself, at least initially, with non-representationalism. But does Brandom want to remain a non-representationalist, or to build representationalism on pragmatic foundations? These are very different projects, as we see we think about the case of truth. There's a big difference between deflationism about truth, and the kind of pragmatism which wants to say what truth is—to give a reductive *analysis* of truth—in terms of practice (for example as what works, or what we converge on in the long run). Deflationism tells us how the term "true" is *used*, and may well explain this use, in the sense of telling us what useful difference it makes to language users to have a term with this usage pattern. But it doesn't tell us what truth *is*. Conversely, a reductive analysis of truth—even in terms of pragmatist raw materials—is not a form of deflationism.[20]

A similar distinction may be drawn in the case of content. There's an important difference between an approach which *analyzes* content, or meaning, in terms of use—which says what it is for an expression to have a particular content, in terms of how it is used—and an account which simply tells us how expressions are used, without thereby claiming to offer an account of *content*. For an account of the latter kind, ascriptions of content may figure as part of the explanandum. Part of the task of such a theory may be to explain the use, and function, of terms such as "content" and "meaning" in ordinary contexts. But just as explaining the use of the term "true" is different from saying what truth *is*, explaining the use of the term "content" is different from explaining what content *is*. A thoroughgoing non-representationalist view just tells us about use. It doesn't explain content by analyzing it in terms of use. It is not entirely clear to me whether Brandom counts as a non-representationalist in this sense—I suspect not.

A lot rests on this issue. Representation is a word–world relation. An account that begins with *terms*, and adds a representation relation, thus ends up including in its ontology what lies at the other end of such a relation—the referents of those terms, or what they represent. And if these objects are not things already present in the naturalistic framework within which we theorize about language, the result is likely to be an embarrassment. Either we find a place for these objects—values, possibilities, numbers, or meanings themselves, for example—in the natural world, or we endow our representation relations with the ability to reach beyond this world. Neither option seems appealing.

20. I say more about these issues in Price (2003).

But as Wittgenstein surely saw, the problem may be self-imposed, a product of our own theoretical preconceptions. If our linguistic theory is non-representational, no such problem arises.[21] Hence the appeal of expressivism in many areas, where ontological commitment seems naturalistically problematic. Of course, these anti-metaphysical advantages require that the expressivist stay non-representationalist, and not proceed to construct representational or semantic relations on pragmatic foundations. If Brandom stands on the side of analysis, the side of constructing representational relations rather than explaining representational idioms, then it is doubtful whether he is entitled to these advantages. Nevertheless, his raw materials are avowedly pragmatic. He takes it that our thoughts and expressions have to earn their representational contents in use. Brandom's approach and mine thus start at the same point, even if they diverge later.

Since neither such approach can start with representational states—states already thought of as possessing content—they need to start with something more basic. Their raw materials need to be psychological states construed in non-representational or non-conceptual terms—behavioral (or more broadly, functional) dispositions of various kinds, or what Brandom calls "knowings how." Assertion can then be thought of, most primitively, as a kind of expression or product of states of this kind. It is not mere involuntary expression, but a kind of deliberate "taking a stand"—in Brandom's terms, a "making explicit"—of one's dispositions in the relevant respect, in a way which invites challenge by fellow speakers who have certain conflicting dispositions.[22]

What point could there be to a linguistic practice for "taking a stand," in this sense? In my view, a plausible answer is that it serves to encourage useful modification of such commitments, in the light of conflict and subsequent resolution of conflict. I'll say a little more about this proposal in a moment, though again, of course, it requires a great deal more elaboration than I can give it here. For the present, the important task is to show that a model of this kind allows for interesting functional plurality *within* the class of assertions—a functional plurality not explained, as in the orthodox picture, merely by differences of representational content.[23]

9. Non-representationalism and Functional Pluralism

To this end, imagine a theoretical inquiry which begins by thinking about the biological functions of the mental states we call beliefs, or commitments, setting their (apparent) semantic properties explicitly to one side. How has it served our

21. I expand on these ideas in Price (2004a).

22. Good question: What counts as conflict? I discuss this issue in Price (1988).

23. Indeed, the direction of explanation is the reverse, in my view. That's what it means to say that this approach explains in pragmatic terms how there come to be particular representational contents.

ancestors to develop the capacity to have such mental states? What role did they play in an increasingly complex psychological life? It would not be surprising to discover that there is no single answer, satisfactory for all kinds of commitments. Perhaps the function of some commitments can be understood in terms of the idea that it is advantageous to have mental states designed to co-vary with certain environmental conditions, but for many commitments, the story might be much more complicated. Consider causal or probabilistic commitments, for example. On anybody's story—even a realist story, if it is minimally adequate—these commitments manifest themselves as dispositions to have certain sorts of expectations in certain sorts of circumstances. Plausibly, there's an interesting story to be told about the biological value of having an internal functional organization rich enough to contain such dispositions.

Or consider any of the other cases in which it has seemed difficult to give a straightforwardly truth-conditional account of the content of judgments of certain kind—the kinds of cases in which non-cognitivism commonly seems an attractive option, for example, and perhaps others as well: universal generalizations, indicative and subjunctive conditionals, logical claims, and so on. Suppose that in each of these cases we have some sense of what the commitments in question enable us to *do*, which we couldn't do otherwise—some sense of the role of the commitments in question in the psychological architecture of creatures like us.

And suppose that we are able to get to this point, without invoking the idea that the states we are talking about have contents, in any substantial sense. (Where we mention the environment, we talk about causal covariance and the like.) So far, then, we'd have a sketch of an understanding of what these various kinds of commitments do for us, but no understanding of why they manifest themselves *as* commitments—no understanding of why we take them to be truth-valued, for example, or expressible in declarative form.

As noted earlier, one option would be to invoke semantic properties to answer this question. We would then incur at least three obligations. First, presumably, we'd need to explain the functions of the various kinds of commitment in terms of their content or semantic properties. (This is the kind of obligation that, at least in some of the cases canvassed, drives non-cognitivists to deny that the commitments concerned do have genuine descriptive content.) Second, we'd need to say what these semantic properties are. And third, we'd need to show how invoking them explains the practice of declarative judgment. Perhaps these obligations can be met, but for the moment let's choose a different course. Let's think in the same explanatory spirit about the functions of the various manifestations of the declarative form. With respect to the various non-representationally characterized commitments we have described, let's think about the question, why do we give voice to *those* mental states in *that* form?

Here deflationists are allies, for they offer us some aspects of a possible answer. They offer us an account of the function of the truth predicate, for example—an account which, as noted earlier, is compatible with the view that commitments serve many different functions. But this is at best only part of the story. We need an account of the function of assertoric discourse, which explains how commitments with many different functions of their own usefully get cast as "public" judgments, presented in language for others to use or to challenge.[24]

It isn't difficult to find a place to start. For social creatures like us, there are often advantages in aligning our commitments across our communities, and especially in copying the commitments of more experienced members of our communities. To some extent we could achieve this kind of alignment by non-linguistic means—deducing the commitments of our fellows from their behavior, for example—but it seems much facilitated by a linguistic means of giving voice to and discussing commitments. That's one kind of thing that assertion seems especially well-suited to *do*. Moreover—and for the moment this is the crucial point—it is something it can usefully do in application to commitments with a wide variety of functional roles of their own.

This approach thus turns on the idea that assertions are intentional expressions of psychological states that are initially construed in non-representational terms. These underlying psychological states may themselves have a variety of functional roles, within the internal psychological architecture of the speakers concerned (or better, within the complex network of relations involving both these internal states and the creatures' external environment). Crucially, then, the possibility of plurality comes from the fact that the states in question are not thought of as *primarily* representational in function. Representational states have a single basic function, namely, to "mirror" reality. Plurality, if any, must then flow from plurality of content—from differences in *what is represented*. But a non-representational starting point allows that the commitments in question have a variety of functional roles; a variety obscured in their expression, when they take on the common "clothing" of the assertoric form.

The view thus leaves space for functional pluralism, and does so precisely in virtue of its non-representationalism. Yet in another sense it still treats assertion as a single tool—in the imagined version, a tool for aligning commitments across a speech community. Assertion thus becomes a multipurpose tool, in much the same way as the handle turns out to be, in the cabin of Wittgenstein's locomotive. In one sense, as Wittgenstein stresses, the various handles have very different functions. Yet they are all "designed to be handled," as Wittgenstein puts it, and *in that sense* members of an important single category (in contrast, as I noted at the beginning, to the assorted tools—"a screw-driver, a rule, a glue-pot, glue . . ."—mentioned in Wittgenstein's tool-box example). Handles as a class are importantly different from pedals as a class, for example (though many jobs could be performed by either).

24. As several writers have noticed, it is puzzling why the deflationist's "same again" notion of truth is not applicable to non-declarative speech acts.

So here's the proposal. Thinking of the function of assertions as uniformly representational misses important functional distinctions—distinctions we can't put back in just by appealing to differences in what is represented. To get the direction of explanation right, we need to begin with pragmatic differences, differences among the kinds of things that the assertions in question *do* (or more accurately, differences among the kinds of things that their underlying psychological states *do*, for complex creatures in a complex environment). And to get the unity right, we need to note that in their different ways, all of these tasks are tasks whose verbal expressions appropriately invoke the kind of multipurpose tool that assertion in general *is*. To say this, we need to say what kind of tool it is—what general things we do with it that we couldn't do otherwise.[25] If the answer is in part that we expose our commitments to criticism by our fellows, then the point will be that this may be a useful thing to do, for commitments with a range of different functional roles (none of them representation as such).

It is worth noting that this kind of explanatory structure also exists elsewhere in biology. A good example—almost a mirror image of the one from Wittgenstein with which we began—is the human hand. The hand and its precursors must have been useful to our ancestors for many distinct survival-enhancing purposes (many of which could also be performed, though perhaps less well, in other ways). Plausibly, the hand's net contribution to our species' biological success turned on the cumulative advantage of these many distinct functions. In explaining the hand's evolution, then, we need to recognize that it is a multipurpose tool.[26]

The same would be true, only perhaps more so, if we simply studied the function of hands in contemporary human life, ignoring their biological origins. We would find that our hands serve a huge range of functions, practically all of which can also be served by other means. Although there is no doubt that hands in themselves are theoretically significant objects of study, we miss their true significance if we fail to recognize that the category of manual tasks—of things done by hand—is not a unitary natural kind. If we say that the function of the hand is *manipulation*, and leave it at that, we miss something very important: we miss the underlying functional diversity. On my reading, Wittgenstein makes a closely analogous point about assertion—a point in which representation plays the role of manipulation, as the notion whose homogeneity needs to be challenged.

25. Or could only do with the help of some different tool—some different solution to the problem that assertion solves for us.

26. As Menand (2001: 361) notes, Dewey too uses the hand as an analogy for what we do with words and thought. In his case, the point is to counter the representationalism of traditional epistemology, but the present use of the analogy seems nicely complementary.

10. The Survival of the Sense–Force Distinction

I claimed earlier that my version of the Wittgensteinian view preserves something analogous to the Fregean sense–force structure. The first thing it preserves, as I've just stressed, is the idea that there is something that assertions have in common. Despite the fact that it introduces a new kind of pragmatic diversity within the class of assertoric utterances—a diversity not found in the Fregean picture—it nevertheless allows that there is some significant sense in which all assertions are "doing the same thing." For they are all applications of the same linguistic tool—a multipurpose tool, certainly, but a single tool for all that.[27]

Of course, an approach of the proposed kind should not restrict itself to the utterances we think of as assertoric, or declarative. Importantly, therefore, the idea that assertions are the applications of a single multipurpose tool has the implication that other utterances are *not* applications of this tool. And when it comes to saying something more positive about non-assertoric utterances, there is an appealing strategy available—a strategy that seems to guarantee that the existing pragmatic elements of the Fregean model will survive in this more general theory.

The strategy turns on the fact that the proposed account seems able simply to help itself to the work of its Fregean rivals, at least wherever a modest theory of meaning is possible—wherever the conceptual resources of the metalanguage are at least as rich as those of the object language. By her own lights, for example, a Fregean owes us an account of the use of the imperative "Make grass green!" in terms of the truth conditions of the sentence "Grass is green." As speakers of a language with the required conceptual resources, we know—modestly, as it were—what those truth conditions are. That is, we know that "Grass is green" is true if and only if grass is green. So we know enough to understand what the Fregean tells us about the use of the imperative sentences. This knowledge surely remains available to us, even if we add our pragmatic account of the origins of the thought that grass is green.

It might be objected that in virtue of its modesty, this account will end up treating too much as part of the theoretical ontology. For example, won't it give an account of use conditions for the imperative "Make grass green!" that actually refers to colors? If so, then we are once more saddled with the problem that nonrepresentationalism promised to avoid, of accommodating within the natural world the objects of color talk, normative talk, causal talk, meaning talk, and all the rest. But the difficulty is merely apparent, I think. If it is to provide a useful account of what a speaker must know in order to use an utterance correctly, the

27. In allowing this much unity to the class of assertions, the account might be thought insufficiently Wittgensteinian. Certainly it conflicts with the radical pluralism of some of his examples, such as that of the toolbox. However, we have seen that taken this literally, his examples are not consistent with one another. And the proposed view is certainly compatible with the pluralism of the less radical examples.

theory must appeal to speakers' *judgments* about colors, not to colors themselves. It will have to say, not that the command is obeyed if grass is made green, but that one should *judge* it to be obeyed when one *judges* grass to have been made green. Judgments of the latter kind are something we already have in the first-stage theory here proposed. So as long as project is ultimately grounded on use or judgment conditions in this way, there will no embarrassing problem of unwelcome ontology.[28]

11. Conclusion

I've argued that to make sense of Wittgenstein's view, we need to reject a representational conception of the core function of assertoric language. As long as this conception remains in place, the key theoretical notions of a theory of language will be sought in the semantic stable. Reference, truth, content, and the like will seem the central notions we need, as linguistic theorists. And the prime task of a theory of meaning will seem to be that of *specifying* these semantically characterized properties, for arbitrary linguistic items of appropriate kinds.

It might appear that abandoning the representationalist conception means abandoning the project of specifying semantic properties. But we need to be careful. We've seen that there are two versions of this project, distinguished by whether the semantic notions play a deflationary or non-deflationary role in the theory in question. I argued that this distinction lines up with the one that Dummett draws between modest and full-blooded versions of a Fregean theory of meaning. Only a full-blooded theory requires the representationalist presupposition, and a modest theory hence survives its rejection.

However, the very resilience of the modest theory perhaps makes it hard to see that the representationalist presupposition really is optional. After all, it seems a truism that we can say something informative about the meaning of a metalanguage sentence *s* by noting that S is true iff P, for some appropriate object language sentence P. It takes sensitivity to the issue of the theoretical role of the truth predicate to see that this truism isn't a vindication of representationalism at all. On the contrary, it is a truism precisely because the use it makes of truth is so "thin."

The resilience of the modest theory may also tend to obscure the fact that it is not the only theory left standing, if we reject representionalism. In addition to the modest theory, there remains a space for a different kind of immodest theory, employing non-representational conceptions of linguistic function. This is where we find the proposed expressivist version of Wittgentstein's linguistic pluralism.

28. The same move enables the proposal to deal with the possibility of imperatives whose significance is inaccessible to us, because we lack the contingent features that the pragmatic account identifies as essential to the use conditions of the thoughts in question.

Getting to this view from a Fregean starting point thus takes two steps. We need to distinguish modest and full-blooded versions of the content-specifying approach. And we need to see that the full-blooded approach is not the only immodest option for linguistic theory. Instead of using the semantic notions in a substantial voice, we have the option of finding a different theoretical vocabulary altogether.[29]

This summary makes the path to the proposed view seem somewhat tortuous. But it all depends on where we start. In one sense, the view should seem easy to reach, from somewhere quite familiar. This fast-track route to expressivism turns on the fact that—as I noted in section 4—everybody needs an account of concept possession. On everybody's view, then, there is some more-or-less use-based fact about what it takes to employ a given concept. In the orthodox picture, the items thus characterised are thought of in representational terms, as "modes of presentation" of worldly objects. What is distinctive about the present view is not that it does *more* but that it does *less*—it just asks about use conditions, without supplementing the resulting theory with truth conditions, semantic relations, and the like.

In one sense, the possibility of this "contraction" of the orthodox picture ought not to seem surprising, to contemporary philosophers. Why? Because the idea that the semantic notions not have a substantial theoretical role is itself a familiar one in contemporary philosophy, in a way in which it wasn't in Wittgenstein's time. Unsurprising does not imply uncontroversial, of course. As long as deflationism itself is controversial, so too will be this corollary. At present, in fact, deflationism probably generates less controversy than it deserves, because its

29. Dummett takes the first step, but apparently not the second. I think that in this respect, despite his advocacy of alternatives to truth as the key concept of a theory of meaning, he stays too close to the Fregean orthodoxy. (This is the source of the tension between Frege and pragmatism in Dummett's work, on which I commented in note 8 above.) Clearly, this is a topic on which much needs to be said. But in my view one relevant distinction, insufficiently drawn in Dummett's work, is between two conceptions of the role of an assertibility condition. As I put it in an early paper:

> [I]t is doubtful whether the view that the meaning of a sentence is determined by its assertion conditions—by *when* it may be correctly asserted—need offer this as a revised account of what it is *that* a person who makes an assertion is claiming to be the case. The alternative is to say that although the content, or sense, of an assertion is ultimately determined by its assertibility conditions, it does not *state* that these conditions hold. "Eric is flying" states that Eric is flying, and not that it is assertible that this is so, even if what it is to state that Eric is flying is ultimately to be understood in terms of *when* this may correctly be stated. (1983b: 163)

In other words, an account of when an assertion is typically or properly *used*, need not be a specification of what it *says*. With this distinction in place, we are already close to recognizing the possibilities (a) that the only kind of content specification is the modest kind, and (b) that use-based accounts are therefore, in the present terminology, immodest but not full-blooded.

consequences are systematically underrated—because people don't see how radical a challenge it poses to the representationalist orthodoxy.

All the same, many philosophical views are both well-known and controversial. In calling attention to global expressivism as a framework within which to make sense of Wittgenstein's linguistic pluralism, I don't claim to have shown that the resulting view should not be controversial. I do claim to have shown that it should be better-known.[30]

30. I am grateful to Richard Holton, Max Kölbel, Bernhard Weiss, and a conference audience in Sydney in June 2002 for helpful comments on previous versions of this piece.

11

Pragmatism, Quasi-realism, and the Global Challenge

> William James said that sometimes detailed philosophical argument is irrelevant. Once a current of thought is really under way, trying to oppose it with argument is like planting a stick in a river to try to alter its course: "round your obstacle flows the water and 'gets there just the same.'" He thought pragmatism was such a river. There is a contemporary river that sometimes calls itself pragmatism, although other titles are probably better. At any rate it is the denial of differences, the celebration of the seamless web of language, the soothing away of distinctions, whether of primary versus secondary, fact versus value, description versus expression, or of any other significant kind. What is left is a smooth, undifferentiated view of language, sometimes a nuanced kind of anthropomorphism or "internal" realism, sometimes the view that no view is possible: minimalism, deflationism, quietism. Wittgenstein is often admired as a high priest of the movement. Planting a stick in this water is probably futile, but having done it before I shall do it again, and—who knows?—enough sticks may make a dam, and the waters of error may subside.
>
> —Blackburn 1998a: 157

So begins Simon Blackburn's contribution to a symposium with Crispin Wright on "Realism and Truth." In opposing this "smooth, undifferentiated view of language," Blackburn takes issue, in particular, with Wright's view of the implications for expressivism of minimalism about truth. Wright is a leading advocate of a widespread view that semantic minimalism provides a straightforward argument for cognitivism, and hence against expressivism. For his part, of course, Blackburn is the principal proponent of a rather subtle version of expressivism, quasi-realism, which he takes to provide the most plausible treatment of a range of philosophical topics: moral, aesthetic, conditional, causal, and probabilistic judgments, for example. Quasi-realism depends on noting *differences* between discourses, and yet Blackburn himself is very sympathetic to semantic minimalism—hence his desire to resist the claim that minimalism is incompatible with expressivism, and to oppose the "undifferentiated view" in general.

For our part, we have considerable sympathy with quasi-realism and with Blackburn's campaign against this homogeneous view of language. We also agree with Blackburn that the latter view is not well described as pragmatism. Indeed, we are going to be calling attention to some respects in which it is quasi-realism that counts as a kind of pragmatism. However, we also want to identify a respect in which quasi-realism differs from pragmatism—a respect which turns on the fact that the quasi-realist view of language remains *too* differentiated, in a sense that we'll explain. Among other things, we maintain, this leaves quasi-realism vulnerable to the argument mentioned above, premised on semantic minimalism, in a way in which more ambitious forms of expressivism (or pragmatism) are not. Indeed, we'll be arguing that the usual version of the argument (as advocated, for example, by Wright) gets the implications of semantic minimalism precisely backward: semantic minimalism provides almost a knock-down argument *for* a strong or global kind of expressivism, not a knock-down argument against it.

This strong kind of expressivism is also a kind of pragmatism. It is an important and appealing position, in our view, but it remains surprisingly invisible in contemporary philosophy.[1] Our main objective here is to try to make it more visible. Blackburn's paper, and the dialectic of the quasi-realist's struggle with minimalism, provides a useful contrastive background. As just noted, we'll be arguing that minimalism turns out to provide a global argument *for* expressivism. So the news is mixed, from a quasi-realist perspective: good news for the expressivist project, but bad news for any merely *local* form of it, such as quasi-realism itself. The stable view is our form of pragmatism.[2]

1. Surprisingly so for two reasons, in our view: first, because the position in question is close in motivation and methodology to familiar views, such as quasi-realism itself; and second, as we'll explain, because the unfamiliar view in question is actually the proper end-point of a familiar line of argument from popular premisses. In both cases, we think, the pragmatist option has been obscured by a dogmatic attachment to an assumption about language with which it conflicts. The assumption in question is often called representationalism, and our point may be put like this: it is surprising that representationalism itself hasn't been more widely challenged, given that the means and motive for doing so have been popular currency for the better part of two decades.

2. As we note in section 8 below, Blackburn himself has entertained this global view in some of his more recent work, and indeed has declared himself "agnostic" (1998b: 318) about the issue that separates it from the older and better-known local version of quasi-realism. Until section 8, for ease of exposition, we take our notional Blackburnian opponent to be the original local kind of quasi-realist. If we think of our true opponent as the real (present-day) Simon Blackburn, it is more accurate to say that our message is that he should come off the fence, and opt for the global version of the view.

The chapter goes like this: In the next section we introduce the variety of pragmatism we have in mind as a particular kind of response to a familiar philosophical puzzle. We then take some care to distinguish it, first, from its neighbors "on the right": from various metaphysical approaches to similar philosophical puzzles. As we'll explain, a key distinguishing feature of pragmatism, in our sense, is that it is metaphysically *quietist*.

Next, we note the position's relation to its neighbors "on the left"—to various familiar forms of expressivism, including quasi-realism. There are certainly affinities, but a major difference is that these familiar views are typically local in scope, intended to apply to some topics or vocabularies but not to others; whereas our kind of pragmatism is necessarily a global view, in the relevant respects. Again, the point turns on quietism. Unlike more familiar forms of expressivism, our pragmatism is quietist (in a sense that we'll explain) about the representational character of various vocabularies. As a result, it provides a natural and stable response to the challenge from minimalism, mentioned above. And it retains the best aspects of the differentiation offered by quasi-realism—while avoiding, via representational quietism, a more problematic kind of differentiation.

1. Pragmatism and the Placement Problem

Our first task is to bring our target variety of pragmatism into view, by contrasting it with some metaphysical views on one side, and some more familiar expressivist views, on the other. Both contrasts are best drawn against the background of a familiar kind of philosophical puzzle—a puzzle that often presents itself as a metaphysical issue about the nature, or essence, of some thing or property: What is mind? What is causation? What is goodness? What is truth? Often, what gives such questions their distinctive flavor is that the thing or property in question seems hard to "place" in the kind of world described by science. In this form, these "placement problems" stem from a presupposition about the ontological scope of science—roughly, the naturalist assumption that all there is is the world as studied by science.[3]

The pragmatist we have in mind wants to dismiss or demote such metaphysical puzzles in favor of more practical questions, about the roles and functions of the matters in question in human life.[4] But what are these "matters," precisely? Not

3. This "naturalist" assumption implies that anything with a good claim "to be real" must in some sense—perhaps under some other description, for example—be the kind of thing recognized in scientific theory. Naturalism of this kind is enormously influential in contemporary philosophy. Here, what we want to stress is its role as a motivation for metaphysics.

4. These questions can be naturalistic, too, of course, but in the sense that they involve a naturalistic reflection on aspects of human behavior. See Price (2004a) for more on the distinction between these two kinds of naturalism.

the metaphysician's objects or properties themselves, presumably, but the words, concepts, and thoughts in terms of which (as we ordinarily put it) we talk and think *about* such things and properties. In other words, a pragmatist about causation doesn't ask about the role of causation itself in human life, but about the role and genealogy of the notion, term or concept "causation." (The former question may be an interesting question, from some philosophical or scientific standpoints, but it isn't the pragmatist's question.)

Pragmatism thus has a second-order, or "linguistic" focus. We acknowledge that the term "linguistic" isn't entirely happy in this context. If we don't want to beg important questions about the relative priority of thought and language, it might seem better to say that pragmatism begins with a focus on *representations*—leaving it open whether the fundamental representations are mental or linguistic in nature. But this terminology has a countervailing disadvantage. The term "representation" equivocates between two meanings that a pragmatist, of all people, needs to distinguish. In one sense, the term refers to a quasi-syntactical item on the page, or in the head, as it were—for example, to the sentence or term, in the strictly linguistic case.[5] In the other sense, it characterizes the (supposed) function of that item (i.e., that it represents). As we'll see, a pragmatist has a strong reason to reject characterizations of this kind—standard representationalist accounts of the functions of the psychological or linguistic items in question. Even if intended only as a label for the meaning-bearing items in question, the term "representation" thus provides an uncomfortable vehicle for a view of this kind.

Accordingly, choosing the lesser of terminological evils, we'll say that pragmatism begins with questions about the functions and genealogy of certain *linguistic* items—emphasizing that unless we stipulate otherwise, we're always assuming that these items may be mental, as well as strictly linguistic (in the ordinary sense).

Pragmatism thus begins with linguistic explananda rather than material explananda; with phenomena concerning the *use* of certain terms and concepts, rather than with things or properties of a non-linguistic nature. It begins with linguistic behavior, and asks broadly anthropological questions: How are we to understand the roles and functions of the behavior in question, in the lives of the creatures concerned? What is its practical significance? Whence its genealogy?

In philosophically interesting cases, such as the ones thought to give rise to placement problems, pragmatists will be looking for answers that explain the distinctive character of the topics in question—that account for the distinctive character of evaluative concepts, for example. Their aim is to dissolve the apparent

5. This will admit of further differentiation, depending on whether we think of symbols as mere marks, or as something like "symbols-in-a-language." These issues are important, but not immediately relevant to the distinctions we're drawing here.

puzzle of these cases, by accounting for the linguistic phenomena at the heart of the puzzle. And their guiding intuition is that if we can explain how natural creatures in our circumstances naturally come to speak in these ways, there is no further puzzle about the place of the topics concerned, in the kind of world described by science.

This intuition isn't self-supporting, however. It needs to be backed up by a case for rejecting a train of thought that otherwise allows the placement problem to reemerge in metaphysical guise, as puzzling as before. As we are about to see, metaphysicians, too, can ask questions about the functions of the relevant parts of language. For a pragmatist, the crucial thing is to resist the invitation to answer these questions in a way which leads back to metaphysics.

2. Two Ways of Starting with Language

At first sight, it might seem that the linguistic focus itself is sufficient to distinguish pragmatism from metaphysical approaches to the placement puzzles. After all, doesn't metaphysics presuppose a material focus? Isn't its interest necessarily in the objects and properties—goodness, causation, mind, or whatever—rather than in the use of the corresponding terms?

But things are not so simple. Let's grant that it is definitive of metaphysics, according to its own self-image, that it has its eyes on the world at large, and not on language specifically. Nevertheless, as the contemporary literature demonstrates, a surprising amount of metaphysical business can be conducted at a linguistic level. Thus contemporary writers interested in the nature of causation, say, or mental states, will often take themselves to be investigating the "truthmakers" of causal claims, or the "referents" of terms such as "belief." They thus characterise their metaphysical targets in *semantic* terms, as the objects, properties or states of affairs at the "far end" of some semantic relation. The item at the "near end" is a term or a sentence, a concept or a proposition, a thought or a belief—in other words (in the broad sense we're presently assuming) something linguistic.[6] In one sense, then, metaphysics of this kind begins with a linguistic focus.[7]

6. We're blurring a distinction here between the case in which the linguistic item in question is something concrete, such as a linguistic token, and the case in which it is something abstract, such as a proposition. A metaphysics that begins with abstract propositions doesn't overlap with pragmatism, in the sense we have in mind here, of course. But in practice, the case for believing in propositions is likely to rest on linguistic practices, so that such a view becomes linguistically grounded, in the present sense, after all.

7. This route to metaphysics needs to be distinguished from a kind of pseudo-linguistic mode permitted by semantic ascent, in Quine's sense. For Quine, talking about the *referent* of the term "X," or the *truth* of the sentence "X is F," is just another way of talking about the *object* X. (As he himself puts it: "By calling the sentence ['Snow is white'] true, we call snow white. The truth predicate is a

Thus a metaphysician, too, may begin her inquiry with a more-or-less anthropological concern to account for certain aspects of human linguistic behavior. If we took that concern to be constituitive of the kind of pragmatism we have in mind, the upshot would be that there is an overlap, in principle, between pragmatism (in this sense) and metaphysics. The choice is terminological, but our interest is in highlighting the view that begins with such an anthropological concern, without treating it as a stepping-stone to metaphysics. Since the stepping-stone is provided by semantic or representationalist assumptions, we'll reserve the term "pragmatism" for the view that rejects such assumptions.[8]

So it isn't a linguistic starting point alone that distinguishes pragmatism from metaphysics. Rather, it is a combination of such a starting point and a rejection of the semantic or "representationalist" presuppositions that otherwise lead our theoretical gaze from language to the world—which turn an anthropological concern into a metaphysical concern, in effect. Diagramatically:

PRAGMATISM = LINGUISTIC PRIORITY without REPRESENTATIONALISM

It is easy to miss the possibility of beginning where pragmatism begins (namely, with an interest in understanding our *use* of terms such as "good," "cause," and "true"), without feeling the pull of the metaphysical questions—without wanting to ask what we are talking *about*. Unless the role of the representationalist assumption is made explicit, it is liable to remain part of the implicit geography of our thought about these matters, a pathway that cannot help but lead us from one place to the other. Once it is properly mapped, however, the presupposition can be challenged. We pragmatists can maintain that our predecessors' mistake was precisely to follow that representationalist path, into the cul de sac of metaphysics.

---

device of disquotation" [Quine 1970: 12].) Quine's deflationary semantic notions are therefore too thin for a genuinely linguistically grounded metaphysical program—too thin to provide the substantial issues *about language* with which such a program needs to begin (viz., substantial issues about referents and truthmakers). See Price (2004a) for more on this point. Blackburn often makes a similar point about semantic ascent construed à la Ramsey. Noting that "Ramsey's Ladder" doesn't take us to a new theoretical level, Blackburn remarks that there are "philosophies that take advantage of the horizontal nature of Ramsey's ladder to climb it, and then announce a better view from the top." (1998b: 78, n25). In our terms, the philosophers that Blackburn has in mind are those who fail to see that the fashionable linguistic methods—talk of truthmakers, truth-conditions, referents, and the like—add precisely nothing to the repertoire or prospects of metaphysics, unless the semantic notions in question are more robust than those of Ramsey and Quine.

8. Our choice has a long and excellent pedigree in the pragmatist tradition, of course. Menand (2001: 361) notes that already in 1905, Dewey writes that pragmatism will "give the *coup de grace* to *representationalism*." In fact, as we'll see later, it turns out to be important to distinguish two different ways of rejecting representationalism. This will be crucial to our disagreement with Blackburn.

3. Three Ways of Rejecting Metaphysics

Our next task is to be clear about the ways in which pragmatism (in our sense) differs from its metaphysical neighbours. It rejects metaphysics, but in a specific sense, which we need to distinguish from two weaker ways of rejecting traditional metaphysical concerns.

No Metaphysics versus Anti-realist Metaphysics

Consider the familiar view that moral values are a useful fiction. This view shares with pragmatism an interest in the role and genealogy of moral concepts in human life. But it retains a metaphysical face: it maintains that, literally speaking, there are no moral values. Clearly, this is an ontological claim. (Similarly for fictionalism about other contentious topics, such as possible worlds, or truth itself.)

There are some senses in which fictionalism does reject metaphysics, of course. Moral fictionalists reject metaphysical inquiries into the nature of moral values. Since there are no such things as moral values, according to the fictionalist, there is no nature to discover (except "within the fiction," as it were). The negative, anti-realist, metaphysical thesis thus disallows a certain kind of positive metaphysical inquiry.

But contrast this anti-realist metaphysics to views that reject metaphysics altogether. Famously, there are global versions of anti-metaphysical theses of this kind, such as that of Carnap's "Empiricism, Semantic and Ontology" (1950) and (at least arguably) Quine's "On What There Is" (1948). There are also local versions, often based on the claim that the metaphysical inquiry, in some area, presupposes a mistaken view of the function of the language in which it is couched. As we note below, quasi-realism provides a particularly explicit version of the latter kind of view.

Either way, globally or locally, the relevant contrast is between views that reject the metaphysical issues altogether, and views that allow anti-realist, existence-denying metaphysics. Orthodox fictionalism is the latter view, the pragmatism we have in mind is the former. Pragmatism in our sense is thus a "no metaphysics" view rather than an anti-realist view, in the metaphysical sense. Pragmatists are metaphysical *quietists*.[9]

No Metaphysics versus Subjectivist Metaphysics

The second contrast we need turns on the fact that there is a way of answering the "what is" question which blurs the contrast with pragmatism, by offering an

9. Such a quietist may well agree with fictionalists about the *genealogy* of moral terms, of course. More on this below.

answer to some degree subjectivist. What is causation, or truth, or value? Not something as objective as we might have thought at first sight, according to this proposal, but something that involves us—something partly psychological in nature, perhaps, or something with an implicit relational aspect. In the contemporary literature, the neo-Lockean notion of response-dependence offers a popular model for views of this kind: to be red, for example, is to be such as to produce a certain response in (normal) human observers, under appropriate conditions. So colors are treated as real properties, fit objects of metaphysical scrutiny, but more subjective (or subject-involving) than we might have supposed.

These views are hybrids. They are metaphysical, in that they take seriously the "what is" questions. But they give the objects or properties or states of affairs a human face, or human foundations—even foundations cast explicitly in terms of use. Again, it is to some extent a terminological matter whether we call these views "pragmatist."[10] But whatever term we use, one sharp way of marking the contrast with what we're here calling pragmatism is to note that these subjectivists are not quietists about semantic or representationalist matters. On the contrary, they think that questions about the truthmakers, or truth-conditions, of sentences, statements, or beliefs, or the referents of terms or concepts, have determinate answers—answers that it is the task of philosophy to uncover. (Their distinctive message is that these things turn out to lie closer to home than we thought.)

Thus subjectivism is best viewed as a form of metaphysics. It takes on board the material questions, and the representational conception of language which leads to them. In particular, therefore, it is not a quietist view, either about the representational status of the language in question, or about associated ontological matters.

No Metaphysics—Pragmatists as Metaphysical Quietists

Thus by pragmatism, henceforth, we mean a view that contrasts both with this kind of subjectivist metaphysics and with the anti-realist metaphysics of fictionalism and error theories. Our pragmatists are (normally[11]) happy to stand with the folk, and to affirm the first-order truths of the domains in question—to affirm that there are beliefs, and values, and causes, and ways things might have been, and so on. What they reject is any distinctively metaphysical theoretical

10. Johnston (1993) treats response-dependence as a variety of pragmatism—as does Price (1991b), at least for dialectical purposes, in arguing that the kind of use-based pragmatism we are defending here provides a better home than response-dependence for Johnston's "pragmatist" intuitions.

11. The exceptions will be the cases in which the pragmatists are *mere* anthropologists, reflecting on a discourse in which they themselves do not participate.

perspective from which to say more about these matters—that they do or don't *really* exist, that they are *really* something subjective, or whatever.

This contrast between metaphysical quietism, on the one side, and fictionalism and subjectivism, on the other, echoes an observation made by David Lewis in one of his last papers (Lewis 2005). Lewis's main claim is that quasi-realism is effectively a form of fictionalism. Lewis notes that fictionalism and quasi-realism both endorse the first-order folk claims of a target discourse, but then offer us what amounts to a second-order qualification. In the case of modal fictionalism, for example, it goes like this: "There are ways things could have been"—that's the first-order claim—"but only in the modal fiction in which we all participate"—that's the fictionalist rider. Lewis seems to suggest that fictionalism and quasi-realism are therefore inferior to the view which accepts such statements without qualification—that is, as he inteprets the unqualified view, to realism.

Let's set aside for the moment the question as to whether Lewis is right to interpret quasi-realism as a form of fictionalism, and focus on the nature of this unqualified alternative, to which Lewis contrasts fictionalism and quasi-realism. What is this unqualified "realism"? Is it the view that *just* says, with the folk, "'There are ways things might have been"? Or is it the view that says "There REALLY ARE ways things might have been"—where the capital letters mark some distinctively philosophical claim? If there's a difference between these two possibilities, and if it's the unqualified position Lewis is looking for—in order to claim a comparative advantage over fictionalism and quasi-realism—then it must be the weaker position. Why? Because the stronger also requires an additional qualification, though this time of a positive rather than a negative kind. (The folk don't add the capital letters, if adding the capital letters adds philosophical theory.)

What if there isn't a difference between the weaker and stronger views? That would imply that—as Carnap (1950) thought, for example—there isn't any distinctively theoretical viewpoint that philosophy can bring to such matters of ontology. In other words, it implies that there isn't any distinct stronger position. Again, then, the unqualified position is the weaker position.

However, this weaker position is effectively our metaphysical quietism. Thus—still bracketing the question as to whether Lewis is right to identify quasi-realism with fictionalism—the distinction that Lewis identifies, between unqualified and qualified ways of speaking with the folk, is essentially the distinction that we need, between pragmatism and its metaphysical neighbors.

So our pragmatists are metaphysical quietists. But note that they are not philosophical quietists *tout court*, if there could be such a view. On the contrary, they take some relevant theoretical matters very seriously indeed: in particular, some broadly anthropological issues about the roles and genealogy of various aspects of human linguistic behavior. It is arguable that these issues are compulsory questions, necessarily addressed, at least implicitly, by all the views we have considered so far. (We return to this issue in section 11.) What distinguishes pragmatism is its commitment to addressing them without the resources of a representationalist model of language. As we are about to see, this is a commitment that pragmatism shares, at least locally, with quasi-realism.

4. Quasi-realism as Local Pragmatism?

We said earlier that we intended to outline a variety of pragmatism according to which quasi-realism counts as a pragmatist view, in significant respects. What we meant by that claim should now be apparent. Consider, say, a quasi-realist view of evaluative discourse. Such a view is certainly anthropological, or genealogical, in the sense outlined above. And it rejects what we called the representationalist assumption with respect to evaluative discourse. In other words, crucially, it rejects the assumption that otherwise leads from a linguistic conception of the original puzzle about evaluative discourse, to metaphysical issues about the nature of value.

So far, of course, quasi-realism keeps company with orthodox non-cognitivism or expressivism on these matters. (Like those views, in particular, it should not be confused for some version of metaphysical subjectivism. It does not say that in claiming that X is good, we *report* our approval of X, or *describe* X as being disposed to elicit our approval.) Where quasi-realism begins to part company with some cruder forms of non-cognitivism is at the choice point between metaphysical anti-realism and metaphysical quietism. Does non-cognitivism about evaluative concepts imply that, literally speaking, there are no values (thus agreeing with fictionalists and error theorists)? Some non-cognitivists seem to have thought so, but Blackburn is not one of them. As he himself often stresses, quasi-realism is not an error theory: on the contrary, as he puts it, "quasi-realism is most easily thought of as the enterprise of showing why projectivism needs no truck with an error theory" (1998a: 175). Elsewhere, responding to this question—"Aren't you really trying to defend our right to talk 'as if' there were moral truths, although in your view *there aren't any really?*"—his answer is emphatic: "No, no, no" (1998b: 319).

Thus Blackburn's view is (i) that when we speak with the folk, we are fully (and literally) entitled to say that there are values—and (ii) that no other legitimate standpoint is available to philosophy, from which we can properly retract such a claim. In our terminology, this amounts to saying that quasi-realism is metaphysically quietist. *Pace* Lewis, in fact, it is precisely this point that distinguishes quasi-realism from fictionalism. Unlike a fictionalist, a quasi-realist who stands with the folk in affirming that there are values (say), does not then proceed to add a negative qualification. (At worst, he merely withholds some further accolade or emphasis or capital letter, to which he takes our "non-quasi" commitments to be entitled. But this means that if it is the extra qualification which is objectionable, as Lewis suggests, then quasi-realism stays on the side of virtue, in the "quasi" cases.)

This reading of Blackburn might seem in tension with his own description of quasi-realism as a variety of anti-realism, and especially with an account of the place and nature of quasi-realism he offers in Blackburn (1993b). In that context, he contrasts quasi-realism with what he calls "immanent realism":

> Immanent realism is the position that the forms of ordinary discourse in the area form the only data, and themselves impose realism. . . . External realism would be a conjunction of the view that (a) there is a further external, metaphysical issue over whether the right theory of the area is realistic, and (b) the answer to this issue is that it is. Immanent realism entails the denial of (a); quasi-realism agrees with (a), but denies (b). (1993b: 368)

Isn't agreeing with (a) incompatible with being a metaphysical quietist? Indeed, isn't it the immanent realist, in Blackburn's sense, who better counts as such a quietist?

No, in our view, although this is perhaps a matter on which Blackburn could usefully have been clearer. For consider the external issue allowed by (a), as seen from the perspective of a quasi-realist. The first external question that arises is not metaphysical, but linguistic. It is the question: "Is the right theory of this area of commitment a theory that treats it as genuinely descriptive?" If the answer is that the area is genuinely descriptive, the orthodox metaphysical questions are thereby deemed appropriate: Is the area in question in good shape, is there really anything (and if so, what) to which its claims answer, and so on? But if the answer to the initial question is that the best theory in this case is not genuinely descriptive, then the quasi-realist regards these metaphysical inquiries as inappropriate—a kind of category mistake, in effect.

In the latter case, moreover, the quasi-realist is an anti-realist not in the sense of endorsing negative, existence-denying metaphysical claims, but only in the sense of not endorsing positive, capital-R Realist, existence-affirming metaphysical claims. (Compare the difference between an anti-theist who denies the existence of God, and an anti-theist who simply rejects the issue altogether, refusing to take sides—or even to label herself as an agnostic—on an issue she regards as in some way ill-founded.)

Thus, once we distinguish these two kinds of anti-realism, and recognize that the kind of external question properly allowed by a quasi-realist is not itself metaphysical—rather, it is the linguistically grounded meta-metaphysical question whether metaphysics is in order, in the domain in question—we can see how it is indeed true, as we claimed, that a quasi-realist is a metaphysical quietist, about those domains he takes to require the quasi-realist treatment.

Quasi-realism thus appears to have all the marks of our species of anthropological pragmatism. In reading quasi-realism in this way, however, we need to stress once more that it is a local pragmatism. It adopts the pragmatist attitude with respect to some areas of discourse, some topics of philosophical puzzlement, but not universally. Elsewhere, as it were, representationalism and metaphysics still reign.[12]

5. The Global Challenge

In our view, however, quasi-realism is untenable in this local form. Like other local forms of expressivism, it faces irresistible pressures toward "globalization"—pressures to concede the field to a view which, approached from this direction, is aptly characterised as *global* quasi-realism, or *global* expressivism. Seen head-on, this new view is the anthropological pragmatism with which we began, in its unrestricted form. Our next task is to explore the sources and consequences of this "global challenge."

It turns out that the pressure toward globalization threatens quasi-realism from two distinct directions, one external and one internal. The internal pressure stems from an argument to the effect that unless quasi-realism becomes a global view, it is condemned to be a victim of its own success: roughly, its own success renders redundant any stronger form of realism, of whatever kind a local quasi-realist wants to invoke in the "non-quasi" cases. We defer this challenge for the time being, however, and turn first to the external challenge.

The external challenge relies on reversing one of the main currents in the river to which Blackburn refers (and which he himself sets out to obstruct), in the passage with which we began. As we noted, semantic minimalism is commonly taken to provide a strong argument against expressivism. In our view, as we said, this gets things precisely backward. In fact, semantic minimalism provides a global argument in favor of expressivism, and this argument is the external challenge to merely local forms of expressivism, such as Blackburn's quasi-realism.

In turning the familiar appeal to semantic minimalism on its head in this way, we end up agreeing with Blackburn in one sense, but disagreeing with him in another. Blackburn is right, in our view, to deny that semantic minimalism implies an undifferentiated, homogeneous, view of language—on the contrary, as Blackburn argues, the important differentation most characteristic of pragmatism and expressivism remains firmly in place. On the other hand, we want to argue that minimalism does sweep away the kind of bifurcation that distinguishes Blackburn's quasi-realism—as a local form of pragmatism—from a more global version of the same kind of view.

12. Note that there is one important sense in which representationalism still reigns for a quasi-realist, even in the "quasi" domains. It is still regarded a contentful theoretical question *whether* the domains in question are genuinely descriptive, or representational (the answer being that they are not). As representational quietists, our pragmatists do not admit such a question. More on this distinction later.

6. The Minimalist Challenge

In its simplest form, the conventional argument that minimalism about truth is an enemy of non-cognitivism and expressivism goes something like this.[13] If there is nothing more to truth than the equivalence schema, then any meaningful sentence "P" whose syntax permits it to be embedded in the form "P is true" immediately possesses truth-conditions, in the only sense available: namely, "P" is true if and only if P. Since moral claims, for example, are certainly embeddable in this way, it is immediate that moral claims are truth-conditional, or truth-evaluable, as the cognitivist maintains. In general, then, the thought is that if truth is minimal, it is easy for sentences to be truth-evaluable—and hence implausible for a non-cognitivist to maintain that a superficially truth-conditional statement is not genuinely truth-conditional.[14]

In our view, as we said, this argument is almost completely wrongheaded. The key to seeing this is to note that expressivism normally makes *two* claims about its target discourse, one negative and one positive. The negative claim says that these terms or statements lack some semantic feature: they are non-referential, non-truth-apt, non-descriptive, non-factual, or something of the kind. The positive claim offers an alternative, non-semantic, account of the functions of the language in question—for example, that it expresses, or projects, evaluative attitudes of the speaker in question. Thus the negative claim is *anti-representational*, the positive claim *expressivist*.

What is the effect on such a combination of views of deflationism about the semantic vocabulary in which the negative claim is couched? If we read the minimalist as claiming, inter alia, that the semantic notions have no substantial theoretical role to play, then the consequence is that the negative claim must be abandoned. For it is a substantial theoretical claim, cast (essentially) in semantic vocabulary. But abandoning this claim does not imply that, qua theoreticians, we must endorse its negation—that is, endorse cognitivism. On the contrary, what's thin for the goose is thin for the gander: if semantic terms can't be used in a thick sense, they can't be used on either side of a (thick) dispute as to whether evaluative claims are genuinely representational.

Consider again the theological analogy. Evolutionary biologists don't think that the species were created by God. Does this mean that they must use the term

13. This section draws heavily on material from Price (2009).

14. An early version of the argument may be found in McDowell (1981), though the point seems to have been in play before that. (It is closely related to some points raised in a filmed discussion between Peter Strawson and Gareth Evans, made for the Open University in 1975.) More recent versions may be found in Boghossian (1990), Wright (1992), and Humberstone (1991). The argument is also endorsed by Jackson, Oppy, and Smith (1994), who propose a response for non-cognitivism, based on the argument that minimalism about *truth* need not imply minimalism about *truth-aptness*, and that it is non-minimalism about truth-aptness that matters for the non-cognitivist's purposes. In our view, non-cognitivism does not need saving: in the important respects, semantic minimalism already represents victory by default.

"God," in their theoretical voice, in order to deny that the species were created by God? Obviously not—they simply offer an account of the origin of the species in which the term "God" does not appear. So rejecting the view that God created the species does not require accepting the following claim: God did not create the species. The alternative—the right alternative, obviously, in this case—is a kind of passive rejection: simply avoiding theological vocabulary, in scientific contexts.

As before, the point of the example is that not affirming is not the same as denying, and the lesson carries over to the present case. From a theoretician's point of view, declining to affirm that a linguistic item stands in semantic relations does not entail denying that it does so. One may simply dismiss the issue, as having no relevant theoretical content.

So what is the effect of deflationism on expressivism? It is to deflate the expressivist's (usual) negative claim, *while leaving intact the positive claim*—the expressivist's pragmatic account of the function of the terms in question. Contrary to the received view, then, semantic minimalism is a friend rather an enemy of expressivism. Provided that we take it that the core of the expressivist position is what we've called a pragmatic account of the key functions of the judgments in question—an account not cast in representational, "descriptive," or semantic terms—then deflationism about the key semantic notions is a *global* motivation for expressivism. It is a global reason for thinking that whatever the interesting theoretical view of the functions of a class of judgments turns out to be, it cannot be that they are referential, or truth-conditional. (To repeat: deflationism amounts to a denial that these notions have a substantial theoretical role.)

Of course, the difficulty for most expressivists is that they are explicit in wanting their expressivism to be a local view. They want a contrast between the domains in which they offer a non-representational account of the functions of the language in question, and the domains they want to regard as genuinely representational. Even more importantly, as we noted above, they want the question "Is this domain genuinely representational?" to be in good order, with substantial content, in both kinds of cases. Deflationism disallows this question, and thereby the contrast that depends on it—but it doesn't disallow the expressivist's positive, pragmatic account of what supposedly lies on the non-representational side of the fence. On the contrary, the problem is with what supposedly lies on the representational side (and hence with the existence of the dividing line itself).

Semantic minimalism thus implies global pragmatism, in our sense. Recall our equation above:

PRAGMATISM = LINGUISTIC PRIORITY without REPRESENTATIONALISM

Semantic minimalism requires that substantial theory about our linguistic behavior must operate without the semantic categories that underpin representationalism—necessarily without REPRESENTATIONALISM, in other words.

Finally, note that this conclusion does not entail a homogeneous, undifferentiated view of language. On the contrary, there's plenty of scope for differentiation, in the pragmatist's functional key. The only differentiation disallowed is that between genuinely and "quasi" representational discourse. So, as we said, it is good news and bad news, from a quasi-realist point's of view: a cheer for expressivism and genealogy, but a boo for one distinctive aspect of the quasi-realist's version of these ideas, namely, the view that quasi-realism can remain a local doctrine.

7. The Eleatic Equivocation

There are two sides to this conclusion, the general pro-expressivist aspect and the more specific anti (local) quasi-realist aspect. One reason that both aspects have been overlooked, presumably, is that the representationalist conception of language is so deeply entrenched that it has been hard to see how directly it is challenged by semantic minimalism—hard to see what a radical thesis semantic minimalism is, in this sense. (So much the worse for semantic realism, perhaps—more on this possibility later.)

Another reason has to do with the dialectics of contemporary expressivist positions. Seeing themselves as local views, these theories come to the field with an interest in maintaining the representationalist picture, while reducing its domain. In that context, writers concerned to defend expressivism against the supposed threat of semantic minimalism seem to have confused two tasks. One task is that of arguing that semantic minimalism leaves plenty of room for differentiation, in an expressivist key—that it doesn't "make everything the same." The other is that of arguing that semantic minimalism leaves room for a particular kind of differentiation, namely, that between genuinely representational and non-representational uses of language. The strength of the expressivist's case for the first point has perhaps obscured the weakness of the argument for the second. The two conclusions haven't been properly distinguished, and the strong argument has tended to shield its weaker sibling.

The most popular argument for the second point—that is, for the defense of the "bifurcation thesis" (as it is called by Kraut [1990], following Rorty)—appeals to what we might call the Eleatic Criterion. The central thought goes something like this. We need to appeal to trees to explain our use of the term "tree," but we don't need to appeal to goodness to explain our use of the term "good." So we should interpret talk of trees "really" realistically, but talk of goodness only quasi-realistically (see Blackburn 1984: 257; 1998b: 80; Kraut 1990; and Dreier 2004, for example, for various versions of this suggestion).

This is an appealing idea, and the Eleatic Criterion may well mark some distinction of interest. However, there are some interesting reasons for doubting whether it draws a line where its proponents would like to draw a line—say, around scientific claims.[15] More importantly for present purposes, semantic minimalism entails that any distinction drawn this way simply can't be a distinction between those utterances that do stand in substantial semantic relations to the world and those that do not. But since that's what it would take to distinguish representational from non-representational uses of language, the Eleatic Criterion can't provide a way of retaining the bifurcation thesis, in the face of semantic minimalism. If the Eleatic Criterion could ground the bifurcation thesis, in other words, that would show that semantic minimalism is simply false—that substantial semantic notions can be built on eleatic considerations.

Thus the Eleatic Criterion can't save expressivists from the following dilemma: either (i) they reject semantic minimalism, building substantial semantic relations on some basis or other (eleatic or otherwise); or (ii) they concede that their expressivism is a global position (albeit one with plenty of scope for distinctions of a non-semantic kind—including some, perhaps, marked by the Eleatic Criterion itself). The latter horn is the one that we recommend—our global anthropological pragmatism, or global expressivism. In a moment, we want to explain why the former horn ought to seem particularly unattractive, from a quasi-realist point of view.

Before we leave the Eleatic Criterion, however, there is another possible move to which we want to call attention. It might be suggested that the proper role of the Eleatic Criterion is not to underpin a *semantic* distinction between genuinely descriptive and quasi-descriptive discourse, but a *metaphysical* distinction, between ontology that deserves our allegiance as realists and ontology that does not.[16] Here, we simply want to point out that this move is out of bounds to a quasi-realist such a Blackburn himself, for at least two reasons. The first is that it would challenge his metaphysical quietism, his insistence in speaking with the folk on the topics to which he applies the quasi-realist treatment—his rejection of error theories, for example. The second is that it would mean that quasi-realism was simply tilling the wrong patch of ground, in taking emulation of realism to be a matter of entitlement to the semantic trimmings: to being treated as "true" and "false," for example. Quasi-realism would require quasi-causation, not quasi-truth.

15. Briefly, one large issue concerns the status of causal discourse, which is arguably both properly treated in expressivist terms, and essential in science. An even deeper issue, perhaps, turns on the status of logical and conceptual generality. Plausibly, the relevant explanations of our use of general terms depends only on the particular instances we and our ancestors happen to have encountered in the past—generality itself seems to play no explanatory role. This point—closely related to the rule-following considerations, apparently—suggests that no interesting part of language really meets the explanatory test. Finally, and in a different vein, it is arguable (see Price 1997a) that much of the appeal of the eleatic intuition rests on a kind of perspectival fallacy: of course the ontology invoked in the explanations in question looks privileged, in those contexts; but so it should, for the explanatory perspective is itself scientific!

16. This is Armstrong's (1997: 41) "Eleatic Principle."

8. Blackburn as Global Quasi-realist?

At some points, Blackburn himself comes very close to accepting the latter horn of the above dilemma. Here, for example, is a passage in which he is arguing that Wright is blind to the distinctions permitted in Ramsey's and Wittgenstein's view of the matter—and blind, in particular, to the fact that these distinctions are thoroughly compatible with Ramsey's thin notion of truth.

> The point is that Ramsey and Wittgenstein do not need to work with a sorted notion of *truth*—robust, upright, hard truth versus some soft and effeminate imitation. They need to work with a sorted notion of a *proposition*, or if we prefer it a sorted notion of *truth-aptitude*. There are propositions properly theorized about in one way, and ones properly theorized about in another. The focus of theory is the nature of the commitment voiced by one adhering to the proposition, and the different functional roles in peoples' lives (or forms of life, or language games) that these different commitments occupy. Indeed, I should say that although a good title for the position might be "non-descriptive functionalism," Wittgenstein could even afford to throw "description" into the minimalist pot. Even if we have to say that all commitments describe their coordinate slices of reality, we can still say that they are to be theorized about in a *distinctive* way. You come at them differently, offering a different theory of their truth-aptitude (again, this ought not to be uncongenial to Wright, since it is only extending the very kind of move he himself makes to rehabilitate versions of the realism debate, in the face of minimalism about truth). You may end up, that is, saying that these assertions describe how things are with values, probability, modality, and the rest. But the way you arrive at this bland result will be distinctive, and it will be the bit that matters. (1998a: 166–167)[17]

Indeed, we say, but where this leads is global quasi-realism! It leads to a view in which all the interesting theoretical work, including any contribution from the Eleatic Criterion, is done on the positive, non-representational, side of the expressivist's account. There is sorting, in other words, but no sorting conducted in a representational key—everything is done in pragmatic terms.[18]

17. Compare Blackburn (1998b: 77–83) for a more detailed discussion of this "Wittgensteinian" option. Note that Blackburn (1990, 1993d) had previously interpreted Wittgenstein as a *local* quasi-realist, so the above view seems to marks a shift.

18. We suspect that Ramsey, too, never saw this point—like Blackburn, his expressivism was a kind of halfway house, whose foundations were considerably weakened by his failure to see that he needed to abandon representationalism altogether, in order to cast the view in a stable form. On a related aspect of this instability, see Holton and Price (2003).

9. The Internal Challenge

To resist this conclusion a (local) quasi-realist needs to take the first horn of the dilemma—in other words, to be non-minimalist about truth and associated semantic notions. As a friend of semantic minimalism, Blackburn himself would find this option highly uncongenial. Indeed, he ought to find it so for a reason more basic than a mere preference for semantic minimalism. This horn of the dilemma is inherently unappealing, from a quasi-realist's point of view, for a reason connected to what we called the internal version of the pressure towards globalization.

To see why, note that what is distinctive and admirable about quasi-realism is that, unlike less careful forms of expressivism, it takes seriously the need to explain the representational appearances—the various respects in which the target discourses "behave like" genuinely representational parts of language. But this exposes it to a familiar challenge, which might be formulated like this:

> "Suppose you (the quasi-realist) succeed in explaining, on expressivist foundations, why non-descriptive claims behave like (what you take to be) genuinely descriptive claims. If these explanations work in the hard cases, such as moral and aesthetic judgements, then it seems likely that they'll work in the easy cases, too—i.e., for scientific judgements. In other words, your "lite" or quasi semantic notions will suffice to explain not only why moral judgements are treated as truth-apt, but equally why scientific claims are treated in this way. But then the claim that the easy cases are genuinely descriptive—i.e., have some more substantial kind of semantic property—seems problematic in one of two ways. Either it is an idle cog, not needed to explain the relevant aspects of the use of the statements in question; or, if it is associated with some characteristic of use that the merely quasi kind of truth cannot emulate, then it shows that quasi-realism is a sleight of hand—it fails to deliver the goods, just where it really matters. If it is really successful by your own standards, in other words, then your quasi-realism inevitably escapes from the box, and becomes a view with global application."

Why, then, is a non-minimalist view of semantic notions necessarily unattractive for a quasi-realist? Because it impales him on the horns of the new dilemma just mentioned: either his own methods render any thick component of his semantic theory an idle cog, unnecessary in accounting for the use of semantic vocabulary; or the failure of his methods to do so reveals a failure to achieve his own professed aims, of explaining how non-descriptive discourse can emulate the real thing.

Thus the option of appealing to a non-minimalist semantic theory, in order to meet the external version of the global challenge—that is, our argument that semantic minimalism entails global expressivism—is not one that a quasi-realist can easily entertain. And the problem turns on the internal version of the global challenge: on the fact that the more successful the quasi-realist program is in its own terms, the greater its difficulty in not swallowing everything. Since the current sweeping the quasi-realist towards globalization is driven by his program's own engines, he cannot invoke substantial semantic notions to stem the flow, without putting a spanner in his own works.

Once again, however, we want to emphasize there is an attractive alternative close at hand. It is global solution represented by our brand of pragmatism, or global expressivism. The near-invisibility of this alternative in contemporary philosophy seems due in large part to the enormous inertia of the representationalist orthodoxy. The point we've stressed is that to the extent that semantic minimalism is taken seriously—as it has been, in many hands, in twentieth-century philosophy—it actually sweeps away the foundations of this orthodoxy. But far from sweeping away, with it, the diversity of the things that expressivists want to claim that we do with assertoric language, the effect is to reveal the underlying diversity to the theoretician's gaze, unencrusted with the dogma that it is all just DESCRIBING.

This concludes the main argument of this chapter. In the two remaining sections, we want to elaborate two aspects of the picture we have outlined so far. In section 10 we sketch the view of language that this form of pragmatism entails. Crucially, as we'll explain, it combines differentiation at one level with homogeneity at another—a single assertoric tool or template, capable of being put to work in the service of many different projects—with both levels being properly investigated in pragmatic terms. In section 11, finally, we return to the theme of quietism, and offer a taxonomy intended to clarify the analogies and disanalogies between the various positions that have been in play.

10. The Puzzle of Many in One

We began with Blackburn's attempts to defend the possibility of linguistic diversity, in the face of a flood of homogeneity thought by some to spring from quietism and minimalism. We've agreed with Blackburn on most points, but argued that the flood does sweep away any merely local version of expressivism or quasi-realism. At this point, however, readers may feel that they've been shown a kind of conjuring trick. As we ourselves have emphasized, our view has less diversity than that of a local quasi-realist, because it lacks a distinction between genuine and merely quasi-description. It is the same thin or quasi-semantic notions, in our picture, across the entire linguistic landscape. But where, then, is the promised diversity? Are we claiming that these same thin semantic notions have different functions in different areas? Surely they are both too thin and too homogeneous for that to be the case?

This challenge calls attention to a feature of our view that deserves greater emphasis. It is, indeed, highly implausible—especially for a semantic minimalist—that there is not a certain unity to basic applications of semantic predicates, in different domains of discourse. If truth is merely a device for disquotation, it has that same function, surely, no matter what the content of the sentences to which it attaches?

One way to see that this needn't be incompatible with the idea that those sentences themselves might have different functions and genealogies, as a pragmatist maintains, is to examine the corresponding point in a broader context. It is highly plausible that there are certain more-or-less universal features of assertion and judgement—for example, to borrow Brandom's (1994) way of looking at these matters, a common practice of undertaking commitments, and "giving and asking for reasons." In some sense, it seems, there is simply one grand language game in which we do these things. The overarching unity of applications of a disquotational truth predicate might be viewed as one small aspect of the broader unity of this "Assertion Game."[19]

What needs to be established is that broad unity at this level is compatible with differentation at a lower level, of the kind our pragmatism requires. It isn't immediately obvious that this is possible, and indeed the task of showing that it is possible takes rather different forms, depending on whether one is a global or merely local pragmatist. Blackburn's local quasi-realist will presumably come to the table with some ready-made (Fregean?) theory of how the relevant phenomena are to be explained in the genuinely descriptive domains, where there isn't a need to accommodate underlying functional diversity (at least of the relevant kind). The task is then to show how bits of language with different basic functions can then properly emulate the surface characteristics of the genuinely descriptive domains.

Global pragmatism requires a different approach. Since it rejects representationalism altogether, it cannot begin by assuming that there is a class of cases for which the explanation of the surface phenomena is already available, at least in principle. In one sense, however, abandoning this assumption makes things easier. We pragmatists can begin with a clean slate, and look for a unitary account of roles and genealogy of the Assertion Game. In particular, we can look for an account which leaves room for underlying diversity, of the kind needed to accommodate the intuitions that we share with merely local quasi-realists, that there are important senses in which different bits of language do different jobs.

We don't have space here to make a detailed case that this is possible, but we want to mention a proposal that one of us has outlined elsewhere (Price 1988,

19. However, it is questionable whether the disquotational account of the function of the truth predicate is adequate, in this context. See Price (1988, 2003) for a defense an alternative version of deflationism, based on the proposal that the truth predicate has a richer, essentially normative, role in discourse.

2004b), to give some sense of how a case might go. The proposal starts with the thought that many of our proto-linguistic psychological states might be such that it would be advantageous, with respect to those states, that we tend toward conformity across our communities. Assertoric language seems to facilitate and encourage such alignment—within the Assertion Game, we give voice to our psychological dispositions in ways that invite challenges by speakers with contrary dispositions. ("That's false" and "That's true" are markers of challenge and concession, respectively—cf. Price [1988; 2003].)

As ordinary speakers, of course, we don't understand that this is what assertoric language is for—we just do it, as it were, and from our point of view, seem to be "saying how things are." But the function of this practice of "saying how things are" is the one in the background—the function of altering our behaviorally significant commitments much more rapidly than our individual experience in the environment could do, by giving us access to the corresponding states of our fellows (and much else besides).

The suggestion is thus that "representational" language is a tool for aligning commitments across a speech community. But though in this sense a single tool, it is a tool with many distinct applications, corresponding to the distinct primary functions of the various kinds of psychological states that take advantage of it—that facilitate their own alignment by expressing themselves in assertoric form. And none of these primary functions is representation as such, in the traditional sense—there are no substantial semantic properties in the picture.

Wittgenstein is well-known for the view that the surface uniformity of language masks underlying diversity, and, as we noted in the previous chapter, one of the analogies he offers in support of this idea in the *Investigations* fits this two-level functional architecture particularly nicely. Speaking of what we see as we look at the linguistic "surface," Wittgenstein offers this comparison:

> It is like looking into the cabin of a locomotive. We see handles all looking more or less alike. (Naturally, since they are all supposed to be handled.) But one is the handle of a crank which can be moved continuously (it regulates the opening of a valve); another is the handle of a switch, which has only two effective positions, it is either off or on; a third is the handle of a brake-lever, the harder one pulls on it, the harder it brakes; a fourth, the handle of a pump: it has an effect only so long as it is moved to and fro. (Wittgenstein 1968: #12)

In one sense, as Wittgenstein's stresses, the various different handles have very different functions. But they are all "designed to be handled." In that sense, then, they are members of a category with a significant functional unity—a unity not possessed by the more assorted tools ("a screw-driver, a rule, a glue-pot, glue . . .") of another of Wittgenstein's examples.

So here's the proposal, as our pragmatist sees it. Thinking of the function of assertions uniformly as representation misses important functional distinctions—distinctions we can't put back in just by appealing to differences in what is represented. To get the direction of explanation right, we need to begin with pragmatic differences, differences among the kinds of things that the assertions in question *do* (or more accurately, perhaps, differences among the kinds of things that their underlying psychological states *do*, for complex creatures in a complex environment). And to get the unity right, we need to note than in their different ways, all of these tasks are tasks whose verbal expressions appropriately invoke the kind of multipurpose tool that assertion in general *is*. To say this, we need to say what kind of tool it is—what general things we do with it that we couldn't do otherwise. If the answer is in part that we expose our commitments to criticism by our fellows, then the point will be that this may be a useful thing to do, for commitments with a range of different functional roles (none of them representation as such).

11. Varieties of Quietism

We began with Blackburn's remarks about a "contemporary river that sometimes calls itself pragmatism." In recommending our own alternative form of pragmatism, we have agreed with Blackburn, in the main, in resisting the "smooth, undifferentiated view of language" that flows from the river in question. Yet as Blackburn notes, the philosophers who ride this river often call themselves minimalists, deflationists, or quietists. We, too, have claimed these labels, at various points—as does Blackburn himself, in certain respects. How, then, do we (and he) avoid being swept downstream?

The trick is to distinguish several different matters with respect to which it is possible to be a philosophical quietist. In this final section, we want to sketch a taxonomy of this kind. This will make it obvious how quietism in one key can be compatible with non-quietism in another—and hence, therefore, how there is room for the kind of stance that we and Blackburn wish to adopt, in opposition to the homogenizing river. As we'll see, it also provides a sharp way of distinguishing our kind of pragmatism from local quasi-realism.

For present purposes, quietism about a particular vocabulary amounts to a rejection of that vocabulary, for the purposes of philosophical theory. This may or may not involve a rejection of the vocabulary in question for other purposes. Thus, to return to our theological example, a theological quietist is not merely agnostic about the issues that divide theists from atheists. She rejects theological discourse altogether, at least as a vocabulary for theoretical investigation. She may reject it for all purposes, simply declining to play that language game at all; or she may regard it as playable with some other point. In the latter case, her attitude is analogous to that of a typical semantic deflationist, who doesn't want to abandon the truth predicate altogether, but merely to insist that it has no independent role to play in marking a legitimate topic of theoretical investigation.

Concerning the issues we have been discussing, there are three main topics or vocabularies, with respect to which quietism is a possibility. The first involves metaphysical issues, the second semantic and representational issues, and the third the broadly anthropological issues about language, emphasized by our kind of explanatory pragmatist. In principle, perhaps, one might be a quietist about any combination of these three topics, giving eight possible variations. In practice, the five options listed in table 11.1 seem particularly significant.

Option A is the position occupied by many contemporary metaphysicians.[20] It accepts that that there is a legitimate metaphysical or ontological standpoint for philosophy, and also a non-minimalist view of semantic notions such as truth and reference. Finally, it also recognizes as a well-founded theoretical inquiry the project of explaining various aspects of linguistic usage—our use of causal or moral terms, for example. It is likely to regard these three areas of theoretical investigation as closely connected, of course. It might regard metaphysics as a search for truthmakers, for example, thus connecting (at least) the first and the second investigations.

Option B represents a different kind of metaphysics, a view that rejects the linguistic methods of contemporary metaphysics on the grounds that the semantic notions are too thin to bear the weight. Stephen Stich (1996) defends a position somewhat like this, arguing that it is a mistake to think of the issue as to whether there are beliefs and desires as the question as to whether the terms "belief" and "desire" actually refer to anything. Stich's case rests not so much on semantic minimalism as such, as on an argument that there is no prospect of a theory of reference that would adequately decide the issue, one way or the other. But semantic minimalism has the same effect.

Table 11.1. **Options for quietism**

	Metaphysical quietism	*Representational quietism*	*Use-explanatory quietism*
A	No	No	No
B	No	Yes	No
C	Yes	No	No
D	Yes	Yes	No
E	Yes	Yes	Yes

20. Jackson (1998) provides a particularly good example.

Option C corresponds to the attitude of local quasi-realism toward the domains it takes to involve "quasi" commitments. Concerning moral discourse, for example, we saw that (the original, non-global) Blackburn was not a quietist about the question whether moral commitments are genuinely descriptive—on the contrary, he regarded it as a substantial theoretical discovery that they are not. Having reached that conclusion, he then regards the metaphysical issues as mute, *for that case*. So he is a metaphysical quietist about the topic in question, but no other kind of quietist: there was the substantial issue just mentioned in the second column, and Blackburn is certainly not a quietist in the third column—on the contrary, that's where he takes the really interesting theoretical work to be.

Option D is our kind of pragmatism. The table helps to make clear what's right and what's wrong about characterizing our view as global quasi-realism, or describing quasi-realism as a local variety of pragmatism. What's right about the characterization is that our view does globally what quasi-realism does locally, *in columns 1 and 3*—namely, it combines metaphysical quietism with an interest in the issues that mark a radically non-quietist attitude to the use-explanatory issues in the third column. What's wrong about the characterization is that the two views never agree in column 2. The quasi-realist holds that there is always a substantial issue as to whether a domain of commitment is genuinely descriptive, or representational (and takes quasi-realism to be appropriate when the answer is that it is not); whereas our pragmatist holds that there is never a substantial issue of this kind.

Option E, finally, recommends quietism in all three modes. Some interpreters of Wittgenstein read him in these terms—among them, presumably, the interpreters that Blackburn has in mind, in the passage with which we began, when he says that Wittgenstein is often admired as a high priest of the crusade to deny differences and celebrate "the seamless web of language." In earlier work, noting that this reading flies in the face of the fact that Wittgenstein repeatedly emphasizes that the surface uniformity of linguistic forms masks deep differences in the things we do with language, Blackburn (1990: 1993d) had proposed that Wittgenstein should be interpreted as a (local) quasi-realist—albeit one who leaves "unfinished business" (1993d: 589), in failing to address the issue of explaining how we can continue to speak of truth, fact, knowledge, and so forth, in the non-descriptive discourses. This is the task undertaken by the quasi-realist, of course. Hence Wittgenstein is only a proto–quasi-realist, on this reading.

As we have already noted, however, Blackburn's view of Wittgenstein seems to have changed. In the paper with which we began, and in another work (1998b) from the same year, Blackburn offers Wittgenstein as a model of what we've termed a global quasi-realist, who throws even the term description "into the minimalist pot." On this view, then—having thrown the representational notions into the pot—Wittgenstein emerges as our kind of pragmatist, a representational quietist, and belongs in row D.

We close by noting that there is another possible reading, which does locate Wittgenstein on row E—a philosophical quietist in all modes—without ignoring his insistence that language is not a "seamless web." The key is to read Wittgenstein as interested in *description*, rather than *explanation*. He calls our attention to the differences, according to this reading of his project, but doesn't regard it as part of the task of philosophy to try to explain them. In particular, he doesn't regard the sideways, third-person stance of our anthropological pragmatists as an available *philosophical* stance.

At this point, there are two possibilities. One takes Wittgenstein to acknowledge that there are significant questions of the kind the pragmatist wants to ask, but to regard them as scientific issues, rather than philosophical issues. The other is more radical, taking Wittgenstein to maintain that there is no legitimate theoretical stance of this kind at all, philosophical or scientific. The former possibility is no challenge to our kind of pragmatism as such, but only its right to call itself philosophy. We have no strong views on this matter. (If pressed, we could always follow Peirce's famous lead, inventing a new name for the enterprise.)

The second possibility is more serious, and connects with deep and interesting issues about the nature and possibility of theorizing about language. These are issues for another time, however. Our task here has been to distinguish our kind of pragmatism from its less quietist neighbors, and especially from quasi-realism. Pragmatism agrees with quasi-realism that the use-explanatory issues in the third column are no place for quietism—on the contrary, they are some of the most interesting issues in philosophy, and worthy of much noise indeed. But the pragmatist insists that the noise should be that of a single voice, singing only in the key that these issues themselves demand, and resisting the temptation to mix its melody with the familiar but discredited themes of metaphysics and representationalism.

For our part, we've urged, in particular, that minimalism about truth and reference leads to this kind of pragmatism. Whistled down the years by such distinguished lips as Wittgenstein, Ramsey, and Quine, semantic minimalism has long been a melody that everybody in philosophy has in their head. What's surprising, in our view, is that so few people have realized how it finishes: with the last quiet gasp of representationalism itself, as pragmatism prepares to sing.

12

The Semantic Foundations of Metaphysics

1. From Metaphysics to Ethics, via Semantics?

In the first chapter of *From Metaphysics to Ethics*, Frank Jackson begins, as he puts it, "by explaining how serious metaphysics by its very nature raises the location problem" (1998: 1). He gives us two examples of location problems. The first concerns semantic properties, such as truth and reference:

> Some physical structures are true. For example, if I were to utter a token of the type "Grass is green," the structure I would thereby bring into existence would be true . . . How are the semantic properties of the sentence related to the non-semantic properties of the sentence? Where, if anywhere, are the semantic properties of truth, content and reference to be found in the non-semantic, physical or naturalistic account of the sentence? (1998: 2)

Jackson notes two possible answers to questions of this kind. The first denies that there are any such semantic properties:

> We might respond with a sceptical or eliminativist position on truth, meaning and reference. Sentences . . . are a species of physical object, and we know that science can in principle tell us the whole story about physical objects. And though we are not, and may never be, in a position actually to give that whole story, we know enough as of now to be able to say, first, that it will look something like . . . a story about masses, shapes, causal chains, behavioural dispositions of language users, evolutionary history, and the like . . . and, secondly, that in any case it will not contain terms for truth, reference and meaning. But if the complete account does not contain truth, reference, and meaning, then so much the worse for truth, reference, and meaning, runs the sceptical response. (1998: 2)

Jackson contrasts this skeptical response with the response he favors, which rests on "distinguishing what appears explicitly in an account from what appears implicitly in it" (1998: 2). This is the idea that he goes on to develop in the book in considerable detail.

The case of the semantic properties deserves its prominence, I think, though for reasons Jackson himself does not mention at this point. Certain assumptions about language, naturally cast in semantic terms, are crucial to Jackson's conception of the task of philosophy in the cases he calls location problems. These assumptions underpin the most natural path to the view that there is a distinctively metaphysical problem for philosophy to address, as opposed to a problem of a broadly anthropological kind, about human linguistic behavior—in this case, about the use of the semantic terms, "true," "refers," and the like.

Jackson is aware of the need for these assumptions, of course. However, I think he underestimates the work needed to justify them, and hence the extent of the threat that they pose to the foundations of his program. By making the assumptions explicit, and by arguing that we need to take seriously the possibility that they might fail,[1] I hope to show that the foundations are in need of reinforcement; indeed, that there is a serious issue about the advisability of the enterprise, at least in Jackson's ambitious form. There's an alternative conception of what philosophy should be up to in this area—a conception, as I said, that regards the main task as more like anthropology than metaphysics. And the issue as to which is the right conception is not to be settled by philosophy, but by the science of human linguistic behavior, broadly construed. So there is an important sense in which the anthropological viewpoint should come first.

Jackson's approach is not peculiarly at fault here. On the contrary, the linguistic assumptions in question are implicit in a great deal of contemporary metaphysics. The attraction of Jackson's program, for my purposes, is that in virtue of its clarity and would-be comprehensiveness, its semantic foundations are comparatively easy to bring into view. But most of the concerns thus exposed apply much more widely, I think.[2]

2. Deflationism and the Location Problem for Semantic Properties

Let's begin with a familiar approach to semantic notions such as reference and truth, namely, *deflationism* or *minimalism*. A number of ideas go under these headings. For present purposes, I'll take the central claim to be that truth and

1. A lot will turn on a distinction between two kinds of failure. Roughly, one involves the endorsement of the negation of the relevant semantic assumptions, the other—the more interesting, in my view—the abandonment *for theoretical purposes* of the semantic notions in terms of which the assumptions are expressed.

2. If Jackson's approach has a distinctive vulnerability, it turns on the fact that it is intended to be comprehensive. More on this later.

reference are not "substantial" properties—not properties needed in the theoretical ontology of a mature science of human linguistic behavior, or of a kind whose nature is properly investigated by science or metaphysics. On the contrary, say deflationists, the task of philosophy is to explain the distinctive role of the semantic *terms*—"true," "refers," and the like—in linguistic practice. And the function of these terms is not to refer to substantial properties, about whose nature there might be a serious philosophical question. Rather, for example, it might be that they play a distinctive grammatical role, providing a logical device for sundry purposes (for example, for expressing infinite conjunctions, as in "Everything Fred says is true").

Deflationist views are cousins of what Jackson calls the "sceptical or eliminativist position" about semantic properties.[3] Like that position, one of their claimed attractions is that they make short work of metaphysical puzzles about reference and truth. For a deflationist, these puzzles rest on a philosophical confusion about the linguistic role of the terms concerned. In Jackson's terms, the claim is that if deflationists are right about the linguistic job of the semantic *predicates*, then there is no location problem for semantic *properties*.

Deflationism is controversial, of course. I have defended a version of it elsewhere (Price 1988; 2003), but won't be trying to do so here—or at least not directly. Rather, I want to use the fact that deflationism is a well-recognized position in the relevant landscape, to call attention to some presuppositions of the program that Jackson advocates in *From Metaphysics to Ethics* and elsewhere. By showing that semantic deflationism would undercut an otherwise attractive foundation for metaphysics as Jackson understands it, I want to show that in its present form, the program presupposes that deflationism is false. This will establish that the program relies on certain empirical assumptions about language, in a way which deserves more prominence than it receives in Jackson's presentation, in my view. I'll argue that these assumptions are harder to justify than Jackson takes them to be.

Jackson's own stance with respect to deflationism also deserves scrutiny, it seems to me. On the one hand, as we'll see, he often seems robustly realist about semantic notions, and the representationalist view of language with which they go hand in hand.[4] On the other hand, in the passage from which I quoted at the

3. Nothing much hangs on how closely deflationism is related to the views Jackson has in mind, but it is worth noting this difference. Deflationism is not typically an eliminativist position—not a view that agrees, as Jackson puts it, that "if the complete [scientific] account does not contain truth, reference, and meaning, then so much the worse for truth, reference, and meaning." On the contrary, say deflationists, it is a mistake to look for truth and reference in the scientific account, and hence no black mark against them if they are not to be found there.

4. Later in the paper, I want to argue that various commonplace observations about language that Jackson appears to take as supporting this view do not bear the weight, being thoroughly compatible with deflationist views.

beginning, he appears to say that it is clear that a scientific account of linguistic tokens—utterances and written sentences, for example—"will not contain terms for truth, reference and meaning." On the face of it, this sounds like a version of the deflationist claim that semantic properties have no essential role in a mature science of human language. If Jackson's view is interpreted this way, then my argument has particular bite. For as things stand, I maintain, the implicit assumption that semantic properties do have an important theoretical role is playing a crucial role in motivating Jackson's view of the task of metaphysics, in the semantic case itself as well as in others.

If I am right about the role of this assumption, there seem to be two ways in which we might try to reconcile it with the view here endorsed by Jackson, that a scientific account of the occurrence of linguistic tokens will not employ semantic terminology. The first would rely on a direct appeal to folk intuitions and practice—to folk use of the semantic vocabulary, in effect. However, leaving aside concerns we should surely feel about allowing the folk to lead us into theoretical territory where science itself declines to tread, we'll see that such an appeal is only helpful if we can *exclude* a deflationary interpretation of the role of the folk vocabulary, which is the very point at issue.

The second option (Jackson's own choice, I think) would be to argue that the semantic facts on which the assumption depends are implicit in the scientific story—the representational view is implicit in the scientific view. This option thus relies on Jackson's proposed solution to the location problem for semantic properties. As I'll argue, however, both the problem and the solution depend on the very assumption here at issue, namely, a semantically characterized representational view of folk use of semantic vocabulary. So there's no comfort here for someone looking for a scientifically respectable reason to believe that assumption.

More at the end of the paper about this apparent circularity problem, and related issues. For the moment, I'm interested simply in exploring the consequences of deflationism for the task and scope of metaphysics as Jackson understands it—in particular, for the existence of location problems. I'll need the following two observations about the commitments of semantic deflationism.

Properties Thick and Thin

First, deflationists needn't say that there are no semantic properties. On the contrary, to the extent that folk usage is committed to claiming that there are such properties, deflationists can concur—can speak with the folk, in effect. But the deflationist insists that once we understand the functions of the corresponding terms in language, we can see that there isn't any metaphysical problem about the nature or "location" of these properties. As Paul Horwich says:

> [I]t is not part of the minimalist conception to maintain that truth is not a property. On the contrary, "is true" is a perfectly good English predicate—and (leaving aside nominalistic concerns about the very notion of "property") one might well take this to be a conclusive criterion for standing for a property of *some* sort. What the minimalist wishes to emphasize, however, is that truth is not a complex or naturalistic property but a property of some other kind. . . . The point behind this jargon is that different kinds of property correspond to different roles that predicates play in our language, and that unless these differences are appreciated, we will be tempted to raise questions regarding one sort that can legitimately arise only in connection with another sort. (Horwich 1998: 37–38)

A caution is needed here about Horwich's use of "standing for." This sounds like a semantic notion, but if so, a deflationist can't expect it to bear theoretical weight. The main point of deflationism is that semantic notions do not bear theoretical weight.

More on this potential inconsistency in a moment. In the present context, one way to avoid it is simply to note—as the rest of the passage says, in effect—that there is a loose and popular use of the notion of a property, according to which, so to speak, where go predicates, there go properties. In this sense, there is certainly a property of truth. But this use of "property" needs to be distinguished from its use in serious science and metaphysics, precisely because these disciplines need to be sensitive to the fact that predicates may play different linguistic roles, in a way which isn't evident on the surface. Truth is thus a property in the loose, popular or "thin" sense, says the deflationist, but not in the scientific, metaphysical or "thick" sense.

Two Ways of Rejecting Semantic Theory

The second point relates to the kind of inconsistency just noted. Paul Boghossian (1990) has argued that irrealism about semantic properties is incoherent, because the irrealist wants to claims that terms such as "true" and "refers" *do not refer to anything*, or that sentences ascribing such semantic properties *lack truth values* (or, perhaps, *are uniformly false*). The essence of Boghossian's objection is that the italicized claims involve, centrally and ineliminably, the very notions with respect to which the semantic irrealist professes irrealism. Surely this involves some sort of vicious circularity?

In the present context, our interest is in a specific form of irrealism about semantic notions, namely, deflationism, characterized as the view that these notions play no substantial or ineliminable role in linguistic theory. Against such a view, Boghossian's charge takes a more specific form. Isn't the deflationist is employing the notions concerned "in her theoretical voice," in characterizing her own deflationist view? This is precisely the inconsistency we noted a moment ago, concerning the semantic notion of "standing for."

But the objection is easily side-stepped. We simply need to distinguish between (i) *denying* (in one's theoretical voice) that ascriptions of semantic properties have semantic properties; and (ii) *saying nothing* (in one's theoretical voice) about whether ascriptions of semantic properties have semantic properties—that is, simply employing different theoretical vocabulary, in saying what one wants to say about such ascriptions. A deflationist cannot consistently do (i), but can consistently do (ii). Let's call (i) *active rejection* and (ii) *passive rejection* of the theoretical claim that ascriptions of semantic properties have semantic properties. (Like passive aggression, then, passive rejection involves strategic silence.)

Here's an analogy: Unlike Creationists, Darwinians don't think that the species were created by God. Does this mean that Darwinians must use the term "God" in their theoretical voice, as it were, in order to *deny* that the species were created by God? Not at all. Darwinians simply offer an account of the origin of the species in which the term "God" does not appear. So *rejecting* the view that God created the species does not require *accepting* the following claim: God did not create the species. The alternative—the correct alternative, surely—is passive rejection: simply avoiding theological vocabulary in scientific contexts.

Similarly, rejecting the view that ascriptions of semantic predicates are referential—rejecting it *as a theoretical view*—does not require that we endorse a *negative* claim, in which the semantic terms are employed in our theoretical voice. Passive rejection provides an alternative, and arguably the only consistent alternative. From now on, then, I assume that semantic deflationism takes this passive form. It doesn't say that ascriptions of semantic properties *lack* semantic properties.

Deflationism thus provides a familiar and apparently coherent view, from standpoint of which the location problem for the semantic properties *seems* not to arise. It might be suggested that this impression is mistaken—that the particular form of deflationism just outlined does not escape the location problem. I'll come back to this, but suppose for the moment that deflationism does avoid the location problem, for the semantic properties. Then, as already noted, it provides a relative of the skeptical or eliminativist approach, that Jackson himself mentions as avoiding this particular location problem. Not particularly new news, in other words.

But there is newer news nearby, I think. I want to argue that semantic deflationism not only provides an example of how the location problem may be defused for the semantic properties themselves, but also a strategy for defusing location problems about other topics. More accurately, semantic deflationism blocks a particular route to location problems—a route that otherwise carries a lot of traffic. Blocking this route doesn't necessarily imply that there are no interesting location problems in metaphysics. There may be other ways of getting to the same place, at least in some cases. But it does suggest that such problems may be rarer than Jackson thinks, and in need of foundations he does not provide.

But does semantic deflationism even promise old news, given the constraints of the two observations made above? It is easy enough to see how the location problem for semantic properties is avoided by someone who says that there are no semantic properties, or that ascriptions of semantic predicates do not represent things as being a certain way. In these cases, of course, there can be no distinctive puzzle raised by semantic language about nature of semantic properties or "ways of being"—or about the relation of such things to the properties or "ways of being" talked about elsewhere. For there simply are no such things, full stop. But if a deflationist agrees that there are semantic properties, at least in the loose and popular sense, and does not actively *deny* that ascriptions of semantic predicates are representational in nature, doesn't the location problem still bite?

I'll meet this challenge by showing that the new news confirms the old news. As I said, I'm going to argue that there is one very general route to location problems that is blocked by the kind of semantic deflationism just canvassed. Having explained why such a semantic deflationism blocks an otherwise appealing route to location problems *in general*, I'll then be able to point out that the argument is self-applicable. This kind of semantic deflationism blocks the same route to the location problem about the semantic properties themselves. The new news thus grounds the old news.

3. Non-cognitivism, Deflationism, and Global Expressivism

The move to side-step metaphysics in the way exemplified by semantic deflationism has a long pedigree. Its most famous incarnation is non-cognitivism in ethics. Accordingly, when Jackson turns to ethics later in his book, he notes that he is assuming cognitivism. As he puts it:

> It is only under the assumption of cognitivism that ethics presents a location problem. If the non-cognitivists are right and ethical sentences do not represent things as being a certain way, there is no question of how to locate the way they represent things as being in relation to accounts told in other terms—descriptive, physical, social or whatever—represent things as being, though there will still, of course, be a need to give an account of the meaning of ethical sentences and of what we are

> doing when we make ethical judgements (where, of course, to make an ethical judgement better not be literally to take things to be some way or other). (1998: 117)

Jackson here relies on an explicitly semantic characterization of the difference between cognitivism and non-cognitivism about ethical claims. Cognitivists take ethical claims to "represent things as being a certain way," and non-cognitivists disagree. So understood, cognitivists and non-cognitivists are both relying on a non-deflationary view of the semantic properties, for they both use semantic or representationalist notions to characterize the function of ethical talk.

What, then, is the impact of adopting deflationism? Exploiting the distinction introduced earlier between active and passive rejection, I want to argue that deflationism about the semantic properties entails a view sufficiently close to non-cognitivism in ethics to defuse metaphysics in precisely the way that non-cognitivism itself does—by ensuring that it is not the case that "ethics presents a location problem" (or, more exactly, by defeating an influential reason for thinking that there is a location problem).

If I am right, the point has wide ramifications. Nothing hangs on the fact that the case in question is that of ethics. Quite generally, then, semantic deflationism blocks a certain route to location problems. As I've stressed, this does not mean that there could not be other routes to the same metaphysical issues. But there seem no candidates of the required generality on offer in Jackson's program, and none in the offing. The upshot is that on Jackson's conception, metaphysics seems to rest on "thick" semantic foundations: in particular, on a non-deflationary view of semantic properties.

In arguing that deflationism favors a view close to non-cognitivism, I'm swimming against the tide. Many writers have suggested that deflationism is an enemy of non-cognitivism. If truth is minimal, the thought goes, then it is easy for sentences to be truth-evaluable, and implausible to claim that moral claims are not truth-evaluable. Versions of the argument may be found in McDowell (1981), Boghossian (1990), Wright (1992), and Humberstone (1991). The argument is endorsed by Jackson himself in Jackson, Oppy, and Smith (1994), a paper proposing an escape route for non-cognitivism, relying on the argument that minimalism about truth need not imply minimalism about truth-aptness, and that it is non-minimalism about truth-aptness that matters for the non-cognitivist's purposes. I'll return to this issue later. For the moment, I'm arguing that the non-cognitivist does not need saving. In important respects, semantic deflationism already represents victory by default.

In my view, then, the orthodox view is almost completely wrongheaded. To see why, note first that non-cognitivism normally makes two claims about its target discourse, one negative and one positive. The negative claim says that these terms or statements lack some semantically characterized feature: they are non-referential, non-truth-apt, non-descriptive, non-factual, or something of the kind. The positive claim offers an alternative account of the functions of the language in question—for example, that it expresses, or projects from, evaluative attitudes. We might say that the negative claim is *anti-representational*, the positive claim *expressivist*.[5]

What is the effect on such a combination of views on deflationism about the semantic vocabulary in which the negative claim is couched? Clearly, the negative claim must be abandoned. But this doesn't imply that, qua theoreticians, we must endorse its negation (i.e., endorse cognitivism). On the contrary, what's sauce for the goose is sauce for the gander. If semantic terms can't be used in a "thick" sense, they can't be used on either side of a (thick) dispute as to whether evaluative claims are representational. Recall the Creationist analogy. If the term "God" has no place in science, then science neither affirms nor denies the sentence "God created the universe." The point of the example was that in cases like this, *not affirming* is not the same as *denying*.

So what is the effect of deflationism on non-cognitivism? It is to deflate the negative claim, while leaving intact the positive claim—the non-cognitivist's expressivist account of the function of the terms in question. Contrary to received wisdom, then, semantic minimalism is a friend and not an enemy of expressivism. If we take it that the expressivist's core claim is that the key functions of the judgments in question are not representational functions, then deflationism about the key semantic notions is a *global* motivation for expressivism—a global reason for thinking that whatever the interesting theoretical conclusion about the function of a class of judgments turns out to be, it cannot be that they are referential, or truth-conditional. For deflationism amounts to a denial that these notions *have* an interesting theoretical role.

One important point: The kind of expressivism thus supported by semantic minimalism is, crucially, *global* expressivism. The orthodoxy is right, in my view, to think that deflationism poses a problem for *local* varieties of non-cognitivism, or expressivism—views that are expressivist about some topics but representationalist about others. If representationalist vocabulary has no theoretical role, it can't be used to characterize the linguistic territory that, from a local expressivist's point of view, lies on the other side of the fence. The whole point is that deflationism implies that there can be no such territory, and hence no such fence. So deflationism does indeed make *local* expressivism unstable—but because it implies global expressivism, not because it implies global cognitivism!

5. This use of the term "expressivist" is to some extent a term of art. For example, disquotationalism about truth is expressivist in these terms, but doesn't rest on idea of expressing a psychological state. The defining feature of an expressivist view, in this sense, is that it theorizes about the use of language without employing semantic properties in its theoretical ontology.

4. Does Global Expressivism Avoid Location Problems?

Semantic deflationism thus implies the view I've called global expressivism.[6] In the form outlined in section 2 it also *exemplifies* such an expressivism. Recall that a crucial feature of that form of deflationism—the feature that enabled it to side-step Boghossian's objection—was that its rejection of the representational view of ascriptions of semantic properties was *passive*, rather than *active*. As a theoretical view, in other words, it makes no recourse to the semantic notions themselves.

At the end of section 2, I noted that it might be claimed that this version of semantic deflationism does not, after all, avoid the location problem for semantic properties. After all, it does not deny that there are semantic properties, or that such ascriptions represent things as being a certain way. On the contrary, it *allows* that there are semantic properties, at least in the loose and popular sense. And it *says nothing* (of a theoretical nature) about whether ascriptions of semantic properties represent things as being a certain way. (No doubt it allows this too, in the loose and popular sense.)

An analogous suggestion carries over quite generally to my modified form of non-cognitivism—the view that keeps the expressivist account of the functions of the part of language in question, while dropping the negative claim that language is not representational. So now we face the question deferred in section 2. Does this view avoid the location problem?

As foreshadowed in section 2, my claim is not that semantic deflationism provides an all-purpose defeater for location problems. Rather, I claim that deflationism blocks a particular route to such problems—albeit an important route, which otherwise provides a powerful and widely applicable theoretical motivation for taking such problems seriously. My claim rests on a distinction between what I'll call *ontologically conservative* and *ontologically non-conservative* ways of theorizing about language. Of course, any way of theorizing about language is going to have some ontological commitments—plausibly, at the very least, commitments to speakers, to speech acts of some kind, and probably to various environmental factors (to help to explain, for example, why such speakers produce such speech acts on such occasions). The distinction between ontologically conservative and ontologically non-conservative theories lies elsewhere. At a first pass, putting the matter in Carnapian terminology, it turns on the question as to whether linguistic theory picks up the *internal* ontological commitments of the linguistic frameworks *theorized about*.

6. Again, the term "expressivism" here means nothing more than that the views in question theorise about language in non-representational terms. See also O'Leary-Hawthorne and Price (1996) and Price (2004a, 2004b).

Recall the analogy I used in section 2 to illustrate the difference between active and passive rejection of a theoretical notion, the use of the notion of creation in biology or cosmology. Assuming for the sake of the example the principle "no creation without a creator," any theory which describes some or all of the entities within its ontology as *created* will thereby incur an ontological commitment to something (possibly) additional—that is, to the existence of one or more creators. For any X such that our theory entails that X is created, the theory thus raises the question "What is the Y, such that X is created by Y?" In one sense, this is a trivial point, turning simply on the fact that "is created by" is relational in form. The bite comes from the fact that as exemplified in Creationism itself, this relation is ontologically non-conservative—it relates biological and physical entities to something not itself part of the biological or physical realm.

Semantic relations have an analogous effect in linguistic theory. If we say as linguistic theorists that the term X *stands for* something, then our linguistic theory itself commits us—in general, at least, though we might want to allow for cases of referential failure—to the existence of something, Y, such that X stands for Y. The question "What is the Y, such that X stands for Y?" is thus a question pressed on us by linguistic theory—even if the Y at issue is something not normally regarded as part of the required ontology of linguistic theory, such as a prime number, or a moral property.

This is what I mean by saying that semantic relations make linguistic theory ontologically non-conservative. Ascribing semantic relations to a body of linguistic utterances commits linguistic theorists to an ontology which mirrors, via the semantic relations in question, the internal ontological commitments of the domain in question.[7] As I put it elsewhere (Price 2004a), semantic relations thus provide a bridge, or ladder, that leads our theoretical gaze from words to things.

It is easy to see how this gives rise to location problems. We find ourselves saying, in our theoretical voice, that terms such as "good," "seven," "cause," "belief," and "truth" do the job of *standing for* something. Naturally, we want an answer to the question "What do they stand for?" which meets various theoretical desiderata—fitting with the other kinds of things we are inclined to say about speakers, their environments and their capacities, for example. Hence, given our starting point, a pressure toward naturalistic answers—toward location problems.

Semantic deflationism generates no such pressure, however. Because it simply doesn't ascribe to terms and sentences such relational properties as *standing for*, *referring to*, or *being made true by*, it raises no such issues about the items at the "world's end" of such relations.

Now a crucial question: Does ontological conservatism require that we reject the representational view actively, affirming in our theoretical voice that the terms in question are non-representational? Or is passive rejection sufficient?

7. Again, this needs to be qualified to allow for the case of systematic referential failure.

A moment's reflection shows that passive rejection is all we need. The ontological non-conservatism of representational approaches is generated by their explicit employment of semantic relations. So long as these relations are simply *absent* from our theoretical vocabulary, no such "extra-linguistic" ontological commitment arises.

Thus the use of semantic notions in linguistic theory generates location problems, by rendering the theory in question ontologically non-conservative. Semantic deflationism blocks this path to location problems, even in the passively non-representational form canvassed in section 2. The kind of expressivism that results from such semantic deflationism provides a global bar to this route to location problems. Moreover, the point is self-applicable, in the way mentioned earlier. That is, this form of semantic deflationism blocks this semantic route to location problems about the semantic properties themselves just as efficiently as it blocks them about other topics.

5. A Reductio?

The argument that semantic deflationism deflates location problems might seem to provide a *reductio* of semantic deflationism. For isn't it obvious that there are some legitimate location problems—for chemical properties in relation to those of physics, for example? Doesn't the argument imply that if deflationism were true, we wouldn't need to worry about the relation of chemistry to physics (perhaps, and surely absurdly, because chemical language and physical language "are simply in different lines of work")?

But the argument implies no such absurdity. It simply implies (as in any case seems highly plausible) that our reasons for being interested in the relation of chemistry to physics don't depend on a lot of implicit linguistic theory. In exhibiting the sense in which chemistry and physics are in the same line of work, we can't simply rely on the claim that they are both representing how things are. If we are semantic deflationists, that characterization is both too thin and too broad to do the work that metaphysics requires of it. (Less metaphorically, relying on representational notions in this way would be incompatible with the central tenet of semantic deflationism, that the semantic properties do no significant theoretical work.)

In the case of chemical properties, one familiar view as to how the required justification should go is provided by David Lewis's account of theoretical identification in science (1970a, 1972). Here, the unifying thread rests on the fact that the theories to which the method is applicable are causal in nature—they are all in the business of ascribing causes and effects. *Modulo* some (perhaps controversial) assumptions about causation—for example, that all causation is ultimately physical causation—this provides a theoretically substantial sense in which all such theories are in the same line of work.

Lewis's program applies to theoretical entities characterizable in terms of their causal role. In taking over some of the key ideas of Lewis's program, however, Jackson is explicit that he wants to generalize beyond the causal realm. As he notes, his proposed "moral functionalism" differs from Lewis's psycho-functionalism in that in the case of moral functionalism, the "principles are not causal principles" (Jackson 1998: 131). What, if anything, plays the role of causation in the wider program? It turns out that *so long as we are not deflationists*, semantic notions will do the trick. To see how this goes, let's consider an abridged version of the two programs.

Consider first Lewis's model. Let "A" be a theoretical term in some scientific theory, and let M(A) be a full specification of A's causal role. (∃x)M(x) is then the Ramsey sentence that results from M(A) by replacing all occurrences of "A" by a bound variable, and (∃!x)M(x) is the version that says that there is a unique realiser "of the A role."

Let's suppose that we have reason to think (∃!x)M(x) true. What do we now know about A? We have the following definite description:

> A is the unique x such that M(x).

How, according to Lewis, do we now address the question "What is A?", or "How do we locate A with respect to the entities described by physics?"? We find, or convince ourselves that in principle we could find, some physical entity D that satisfies the Ramsey sentence for A—that is, such that D is also the unique x such that M(x). A and D then satisfy the same definite description, and are hence the same entity.

What grounds our confidence that there is some such D to be found, at least in principle? If we follow Lewis, it is a thesis about causation—the thesis of "the explanatory adequacy of physics," as Lewis puts it at one point. Taken together with the fact that M(A) encodes the causal facts about A, this gives us what we need.

Thus our confidence that there some such D to be found *does not rest on a semantic thesis*. Although I used a semantic notion a moment ago—I wrote "some physical entity D that *satisfies* the Ramsey sentence for A"—it is clear, I think, that this use is inessential, and thoroughly compatible with a deflationary view of semantic properties. (Indeed, I went on to gloss what I needed to say without using the notion.)

But what happens if we want to generalize Lewis's program beyond the realm of things with causes and effects?[8] In this case we won't in general have definite descriptions in causal terms. But we will have them in semantic terms—descriptions of the form

8. Or when we want to apply it to the causal terms themselves, for that matter.

B is the (unique) x that satisfies the Ramsey sentence $(\exists! x)N(x)$

(where N(B) is our theory of some such notion B).

Problems of uniqueness aside, it is (relatively) trivial that we can form the Ramsey sentence for a given term B in this way. And hence there can be no objection to our proceeding to ask the question "What is B?" by asking

What is the (unique) x that satisfies the Ramsey sentence $(\exists! x)N(x)$?

What is non-trivial, and dependent on a non-deflationary account of satisfaction, is the view that this is anything other than asking

What is the (unique) x such that N(x)?

and that this question has anything other than a trivial answer—"Why, it is B, of course!"[9]

Non-deflationary semantics holds out a promise of a more interesting answer. It gives us a potential handle on the identity question, in precisely the way that causation does in the Lewisean case. That is, it gives us—at least if combined with semantic naturalism of some kind—a new sort of question to investigate: What is the (natural or physical) thing that *stands in this semantic relation* to the Ramsey sentence? If deflationists are right, however, there can be no new theoretical question of this kind—and no material with which to fashion a semantic principle supporting physicalism, analogous to Lewis's principle of the explanatory adequacy of physics.[10]

For the moment, the main point is that the fact that deflationism provides a global challenge to Jacksonian metaphysics does not imply, absurdly, that the kind of questions such a metaphysical program raises are never appropriate. It simply implies that extra work is needed to show that they are appropriate, in any particular case—work that could otherwise be done by semantic notions. But in the cases that would otherwise generate an obvious absurdity, such as that of chemical properties, we have a reasonably good idea how the extra work should go. Arguably, Lewis has done it all for us.[11]

9. Note that to say that the question "What is B?" has no non-trivial answer is not to say that there is no non-trivial theory in the vicinity. There may well be a non-trivial account to be told—in non-representational theoretical vocabulary—about how the speakers in question come to talk in B terms.

10. In effect, this point simply reiterates the contrast drawn in section 4 between ontologically non-conservative and ontologically conservative modes of linguistic theory.

11. In other contexts I would myself be inclined to contest this argument, maintaining that causation is in various ways unsuited to bear this sort of metaphysical weight (being too anthropocentric and too contextual, for example—see Price [2001]). But here my interest is in the contrast between this causally grounded approach to metaphysics, and a more general, semantically grounded, approach.

6. Is Deflationism Obviously False?

I have argued that *if* semantic deflationism is true, then there are likely to be fewer genuine location problems than Jackson imagines. One might concede this conditional claim, and yet argue that its antecedent is obviously false. One might argue, in other words, that it is uncontroversial that much of language is "substantially" representational, in the way apparently denied by semantic deflationists. In *From Metaphysics to Ethics* and elsewhere, Jackson often makes observations about language which might be taken in this spirit. For example:

> Why do foreign-language phrase books sell so well? Because they help us find food, shelter, museums and airports when we travel outside our own language communities. Our need for them highlights what is anyway obvious: much of language is a convention-generated system of representation.
>
> Although it is obvious that much of language is representational, it is occasionally denied. I have attended conference papers attacking the representational view of language given by speakers who have in their pockets pieces of paper with writing on them that tell them where the conference dinner is and when the taxis leave for the airport. How could this happen? I surmise that it is through conflating the obviously correct view that much of language is representational with various controversial views. (1997: 270)

For my part, I agree with Jackson that there is a sense in which it is obvious that much of language is representational, and a sense in which it is controversial. Roughly, the obvious sense is the loose and popular sense, which simply tracks folk usage. The non-obvious sense is the theoretical sense, in which representational and semantic notions are called on to do various sorts of theoretical work, in philosophy and elsewhere. As we'll see, Jackson's own examples establish that what is obvious in the former sense need not be obvious in the latter—there are cases which are clearly representations in the loose and popular sense, about which, as Jackson himself emphasizes, it is a live theoretical issue as to whether they count as representations in the theoretical sense.

Once it is conceded that the popular sense and the theoretical sense come apart in this way, and that the latter is non-obvious, it is open for a deflationist to suggest that there might turn out to be no legitimate theoretical sense—no relevant notion of representation that survives into mature theory about language. Jackson's appeals to what is obvious and uncontroversial about language seem intended to block this possibility. However, once a wedge has been driven between the obvious and the non-obvious issues—between the loose sense in which language is undoubtedly representational, and the controversial theoretical sense—the former has lost its authority as a guide to theory, and cannot exclude thoroughgoing representational deflationism. Or so it seems to me.

In order to make it clear that I'm not relying on judicious choice of examples, let me reproduce some more of Jackson's illustrations of the representational character of language:

> We use language to tell our community and our later selves how things are. Telling how things are requires representational devices, structures that somehow effect a partition in the possibilities. For we say how things are by saying what is ruled in and what is ruled out. (1998: 53)
>
> [T]ypically we know something useful . . . and are giving voice to this knowledge when we classify happenings as examples of grooming behaviour, pain, rational inference, and so on. For only then can we explain the manifestly useful information we give about what the world is like each other and to our later selves, through diary entries and notes on fridges, when we use words like "pain," "grooming behaviour," "electricity bill," "belief," "rational," and so on. (1998: 64–65)
>
> Consider what happens when I utter the sentence, "There is a land-mine two metres away." I tell you something about how things are, and to do that is precisely to tell you which of various possibilities concerning how things are is actual. . . . The sports section of any newspaper is full of speculations about possible outcomes, conveyed by sentences that discriminate among the outcomes in a way we grasp because we understand the sentences. Again, we find our way around buildings by reading or hearing sentences that we understand like "The seminar room is around the corner on the left." There are many different places the seminar room might be located, but after seeing or hearing the sentence, and by virtue of understanding it and trusting the person who produces it, we know which of the possibilities is actual. (1998: 71–72)

The representationalist vocabulary in these examples is, as Jackson intends, unremarkable and uncontroversial. But it remains equally uncontroversial, surely, when we substitute examples like these:

> What Jane told you is *true*
> David Wenham's new performance is *superb*
> It is *probably* going to rain on Friday
> You *should* take an umbrella
> It's *possible* I'll be *able* to get to the party
> *If* I get there, *then* I'll be a little late
> The delay last week was *caused* by late arrival of the inbound aircraft.

In notes on fridges and in pockets, all of these sentences may be used to "partition the possibilities," provide "manifestly useful information," and so on. All of them provide examples of things we may learn by understanding and trusting people who say these things. On the face of it, in other words, they all have all the features that Jackson takes to characterize representational uses of language.

Yet the italicized parts of these claims pick out elements with respect to which expressivist explications are already reasonably well-known. In each case, in other words, we have some idea of how a *theoretical* account of the function of relevant terms might proceed, without employing representationalist vocabulary *at the theoretical level.*

Jackson himself notes some possibilities of this kind. He notes that it is controversial whether ethical claims and indicative conditionals are genuinely representational—in such cases, non-cognitivism is an arguable position. But it seems to me that in admitting this possibility in particular cases, and yet continuing to maintain that in general, our intuitions about the representational character of language are a good guide to theory—a good reason for thinking that much of language is representational, in a theoretical sense—Jackson is guilty of a kind of double standard. "Thick" representational character simply can't be obvious in one case and yet not obvious in another, without some (obvious and obviously relevant!) difference in the surface phenomena.

The tension in Jackson's position here is masked, I think, because the sort of non-cognitivism he has in mind is the orthodox variety, which includes *among its theoretical claims* the assertion that the language in question is non-representational. Thus his imagined opponents about the status of ethical claims and indicative conditionals are people who agree that much of the rest of language is representational. From this standpoint, it is easy to overlook the more radical opponent, who—as a semantic deflationist—claims that none of language is representational in a substantial theoretical sense. But Jackson himself acknowledges the gap between what theory tells us about language and what we can read off its surface. Once in play, this gap serves the purposes of the more radical opponent just as well as it serves those of the conventional opponent. (If anything, in fact, it serves the radical opponent better, because unlike her more conventional colleagues, she does not have to explain why surface structure is a guide to underlying function in some cases but not others.)[12]

12. When Jackson mentions the claim that indicative conditionals do not have truth-conditions, he offers what might perhaps be read as an objection to deflationism. He considers the suggestion that it is a trivial matter that indicative conditions have truth-conditions, because it is trivial that "If it rains then the match will be canceled" is true iff if it rains then the match will be cancelled. (Clearly, this is the sort of thing deflationists are eager to say.) Jackson responds that "this is a grammatically fine, but the issue is not about grammar" (1998: 117).

Jackson is right, of course, that grammar can't be the end of the story. But it doesn't follow that semantic properties provide the appropriate theoretical vocabulary to tell the rest of the story—to say what lies behind the grammar, so to speak. Hence it is open to a deflationist to maintain that it is a trivial issue whether indicative conditionals have truth-conditions, or are representational—of course they do, and are. What isn't open, in this case, is to deny that there are further theoretical questions to be raised about such conditionals, in non-representational terms.

7. Truth-aptness to the Rescue?

As noted earlier, Jackson, Oppy, and Smith (1994) offer non-cognitivists a response to the standard charge that minimalism about truth vindicates cognitivism. They argue that minimalism about truth is compatible with non-minimalism about truth-aptness, and that the latter is what the non-cognitivist needs. I have suggested that this is a cure for a nonexistent disease. In the respects that matter, minimalism about truth is a friend rather than an enemy of non-cognitivism. At least, it is a friend of expressivism, in the broad sense identified above—the view that accords the semantic and representational notions no "thick" role in linguistic theory.

It might be objected that deflationism about truth-aptness is in any case highly implausible. After all, the application of the terms "true" and "false," and related marks of the declarative or assertoric use of language, are very prominent features of language. How likely is it that they don't "track" some theoretically significant underlying characteristic of the speech acts concerned? Such a characteristic—call it the *truth-aptness basis*, or TAB, for short—will be what makes those speech acts truth-apt, in one important sense of the term. And once we've found it, won't we have found a substantial distinguishing mark of the representational uses of language?

No, because the argument rests on an equivocation—a kind of use–mention confusion, in fact. Does "truth-apt" mean "such as to be *treated* as truth-evaluable"—that is, such that competent speakers *apply* the terms "true" and "false" to the sentence in question? Or does it mean "such as to be capable of *being* true or false"? From an anthropological perspective it does seem plausible (let us suppose) that there is some property TAB underlying the declarative use of language, including the use of the terms "true" and "false" in conjunction with some kinds of utterances but not others. So it is plausible, as we might put it, that being *use-of-"true"-apt* is a substantial theoretical property, waiting to be investigated. But being use-of-"true"-apt does not imply being *representational*. It merely implies being *treated as "representational*." (Compare: religious studies, in its anthropological incarnation, does not require theological ontology.)

We can confirm this diagnosis by noting that there is no guarantee whatsoever that TAB itself be representational in nature. In the next section I'll sketch an account with this character. The crucial point is that the underlying property that determines truth-aptness—TAB, as we put it—need not involve any "word–world" surrogate for a semantic relation, of a kind which would be useful to metaphysics, or ground a "thick" representational view of language.[13]

13. The argument criticized here is not that of Jackson, Oppy, and Smith (1994). Their strategy is different. They suggest that sentences acquire truth-aptness by being conventional expressions of truth-apt mental states, namely, beliefs. And they argue "that it is not a minimal matter whether or

8. The Expressivist Alternative

Let's think about the biological functions of the mental states we call beliefs, setting their (apparent) semantic properties explicitly to one side.[14] Or rather, let's simply take advantage of the fact that the semantic properties do not appear explicitly in an account of the functional roles of the states in question, and neglect the familiar problem of how to fashion representational content from such functional materials. Let's begin somewhere familiar, in other words, with the idea that there is some functional characterization of our cognitive lives, in which intentional and semantic terms do not explicitly appear. (In fact, this familiar place is just a rough psychological analogue of what, in a passage quoted at the beginning, Jackson asked us to find plausible with respect to language, namely, a scientific account in which semantic terms do not appear.)

How did it serve our ancestors to develop a psychology rich enough to contain such mental states? What role did those states play in increasingly complex lives? It is plausible, in my view, that there is no single answer, appropriate for all kinds of beliefs. Perhaps the function of some beliefs can be understood in terms of the idea that it is useful to have mental states designed to co-vary with certain environmental conditions, but for many, the story is surely more complicated. Consider causal or probabilistic beliefs, for example, which manifest themselves as dispositions to have certain sorts of expectations (and hence to make certain sorts of decisions) in certain sorts of circumstances. Plausibly, there's a interesting story to be told about the biological value of having an internal functional organisztion rich enough to contain such dispositions.

Or consider some of the other cases in which expressivism has often seemed appealing—universal generalizations, indicative and subjunctive conditionals, modal and moral claims, and so on. In each of these cases we have some sense of what the associated beliefs enable us to *do*, which we couldn't do otherwise—some sense of the distinctive role of the states in question in the psychological

---

not a state is a belief" (Jackson, Oppy, and Smith 1994: 296). There is a sense in which this is relatively uncontroversial, I think. Roughly, it is a parallel to the sense in which it is uncontroversial, or at least plausible, that there is some property TAB that underlies the fact that certain speech acts get cast in declarative form. But as in that case, there is no guarantee that this property is representational in nature (rather than, say, a matter of the place of the state in question in a certain internal architecture).

Jackson, Oppy, and Smith also defend non-minimalism about beliefs by appealing to certain folk intuitions or platitudes about belief. These platitudes do have a representationalist character. For example, they speak of the "truism about belief that it is a state designed to fit the facts" or "designed to fit the way things are" (JOS 1994: 296–297). As in the case of the various intuitions and platitudes that Jackson offers in support of a representational view of language, it seems to me that these psychological platitudes have two interpretations, one obvious and one controversial. The obvious reading doesn't challenge deflationism and global expressivism.

14. This section overlaps to a considerable extent with section 9 of Price (2004b).

architecture of creatures like us. Suppose we get to this point without explicitly invoking the idea that states we are talking about have representational contents. Then we have the beginnings of an understanding of what these various kinds of states do for us—why it's useful to develop a psychological architecture rich enough to contain them—but no understanding of why they manifest themselves as *commitments*. Why do we take them to be truth-evaluable, for example, or expressible in declarative form?

This issue can be approached in the same explanatory spirit, I think. With respect to the various functionally characterized states we've described, we want to consider the question, why do we give voice to *those* mental states in *that* form? And notice a prima facie puzzle. If our account up to this point has emphasized the fact that the states in question have various different functions, it may seem odd that states with different functions all get expressed in a similar way, as truth-evaluable declarative judgments.[15]

However, it isn't difficult to find a place to start. Plausibly, many of our psychological states are such that it is often advantageous, with respect to those states, that we tend to toward conformity across our linguistic communities. A prime function of assertoric language seems to be that it facilitates and encourages such alignment. It leads us to "express" or give voice to our psychological dispositions in ways that invite challenge by speakers with contrary dispositions. And "That's false" and "That's true" are markers of challenge and concession, respectively.[16]

As ordinary speakers, we don't understand that this is what assertoric language is for—we just do it, as it were, and from our point of view, we seem to be "saying how things are." But the function of this practice of "saying how things are" is the one in the background—the function of altering our behaviorally significant commitments much more rapidly than our individual experience in the environment could do, by giving us access to the corresponding states of our fellows (and much else besides). At any rate, that's one kind of thing that assertion seems especially well-suited to *do*. Moreover—and for the moment this is the crucial point—it is something it can usefully do in application to commitments with a wide variety of functional roles of their own (none of them representation as such).

The suggestion is thus that assertions are intentional expressions of psychological states with a variety of (not representationally characterized) functions within the internal psychological architecture of the speakers concerned—or better, within the complex network of relations involving both these internal

15. In contrast, a representational view has it easy at this point. The commonality of linguistic expression reflects the commonality of representational function. But the bump in the rug then shows up somewhere else, when functional differences need to be explained in terms of differences in representational content.

16. Of course, the details of this need to be spelled out rather carefully—especially if we want to avoid simply helping ourselves to the representational notions. See Price (1988, 1990, 2003).

states and the creatures' external environment—a variety obscured in their expression, when they take on what Wittgenstein calls the "clothing" of assertoric language.[17] Clearly, there has to be common clothing internally, too. Roughly, the states in question come to participate in a belief-like or rational cognitive architecture, and an important set of issues concerns the relations of precedence between thought and talk at this point. Does belief, or at least full-blown rationally governed belief, rely on internalising the dialogical structures which come with the development of assertoric language?

Leaving these issues of priority to one side, the proposal is thus that representational language and thought is a tool for aligning commitments across a speech community (and, perhaps, within a single head). But though in one sense a single tool, it is a tool with many distinct applications, corresponding to the distinct primary functions of the various kinds of psychological states that take advantage of it—that facilitate their own alignment by expressing themselves in assertoric form.[18]

As I've stressed in other work, this approach leads to a very different view from Jackson's of the phenomena that he takes to give rise to location problems. Jackson and I begin in the same place, I think, with an interest in making sense of a range of distinct "packets" of linguistic usage—talk of semantic properties, talk of ethical properties, and so on. And we'll agree, presumably, in accepting what science tells us about such talk—as Jackson puts it, in the passage I quoted at the beginning, "a story about masses, shapes, causal chains, behavioural dispositions of language users, evolutionary history, and the like." But then Jackson takes a theoretical move that I want to resist. He takes the talk to be representational, and is led by the path we've described to an issue about the various worldly relata of the semantic relations thus in question. Having framed the problem in those terms, he is then rightly troubled by the resulting ontological plurality, and faces location problems.

By contrast, the expressivist approach stays at the level of the "story about . . . behavioural dispositions of language users, evolutionary history, and the like." In particular, it investigates the functions of the linguistic usage in question, and associated psychology, in non-representational terms, and then tries to account

17. A major theme of the early sections of the *Investigations* is that philosophy misses important distinctions about the uses of language, distinctions hidden from us by "the uniform appearances of words" (Wittgenstein 1968: #11). As Wittgenstein puts it later, "We remain unconscious of the prodigious diversity of all the everyday language-games because the clothing of our language makes everything alike" (1998: 224).

18. This kind of multifunctional explanatory structure exists in other places in biology. As I have noted elsewhere (Price 2004b), a good example is the human hand. If we say that the function of the hand is *manipulation*, and leave it at that, we miss something very important: we miss the underlying functional diversity. On my reading, Wittgenstein makes a closely analogous point about assertion—a point in which representation plays the role of manipulation, as the notion whose homogeneity needs to be challenged.

for the representational "clothing" in the way just described. There's no location problem as such. Instead there is an issue of the same cardinality, so to speak, about the various functions of the various groups of terms and concepts—semantic terms, ethical terms, and the rest. However, this is a problem about human psychology and linguistic behavior—a broadly anthropological problem, as I put it earlier—not a problem in metaphysics. And of course we expect human behavior to be functionally pluralistic. So we have unsurprising plurality, in a familiar and scientifically tractable place, in place of the concerns that motivate Jackson's "serious metaphysics."

9. What if Deflationism Is False?

Let's recap. So far I've been trying to highlight the semantic presuppositions of Jackson's program, by exhibiting the effects on the program of assuming semantic deflationism. I haven't argued for semantic deflationism as such, though I have defended it against two objections: first, that in the light of my own argument, it would lead to the absurd consequence that there are no location problems whatsoever; and second, that its falsity is in any case obvious, something that can be read off from what we all know to be true about language. For all I've said so far, however, deflationism may nevertheless be false. Wouldn't Jackson's metaphysical program then be out of the woods? No problem with semantic presuppositions, surely, so long as they are true?

I want to close by mentioning two reasons for pessimism—two reasons for thinking that metaphysics grounded on semantics isn't out of the woods, even if we reject deflationism about the semantic properties. These reasons take us back to some concerns I touched on at the beginning.

For the first problem, I'll do little more than allude to an excellent discussion of a closely related issue by Stephen Stich, in the first chapter of *Deconstructing the Mind* (Stich 1996). Stich is concerned with eliminativism about the notions of folk psychology—belief, desire, and so on. He notes that many philosophers take the eliminativist thesis to be that the terms "belief" and "desire" *do not refer*. In other words, they take the thesis to be couched in these semantic terms. But if that's what eliminativism is, Stich argues, then in order to assess it we need a theory of reference—a theory capable of guiding our judgment about whether these terms actually do succeed in referring to anything.

Stich argues that this leaves metaphysics in an unenviable position. For one thing, it leaves it hostage to the almost inevitable indeterminacies in a scientific theory of reference. In other words, it means that we can't decide whether eliminativism is true until we sort out the issue between competing theories of reference—and that's likely to mean "never," given the nature of scientific theory. (The threat of deflationism lurks in the background here, of course, but we are now leaving that aside.)

Even worse, in would seem that in crucial cases, the metaphysics needs to *precede* the theory of reference. In order to decide what relation reference is, we need to be able to examine typical cases. In other words, we need to be able to study the various relationships that obtain between words or thoughts or the one side, and the items to which they (supposedly) refer on the other. But how can we do this in the case of "belief" and "desire," while it is up for grabs whether these terms refer to anything? In order to know where to look, we'd have to know not only *that* they refer, but also *to what*. To put this in terms of the location problem: If we need reference to locate belief and desire, we'll find that we need to locate reference, before we can put it to work. Yet we can't locate reference until we've located its worldy relata.

Thus we have two problems for eliminativism, if it is to rely on semantic relations such as reference. (Let's call the first the "referential indeterminacy problem" and the second "the precedence problem.") It's clear, I think, that both problems arise not simply for eliminativism, but for any metaphysical view that relies on reference in this way. In other words, both problems apply just as much if the question is "What is belief?," if this is to be understood as "To what does the term 'belief' refer?," as they do to the question "Are there beliefs?," understood as "Does the term 'belief' refer to anything?"

Quite apart from the threat of deflationism, then, there are reasons for doubting whether metaphysics can rest on semantic foundations. Stich's own response to the problem is simply to abandon semantics, and ask the questions in material form: "Are there beliefs?," in place of "Does the term 'belief' refer to anything?" However, while this certainly seems the right move in some cases—folk psychology might be more controversial than Stich thinks, perhaps, but chemistry isn't, for example—it's clear that Jackson can't follow Stich down this non-semantic path. To do so would be to abandon the global semantic route to location problems. In my view, then, Jackson's program remains vulnerable to Stich's objections, even if we ignore deflationism.

10. The Circularity Issue

Stich's objection applies to the use of semantic notions in the metaphysics of other topics. It argues, in effect, that even if not deflationary, these semantic notions aren't up to the job. It's not that they won't bear the weight, but rather that they can't tell us where the weight is born—which is what we want to know in metaphysics—in advance of an answer to that very question. The semantic legs connect thought and talk to the ground. So we can investigate the ground by following the legs to their feet. But we can't distinguish the real legs from rivals, until we know where the feet are actually located.

But what about the legs themselves? Is there an additional problem about using these semantic props to investigate themselves—to ground the metaphysics of the semantic properties themselves? I think that there is an additional problem. Let's go back to section 5. There, I compared the role of the semantic notions in Jackson's program to that of causation in Lewis's program. Lewis's technique for theoretical identification proceeds in two steps. The first step constructs a Ramsey sentence, to give us a definite description of the theoretical entity or property in question, *couched in causal terms*. The second step turns to science, to discover what it is—couched in other terms—that fulfills that definite description. In setting out to take the second step, we display our confidence in some principle about causation—for example, that all causation is grounded in physical causation.

In section 5 we noted that so long as we can help ourselves to "thick" semantic notions, there is a global variant of this program. In this case, our definite description of our target entity or property tells us that it is the thing or property that satisfies or makes true the description encoded in the non-semantic part of the Ramsey sentence. Formally speaking, this works fine so long as our target entity or property is not itself semantic in nature. Whether it is really any use in metaphysics is another matter, the matter we've just raised.[19] Formally, however, there's no problem.

But consider what happens when our targets are the semantic properties and relations themselves. Here the technique is surely disallowed, because in this case the construction of the Ramsey sentence is supposed to eliminate the semantic terms. This brings us back to the circularity noted at the beginning. Whatever the role that semantic properties play in grounding the location problem for other kinds of properties, they surely can't play that role on their own behalf. Semantic properties cannot bootstrap metaphysics, on other words, but need to be assumed as primitive brute facts. Thus representationalism becomes a kind of surd for Jackson's program, both essential and inaccessible to its methods.

The trajectory from metaphysics to semantic primitives thus goes something like this. Metaphysics begins with an interest in the nature of things. Semantics seems to guarantee a new mode of description of those things, and a new mode of inquiry: describe the things in question as the *referents* of our terms, the *truthmakers* of our sentences, and set out to seek these semantic relata. Scaling down the ladder metaphor, semantic relations thus come to play the role of white canes, for metaphysicians who take us to be the victims of a kind of world-blindness.

As we have seen, deflationists argue that these semantic canes are not sufficiently substantial to do the job.[20] And Stich argues, in effect, that even if they are

19. One reason for being doubtful whether it helps is Quinean. What it relies on, formally speaking, is simply semantic ascent, and as Quine emphasizes, that takes us nowhere new. (Compare Simon Blackburn on Ramsey's ladder, in *Ruling Passions* [1998b].)

20. My aim has been not so much to side with deflationists on this point, but to use the fact that this kind of metaphysics is vulnerable to this charge to highlight the role of the semantic presuppositions in question.

sufficiently substantial, they are too ill-constrained to be useful to metaphysics—there are too many competing canes, and we don't know where a given cane leads unless we are already acquainted with what lies at the far end of it. Setting Stich and deflationists aside, however, the circularity concerns remain. These arise, from this perspective, when we try to use our white canes to guide us to themselves—that is, when we set out to investigate (or "locate") the semantic properties.

There are a number of forms the concern might take. The one just mentioned objects that in the case of the semantic terms themselves, we can't avail ourselves of the generalized Ramsey-Lewis program, in which semantics plays the role that causation does for Lewis himself. As noted, it might be suggested that this is something metaphysics needs to live with. Perhaps semantic properties need to be accepted as "brute primitives."

However, this primitivism amounts to philosophy's *imposing* a view about the functions of human language. This alone should surely concern naturalists, but all the more so if we agree with the remarks of Jackson that I quoted at the beginning, to the effect that semantic properties are likely to be no part of the "surface" scientific story about language. It is bad enough if the semantic categories claim a prior entitlement to a seat at the scientific table, but worse still if they have no other credible reason to be there.

We have seen that for Jackson himself, the claim of the semantic properties seems to rest on the proposal that they are implicit in the scientific story. There's no comfort here for a naturalist bothered by primitivism, however, because in the case of semantic properties, as in other cases, Jackson's conception of the task assumes a representational view of semantic vocabulary in question. Hence it assumes precisely what such a naturalist is seeking reason to accept.

These issues are admittedly very difficult, and it would be premature to insist that there's no non-vicious way to complete this circle, whether in a form acceptable to naturalists or otherwise. Still, in the absence of further clues as to how the solution might go, I think that there are serious grounds for concern. Representationalism seems to operate as kind of transcendental foundation for Jackson's program (and, though perhaps less explicitly, for much of contemporary metaphysics). If so, then at the very least this is something that needs to be clearly acknowledged. (Novices should be told that there are alternative conceptions of the task of philosophy, which don't depend on such a primitive.)

With those alternatives clearly in view, we could proceed to consider what seem to me the hard and important questions in this area. Are these circularities inevitably vicious, from a naturalistic perspective, or should we regard representationalism as a coherent and open question, a matter to be settled by future science? Without alternatives in view, the possibility that representationalism is deeply incoherent looks disastrous, a kind of scepticism that philosophy cannot afford seriously to entertain. With alternatives, it simply looks like a fascinating (possible) philosophical discovery, namely, that semantic properties are too "queer" to be part of a scientific account of language.

11. Philosophy Without Ladders

Representationalist philosophy has been to this point before, I think. Semantic relations seem an essential ladder for serious metaphysics, but a ladder which is itself unreachable by its own rungs. Serious metaphysics thus seems close to the point that Wittgenstein reaches at the end of the *Tractatus*, when he offers us a view of the relation between language and the world that can't be talked about—a view inaccessible by its own lights. (There are other similarities, too, I think. Jackson's generalized Ramsey-Lewis structuralism seems to offer us at the level of theories, or perhaps conceptual clusters, what Wittgenstein's picture theory of meaning offers us at the level of sentences: a view in which linguistic structure mirrors ontological structure, via semantic mappings.)

Famously, that (early) Wittgenstein urged us to kick away the ladder. Whatever he meant by that, he later advocated something less paradoxical. He turned away from the kind of philosophy that required such a ladder. Rather than climbing it and kicking it away, his later recommendation seems to have been to avoid it altogether:

> I might say: if the place I want to get to could only be reached by way of a ladder, I would give up trying to get there. For the place I really have to get to is a place I must already be at now. Anything that I might reach by climbing a ladder does not interest me. (1980: 7e)[21]

The nature of Wittgenstein's later philosophy is a matter for much dispute, of course. Under at least one interpretation (Price 1992, 2004b), however, it is close to what I have called global expressivism—a view that sees the right question, everywhere, as a question posed in non-representationalist terms. What are creatures like us doing with *this* bit of language? As I have emphasized elsewhere (Price 1992, 1997a, 2004a) this is a thoroughly naturalistic viewpoint. Wittgenstein thus becomes a kind of pragmatic naturalist, interested in explaining our use of philosophically puzzling concepts—value, causation, modality, meaning, or whatever—in terms of their role in our cognitive and practical lives.

Another of Wittgenstein's later themes is that philosophy is a kind of self-help therapy, whose role is to help us to overcome our own philosophical cravings—the craving for metaphysics, for example. In my terms, this therapy takes a specific

21. I am indebted to Brad Weslake for this reference.

form. Its goal is to cure the delusion that we are world-blind, to correct the particular form of philosophical hypochondria that leads us to believe that there is a problem that semantic white canes can solve. The key to the cure is to see that the delusion results from imbibing an unhealthy combination of naturalism and representationalism. Some philosophers[22] recognize that this combination is unhealthy, and seek relief by abandoning naturalism. Some think that this is Wittgenstein's prescription. But in my view the right choice, and arguably Wittgenstein's choice, is the other one. We should keep the naturalism and dispense with the representationalism.

Either way, the question of status of the semantic properties well deserves the prominence that Jackson's book accords it, even if for reasons that he himself does not highlight. For naturalists, in my view, this question is the watershed between two radically different conceptions of the task of a scientifically grounded philosophy. On one side lies metaphysics; on the one other, scientific anthropology and the study of certain aspects of human linguistic behavior and psychology. Though Jackson turns the wrong way at the divide, in my view, his book provides the best existing map of the territory on that side. We expressivists—comparatively lonely, these days, on what remains the shady side of the ridge—should surely hope for a Jackson to call our own.

22. For example, perhaps, Paul Boghossian (1990).

13

Metaphysics after Carnap: The Ghost Who Walks?

1. The Carnap Case

Imagine a well-trained mid-twentieth-century American philosopher, caught in a rare traffic jam on the New Jersey Turnpike, one still summer afternoon in 1950. He dozes in his warm car . . . and awakes in the same spot on a chill fall evening in 2008, remembering nothing of the intervening years. It is as if he has been asleep at the wheel for almost sixty years!

Suppose that he sees the upside of his peculiar situation. Phenomenologically, it is on a par with time travel, and what red-blooded philosopher could fail to be excited by that? Of course, he realizes that it is far is more likely that he is suffering from amnesia than that he has actually been transported more than half a century into the future, or survived for that long on the Turnpike—but all the more reason to savor the experience while he can, lest his memory should soon return.

Indeed, he soon becomes a celebrity, written up by Oliver Sacks in *The New Yorker*. Irreverent graduate students call him (with apologies to Beth [1963: 478]) the Carnap* of contemporary philosophy, and everyone is interested in his impressions of modern life. What will surprise him about the society in which he finds himself? Any Australian philosopher who knows contemporary New York will find it easy to imagine some of the things that might stand out: the number of people who ask for change for a cup of coffee, the mind-numbing range of options available when he buys his own cup of coffee, the sheer size of even the smallest, and so on. But let's suppose that Carnap* has the true philosopher's ability to ignore all of this. He wants to know what has happened to his own beloved discipline. "To hell with the beggars and the Starbucks!," he exclaims, "'Where are the big strides in philosophy this past half century?"

At this point, I think, Australian intuitions are less reliable. Australian philosophical audiences find familiar one of the features of contemporary philosophy that Carnap* will find most surprising, namely, the apparent health of metaphysics. Back in the late 1940s, Carnap* recalls, metaphysics, like poverty, was supposed to be on its last legs. Yet everywhere that he turns these days, there is a philosopher espousing a metaphysical position—someone claiming to be a "realist" about this, an "irrealist" about that, a "fictionalist" about something else. Out in the college towns of New Jersey and New England, Carnap* finds, there are more ontological options than kinds of coffee, more metaphysicians than homeless people. And it isn't simply an affliction of the aged, infirm and mentally ill. Like the Great War of his parents' day, contemporary metaphysics seems to have claimed the best and brightest of a generation. "When will they ever learn?," Carnap* hums to himself—a sign perhaps to us, if not to him, that his memory of the intervening years is beginning to return.

If Carnap* were to ask where the battle against metaphysics was lost in twentieth-century philosophy, he would do well to turn his attention to a skirmish between his famous namesake and Quine in the early 1950s. In philosophy, as in less abstract conflicts, single engagements are rarely decisive, but this particular clash does seem of special significance. By the late 1940s, Carnap's position seems to represent the furthest advance of the anti-metaphysical movement, at least on one of its several fronts. The fact that the position was never consolidated, and the ground lost, seems to owe much to Quine's criticism of Carnap's views. Ironically, Quine's criticism was friendly fire, for (as I want to emphasize below) Quine, too, was no friend of traditional metaphysics. But the attack was no less damaging for the fact that it came from behind, and its effect seems to have been to weaken what—at that time, at any rate—seems to have been Quine and Carnap's common cause.

Indeed, Carnap* would soon find another reason for blaming Quine for the apparent health of metaphysics. In fact, he'd discover that Hilary Putnam had recently answered his question explicitly:

> "How come," the reader may wonder, "it is precisely in *analytic* philosophy—a kind of philosophy that, for many years, was *hostile* to the very word 'ontology'—that Ontology flourishes?"
>
> If we ask *when* Ontology became a respectable subject for an analytic philosopher to pursue, the mystery disappears. It became respectable in 1948, when Quine published a famous paper titled "On What There Is." It was Quine who single handedly made Ontology a respectable subject. (Putnam 2004: 78–79)

At least in part, then, the contemporary confidence and self-image of metaphysics rests on a conception of its own history in which Quine plays a central role. According to this popular narrative, it was Quine—perhaps Quine alone—who rescued metaphysics from positivism and other threats in those dark days after World War II (when the world itself seemed at risk). With one hand, Quine wrote "On What There Is," and thus gave ontology a life-saving transfusion. With the other, he drove a stake through the heart of Carnap's "Empiricism, Semantics and Ontology" (1950), and thus dispatched the last incarnation of the Viennese menace.

In my view, this metaphysical rebirthing myth is in large part bogus, in the sense that neither of Quine's achievements actually supports what is now widely taken to rest on it. On the one hand, the ontology that Quine revived in "On What There Is" is itself a pale zombie, compared to the beefy creature that positivists since Hume had being trying to put down. And on the other, Quine's stake missed the heart of Carnap's metaphysics-destroying doctrine completely, merely lopping off some inessential appendages, and leaving the argument, if anything, stronger than before.

If I'm right, then the truth that confronts Carnap* about the fate of philosophy is disturbing indeed. What's haunting the halls of all those college towns—capturing the minds of new generations of the best and brightest—is actually the ghost of a long-discredited discipline. Metaphysics is actually as dead as Carnap left it, but—blinded, in part, by these misinterpretations of Quine—contemporary philosophy has lost the ability to see it for what it is, to distinguish it from live and substantial intellectual pursuits. As his memory begins to return, Carnap* finds himself gripped by a terrifying thought. What if he, too, should soon relapse into blindness, unable to see metaphysics for what it is? What if he, too, should be reclaimed by the living dead?

My main theme in this chapter is, as I put it a moment ago, that metaphysics is as dead, or at least deflated, as Carnap left it. In support of this thesis, I want to do two things. First, I want to show that Quine's famous criticisms of Carnap leave Carnap's anti-metaphysical doctrines substantially intact. I'll argue that the twin-chambered heart of Carnap's view comprises a deflationary view of metaphysics with which Quine concurs, and a pluralism about the functions of existentially quantified discourse, with which Quine does not concur, but against which he offers no significant argument.[1]

Second, I want to call attention to what seems to me to be a persistent misinterpretation of Quine's views on ontology—a way of taking them that would indeed support inflationary metaphysics, but cannot be what Quine intended. I'll argue that the misinterpretations rest on a failure to resolve an important ambiguity, between what we may call thick and thin readings of Quine's conclusions in "On What There Is." It seems to me that many who appeal to Quine in support of their metaphysical investigations rely on the thick reading, while at the same time displaying a kind of false modesty—helping themselves to a cloak of plain-speaking ontological frugality that belongs to the thin reading. Metaphysics thus gets away

1. While it will be clear that I am sympathetic to Carnap's criticisms of metaphysics, I want to stress that my aim here is not to offer new positive arguments in support of Carnap's conclusions, but simply to show that they are not undermined by Quine's famous objections. (On the contrary, I'll argue, Quine and Carnap are playing for the same team.) In principle, it would be compatible with this conclusion that there might be other objections to Carnap's arguments, and hence that metaphysics survives for other reasons. My claim is simply that Quine is not its savior.

with working both sides of the street, because the two readings are not properly distinguished. It is therefore important to take the trouble to draw the distinction, and to show that only the thin reading can really be regarded as legitimate, by Quine's own lights.

2. Carnap's Deflationism

First, then, to Carnap: Carnap thought that much of traditional metaphysics and ontology rests on a mistake. In explaining why, he relies on the notion of a linguistic framework. Roughly, a linguistic framework is the set of rules (supposedly) governing the use of a group of terms and predicates—say, the terms we use in talking about medium-sized objects, or in talking about numbers. Carnap thought that adopting such a framework, or way of talking, typically brings with it ontological methods and questions. These are "internal" questions, questions that arise within the framework, and their nature depends on the framework in question. They may be empirical, as in science, or logical, as in mathematics.

However, Carnap continues, these internal questions do not include the metaphysical questions typically asked by philosophers: "Are there material objects?," for example, or "Are there numbers?" Carnap says that in this form these "external" questions are simply mistakes: "They cannot be asked because they are framed in the wrong way." The only legitimate external questions are pragmatic in nature: Should we adopt this framework? Would it be useful?

In my view, it is helpful to frame Carnap's point in terms of the use–mention distinction. Legitimate *uses* of the terms such as "number" and "material object" are necessarily internal, for it is conformity (more-or-less) to the rules of the framework in question that constitutes use. But as internal questions, as Carnap notes, these questions could not have the significance that traditional metaphysics takes them to have. Metaphysics tries to locate them somewhere else, but thereby commits a use–mention fallacy. The only legitimate external questions simply *mention* the terms in question.

Carnap thus becomes a pluralist about ontological commitment—explicitly so, in the sense that he associates distinct ontological commitment with distinct linguistic frameworks, and at least implicitly so in a deeper "functional" or pragmatic sense. After all, the key to Carnap's accommodation of abstract entities is the idea that the framework that introduces talk of such entities may serve different pragmatic purposes from the framework that introduces talk of physical objects—and this could only be so if there is some sense in which the two frameworks "do different jobs."[2]

2. I'm not sure to what extent this kind of pluralism was actually explicit in Carnap's own views about these issues. My claim here is that it is a necessary corollary of his view, if the suggestion that these pragmatic issues are addressed on a framework-by-framework basis is not to collapse into triviality. Henceforth, on this basis, I'll treat this pragmatic pluralism as part of the Carnapian package.

However, Carnap's view is not simply a recipe for more inclusive realism. For if what is meant by realism is a metaphysical view, in the old sense, then Carnap's position amounts to a *rejection* of all such views. By that realist's lights, then, Carnap's view is a form of global irrealism. Yet his view is not traditional anti-realism, either. It is a third position, which rejects the traditional realist–anti-realist dichotomy. Here is Carnap's own negotiation of this critical point, from "Empiricism, Semantics and Ontology":

> The non-cognitive character of the questions which we have called here external questions was recognized and emphasized already by the Vienna Circle under the leadership of Moritz Schlick, the group from which the movement of logical empiricism originated. Influenced by ideas of Ludwig Wittgenstein, the Circle rejected both the thesis of the reality of the external world and the thesis of its irreality as pseudo-statements; the same was the case for both the thesis of the reality of universals (abstract entities, in our present terminology) and the nominalistic thesis that they are not real and that their alleged names are not names of anything but merely *flatus vocis*. (It is obvious that the apparent negation of a pseudo-statement must also be a pseudo-statement.) It is therefore not correct to classify the members of the Vienna Circle as nominalists, as is sometimes done. However, if we look at the basic anti-metaphysical and pro-scientific attitude of most nominalists (and the same holds for many materialists and realists in the modern sense), disregarding their occasional pseudo-theoretical formulations, then it is, of course, true to say that the Vienna Circle was much closer to those philosophers than to their opponents. (1950: 215)[3]

Thus Carnap's view combines pluralism about ontological commitment with a strikingly deflationary attitude to metaphysics in general. This is a combination that needs to be espoused with some care. If Carnap's pluralism were cast as pluralism about ontology per se, it would sound like a metaphysical position in its own right: pluralism about the furniture of reality, as it were. Hence the need to stress that it is a pluralism about language—about the linguistic frameworks in which, and the purposes for which, we go in for the business of ontological *commitment*.

This pluralist aspect of Carnap's view is one of Quine's main targets. Elsewhere, Quine is also a critic of other manifestations of pluralism about existence and existential quantification, notably that of Ryle. I want to show that these Quinean arguments contain little to trouble Carnap's combination of deflationism about metaphysics and pluralism about the functions of linguistic categories. As a

3. Carnap is here endorsing the views he ascribes to the Vienna Circle, of course.

result, they provide no serious obstacle to the suggestion that in virtue of such pluralism, not all first-order ontological commitment need be scientific ontological commitment.

Quine's objections to Carnap on this matter also offer an apparent defense of metaphysics against Carnap's criticisms—a defense in tension, it may seem, with my suggestion that Quine, too, is really a deflationist about ontological issues. Before turning to the issue of pluralism, I want to show that in fact there is no tension here. For all practical purposes, Quine agrees with Carnap about the status of metaphysical issues. If anything, he is more of a pragmatist than Carnap, arguing that Carnap is mistaken in assigning a more robust status to scientific matters.

3. Quine's Defense of Metaphysics: The Bad News

Much of Quine's attack on Carnap—indeed, the "basic point of contention" (1966: 133), as Quine puts it—rests on the objection that Carnap's notion of a linguistic framework presupposes the analytic–synthetic distinction. Quine argues that in virtue of the failure of the analytic–synthetic distinction, even internal questions are ultimately pragmatic. Referring to Carnap's view that, as Quine puts it, "philosophical questions are only apparently about sorts of objects, and are really pragmatic questions of language policy," Quine asks: "But why should this be true of the philosophical questions and not of theoretical questions generally? Such a distinction of status is of a piece with the notion of analyticity, and as little to be trusted" (1960: 271). In other words, Quine's claim is that there are no purely internal issues, in Carnap's sense. No issue is ever entirely insulated from pragmatic concerns about the possible effects of revisions of the framework itself. Pragmatic issues of this kind are always on the agenda, at least implicitly. In the last analysis, all judgments are pragmatic in nature.

Grant that this is true. What effect does it have on Carnap's anti-metaphysical conclusions? Carnap's internal issues were of no use to traditional metaphysics, and metaphysics does not lose if they are disallowed. But does it gain? Science and mathematics certainly lose, in the sense that they become less pure, more pragmatic, but this is not a gain for metaphysics. And Quine's move certainly does not restore the non-pragmatic external perspective required by metaphysics. In effect, the traditional metaphysician wants to be able to say, "I agree it is useful to say this, but is it true?" Carnap rules out this question, and Quine does not rule it back in.[4]

4. Roughly, Carnap allows us to ask about truth only for internal questions. Quine agrees, but says that there are no such questions, in the last analysis, because there are no firm linguistic rules. As we shall see, some people attribute to Quine a stance according to which truth reemerges from the pragmatist fire, as it were, in the sense that *usefulness* is taken to be a *reason* for believing *true;* but as I want to argue, this is surely a misinterpretation.

Quine sometimes invites confusion on this point. He says that

> if there is no proper distinction between analytic and synthetic, then no basis at all remains for the contrast which Carnap urges between ontological statements [i.e., the metaphysical statements that Carnap wants to disallow] and empirical statements of existence. Ontological questions then end up on a par with the questions of natural science. (1966: 134)

This sounds like good news for ontology, but actually it isn't. Quine's criticism of Carnap cannot provide vindication of traditional metaphysics, for if all issues are ultimately pragmatic, there can't be the more-than-pragmatic issue of the kind the metaphysician requires. The main effect of abandoning the analytic–synthetic distinction is that Carnap's distinctions are no longer sharp—there are no purely internal (non-pragmatic) issues, because linguistic rules are never absolute, and pragmatic restructuring is never entirely off the agenda. But a metaphysician who takes this as a vindication of his position—who announces triumphantly that Quine has shown us that metaphysics is in the same boat as natural science, that "ontological questions [are] on a par with the questions of natural science"—is someone who has not been told the terrible news. Quine himself has sunk the metaphysicians' traditional boat, and left all of us, scientists and ontologists, clinging to Neurath's Raft.

As Quine himself puts it in the same piece:

> Carnap maintains that ontological questions . . . are questions not of fact but of choosing a convenient scheme or framework for science; and with this I agree only if the same be conceded for every scientific hypothesis. (1966: 134)[5]

Thus Quine is not returning to the kind of metaphysics rejected by the logical empiricists. On the contrary, he is moving forwards, embracing a more thoroughgoing post-positivist pragmatism. In this respect, far from blocking Carnap's drive toward a more pragmatic, less metaphysical destination, Quine simply overtakes him, and pushes further in the same direction.

It might be objected that news still looks much better for metaphysics than Carnap would have had us believe. Granted, there is no longer any pure, non-pragmatic science to be had, and no non-pragmatic metaphysics, either. But if metaphysics nevertheless ends up "on a par" with the kinds of questions investigated at CERN and Bell Labs, isn't that a kind of respectability worth having?

5. Note Quine's revealing use of the phrase "for science." It is far from clear that for Carnap, the convenience of adopting a linguistic framework is always convenience *for science*.

However, this suggestion trades on an excessively optimistic reading of the phrase "on a par." After all, consider the implications of Quine's rejection of the analytic–synthetic distinction (on which the present objection to Carnap depends): in one sense, it means that the question whether there exist bachelors either female or married is now "on a par" with the kind of matters investigated at CERN, such as the existence of the Higgs boson. But "on a par" simply means "not sharply distinguished, as empiricism had traditionally assumed." Nobody should take the news to recommend a serious sociological investigation into the gender and marital status of bachelors.

Conversely, the news that science is ultimately pragmatic does not mean that CERN and Bell Labs should be hiring pragmatists. There is still a big difference, in practice, between the day-to-day business of empirical science and the sort of rare occasions on which Quinean science has to confront its pragmatic foundations. At best, it is with these rare situations that Quine's response to Carnap can compare metaphysics—and patently, they are no serious challenge Carnap's objections to traditional metaphysics. Once again, the force of Quine's remarks is not that metaphysics is like science as traditionally (i.e., non-pragmatically) conceived, but that science (at least potentially, and at least in extremis) is like metaphysics as pragmatically conceived.

4. Against Pluralism?

But Quine has another card to play. Carnap's objections to traditional metaphysical issues turn in part on the idea that they involve an illegitimate theoretical stance, "external" to the linguistic frameworks that give their concepts sense. I've suggested above that for Carnap, this external stance is disallowed because if we step back this far, we step outside the relevant game altogether, and can no longer use the notions that have their home there. But how do we count linguistic games? In particular, what is to stop us treating all ontological issues as internal questions within a single grand framework? Why shouldn't we introduce a single existential quantifier, allowed to range over anything at all, and treat the question of the existence of numbers as on a par with that of the existence of dragons?

This is Quine's objection to Carnap's pluralism. Quine characterizes Carnap's views as follows:

> It begins to appear, then, that Carnap's dichotomy of questions of existence is a dichotomy between questions of the form "Are there so-and-so's?" where the so-and-so's purport to exhaust the range of a particular style of bound variables, and questions of the form "Are there so-and-so's?" where the so-and-so's do not purport to exhaust the range of a particular style of bound variables. Let me call the former questions

> *category* questions, and the latter ones *subclass* questions. I need this new terminology because Carnap's terms "external" and "internal" draw a somewhat different distinction which is derivative from the distinction between category questions and subclass questions. The external questions are the category questions conceived as propounded before the adoption of a given language; and they are, Carnap holds, properly to be construed as questions of the desirability of a given language form. The internal questions comprise the subclass questions and, in addition, the category questions when these are construed as treated within an adopted language as questions having trivially analytic or contradictory answers. (1966: 130)

Accordingly, Quine continues,

> the question whether there are numbers will be a category question only with respect to languages which appropriate a separate style of variables for the exclusive purpose of referring to numbers. If our language refers to numbers through variables which also take classes other than numbers as values, then the question whether there are numbers becomes a subclass question, on a par with the question whether there are primes over a hundred . . .
>
> Even the question whether there are classes, or whether there are physical objects, becomes a subclass question if our language uses a single style of variables to range over both sorts of entities. Whether the statement that there are physical objects and the statement that there are black swans should be put on the same side of the dichotomy, or on opposite sides, comes to depend on the rather trivial consideration of whether we use one style of variables or two for physical objects and classes. (1966: 131)

In effect, then, Quine is arguing that there is no principled basis for Carnap's distinction of language into frameworks, where this is to be understood in terms of the introduction of new quantifiers, ranging over distinct domains of entities. If there is only one existential quantifier, ranging over entities of any kind, then there would appear to be nothing to whose existence we are necessarily committed by virtue of using a particular system of concepts. We can always step back, consider the broader range of entities, and ask ourselves whether anything within this range answers to the concepts in question.

If Quine is right, then supposedly metaphysical issues—"Are there numbers?," for example—would seem to be on a par with the ontological issues that Carnap wants to regard as internal. It is true that all ontological questions have a pragmatic ingredient, by Quine's lights, but this is no longer quite the comfort that it was before. At that stage, the point was that Quine's attack on the analytic–synthetic distinction seemed to worsen things for science, without improving things for metaphysics—it didn't challenge the idea that metaphysics involves a linguistic mistake. But it now looks as though Carnap's main objection to metaphysics rests on an unsupported premise, namely the assumption that there is some sort of principled plurality in language which blocks Quine's move to homogenise the existential quantifier.

So far as I can see, Carnap himself does not have a satisfactory defense of this doctrine. In Quine's terms, he does not have any principled way to distinguish between category questions and subclass questions. What he needs, in effect, is an argument that there is some sort of *category mistake* involved in assimilating issues of the existence of numbers (say) and of the existence of physical objects. He takes for granted that this is so, and his model for the construction of languages reflects this assumption: roughly, speaking, the model requires that we mark the category boundaries in our choice of syntax—a different quantifier for each category, for example. But he does little to defend the assumption that the boundaries are there to be marked, prior to our syntactical choices—and this is what Quine denies.

Tradition seems to assume that Quine has an argument for the opposing view—an argument for *monism*, where Carnap requires *pluralism*, as it were. I want to show that this is a mistake, and rests on a confusion between two theoretical issues concerning language. For Carnap's pluralism operates at two levels. On the surface, most explicitly, it is a doctrine expressed in terms of the logical syntax of language—the view that language may be significantly factored into distinct linguistic frameworks, each associated with "a particular style of bound variables," as Quine puts it (1966: 130). Underlying this logico-syntactical pluralism, however, is the pragmatic or functional pluralism that provides its motivation. Carnap holds that there is some sort of category mistake involved in assimilating issues of the existence of classes, say, and the existence of physical objects. His model for the construction of linguistic frameworks reflects this assumption, requiring that we mark the category boundaries in our choice of syntax—a different quantifier for each category, for example. But the distinctions in question are not grounded at the syntactical level.

This is important, because Quine's challenge to Carnap's pluralism rests on a challenge to its logico-syntactical manifestation. Quine argues that it cannot be more than "a rather trivial consideration" whether we use different quantifiers for numbers, classes, and physical objects, for example, or use a single existential quantifier ranging over entities of any of these kinds. I want to argue that we can allow that Quine is right about this, while insisting that it makes no difference at all to the issue that really matters: namely, whether Carnap is right about the underlying functional distinctions, and right about category mistakes.

5. Carnap, Quine and Ryle on the "Mixing of Spheres"

The notion of a category mistake was familiar to the logical positivists of the 1920s and 1930s. In the *Aufbau* of 1928, Carnap himself uses the term "mixing of spheres" *(Sphärenvermengung)* for, as he puts it later (Schilpp 1963: 45), "the neglect of distinctions in the logical types of various kinds of concepts." But for contemporary audiences the notion is particularly associated with Ryle. Ryle is quite clear that it has implications for ontological issues, and in a famous passage in *The Concept of Mind*, touches on the question as to whether existence is a univocal notion:

> It is perfectly proper to say, in one logical tone of voice, that there exist minds, and to say, in another logical tone of voice, that there exist bodies. But these expressions do not indicate two different species of existence, for "existence" is not a generic word like "coloured" or "sexed." They indicate two different senses of "exist," somewhat as "rising" has different senses in "the tide is rising," "hopes are rising" and "the average age of death is rising." A man would be thought to be making a poor joke who said that three things are now rising, namely the tide, hopes and the average age of death. It would be just as good or bad a joke to say that there exist prime numbers and Wednesdays and public opinions and navies; or that there exist both minds and bodies. (1949: 23)

Given Quine's response to Carnap, it isn't surprising that he has little sympathy for Ryle's apparent ontological pluralism. In a section of *Word and Object* devoted to ambiguity, Quine takes the opportunity to put on record his objection to Ryle's view:

> There are philosophers who stoutly maintain that "true" said of logical or mathematical laws and "true" said of weather predictions or suspects' confessions are two uses of an ambiguous term "true." There are philosophers who stoutly maintain that "exists" said of numbers, classes and the like and "exists" said of material objects are two uses of an ambiguous term "exists." What mainly baffles me is the stoutness of their maintenance. What can they possibly count as evidence? Why not view "true" as unambiguous but very general, and recognize the difference between true logical laws and true confessions as a difference merely between logical laws and confessions? And correspondingly for existence? (1960: 131)[6]

6. The above passage from Ryle's *The Concept of Mind* is one of two places to which Quine refers his readers for "examples of what I am protesting."

But what is the disagreement between Quine and Ryle? For Quine, matters of ontology reduce to matters of quantification, and presumably Ryle would not deny that we should quantify over prime numbers, days of the week and dispositions. Indeed, Ryle might reinforce his own denial that there are "two species of existence" by agreeing with Quine that what is essential to the single species of existence is its link with quantification. Ryle simply needs to say that what we are doing in saying that beliefs exist is not what we are doing in saying that tables exist—but that this difference rests on a difference in talk about tables and talk about beliefs, rather than on any difference in the notions of existence involved. So far this is exactly what Quine would have us say. The difference is that whereas Quine's formulation might lead us to focus on the issue of the difference between tables and beliefs per se, Ryle's functional orientation—his attention to the question as to what a linguistic category *does*—will instead lead us to focus on the difference between the *functions* of talk of beliefs and talk of tables; on the issue of what the two kinds of talk are *for*, rather than that of what they are *about*.

Moreover, it is open to Ryle (and again, entirely in keeping with his use of the analogy with "rising") to say that in one important sense, it is *exactly the same* existential quantifier we use in these different cases. It is the same logical device, but employed in the service of different functional, pragmatic or linguistic ends. This move is important, because it goes a long way to defusing Quine's objection to Carnap.

By way of comparison—picking up on Quine's own second concern in the passage above—consider the familiar view that the truth predicate is a grammatical device to meet certain logical and pragmatic needs: a device for disquotational or prosentential purposes, say. As a number of writers have noted (see, e.g., Horwich 1990: 87–88; Blackburn 1984) this account is compatible with the view that declarative sentences can perform radically different functions, in a way which isn't captured merely by noting differences in content. Consider projectivism about moral or causal claims, for example. A deflationist may say that although it is the same deflated notion of truth we use when we say there are moral truths, or that there are causal truths, moral and causal claims have quite different functions (both with respect to each other, and with respect to other kinds of declarative claims).

An analogous move seems to provide the best way to preserve the pluralist insights of Carnap and Ryle in the face of Quine's objections. We should concede to Quine that there is a single logico-syntactic device of existential quantification, just as there is a single device of disquotational truth—if Carnap was really committed to the view that there are different existential quantifiers, one for each framework, then he was wrong about that.[7] But we should insist that this device has application

7. Though it is hard to see that there could really be a substantial difference of opinion here. We could index our disquotational truth predicates in a way that distinguished the predicate we apply to moral claims from the predicate we apply to causal claims, but this trivial syntactical exercise wouldn't

in a range of cases, whose functional origins are sufficiently distinct that naturalism is guilty of a serious error, in attempting to treat them as all on a par.

On this view, the subject–predicate form and indeed the notion of an object itself have a one–many functional character. In one sense, it is the same tool or set of tools we employ wherever we speak of objects, or whenever we use the subject–predicate form, or—what seems part of the same package—whenever we use the existential quantifier. However, there's no further unitary notion of *object*, or *substance*, or metaphysical bearer of properties, but "only a subject position in an infinite web of discourses."[8] Similarly, it is the same tool or set of tools we use whenever we speak of truth, whenever we make a judgment or an assertion. But in each case, the relevant tool or set of tools may have incommensurable uses, if there are important senses in which the bits of language they facilitate have different functions (in a way that doesn't simply collapse into differences in the objects *talked about*).

Thus the right way to read Ryle seems to be something like this. Terms such as "exists" and "true" are not ambiguous, for they serve a single core purpose in their various different applications. In that sense, they are univocal but very general terms, as Quine himself suggests. In virtue of the preexisting functional differences between the concepts with which they associate, however, the different applications of these terms are incommensurable, in an important sense. Many terms in language seem to fit this pattern, in having a single core meaning or function, with application in several quite distinct cases. A good example is the term Ryle himself offers by way of comparison with "exists," namely "rising." "Rising" certainly has a core meaning. It refers to the increase in some quantity over time. But in virtue of the incommensurability of different kinds of quantities, different risings may themselves be incommensurable. It doesn't make sense to ask whether the average age of death is rising faster than the cost of living, for example.

Similarly for existence, Ryle seems to want to say. The term has a single core meaning or function, tied to that of the existential quantifier. But because the notions of mind and body "belong to different logical categories"—that is, as I

---

prevent it from being the case that the resulting predicates both serve the same disquotational function. It is surely uncharitable to Carnap to suggest that he was confused about the analogous point, in the case of the existential quantifier. A champion of less deflationary metaphysics might think that there were significant distinctions for such syntactical conventions to mark, but why should Carnap think so?

8. To reverse the sense of a remark by one of David Lodge's characters, who is characterizing the view that there is no such thing as the Self. In this context, I note that Hilary Putnam does want to distinguish between "speaking of objects" and "using the existential quantifier," and wants to use the term object in a more restricted sense (see Putnam 2004: 52ff; 2001: 140–194). However, there doesn't seem to be much at issue here. Certainly, the Carnapian view I am recommending seems close to Putnam's "pragmatic pluralism" (2004: 21–22).

would put it, have importantly different functions in language—it doesn't make sense to think of the existence of minds as on a par with the existence of bodies. Ryle himself glosses this incommensurability in terms of the oddity of conjunctions such as "There are beliefs and there are rocks," but this doesn't seem to get to the heart of the matter. The crucial point is that attempts to make ontological comparisons between entities in the two domains go wrong in just the way that attempts to compare different kinds of risings go wrong.[9]

Of course, more needs to be said about the relevant notion of linguistic function. In some sense, talk of chairs serves a different function from talk of tables, simply because chairs and tables are different kinds of furniture. Yet Ryle (and I) don't want to say that "chair" and "table" belong to different logical categories. So we need a story about which functional differences are the important ones. Indeed, we want a story on two levels. We want an account of the kind of logical and linguistic symptoms that indicate the presence of one of the distinctions in question—a joint between logical categories. And we want to know what underlies and explains those symptoms—what *constitutes* the distinctions in question.[10]

Whatever the best story about these matters, an appealing thought is that if there are joints of this kind in language to be mapped and explained, they will turn out to line up with what, viewed from a different angle, present as some of the "hard cases" of contemporary metaphysics—the status and nature of morality, modality, meaning and the mental, for example. Ryle himself certainly thought that proper attention to categorical distinctions could deflate such metaphysical issues; and so too, at least to a limited extent, did Carnap. (So too did Wittgenstein, of course.) What's striking, from the point of view we imagined at the beginning of the chapter, is how invisible this approach became in the later decades of the twentieth century. Much of analytic philosophy came to forget about Wittgenstein, Carnap, and Ryle, and to take for granted, once more, that the relevant issues are metaphysical: Are there *really* entities or facts of the kinds in question (and if so, what is their nature)?

True, some people who began with these questions would go on to ask about linguistic functions. If we want to say that there are no such entities, for example, what account can we give of the language that seems to refer to such things? Even here, however, the linguistic point is subsidiary to the ontological point. It isn't Carnap's point, or Ryle's point, namely that the ontological question itself rests on a philosopher's confusion about language—on a failure to notice the joints.

9. In both cases it is debatable whether we should say that the comparisons are senseless, or merely false. I suspect that it makes little difference, as long as we recognize that even if we call it falsity, it involves a different kind of error from that involved in mistaken intra-category comparisons.

10. Ryle himself seems to pay much more attention to the former question than to the latter; see especially his "Categories" (1938).

Quine seems poorly placed to reject the suggestion that there might be important functional differences of this kind in language. The issue is one for science. It is the anthropologist, or perhaps the biologist, who asks, "What does this linguistic construction do for these people?" Quine can hardly argue that the results of such investigations may be known a priori.

True, Quine himself often seems to take for granted that language has a well-defined core descriptive function, common to all well-founded assertoric discourse. This assumption underpins his claim that some apparently assertoric discourses—those of intentional psychology or morality, for example—do not serve this function, being rather expressive or instrumental. But as Chris Hookway (1988: 68–69) notes, it is far from clear that this assumption is defensible, in Quine's own terms. For example, given Quine's own minimalism about truth, it is no use his saying that descriptive discourse aims at truth. Why shouldn't a minimal notion of truth be useful in an expressive or instrumental discourse? In other words, why shouldn't a minimalist allow that truth itself is a multifunctional notion, in our earlier sense? And why shouldn't the notion of description be as minimal as that of truth—thus undermining the assumption that description itself comprises a significant functional category? These are difficult matters, but that fact in itself supports the rather weak conclusion I want to draw. Quine's criticism of Carnap and Ryle's ontological pluralism is inconclusive, to say the least, because the issue depends on substantial issues about language on which the jury is still out.

Perhaps it would be better to say that the jury has been disbanded, for contemporary philosophy seems to have forgotten the case. I have argued that there is no justification for this amnesia in Quine's response to Carnap and Ryle. We have seen that Quine agrees with Carnap in rejecting an external, non-pragmatic standpoint for metaphysics (and that Quine's appeal to the failure of the analytic–synthetic distinction is largely a red herring at this point). Carnap's claim that traditional metaphysics is also guilty of a more local kind of error turns out to rest on foundations that Carnap himself does not supply—in effect, functional foundations for Ryle's notion of a category mistake. Nothing in Quine's criticism of Carnap's and Ryle's pluralism seems to count against the existence of such foundations, and so the verdict on the Carnap-Ryle view must await excavations—first-order scientific inquiries into the underlying functions of language in human life. The importance of this kind of investigation is much less appreciated in contemporary philosophy than it was in the 1950s, I think; and Quine, or at least his interpreters, deserve some of the blame.

6. Saving Ontology?

I noted at the beginning that there seem to be two main grounds to hold Quine responsible for the apparent health of metaphysics in contemporary philosophy, of which the first was the impact of his criticisms of Carnap. The second was the impact of "On What There Is," with which, as Putnam puts it, "Quine . . . single handedly made Ontology a respectable subject." In the remainder of the chapter I want to call attention by example to what seems to me a persistent misinterpretation of the significance of Quine's position on ontology—a misinterpretation that has the effect of making Quinean ontology a much more substantial metaphysical program than it really is. I offer two examples. Each is associated with one of the major figures of the post-Quinean analytic philosophy—Hilary Putnam and David Lewis, respectively—and perhaps the weight of these giants has contributed to the persistence of the misinterpretation.

7. Is There an Argument from Indispensability?

The first example comes from philosophy of mathematics. In debates between realists and anti-realists about mathematical entities, both sides commonly concede the force of the so-called Quine-Putnam indispensability argument. Here's a formulation of this argument from Hartry Field—perhaps the leading contemporary writer on the irrealist side of these debates—who attributes it particularly to Putnam:

> Putnam 1971 is the *locus classicus* for the view that we need to regard mathematics as true because only by doing so can we explain the utility of mathematics in other areas: for instance, its utility in science . . . and in metalogic . . . The general form of this Putnamian argument is as follows:
>
> (i) We need to speak in terms of mathematical entities in doing science, metalogic, etc.;
>
> (ii) If we need to speak in terms of a kind of entity for such important purposes, we have excellent reason for supposing that that kind of entity exists (or at least, that claims that on their face state the existence of such entities are true). (2001: 328–329)

Field takes it that in order to avoid the conclusion of this argument—that is, as he sees it, to avoid mathematical realism—anti-realists need to deny the truth of the first premise. (Hence his interest in the project of "science without numbers.")

Here's another formulation of the indispensability argument, this time from Mark Colyvan (2003), on the realist side of the debate:

> For future reference I'll state the Quine-Putnam indispensability argument in the following explicit form:
>
> (P1) We ought to have ontological commitment to all and only the entities that are indispensable to our best scientific theories.

(P2) Mathematical entities are indispensable to our best scientific theories.

(C) We ought to have ontological commitment to mathematical entities.

In my view, as I said, these arguments involve a subtle misinterpretation of Quine, and perhaps also of Putnam—though admittedly a misinterpretation that neither Quine nor Putnam seems to have done much to discourage. Here is Putnam's own version of the argument, from the source cited by Field:

> So far I have been developing an argument for realism along roughly the following lines: quantification over mathematical entities is indispensable for science, both formal and physical; therefore we should accept such quantification; but this commits us to accepting the existence of the mathematical entitites in question. This type of argument stems, of course, from Quine, who has for years stressed both the indispensability of quantification over mathematical entitites and the intellectual dishonesty of denying the existence of what one daily presupposes. (1971: 347)

Let's pay particular attention to Putnam's final remark here—his gloss of Quine. Putnam says that if quantification over mathematical entitites is indispensable, it is "intellectually dishonest" to deny the existence of such entities. The crucial point—a point missed by Putnam himself here, so far as I can see—is that a principled exclusion of arguments *against* the existence of entities of a certain kind does not in itself comprise an argument *for* the existence of such entities, of the kind supposedly captured by the above formulations.[11]

One way to highlight this distinction is to note that if there were an argument usable by ontologists in this vicinity, then by Quine's lights it would also be an argument usable by scientists and mathematicians themselves. After all, Quine insists that philosophy is not separate from science—we're all adrift in the same boat. But think about the (supposed) argument as used by scientists themselves. To secure premise (P2) (in Colyvan's notation), they must come to accept that quantification over mathematical entities is indispensable—not merely something that they just happen to go in for as scientists, but something that survives under reflection—something they think that they don't have a choice about, if they are to continue to do science at all.

11. In other words, what Putnam's gloss of Quine actually entitles us to is not (P1), but a strictly weaker principle something like this:
(P1*) Philosophers have no business disowning entities indispensable in science.
The crucial point I want to make is that although (P1*) prohibits *anti-realist* metaphysics, it doesn't support or mandate *realist* metaphysics; for it doesn't exclude Carnap's deflationary alternative to both.

But for Quine, of course, there is no space between ontological commitment—belief that there are mathematical entities—and acceptance of quantification over mathematical entities. So, by Quine's lights, to be in a position to accept (P2) is to accept not only that one believes that there are mathematical entities, but that one is justified in doing so, by the lights of best (philosophically informed) scientific practice. It is to believe not only that there are mathematical entities, but that one ought to believe that there are (by the standards of scientific practice), having properly considered the alternatives.

Imagine our scientists, thus equipped with premise (P2). If they accept premise (P1), they are thus led to the conclusion, (C), that they ought to believe that there are mathematical entities. But they believed that already, by assumption, if "ought" means something like "by the internal standards of science." So the argument could only take them somewhere new if there were some other standards—some other standpoint, from which to assess the question as to whether there are mathematical entities.

There are two problems with this last idea (i.e., that there is some other standpoint from which to assess the question). One is that it flatly contradicts Quine, who insists that there is no separate standpoint for ontology, outside that of science. The other is that by introducing two standards for ontological commitment—the second-rate "as-if" kind of commitment at the first stage, as compared to the first-rate, meaty kind of commitment at the second—it pulls the rug from beneath the entire argument. If there is a second-rate kind of ontological commitment, why should *that* kind of commitment be a guide to what there is? On the contrary, presumably, what makes it second-rate is that it isn't a (first-rate) guide to what there is.

In defense of the argument from indispensability, it might be said that Quine insists that if science reaches that stage of accepting (P2), then there is no philosophical standpoint from which it makes sense to doubt that there are mathematical entities—to ask "But are there REALLY mathematical entities?" Doesn't this imply that if science reaches the stage of accepting (P2), then we are justified in affirming that there are mathematical entities—after all, aren't we justified in affirming what it makes no sense to doubt?

Well, it depends. Perhaps we are justified in repeating what science says. But even if so, this involves no inference from the fact that science says it: no argument, simply concurrence. The Quinean doctrine that if science reaches that stage of accepting (P2), then there is no philosophical standpoint from which it makes sense to doubt that there are mathematical entities—to ask "But are there REALLY mathematical entities?"—does put paid to a certain sort of ontological scepticism, or anti-realism. But it doesn't imply that there is an argument *from* the needs of science *to* ontological conclusions—*for* realism. On the contrary, it deflates or disallows a certain sort of ontological debate: a debate taking place outside science, about whether there are things of the kind science quantifies over. After all, think of "REALLY" as a metaphysician's term of art. The argument that it makes no sense to ask "But are there REALLY mathematical entities?" does not imply that we should say "There REALLY are mathematical entities." Perhaps we should simply forget about "REALLY."

The difficulty with the argument just given is that our realist opponents will deny that they ever meant anything special (namely, "REALLY") by "really." A familiar dispute then ensues about whose position is the more modest—about who holds the metaphysical low ground, so to speak. From the deflationist's point of view, the right strategy is to present one's opponent with issues on which she must take a stand, one way or the other. The aim is to show that if she agrees, she is being more deflationist than she wants to be; while if she disagrees, she holds commitments sufficiently inflated to be targets.

The claimed argument from indispensability provides one such choice point, in my view. Once we distinguish the strong (realist metaphysics supporting) version of the argument from the weak (anti-realist metaphysics rejecting) version of the argument, then we deflationists can offer an opponent a choice between the two. If she chooses the strong version, we argue, as above, that she is no true Quinean. If she insists, instead, that she accepts the argument only in the modest, anti-realist dismissing sense, then we have no reason to disagree. On the contrary, we should welcome her to the anti-metaphysical club—to the enlightened circle who agree with Carnap, in rejecting "both the thesis of the reality of the external world and the thesis of its irreality."

8. How Metaphysical Is Modal Realism?

I now turn to a second appeal to the Quinean recipe for ontology—perhaps the most famous in twentieth-century metaphysics. It is David Lewis's argument for modal realism. Lewis begins by emphasizing that his modal realism is simply an ontological thesis:

> [M]y modal realism is simply the thesis that there are other worlds, and individuals inhabiting those worlds; and that these are of a certain nature, and suited to play certain theoretical roles. It is an existential claim, not . . . a thesis about our semantic competence, or about the nature of truth, or about bivalence, or about the limits of our knowledge. For me, the question is of the existence of objects—not the objectivity of the subject matter. (1986: viii)

"Why believe in [such] a plurality of worlds?," Lewis asks. "Because the hypothesis is serviceable," he replies, "and that is a reason to think that it is true" (1986: 3). He compares this argument to the mathematical case, cast explicitly in Quinean form:

> Set theory offers the mathematician great economy of primitives and premises, in return for accepting rather a lot of entities unknown to

> *Homo javanensis*. It offers an improvement in what Quine calls ideology, paid for in the coin of ontology. It's an offer you can't refuse. The price is right; the benefits in theoretical unity and economy are well worth the entities. Philosophers might like to see the subject reconstructed or reconstrued; but working mathematicians insist on pursuing their subject in paradise, and will not be driven out. Their thesis of the plurality of sets is fruitful; that gives them good reason to believe that it is true. (1986: 4)

In sum, then, Lewis's argument for modal realism comes down to this:

> [There are] many ways in which systematic philosophy goes more easily if we may presuppose modal realism in our analyses. I take this to be a good reason to think that modal realism is true, just as the utility of set theory in mathematics is a good reason to believe that there are sets. (1986: vii)

The first point I want to make about this argument is that it simply ignores the distinction a Carnapian will want to draw between pragmatic and traditional evidential reasons for "believing true." Clearly, a Carnapian might accept that the utility of talk of possible worlds (or sets) is a good *pragmatic* reason for adopting the vocabulary in question, without reading this as in any sense an argument for the *truth* of a metaphysical conclusion. To distinguish his position from such a Carnapian case for talk of possible worlds, Lewis needs to interpret the argument in a stronger sense. The question is, does Quine really offer any grounds for doing so?

Defenders of the argument from indispensability would answer "yes" at this point, and see Lewis as an ally in their own cause. But I have argued that this misrepresents Quine: the right conclusions to draw from the appeal to indispensability are simply the illegitimacy of any *metaphysical* stance, whether positive or negative on the ontological matter in question; coupled with the affirmation of the *pragmatic* case for continuing to use the vocabulary in question. Once more, this is entirely in keeping with Carnap's pragmatism and metaphysical deflationism.

If I am right, then the rather surprising upshot is that Lewis's modal realism—the most visible and controversial thesis of perhaps the most respected figure in late-twentieth-century metaphysics—doesn't really need to be thought of as *metaphysics* at all, in the sense of the subject that Carnap and his predecessors attacked. I don't claim this as an original insight. Simon Blackburn, for one, has long urged that the distinctively metaphysical "oomph" of Lewis's modal realism is surprisingly hard to pin down (and hard to distinguish, in particular, from Blackburn's own quasi-realism about modality). But the message has fallen on deaf ears. Many people *think* that they are doing metaphysics, in Lewis's footsteps—as Lewis himself intended, obviously, when he took those steps in the first place.

Lewis himself was aware of the threat from this quarter, and in one of his last papers (2005), he seeks to equate quasi-realism with a self-consciously metaphysical position, namely fictionalism.[12] He notes that both views (fictionalism and quasi-realism) endorse the first-order folk claims of a target discourse, but then offer us a second-order qualification. Thus in the modal case, for example, it goes like this: "There are ways things could have been"—that's the first-order claim—"but only in the modal fiction in which we all participate"—that's the fictionalist rider. Lewis seems to suggest that fictionalism and quasi-realism are therefore inferior to the view which accepts such statements without qualification—that is, as he interprets the unqualified view, to realism.

Set aside for the moment the question as to whether Lewis is right to interpret quasi-realism as a form of fictionalism, and focus first on the nature of this unqualified alternative, to which Lewis contrasts fictionalism and quasi-realism. What is this unqualified "realism"? Is it the view that *just* says, with the folk, "There are ways things might have been"? Or is it the view that says "There are REALLY ways things might have been"—where the capital letters mark some distinctively philosophical claim? If there's a difference between these two possibilities, and if it's the unqualified position we're after, then it must be the weaker position. Why? Because the stronger also requires an additional qualification, though this time of a positive rather than a negative kind. (The folk don't add the capital letters, if adding the capital letters adds philosophal theory.)

What if there isn't a difference between the weaker and stronger views? That would imply that, as Carnap thought, there isn't any distinctively theoretical viewpoint that philosophy can bring to such matters of ontology. In other words, it implies that there isn't any distinct (and legitimate) stronger position. Again, then, the unqualified position is the weaker position.

All the same, Lewis's argument may seem to pose a threat to what I am offering as the most attractive version of the Carnapian program, in the following sense. I have suggested that in order to meet Quine's objections to pluralism, a Carnapian needs to emphasize what I called the functional pluralism that already seems implicit in Carnap's view. In other words, the Carnapian needs to emphasize the plurality of the things we do with language (and with existentially quantified language, in particular).

However, this functionalist or genealogical orientation seems to have much in common with Blackburn's quasi-realism. And this raises the possibility that Lewis's argument might be able to establish that my Carnapian position is more metaphysical than I take it to be: metaphysical in the negative sense, in that—like fictionalism—it is committed to metaphysical claims of an anti-realist nature.

12. I am not sure whether Lewis thought of this paper as a response to the threat just mentioned; but he can hardly have been unaware that if his argument succeeded, it would serve this purpose.

Lewis's argument turns on the observation that there are qualifications we can add to what would otherwise be an assertion (or series of assertions), which have the effect of canceling the assertoric force. He gives several examples—for example, "I shall say much that I do not believe, starting *now*," and "According to the Sherlock Holmes stories . . ." (2005: 315)—and notes that an expression of metaphysical fictionalism (about moral discourse, say) has the same effect: it amounts to preceding one's moral assertions with the remark that they are not really true. Lewis claims that the same is true of quasi-realism—it, too, amounts to a "disowning preface" (2005: 315) of this kind: "That preface is to be found in the endorsement of projectivism that precedes and motivates [Blackburn's] advocacy of quasi-realism. . . . It is something the quasi-realist says that the realist will not echo" (2005: 315).

In the present context, the relevant question is whether projectivism, or some other broadly functionalist or expressivist genealogy for a Carnapian domain of existential commitment, does amount to a "disowning preface," in a way that creates any sort of difficulty for the combination I have recommended, of functional pluralism and metaphysical deflationism. Can we adopt a domain of existential quantification in a pragmatic Carnapian spirit, and *say* that that is what we are doing, without canceling the assertoric force of the claims (including the existential claims) that we make in that domain?

The first point to note is that such a functional story will certainly count as a disowning preface to some claims that a metaphysical realist might want to make—in particular, claims that entail, explicitly or implicitly, some alternative account of the function and genealogy of the language in question. But no problems here for a deflationist, presumably, who won't be endorsing such claims in the first place.[13] The relevant issue isn't whether quasi-realism disowns what the capital-R Realist *adds* when he affirms that there are REALLY moral truths. It is whether it disowns the ordinary unqualified affirmation of moral truths.

So, does genealogy amount to taking something back, or merely to adding more? Note, first, that not all ways of adding more take something back. Consider this case, for example:

> The butler wasn't at Starbucks on the night of the murder. (I've known that since last week.)

13. This issue is a tricky one for Blackburn, perhaps, in that his quasi-realism may commit him to some implicit metaphysical picture associated with the idea of genuinely representational discourse—the cases to which he wants to contrast the domains in which *quasi*-realism is the appropriate strategy. But no such problem arises for global quasi-realism, a view that Blackburn sometimes seems tempted by (and associates with Wittgenstein), and that I myself have recommended. See Blackburn (1998a: 166–167; 1998b: 77–83), Price (1992, 2004b), and Macarthur and Price (2007).

This shows that there are some ways we can "fill in some of the background" to an assertion, without disowning that assertion. More interestingly, it appears that there are some ways in which we can diminish the force of an assertion by adding a qualification, without in any sense undermining its *truth:*

> It turns out that the butler did it. (I speak, of course, as a fallible human being.)

Here, the addition does indeed seem to diminish the force of the preceding assertion. But the corresponding addition would be true (and in normal circumstances we would know perfectly well that it would be true) for almost any assertion whatsoever. So although *mentioning it* counts as some sort of retraction, that's no reason to doubt the truth of the qualification itself, or to question a straightforwardly realist construal of the original sentence. This shows that there is space for (true) genealogy to be both conversationally "disowning," and yet entirely compatible with realism—at least if realism here means simply taking a claim at face value, rather than adding some rival genealogy.

The lesson seems to be that we need to distinguish a broad sense of "disowning" or diminishing the force of an assertion, from a stricter sense which amounts to something like *contradicting*, or *implying the falsity*, of the original assertion. The examples above suggest that in some but not all cases, genealogy disowns in the former sense. It is not entirely clear which side of the line quasi-realist genealogy falls on, I think, but for present purposes it doesn't matter. For present purposes the latter kind of disowning—"implying the falsity," as I put it—is the crucial one.

Fictionalism certainly disowns in this latter sense, but quasi-realism does not. One way to convince ourselves of this is to keep a clear eye on the use–mention distinction. Fictionalism needs to *use* moral vocabulary, in order to deny that there are values, literally speaking; whereas Carnapian or Blackburnian genealogy need only *mention* it (in explaining what the folk do, when they *use* it). Quasi-realism talks *about* the talk, as it were, without actually talking the talk. Hence it simply lacks the vocabulary to say (or imply) that moral claims are false.

If Lewis were right to equate quasi-realism with fictionalism, it would be much harder to be a metaphysical deflationist than Carnap takes it to be—contrary, clearly, to his own intentions, Carnap's view would be metaphysics in disguise. But Lewis hasn't made a case for the equation. And in a sense, his argument fails precisely because it is blind to the distinction between what we might call a metaphysical stance with respect to a vocabulary—a stance which takes the primary question to be whether the claims distinctive of the vocabulary are *true*—and a genealogical or anthropological stance, which is interested in why creatures like us come to employ the vocabulary in the first place. Reflections from the latter stance may not always be neutral with respect to the moves we make within the game—the assertions we make as we employ the vocabulary ourselves. (In some cases, indeed, they cause us to abandon the game altogether.) But as long as we keep the stances distinct in the first place, there's no excuse for confusing this lack of neutrality for the adoption of a position within the game itself.

Thus it appears that neither Lewis's own argument for modal realism, nor his late attempt to equate quasi-realism with fictionalism, offers any significant obstacle to a Carnapian combination of metaphysical deflationism and pragmatic functional pluralism. Once again, it turns out to be simply an illusion to think that Quine offers a recipe for any more substantial kind of metaphysics. I conclude that, Quine's objections notwithstanding, metaphysics remains where Carnap left it. The challenge of "Empiricism, Semantics and Ontology" remains unanswered.[14]

14. This chapter draws substantially on two earlier publications. The first five sections include an updated version of much of the material in a paper in *The Electronic Journal of Analytic Philosophy* (Price 1997), in some cases via a second incarnation in a recent paper in *The Journal of Philosophy* (Price 2007). Section 7 is also based on a section of the latter paper. I am also much indebted to Amie Thomasson and Matti Eklund, for many helpful comments on an earlier version.

14

One Cheer for Representationalism?

1. Paradise Postponed?

When Dewey declared in 1905 that pragmatism would "give the *coup de grace* to *representationalism*,"[1] he had (to say the least) underestimated the tenacity of the intended victim. Even as he wrote, Russell was at work on the wagons that were to carry so much of philosophy into new lands—regions where Frege's referentialism was part of the bedrock (or so it seemed). A century later, despite renewed resistance by such giants as Wittgenstein and Richard Rorty, representationalism seems to many to be not only alive but unassailable—part of the constitution of the analytic republic, and almost too obvious to challenge.[2]

1. From a letter quoted by Menand 2001: 361.

2. Anti-representationalism often meets with something close to incomprehension, as in these remarks from Frank Jackson, for example:

> Although it is obvious that much of language is representational, it is occasionally denied. I have attended conference papers attacking the representational view of language given by speakers who have in their pockets pieces of paper with writing on them that tell them where the conference dinner is and when the taxis leave for the airport. (Jackson 1997: 270)

Similarly, referring directly to Rorty's anti-representationalism, Simon Blackburn writes:

> [L]anguage is not there to represent things—how ridiculous! . . . For, after all, a wiring diagram represents how things stand inside our electric bell, our fuel gauge represents the amount of petrol left in the tank, and our physics or history tells how things stand physically or historically. (2005a: 153)

(I return to Blackburn's remarks below.) Moreover, as Brandom points out, it isn't only in analytic philosophy that representationalism tends to be taken for granted:

> [A] representational paradigm reigns not only in the whole spectrum of analytically pursued semantics, from model-theoretic, through possible worlds, directly counterfactual, and informational approaches to teleosemantic ones, but also in structuralism inheriting the broad outlines of Saussure's semantics, and even in those later continental thinkers whose poststructuralism is still so far mired in the representational paradigm that it can see no other alternative to understanding meaning in terms of signifiers standing for signifieds than to understand it in terms of signifiers standing for other signifiers. (2000: 9–10)

Look a little more closely at the contemporary shape of this Fregean domain, however, and we pragmatists may find grounds for Deweyan optimism about its eventual fate—signs that the representationalist republic may be crumbling from within. One promising sign is the virulence of a virus of which Frege himself is one of the progenitors, namely, "semantic minimalism": a quietist, deflationary attitude to some of the foundational conceptual machinery of representationalism. Doesn't minimalism eat away at representationalism from the inside, depriving it of the theoretical vocabulary it needs to be telling us anything substantial about human thought and language? If so, then perhaps representationalism is dead after all, still flying the flag over the shell of an empire when the interesting conversation has moved elsewhere.

The second hopeful sign for Deweyan optimists, in my view, is the persistence, within the borders of representationalism, of a series of breakaway movements—each contending that the representationalist framework claims no proper dominion over some *local* region of its apparent territory, and offering an alternative, "expressivist," account of the region in question. While most of these breakaway movements are (perhaps hopelessly) local in their ambitions, I think that the threat they pose collectively is substantial (and underrated). I'll call it the threat of *functional pluralism*: a challenge to the homogeneity of the representationalist empire. Interpreted in this optimistic light, these breakaway views do locally what Wittgenstein did globally.[3] They challenge the assumption that language has a single core function, namely, to "represent how things are."

Thus semantic minimalism and expressivist functional pluralism—two homegrown products of the analytic tradition—offer some prospect that Dewey may have been right about the eventual fate of representationalism. Moreover, it is easy to read both movements as products of pragmatist seeds, within the analytic mainstream. After all, semantic minimalism offers a self-consciously non-metaphysical approach to truth, while focusing on practical questions about what we can *do* with a truth predicate that it would be difficult or impossible to do without it. And expressivism focuses directly on the distinctive use of (say) moral or modal vocabulary—thereby, once again, sidestepping traditional metaphysical concerns about nature of moral or modal states of affairs. In both cases, then, we see some of the defining characteristics of pragmatism, such as an interest in the practical utility of words and forms of thought, and a rejection of metaphysics. So optimism on either ground about the fate of representationalism is "Dewey-eyed" not merely in predicting a coup de grâce, but in anticipating that the fatal blow will come from pragmatism.

Dewey was the first author to be honoured in the *Library of Living Philosophers* series, and hence it seemed fitting for me to write for Richard Rorty's volume on

3. "We remain unconscious of the prodigious diversity of all the everyday language-games because the clothing of our language makes everything alike" (Wittgenstein 1968: 224; see 23–24 for similar remarks).

what is so strikingly a Deweyan as well as a Rortyan theme. In this chapter I want to try to fill out the above remarks, concerning what strikes me as a confirmation of a Dewey-Wittgenstein-Rorty anti-representationalism from sources within the analytic domain. In particular, I want to distinguish several grades of anti-representationalism, and to recommend what seems to me the most attractive grade. I'll draw these distinctions with reference to a pragmatist who can easily seem to be more of friend of representationalism than Dewey, Wittgenstein or Rorty, namely Bob Brandom. I suspect that Rorty may feel that the position I recommend concedes too much to representationalism; and Brandom, perhaps, that it concedes too little. If so, so be it: I am between Rorty and Brandom. By my lights, one could do a lot worse than that.

2. Dissent among the Dissenters?

First, an objection to the idea that we might build a challenge to representationalism on the twin pillars of semantic minimalism and expressivist pluralism: It is often held that these two views are themselves in conflict (in which case an anti-representationalism based on both would be less Dewey-eyed than cross-eyed). The claimed conflict rests on the thought that semantic minimalism undermines expressivism, by lowering the bar: by making it easy for a declarative discourse to be truth-conditional, in the only sense that minimalism allows.

This has been a popular challenge to expressivism, propounded by John McDowell and Crispin Wright, among others (see, e.g., McDowell 1981; Boghossian 1990; Humberstone 1991; Wright 1992; Jackson, Oppy, and Smith 1994) But it is a deeply puzzling objection, for the appeal to minimalism actually *supports* what is surely the core doctrine of expressivism, namely, that we should not theorize about vocabularies in a semantic key. Concerning evaluative or normative vocabulary, for example, the expressivist's core claim is that we should concern ourselves with the use, function, and pragmatic significance of the vocabularies concerned, rather than with their semantic attributes. If we follow the expressivist in making this theoretical shift, how could it trouble us if semantic minimalists insist that the issue of semantic attributes is theoretically empty? As expressivists, we were already committed to the view that the interesting theoretical conversation takes place somewhere else. So isn't it good news—a kind of automatic confirmation of our instincts—if the semantic minimalist tells us that there is in any case no interesting theorising to be done in semantic terms?

I think that the availability of this response to the minimalist challenge to expressivism has been obscured by the fact that expressivism is usually a local position. Typically, expressivists want to abandon the semantic framework for a particular vocabulary—again, evaluative vocabulary, for example—while retaining it elsewhere. This does render them vulnerable to the minimalist challenge . . . but because of what they *retain* of the representationalist picture, not because of what they *adopt* of the expressivist picture! The minimalist challenge does indeed threaten the contrast that local expressivists usually want to draw between genuinely descriptive and expressive vocabularies—but because it threatens the former category, not because it threatens the latter.

This reading of the true relevance of minimalism to expressivism meshes nicely, I think, with the way Simon Blackburn interprets Wittgenstein, as someone who combines semantic minimalism and expressivism (arguably, in fact, *global* expressivism). Responding to Crispin Wright's version of the usual minimalist challenge to expressivism, and to a general tendency to read Wittgenstein as the kind of minimalist who wants to "homogenize" language, Blackburn points out, in effect, that the fact that distinctions go missing in a semantic key—the fact that Ramsey's or Wittgenstein's semantic minimalism denies us the right to theorize about differences in one way—does not imply at all that we cannot theorize about differences in another way. The relevant differences are pragmatic, not semantic; and minimalism makes this easier to say, not harder!

> The point is that Ramsey and Wittgenstein do not need to work with a sorted notion of *truth*—robust, upright, hard truth versus some soft and effeminate imitation. They need to work with a sorted notion of a *proposition*, or if we prefer it a sorted notion of *truth-aptitude*. There are propositions properly theorized about in one way, and ones properly theorized about in another. The focus of theory is the nature of the commitment voiced by one adhering to the proposition, and the different functional roles in peoples' lives (or forms of life, or language games) that these different commitments occupy. Indeed, I should say that although a good title for the position might be "non-descriptive functionalism," Wittgenstein could even afford to throw "description" into the minimalist pot. Even if we have to say that all commitments describe their coordinate slices of reality, we can still say that they are to be theorized about in a *distinctive* way. You come at them differently, offering a different theory of their truth-aptitude (again, this ought not to be uncongenial to Wright, since it is only extending the very kind of move he himself makes to rehabilitate versions of the realism debate, in the face of minimalism about truth). You may end up, that is, saying that these assertions describe how things are with values, probability, modality, and the rest. But the way you arrive at this bland result will be distinctive, and it will be the bit that matters. (Blackburn 1998a: 166–167)[4]

In my view, in fact, Blackburn understates the case: it is not that Wittgenstein could afford to throw "description" into the minimalist pot, but rather that—as a semantic minimalist—he cannot afford *not* to throw it into the pot. In other

4. Cf. Blackburn 1998b: 77–83, for a more detailed discussion of this "Wittgensteinian" option.

words, the *only* satisfactory resolution of the apparent tension between minimalism and expressivism comes from seeing that minimalism implies that there can be no half measures. Given minimalism, expressivism is *necessarily* a global viewpoint, because minimalism deprives us of the theoretical vocabulary needed for any alternative viewpoint.

In failing to see that minimalism actually mandates expressivism in this way, Blackburn fails to see quite how completely wrongheaded is the usual charge that minimalism defeats expressivism. Nevertheless, I think Blackburn gets closer to the truth on this matter than most people—a fact which makes it all the more puzzling that, as I noted at the beginning, he is one of those who dismisses Rorty's anti-representationalism as an "absurd" position. In Blackburn's case, the charge comes from someone whose major contribution has been to show us how subtle the question of whether a vocabulary is really in the representing business can be; to argue that ways of talking which *look* for all the world as if they are genuinely representational—moral talk, or modal talk, for example—can actually be playing some different role.

We have just seen that in enlisting Wittgenstein as a patron of his own "quasi-realist" program, Blackburn has even canvassed sympathetically the idea that there is no distinction between the descriptive and the non-descriptive. There are two ways to read the implications of this suggestion for representationalism: either it amounts to a global rejection of representationalism, a way of saying *globally* what expressivists and non-cognitivists usually say *locally*. Or it saves representationalism, but at the cost of stripping it of all theoretical content—of deflating the notion so much that it no longer plays any role in our theorizing about the relationship of language and thought to the world. But it is hard to see how either reading differs significantly from Rorty's rejection of representationalism; hard to see how someone who finds himself close to Wittgenstein on these matters could possibly be far from Rorty.

The real moral of the case is thus that semantic minimalism and expressivist pluralism are not only not in conflict, but actually reinforce one another. In white-anting representationalism, minimalism leaves the field clear for global expressivism (i.e., for a global assemblage of local expressivisms); while expressivism in its local varieties gives us an indication of what the theoretical conversation is going to be about, given that it is not to be conducted in a semantic key. All in all, then, a bright future for the Deweyan vision, albeit a century late.

3. Brandom as Counter-revolutionary?

But a shadow falls over this Dewey-eyed vista from an unlikely quarter. My optimist—who sees representationalism as undermined by a resurgence of pragmatist themes within the analytic encampment, and sets off, *sans* mirrors, on the trail blazed by Dewey, Wittgenstein, and Rorty—finds his way blocked by a pragmatist of comparable stature, who may appear to be moving in the opposite direction. This counter-revolutionary figure is Robert Brandom, whose pragmatism sometimes seems intended not so much to deliver Dewey's coup de grâce to representationalism, as an old-fashioned coup d'état—to take over the representationalist empire intact, by rebuilding its walls on properly pragmatic foundations.

The matter is complex, partly because Brandom, too, is certainly opposed to many elements of traditional non-pragmatist representationalism, and partly because his view can be read in different ways. In the interests of sharpening matters up, I want to try to distinguish four possible positions, on a spectrum ranging from complete rejection of representationalism, on the left, to full-blown three-cheers endorsement of representationalism, on the right. On the assumption that Wittgenstein and Rorty occupy the left-most (no cheers) position, I want to locate my counter-revolutionary reading of Brandom two steps further to the right, one cheer short of full-blown representationalism. And I want to recommend the position between Rorty and (this version of) Brandom: one cheer for representationalism.[5]

As I shall explain, however, the scale is not linear. The difference between one and two cheers marks a sea change in one's implicit philosophical outlook, a kind of Dewey Line for pragmatism: stay to the left of it, and one's pragmatism is a genuinely progressive position, an alternative to metaphysics. Move to the right of it, and one is at best a metaphysician in pragmatist's clothing. So this is not a gap anyone can comfortably straddle, and my message to Brandom is that he needs to take a stand, on one side or other.

4. Does Language Have a Downtown?

Brandom emphasizes that in contrast to Wittgenstein, his view requires that language "has a downtown"—that *assertion* is a fundamental linguistic activity on which others depend. At the heart of Brandom's entire project is a pragmatic, *inferentialist* account of what is fundamental to this core activity.

> By contrast to Wittgenstein, the inferential identification of the conceptual claims that language . . . has a *center;* it is not a motley. Inferential practices of producing and consuming *reasons* are *downtown* in the region of linguistic practice. Suburban linguistic practices utilize and depend on the conceptual contents forged in the game of giving and asking for reasons, are parasitic on it. (2000: 14)

5. Thus there are two apparent points of conflict between Brandom's position and what I'm treating as the Dewey-Wittgenstein-Rorty position, and broadly speaking I want to agree with Brandom on the first and disagree on the second—though, as I said, the disagreement turns on a particular interpretation of Brandom's views.

Doesn't this challenge Wittgensteinian pluralism, especially as appropriated by Blackburn? Where the expressivist wants to see a variety of superficially assertoric language games, differently related to various functions and psychological states, Brandom shows us a single practice of making commitments, offering entitlements, giving and asking for reasons. And for Brandom, surely, it isn't an option to throw assertion "into the minimalist pot": on the contrary, assertion is *the* fundamental language game, and the core of Brandom's whole project is an investigation of the nature of this fundamental game.

In my view, however, there's actually no deep conflict here. After all, even Wittgenstein acknowledges the common "clothing," which makes different language games superficially similar (and thereby misleads us into thinking that they are all doing the same job). It is open to us to say that the key similarity is precisely that various of the different language games all avail themselves of the same inferential machinery. This is thoroughly compatible with underlying pluralism, so long as we also maintain that the various different kinds of commitments answer to different needs and purposes—have different origins in our complex natures and relations to our physical and social environments. It is open to us to say this as long as we reject what is otherwise a competing account of the significance of assertions, namely, that they exhibit a common relation to preexisting conceptual contents (which puts the basic pluralism at the level of differences of content, rather than differences of function).

Thus I think we can follow Brandom here—agree that language has a downtown—without sacrificing key pragmatist territory. What we need is the idea that although assertion is indeed a fundamental language game, it is a game with multiple functionally distinct applications—a multifunction tool, in effect.[6] So long as the right way to theorize about these applications is in the expressivist's use-based vocabulary, the position is compatible with the kind of functional pluralism of Blackburn's version of Wittgenstein.

Indeed, Brandom's project seems not only compatible with this kind of pragmatic functional pluralism, but committed to it. Brandom characterizes his project as follows:

> Starting with an account of what one is *doing* in making a claim, it seeks to elaborate from it an account of what is said, the content or proposition—something that can be thought of in terms of truth conditions—to which one commits oneself by making a speech act. (2000: 12)
>
> Pragmatism about the conceptual seeks to understand what it is explicitly to *say* or *think that* something is the case in terms of what one must implicitly know *how* (be able) to *do*. (2000: 18)

6. Brandom warns us against misuse of the idea that language is a tool—that language has a *purpose*—but nothing I say here treads on controversial ground in this respect. (On the contrary, as I'm about to explain, the functional pluralism I have in mind here is of a kind that Brandom himself wants to highlight.)

Thus Brandom aims to show how conceptual content arises from pragmatic function, and this could only fail to involve some sort of pragmatic functional pluralism if Brandom were to offer us the *same* functional story for every sort of content. That is obviously not what he intends, however. On the contrary, what's exciting about Brandom's project is the way in which he links different kinds of vocabulary to different kinds of pragmatic tasks—the dazzle is in these details, as it were. And it couldn't be what he intends, surely, on pain of falling back into his opponent's camp. If Brandom were to say that we were *doing* the same thing, in the relevant sense, in making any assertion whatsoever, then he would merely have offered us a pragmatic account of assertoric *force*—by coarse-graining to this extreme, his account would simply fail to connect with what varies from assertion to assertion, and hence would have nothing to say about *content* (or the dimension of variability it represents).

So although Brandom's account may impose a degree of uniformity on language that Wittgenstein might wish to reject—offering us a uniform account of the way in which Wittgenstein's common linguistic "clothing" is held together, so to speak—it not only *allows* but actually *requires* that this uniformity coexist with an underlying pragmatic diversity. Different pieces of clothing do different things, even though there is an important sense in which they are all put together in the same way.

Note also that although Brandom cannot throw the term "assertion" into "Wittgenstein's minimalist pot," it doesn't follow that he cannot throw in terms such as "description," "truth," "reference," and "representation" itself. It is open to Brandom to maintain (and at least in the case of "truth" and "reference" he does explicitly maintain) that his substantial account of assertion—as the core, downtown, language game—doesn't depend on substantial "word–world" relations, of the kind these terms are taken to denote in conventional representationalist views.

But does Brandom want to throw all these terms into the minimalist pot? This seems to me to be a matter on which Brandom could usefully be clearer. Certainly he sometimes speaks as if his project is not to deflate representational and referential notions, but rather to show how they can be constructed from pragmatic materials:

> The major explanatory challenge for inferentialists is rather to explain the representational dimension of semantic content—to construe *referential* relations in terms of *inferential* ones. (1994: xvi)

> The representationalist tradition has, beginning with Frege, developed rich accounts of *inference* in terms of *reference*. How is it possible conversely to make sense of reference in terms of inference? In the absence of such an account, the inferentialist's attempt to turn the explanatory tables on the representationalist tradition must be deemed desperate and unsuccessful. (1994: 136)

In the observance, however, what Brandom actually does is not to "construe referential relations" (as having such-and-such a nature, for example), or to "make sense of reference" (itself), but rather to offer us an account of the use of referential *vocabulary:* he tells us about the use of the *term* "refers," not about the reference *relation*—about *ascriptions* of reference, not about reference itself.

Why does this distinction matter? In my view, it matters because it is crucial to avoiding a certain kind of philosophical cul de sac—roughly, metaphysics, or at least a distinctively misguided and self-inflicted kind of metaphysics, to which philosophy has long been subject. One of the lessons I think that Brandom might well learn from the analytic expressivist tradition concerns the importance and rewards of treading carefully on these matters. I want to summarize what I take to be some of the insights of that tradition, in order to explain where I take it that Brandom should place his feet (and to describe the gap that I think he currently straddles).

5. The Lessons of Humean Expressivism

The expressivist views I have in mind are responses to what are now called "location" or "placement" problems. Initially, these present as metaphysical or perhaps epistemological problems, within the context of some broad metaphysical or epistemological program: empiricism, say, or physicalism. By the lights of the program in question, some of the things we talk about seem hard to "place," within the framework the program dictates for reality or our knowledge of reality. Where are moral facts to be located in the kind of world described by physics? Where is our knowledge of causal necessity to go, if a posteriori knowledge is to grounded on the senses?

The expressivist solution is to move the problem cases outside the scope of the general program in question, by arguing that our tendency to place them within its scope reflects a mistaken understanding of the vocabulary associated with the matters in question. Thus the (apparent) location problem for moral or causal *facts* was said to rest on a mistaken understanding of the function of moral or causal *language*. Once we note that this language is not in the business of "describing reality," says the expressivist, the location problem can be seen to rest on a category mistake.

Note that traditional expressivism thus involved both a negative and a positive thesis about the vocabularies in question. The negative thesis was that these vocabularies are not genuinely representational, and as I noted earlier, expressivists here took for granted that some parts of language are genuinely representational (and, implicitly, that this was a substantial matter of some sort). The positive thesis proposed some alternative account of the function of each vocabulary in question. My inversion of the common minimalist objection to expressivism rests on the observation that the positive thesis not only survives deflation of the negative thesis by semantic deflationism—it actually wins by default, in the sense that semantic deflationism *mandates* some non-representational account of the functions of the language in question.

But what is happening at this point on the metaphysical side—that is, to those metaphysical issues that expressivism originally sought to evade? Note first that traditional expressivism tended to be an explicitly anti-realist position, at least in those versions embedded in some broader metaphysical program. In ethics, for example, non-cognitivism was seen as a way of making sense of the language of morals, while denying that there are really any such things a moral values or moral facts. But this was always a little problematic: if moral language was non-descriptive, how could it be used to make even a negative metaphysical claim? Better, perhaps, to say that the traditional metaphysical issue of realism versus anti-realism is simply ill-posed—an attitude to metaphysics that has long been in play, as Carnap makes clear:

> Influenced by ideas of Ludwig Wittgenstein, the [Vienna] Circle rejected both the thesis of the reality of the external world and the thesis of its irreality as pseudo-statements; the same was the case for both the thesis of the reality of universals . . . and the nominalistic thesis that they are not real and that their alleged names are not names of anything but merely *flatus vocis*. (1950: 215)

Famously, Carnap recommends this kind of metaphysical quietism quite generally, and this is surely a desirable stance for an expressivist, especially when semantic minimalism deflates what I called the expressivist's negative thesis. An expressivist wants to allow that as users of moral language, we may talk of the existence of values and moral facts, in what Carnap would call an internal sense. What's important is to deny that there is any other sense in which these issues make sense. Here Carnap is a valuable ally, but a general Carnapian prohibition on "external" ontological questions isn't sufficient at this point. My expressivist needs to show that like her more traditional colleagues, she escapes a certain kind of dog-leg, which—Carnapian prohibitions notwithstanding—threatens to take us from linguistic theory to metaphysics.

To explain what I mean by this, I need a distinction between ontologically *conservative* and ontologically *profligate* ways of theorizing about language. Any way of theorizing about language has some ontological commitments, of course—at the very least, presumably, commitments to speakers, to speech acts of some kind, and to various environmental factors (e.g., to explain why such speakers produce such speech acts on certain occasions but not others). An ontologically conservative theory commits us to no more than this. Whereas—again putting the matter in Carnapian terms—an ontologically profligate theory also picks up the *internal* ontological commitments of the linguistic frameworks *theorized about*.

How can this happen? Easily, if our theories invoke representational notions. If we say as linguistic theorists that a term X *stands for* something, then the question "What is the Y, such that X stands for Y?" becomes a question pressed on us by our linguistic theory itself—even if the Y at issue is something not normally regarded as part of the required ontology of linguistic theory, such as a moral property, or a prime number.

Employing substantial semantic relations thus makes linguistic theory ontologically profligate. Ascribing semantic relations to a vocabulary commits linguistic theorists to an ontology that mirrors—via the semantic relations in question—the internal ontological commitments of the vocabulary in question. Semantic relations thus provide a kind of bridge that cannot help but lead our theoretical gaze from words to things.

It is easy to see how this gives rise to location problems. As theorists studying human language as a natural phenomenon, we find ourselves saying in our theoretical voice that terms such as "goodness," "seven," "cause," "knowledge," and "truth" do the job of *referring*—in other words, that they stand at one end of a relation of some significant kind. We then feel the need for an answer to the question, "What lies at the other end of this relation?," which meets various theoretical desiderata—meshing with the other kinds of things we are inclined to say about speakers, their environments and their capacities, for example. Hence, given our starting point, a pressure toward naturalistic answers and towards location problems.

Traditional expressivism relieves this pressure by arguing that the semantic properties were wrongly ascribed, in the problem cases. My deflationary expressivism needs to sail closer to wind, and it isn't immediately obvious that it can stay on the conservative side of the line. The crucial point is that the ontological profligacy of representational approaches is generated by their explicit employment of semantic relations, *for theoretical purposes*. So long as the semantic terms are simply *absent* from our theoretical vocabulary, no such "extra-linguistic" ontological commitment arises. The trick is to find a way of ensuring that we stay on the side of virtue here, while allowing ourselves (and our subjects) the harmless deflationary use of the semantic vocabulary.

The solution lies in close attention to a use–mention distinction. The expressivist's motto should be that vocabularies should be *mentioned* but not *used*—theorized about but not employed, at least in the armchair. As long as the expressivist keeps this in mind—ensures that her initial theoretical perspective only *mentions* the target vocabulary—there's no danger that her own casual deflationary use of the metalinguistic semantic vocabulary will lead her into the metaphysical trap; and no danger, either, that her subjects' use of the corresponding vocabulary of the object language will draw her into their ontological web. With the use–mention distinction properly in mind, then, semantic deflationism does provide the required guarantee. It ensures that the expressivist is never going to find herself committed to a claim of the form "X *refers* to Y," where X is a term of the object language. (After all, the essence of a deflationary view of reference is that the notion has no such theoretical use.)

Summing up, what is at stake is the ability of pragmatism to escape certain sorts of metaphysical or ontological questions. One of the great virtues of expressivism is the way that it replaces metaphysical questions with questions about human thought and language. In place of metaphysical questions about the nature of value, or modality, say, it offers us questions about the role and genealogy of evaluative and modal vocabularies—and these are questions about human behavior, broadly construed, rather than questions about some seemingly puzzling part of the metaphysical realm. This shift is one of the things that makes Humean expressivism attractive to naturalists. It simply sidesteps the problem of finding a place for value (or indeed causal necessity!) in the kind of world that physics gives us reason to believe in. (There are concomitant epistemological virtues, too, as was also clear to Hume.) So naturalists should embrace the pragmatist–expressivist shift from philosophizing about objects to philosophizing about vocabularies, in my view—embrace the lesson that a proper naturalism about subjects may undercut the motivation for a common form of naturalism about objects.

This is why it matters, and why virtue requires that we stay on what I want to identify as the Dewey-Wittgenstein-Rorty side of the fence: resolutely opposed to the kind of representationalism that gives metaphysics a free ride (on the back of the study of vocabularies). Expressivism isn't a way of doing metaphysics in a pragmatist key. It is a way of doing something like anthropology.

6. Where Does Brandom Stand?

Where does Brandom stand with respect to this distinction between metaphysics and anthropology? As I said earlier, my impression is that he straddles the divide. This is a large topic, deserving a more detailed treatment elsewhere, but I want to sketch some reasons in support of this assessment.

On the one hand, as I have already noted, Brandom often writes as if his project is metaphysical, in the present sense—as if he is concerned to give us an account of the nature and constitution of matters of philosophical interest, such as conceptual content and the referential aspect of language:

> The primary treatment of the representational dimension of conceptual content is reserved for Chapter 8 . . . [where] the representational properties of semantic contents are explained as consequences of the essentially *social* character of inferential practice. (1994: xvii)

On the face of it, this is both "metaphysical" about reference itself, and a path to more general metaphysical issues, in the way I've described. Moreover, some of

Brandom's own (apparent) metaphysical aims are more general and more ambitious:

> [T]he investigation of the nature and limits of the explicit expression in principles of what is implicit in discursive practices yields a powerful transcendental argument—a . . . transcendental expressive argument for the existence of objects . . . . (1994: xxii–xxiii)

On the other hand, Brandom often makes it clear that what is really going on is about the forms of language and thought, not about extra-linguistic reality as such. The passage I have just quoted continues with the following gloss on the transcendental argument in question: it is an "argument that (and why) the *only* form the world *we can talk and think of* can take is that of a world of facts about particular objects and their properties and relations" (1994: xxii–xxiii, second emphasis added).

Similarly, at a less general level, Brandom often stresses that what he is offering is primarily an account of the *attribution of terms*—"truth," "reference," "represents," and so on—not of the properties or relations that other approaches take those terms to denote. Concerning his account of knowledge claims, for example, he says:

> Its primary focus is not on knowledge itself but on *attributions* of knowledge, attitudes towards that status. The pragmatist must ask, What are we doing when we say that someone knows something? (1994: 297)

But a few sentences later, continuing the same exposition, we have this: "A pragmatist phenomenalist account *of knowledge* will accordingly investigate the social and normative significance of acts of attributing knowledge" (1994: 297, emphasis added). Here, the two stances are once again run together: to make things clear, a pragmatist should deny that he is offering an account *of* knowledge at all. (That's what it means to say that the project is anthropology, not metaphysics.)

It might seem that I am being uncharitable to Brandom here, taking too literally his claim to be giving an account *of* knowledge (and similar claims about other topics). By way of comparison, isn't it harmless to say, at least loosely, that disquotationalism is an account of truth, even though it isn't literally an account *of* truth, but rather of the functions of the truth predicate? But I think there are other reasons for taking Brandom to task on this point—more on this in a moment.

Another point in Brandom's favor (from my Humean perspective) is that he often makes it clear that he rejects a realist construal of reference relations (and hence, as I've pointed out, of the theoretical bridge that is otherwise to liable to lead from anthropology back to metaphysics). Thus, concerning the consequences of his preferred anaphoric version of semantic deflationism, he writes as follows:

> One who endorses the anaphoric account of what is expressed by "true" and "refers" must accordingly eschew the reifying move to a truth property and a reference relation. A line is implicitly drawn by this approach between ordinary truth and reference talk and variously specifically philosophical extensions of it based on theoretical conclusions that have been drawn from a mistaken understanding of what such talk expresses. Ordinary remarks about what is true and what is false and about what some expression refers to are perfectly in order as they stand; and the anaphoric account explains how they should be understood. But truth and reference are philosophers' fictions, generated by grammatical misunderstandings. (1994: 323–324)

> Various word–world relations play important explanatory roles in theoretical semantic projects, but to think of any one of these as what is referred to as "the reference relation" is to be bewitched by surface syntactic form. (1994: 325)

On the other hand, Brandom's strategy at this point suggests that in some ways he is still wedded to a traditional representational picture. Consider in particular his reliance on syntactic criteria in order to be able to deny, as he puts it,

> that claims expressed using traditional semantic vocabulary make it possible for us to state specifically *semantic facts*, in the way that claims expressed using the vocabulary of physics, say, make it possible for us to state specifically *physical facts*. (1994: 326)

Here Brandom sounds like a traditional (*local*) expressivist, who is still in the grip of the picture that some parts of language are genuinely descriptive, in some robust sense. He hasn't seen the option and attractions of allowing one's semantic deflationism to deflate this picture, too; and remains vulnerable to the slide to metaphysics, wherever the syntactical loophole isn't available.

This reading is born out by the fact that at certain points he makes to confront these traditional metaphysical issues head-on. "None of these is a naturalistic account," he says (2000: 27), referring to various aspects of his account of the referential, objective and normative aspects of discourse. And again:

> Norms . . . are not objects in the causal order. . . . Nonetheless, according to the account presented here, there are norms, and their existence is neither supernatural nor mysterious. (1994: 626)

Once again, this passage continues with what is by my lights exactly the right explanation of what keeps Brandom's feet on the ground: "Normative statuses are domesticated by being understood in terms of normative attitudes, which *are* in the causal order" (1994: 626). But my point is that he shouldn't have to retreat in this way in the first place. His account only looks non-naturalistic (to him) because he tries to conceive of it as metaphysics. If he had stayed on the virtuous (anthropological) side of the fence to begin with, there would have been no appearance of anything non-naturalistic, and no need to retreat.

One final example, which seems to me to illustrate Brandom's continuing attraction to what I am thinking of as the more representationalist side of the fence—the side where we find the project of *reconstructing* representational relations using pragmatic raw materials. It is from Brandom's closing John Locke lecture, and is a characterization he offers of his own project, in response to the following self-posed challenge—"Doesn't the story I have been telling remain too resolutely on the 'word' side of the word/world divide?":

> Engaging in discursive practices and exercising discursive abilities is using words to say and mean something, hence to talk about items in the world. Those practices, the exercise of those abilities, those uses, *establish* semantic relations between words and the world. This is one of the big ideas that traditional pragmatism brings to philosophical thought about semantics: don't look to begin with to the relation between representings and representeds, but to the nature of the doing, of the process, that institutes that relation. (2008: 177–178)

I have been arguing that the right course—and the course that Brandom actually often follows, *in practice*—is precisely to remain "'resolutely on the 'word' side of the word/world divide." This resolution doesn't prevent us from seeking to explain referential *vocabulary*—the ordinary *ascriptions* of semantic relations, whose pervasiveness in language no doubt does much to explain the attractiveness of the representational picture. Nor does it require, absurdly, that we say nothing about word–world relations. On the contrary, as Brandom himself points out in a remark I quoted above:

> Various word–world relations play important explanatory roles in theoretical semantic projects, but to think of any one of these as what is referred to as 'the reference relation' is to be bewitched by surface syntactic form. (1994: 325)

And the resolution has the payoff that I've been trying to emphasize: by ensuring that our linguistic theory remains ontologically conservative, it keeps us safe from metaphysics.

In calling this kind of liberation from metaphysics an insight of Humean expressivism, I don't mean, of course, to belittle the respects in which pragmatism has moved on from Hume. Brandom notes that Wilfred Sellars characterized his own philosophical project as that of moving analytic philosophy from its Humean phase to a Kantian phase, and glosses the heart of this idea as the view that traditional empiricism missed the importance of the conceptual articulation of thought. Rorty, in turn, has described Brandom's project as a contribution to the next step: a transition from a Kantian to an Hegelian phase, based on recognition of the social constitution of concepts, and of the linguistic norms on which they depend. For my part, I've urged merely that Brandom's version of this project is in need of clarity on what I think it is fair to describe as a Humean insight. Hume's expressivism may well be a large step behind Kant, in failing to appreciate the importance of the conceptual; and a further large step behind Hegel, in failing to see that the conceptual depends on the social. But it is still at the head of the field for its understanding of the way in which what we would now call pragmatism simply turns its back on metaphysics. (We Humeans expect this kind of blindness from mainstream representationalists, for we can see how their representationalism leads them astray. But we hope for better from our fellow pragmatists.)

7. Between Rorty and Brandom

I want to finish with an analogy, intended to give some sense of the progressive pragmatist program, as I see it; and of the key elements which may distinguish my sense of the way forward from that of Rorty, on one side, and Brandom, on the other.

Imagine a large structure such as a sports stadium, built as a three-dimensional network of steel beams. Imagine it illuminated by the sun from overhead: each beam casts a shadow on the pitch beneath. Now imagine a photograph of the scene, in the hands of alien anthropologists (from a grey, cloud-bound planet, perhaps, where shadows are uncommon). The aliens realize that the stadium is an artifact of some kind, and wonder about the intentions of the creatures who designed it. Noticing the correspondence between beams and dark lines on the green surface underneath, they postulate that the function of a beam is to *represent* the corresponding line in pattern below. (Perhaps the more radical among them postulate that the representation is irreducibly perspectival: the stadium represents the pattern of dark lines on the grass, *as seen from the viewpoint of the sun*.)

The alien hypothesis gets things back to front, of course. The pattern on the grass is a projection of the structure of the stadium, rather than vice versa. Less obviously, but in my view even more importantly, the hypothesis is blind to the fact that beams have many different functions, within the structure as a whole. Some are vertical supports, transferring load to the ground; some are "pushers," designed to keep other things apart; some are "pullers," designed to hold other things together; some, such as supports for scoreboards, seats, and cameras, may be related to the use of the stadium as a sports venue; some may be merely decorative; and many, of course, may serve multiple functions, functions that only make sense within the context of the structure as a whole. So although all the beams have something in common—they are all *beams*, after all—they are also different in important respects. And to understand the structure, its relation to the ground on which it sits, and its role in the lives of the creatures who built it, we need to understand these differences.

Language and thought are not human artefacts. No one designed them, and they have a purpose, at best, only in the ersatz evolutionary sense. Nevertheless, just as we can speak of the functions (in this sense) of organs and structures within the human body, at various levels of organization, and their contribution to the overall interaction between ourselves (individually and collectively) and our environment, so we can ask similar questions about the functions and contributions of thought and language, and of their various components. Much of science and philosophy is dominated by a view of the functions of thought and language which is analogous to the alien hypothesis about the stadium, namely, that their primary function is to "represent" external patterns. Anti-representationalists agree that this view is mistaken in important ways, but disagree about precisely which ways, and about what we should say instead.

For my part, I want to argue that the representationalist orthodoxy makes two basic mistakes. It misses important respects in which patterns in the conceptual realm depend on aspects of us, rather than aspects of our environment. And it misses a crucial dimension of functional diversity, within the conceptual realm—important respects in which different vocabularies do different jobs in our complex relationship to our physical environment. However, I think that this functional pluralism needs to come with an important rider. Just as we shouldn't ignore what the steel beams in the stadium have in common—their common attributes, such as length, mass, and load-bearing capacity, which underpin their various different applications—so we shouldn't overlook an important kind of homogeneity within language, comprising the ubiquity and centrality of assertion, of Brandom's "downtown."

I suspect that Rorty may be skeptical about the prospects for interesting theoretical work from this perspective. However, there is no doubt that it resonates with some Rortyan themes—especially with the view that language is for "coping not copying," to mention one of Rorty's favorite Deweyan slogans. I've urged that we should embroider this theme in two ways. First, we should anticipate that language makes various interestingly different kinds of contributions to coping, associated broadly with variation in us, as well as variation in our environment; and hence expect a theoretically interesting functional pluralism. This doesn't commit us to the view that all differences are theoretically interesting, of course, or that all have the same kind of explanation or genealogy. On the contrary, as elsewhere in biology and anthropology, we should expect differences with respect to the depth and contingency of variations, as well as with respect to function. Some functions are likely to be basic and perhaps hard-wired; others, simply cultural fads. No matter: the basic point is that "coping" brings a new dimension of variability to linguistic theory, a dimension that "copying" necessarily suppresses.

We should be amazed, indeed ashamed, if our ancestors have not managed to exploit this potential diversity, in theoretically interesting ways.

Second, we should recognize that superimposed on this functional diversity is an important kind of unity: a central kind of practice—namely, assertion—which is put to work in the service of many (though not all) of these diverse functions. Here, too, of course, there's an issue about historical contingency and cultural difference. It is an interesting question how general this device is, and what sort of variation it displays, from culture to culture and era to era. If Brandom is right then the answer must be "very little," because assertion is fundamental to anything that counts as a language at all. But even to bring this question into focus, we need to understand our home territory, how it works for us—and here, I think, Brandom's account is the most illuminating we have.

In according this kind of centrality to assertion, I'm one step closer to the orthodoxy than the view—arguably Wittgenstein's, and perhaps Rorty's—that even this much representationalism is too much: hence my one cheer for representationalism. But I am one step further from the orthodoxy than the view that Brandom appears at least tempted to adopt, which aims to build a substantial notion of representational content from expressivist and pragmatist raw materials.[7] And that view, in turn, is importantly distinct from full-blown primitive representationalism—from what Brandom calls platonism about semantic content. Rorty, Brandom, and I are agreed on the need to follow Dewey's lead, in draining that traditional tub. If we disagree, it is about whether to expect a baby, and if so of what shape and origins. Rorty, I think, expects nothing. Brandom, I think, sometimes hopes for a kind of hybrid—a sort of semantic Christ-child, its platonic properties reborn of human stock. And I expect something more modest and mortal, a complex little creature of flesh and blood—no analytic angel, certainly, but none the worse for that.

7. In a different way, Blackburn, too, seems tempted by this position, in the form of what he calls *success semantics:* "the view that a theory of success in action is a possible basis for a theory of *representation*, or a theory of *content or intentionality*" (Blackburn 2005b).

REFERENCES

Abrams, M. H. (1953). *The Mirror and the Lamp: Romantic Theory and the Critical Tradition*. New York: Oxford University Press.

Armstrong, D. (1983). *What Is a Law of Nature*. Cambridge: Cambridge University Press.

Armstrong, D. (1997). *A World of States of Affairs*. Cambridge: Cambridge University Press.

Beth, E. (1963). "Carnap on Constructed Systems," in P. Schilpp (ed.), *Library of Living Philosophers*, Vol. XI: *The Philosophy of Rudolf Carnap*. La Salle, IL: Open Court, 469–502.

Blackburn, S. (1971). 'Moral Realism', in J. Casey (ed.), *Morality and Moral Reasoning*. London: Methuen, 101–124.

Blackburn, S. (1984). *Spreading the Word*. Oxford: Oxford University Press.

Blackburn, S. (1985). "Supervenience Revisited," in Hacking (ed.), *Exercises in Analysis: Essays by Students of Casimir Lewy*. Cambridge: Cambridge University Press, 47–67.

Blackburn, S. (1988). "Attitudes and Contents." *Ethics*, 98: 501–517.

Blackburn, S. (1990). "Wittgenstein's Irrealism," in J. Brandl and R. Haller (eds.), *Wittgenstein: Eine Neubewehrung*. Vienna: Holder-Richler-Temsky.

Blackburn, S. (1993a). *Essays in Quasi-Realism*. Oxford: Oxford University Press.

Blackburn, S. (1993b). "Realism, Quasi, or Queasy," in J. Haldane and C. Wright (ed.), *Reality, Represenation, and Projection*. Oxford: Oxford University Press, 365–384.

Blackburn, S. (1993c). "Wittgenstein and Minimalism," in B. Garrett and K. Mulligan (eds.), *Themes from Wittgenstein, Working Papers in Philosophy*, 4. Canberra: Philosophy Program, Research School of Social Sciences, ANU, 1–14.

Blackburn, S. (1993d). "Review of Paul Johnston." *Wittgenstein and Moral Philosophy, Ethics*, 103: 588–590.

Blackburn, S. (1998a). "Wittgenstein, Wright, Rorty and Minimalism." *Mind*, 107: 157–182.

Blackburn, S. (1998b). *Ruling Passions: A Theory of Practical Reasoning*. Oxford: Oxford University Press.

Blackburn, S. (2005a). *Truth: A Guide for the Perplexed*. London: Allen Lane.

Blackburn, S. (2005b). "Success Semantics," in H. Lillehammer and D. H. Mellor (eds.), *Ramsey's Legacy*. Oxford: Oxford University Press.

Boghossian, P. (1989). "The Rule-Following Considerations." *Mind* 98: 507–549.

Boghossian, P. (1990). "The Status of Content." *Philosophical Review*, 99: 157–184.

Brandom, R. (1983). "Asserting." *Noûs*, 17: 637–650.

Brandom, R. (1984). "Reference Explained Away." *The Journal of Philosophy*, 81: 469–492.

Brandom, R. (1988). "Pragmatism, Phenomenalism, and Truth Talk." *Midwest Studies in Philosophy*, 22: 75–93.

Brandom, R. (1994). *Making it Explicit*. Cambridge, MA: Harvard University Press.

Brandom, R. (2000). *Articulating Reasons: An Introduction to Inferentialism*. Cambridge, MA: Harvard University Press.

Brandom, R. (2008). *Between Saying and Doing: Towards an Analytic Pragmatism*. Oxford: Oxford University Press.

Campbell, J. (1993). "A Simple View of Colour," in J. Haldane and C. Wright (eds.), *Reality, Representation and Projection*. Oxford: Oxford University Press.

Carnap, R. (1950). "'Empiricism, Semantics and Ontology." *Revue Internationale de Philosophie*, 4: 20–40. Reprinted in *Meaning and Necessity: A Study in Semantics and Modal Logic*, 2nd enlarged ed., Chicago: University of Chicago Press, 1956, 205–221. Page references are to the latter version.

Chalmers, D. (1996). *The Conscious Mind: In Search of a Fundamental Theory*. New York: Oxford University Press.

Chomsky, N. (1957). *Syntactic Structures*. The Hague: Mouton.

Chomsky, N. (1975). *Logical Structure of Linguistic Theory*. New York and Chicago: Plenum; University of Chicago Press

Chomsky, N. (1995). "Language and Nature." *Mind*, 104: 1–61.

Cohen, J. (1977). *The Probable and the Provable*. Oxford: Oxford University Press.

Collins, J. (1988). "Belief, Desire and Revision". *Mind*, 97: 333–342.

Colyvan, M. (2003). "Indispensability Arguments in The Philosophy of Mathematics," in Edward N. Zalta (ed.), *The Stanford Encyclopedia of Philosophy*, Spring 2003 ed. Stanford, CA: Center for the Study of Language and Information.

Davidson, D. (1974). "On the Very Idea of a Conceptual Scheme." *Proceedings and Addresses of the American Philosophical Association*, 47: 5–20.

Dennett, D. (1991). "Real Patterns." *Journal of Philosophy*, 88: 27–51.

Drier, J. (2004). "Meta-Ethics and the Problem of Creeping Minimalism." *Philosophical Perspectives* 18, *Ethics*: 23–44.

Dummett, M. (1973). *Frege: Philosophy of Language*. London: Duckworth.

Dummett, M. (1975). "What Is a Theory of Meaning? (I)," in S. Guttenplan (ed.), *Mind and Language*. Oxford: Clarendon Press, 97–138.

Dummett, M. (1978). "The Philosophical Basis of Intuitionist Logic." *Truth and Other Enigmas*. London: Duckworth, 215–247.

Dummett, M. (1979). "The Appeal to Use in a Theory of Meaning," in A. Margalit (ed.), *Meaning and Use*. Dordrecht: Reidel, 123–135.

Dummett, M. (1993). "The Source of the Concept of Truth." *The Seas of Language*. Oxford: Clarendon Press, 188–201.

Field, H. (1994). "Deflationist Views of Meaning and Content." *Mind*, 103: 249–285.

Field, H. (2001). "Mathematical Objectivity and Mathematical Objects," in his *Truth and the Absence of Fact*. Clarendon Press: Oxford, 315–331.

Frege, G. (1960). "Negation," in P. Geach and M. Black (eds.), *Translations from the Philosophical Writings of Gottlob Frege*. Oxford: Oxford University Press.

Geach, P. (1960). "Ascriptivism." *Philosophical Review*, 69: 221–225.

Geach, P. (1965). "Assertion." *Philosophical Review*, 74: 449–465.

Gentzen, G. (1933). "Über das Verhältnis zwischen intuitionistischer und klassischer Arithmetik." Unpublished at the time; English translation in Szabo, M. (ed.), (1969). *The Collected Papers of Gerhard Gentzen*. Amsterdam: North Holland, 53–67.

Gibbard, A. (1990). *Wise Choices, Apt Feelings: A Theory of Normative Judgement*. Cambridge, MA: Harvard University Press.

Gödel, K. (1933). "Zur intuitionistischen Arithmetik und Zahlentheorie." *Ergebnisse eines mathematischen Kolloquiums*, 4: 34–38. English translation in (1986) *Collected Works*, Vol. I. New York: Oxford University Press, 287–295.

Goodman, N. (1983). *Fact Fiction and Forecast*, 4th ed. Cambridge, MA: Harvard University Press.

Hare, R. M. (1971). *Practical Inferences*. London: Macmillan.

Hare, R. M. (1976). "Some Confusions about Subjectivity," in J. Bricke (ed.), *Freedom and Morality: the Lindley Lectures Delivered at the University of Kansas*. Lawrence: University of Kansas.

Hazen, A. (1986). "A Fallacy in Ramsey." *Mind*, 95: 496–498.

Heyting, A. (1930a). "Die formalen Reglen der intuitionistischen Logik." *Sitzungsberichte der Preussischen Akademie der Wissenschaften, physikalisch-mathematische Klasse*, 42–56.

Heyting, A. (1930b). "Die formalen Reglen der intuitionistischen Mathematik." *Sitzungsberichte der Preussischen Akademie der Wissenschaften, physikalisch-mathematische Klasse*, 57–71, 158–169.

Holton, R., and Price, H. (2003). "Ramsey on Saying and Whistling: A Discordant Note." *Noûs*, 37: 325–341. Reprinted as chapter 7 in the present volume.

Hookway, C. (1988). *Quine*. Stanford: Stanford University Press.

Horwich, P. (1990). *Truth*. New York: Basil Blackwell.

Horwich, P. (1993). "Gibbard's Theory of Norms." *Philosophy and Public Affairs*, 22, 1: 67–78.

Horwich, P. (1998). *Truth*, 2nd ed. Oxford: Oxford University Press.

Humberstone, I. L. (1991). "Critical Notice of F. Jackson, *Conditionals*." *Philosophy and Phenomenological Research* LI: 227–234.

Jackson, F. (1982). "Epiphenomenal Qualia." *Philosophical Quarterly*, 32: 127–136.

Jackson, F. (1994). "Armchair Metaphysics," in M. Michael and J. O'Leary-Hawthorne (eds.), *Philosophy in Mind: The Place of Philosophy in the Study of the Mind*. Dordrecht: Kluwer, 23–42.

Jackson, F. (1997). "Naturalism and the Fate of the M-Worlds II," *Proceedings of the Aristotelian Society*, 71 (Supp.): 269–282.

Jackson, F. (1998). *From Metaphysics to Ethics*. Oxford: Clarendon Press.

Jackson, F., Oppy, G., and Smith, M. (1994). "Minimalism and Truth Aptness." *Mind*, 103: 287–302.

Jackson, F., and Pettit, P. (1995). "Moral Functionalism and Moral Motivation." *Philosophical Quarterly*, 45: 20–40.

Johnston, M. (1989). "Dispositional Theories of Value." *Proceedings of the Aristotelian Society*, 63 supp.: 139–174.

Johnston, M. (1993). "Objectivity Refigured," in J. Haldane and C. Wright (eds.), *Reality, Representation and Projection*. Oxford: Oxford University Press, 85–130.

Keynes, J. M. (1921). *A Treatise on Probability*. London: Macmillan.

Kraut, R. (1990). "Varieties of Pragmatism." *Mind*, 99: 157–183

Kripke, S. A. (1982). *Wittgenstein on Rules and Private Language*. Cambridge, MA: Harvard University Press.

Lance, M., and O'Leary-Hawthorne, J. (1997). *The Grammar of Meaning*. Cambridge: Cambridge University Press.

Leiter, B. (2004). "Introduction: The Future for Philosophy." in B. Leiter (ed.), *The Future for Philosophy*. Oxford: Clarendon Press, 1–23.

Lewis, D. (1966). "An Argument for the Identity Theory." *Journal of Philosophy*, 63: 17–25.

Lewis, D. (1970a). "How to Define Theoretical Terms." *Journal of Philosophy*, 67: 427–446.

Lewis, D. (1970b). "General Semantics." *Synthese*, 22: 18–67.

Lewis, D. (1972). "Psychophysical and Theoretical Identifications." *Australasian Journal of Philosophy*, 50: 249–258.

Lewis, D. (1975). "Languages and Language," in K. Gunderstone (ed.), *Minnesota Studies in the Philosophy of Science*, Volume VII. Minneapolis: University of Minnesota Press.

Lewis, D. (1983). "General Semantics." *Philosophical Papers*, Volume I. Oxford: Oxford University Press, 198–232.

Lewis, D. (1986a). *Philosophical Papers*, Volume II. Oxford: Oxford University Press.

Lewis, D. (1986b). *On the Plurality of Worlds*. Oxford: Blackwell.

Lewis, D. (1988). "Desire as Belief." *Mind*, 97: 323–332.

Lewis, D. (1994). "Reduction of Mind," in S. Guttenplan (ed.), *A Companion to Philosophy of Mind*. Oxford: Blackwell.

Lewis, D. (2005). "Quasi-realism is Fictionalism," in Mark Kalderon (ed.), *Fictionalist Approaches to Metaphysics*. Oxford: Oxford University Press, 314–321.

Loar, B. (1980). "Ramsey's Theory of Belief and Truth," in D. H. Mellor (ed.), *Prospects for Pragmatism*. Cambridge: Cambridge University Press, 49–70.

Macarthur, D., and Price, H. (2007). "Pragmatism, Quasi-realism and the Global Challenge," in Cheryl Misak (ed.), *The New Pragmatists*. Oxford: Oxford University Press, 91–120. Reprinted as chapter 11 in the present volume.

McDowell, J. (1981). "Anti-realism and the Epistemology of Understanding," in J. Bouveresse and H. Parret (eds.), *Meaning and Understanding*. Berlin: W. de Gruyter.

Mackie, J. L. (1977). *Ethics: Inventing Right and Wrong*. Harmondsworth: Penguin Books.

Majer, U. (1989). "Ramsey's Conception of Theories: An Intuitionistic Approach." *History of Philosophy Quarterly*, 6: 233–258.

Majer, U. (1991). "Ramsey's Theory of Truth and the Truth of Theories." *Theoria*, 57: 162–195.

Mellor, H. (1971). *The Matter of Chance*. Cambridge: Cambridge University Press.

Menand, L. (2001). *The Metaphysical Club: A Story of Ideas in America*. New York: Farrar, Strauss and Giroux.

Menzies, P., and Price, H. (1993). "Causation as a Secondary Quality." *British Journal for the Philosophy of Science*, 44: 187–203.

Moore, A. (1990). *The Infinite*. London: Routledge.

Moore, G. E. (1903). *Principia Ethica*. Cambridge: Cambridge University Press.

North, C. (1832). "Tennyson's Poems." *Blackwood's Edinburgh Magazine*, 31: 721–741.

O'Leary-Hawthorne, J., and Price, H. (1996). "How to Stand Up for Non-cognitivists." *Australasian Journal of Philosophy*, 74 (2): 275–292. Reprinted as chapter 5 in the present volume.

Pettit, P. (1988). "Humeans, Anti-Humeans and Motivation'. *Mind*, 97: 530–533.

Pettit, P. (1991). 'Realism and Response-Dependence'. *Mind*, 100, 587–626.

Pettit, P., and Price, H. (1989). "Bare Functional Desire." *Analysis*, 44: 162–169.

Price, H. (1983a). "Does "Probably" Modify Sense?." *Australasian Journal of Philosophy*, 61: 396–408.

Price, H. (1983b). "Sense, Assertion, Dummett and Denial." *Mind*, 97: 174–188.

Price, H. (1986). "Conditional Credence." *Mind*, 95: 18–36.

Price, H. (1988). *Facts and the Function of Truth*. Oxford: Basil Blackwell.

Price, H. (1989). "Defending Desire-as-Belief." *Mind*, 98: 119–127.

Price, H. (1990). "Why "Not"?." *Mind*, 99: 221–238.

Price, H. (1991a). "Agency and Probabilistic Causality." *British Journal for the Philosophy of Science*, 42: 157–176.

Price, H. (1991b). "Two Paths to Pragmatism." *Working Papers in Philosophy*. Canberra: Research School of Social Sciences, ANU. Reprinted as chapter 4 in the present volume.

Price, H. (1992). "Metaphysical Pluralism." *Journal of Philosophy*, 89: 387–409. Reprinted as chapter 2 in the present volume.

Price, H. (1994). "Semantic Minimalism and the Frege Point," in S. L. Tsohatzidis (ed.), *Foundations of Speech Act Theory: Philosophical and Linguistic Perspectives*. London: Routledge. Reprinted as chapter 3 in the present volume.

Price, H. (1997a). "Naturalism and the Fate of the M-Worlds." *Proceedings of the Aristotelian Society*, 71: 247–267. Reprinted as chapter 6 in the present volume.

Price, H. (1997b). "Carnap, Quine and the Fate of Metaphysics," *The Electronic Journal of Analytic Philosophy*, 5 (Spring).

Price, H. (1998). "Three Norms of Assertibility, or How the MOA Became Extinct." *Philosophical Perspectives*, 12: 41–54.

Price, H. (2001). "Causation in the Special Sciences: The Case for Pragmatism," in D. Costantini, M. C. Galavotti, and P. Suppes (eds.), *Stochastic Causality*. Stanford: CSLI Publications, 103–120.

Price, H. (2003). "Truth as Convenient Friction." *The Journal of Philosophy*, 100: 167–190. Reprinted as chapter 8 in the present volume.

Price, H. (2004a). "Naturalism Without Representationalism," in M. de Caro and D. Macarthur (eds.), *Naturalism in Question*. Cambridge, MA: Harvard University Press. Reprinted as chapter 9 in the present volume.

Price, H. (2004b). "Immodesty Without Mirrors—Making Sense of Wittgenstein's Linguistic Pluralism," in M. Kölbel and B. Weiss. (eds.), *Wittgenstein's Lasting Significance*. Boston: Routledge & Kegan Paul, 179–205. Reprinted as chapter 10 in the present volume.

Price, H. (2007a). "Quining Naturalism." *Journal of Philosophy*, 104: 375–405.

Price, H. (2007b). "Causal Perspectivalism," in H. Price and R. Corry (eds.), *Causation, Physics and the Constitution of Reality: Russell's Republic Revisited* (OUP), 250–292.

Price, H. (2008). René Descartes Lectures, Tilburg. Available online at http://philsci-archive.pitt.edu/archive/00004430/

Price, H. (2009). "The Semantic Foundations of Metaphysics," in I. Ravenscroft (ed.), *Minds, Worlds and Conditionals: Essays in Honour of Frank Jackson*. Oxford: Oxford University Press, 111–140. Reprinted as chapter 12 in the present volume.

Putnam, H. (1971). "Philosophy of Logic," in his *Mathematics, Matter and Method: Philosophical Papers*, Volume 1 (2nd ed.). Cambridge: Cambridge University Press, 323–357. (Originally published in 1971 as *Philosophy of Logic*, New York: Harper Torchbooks.)

Putnam, H. (1978). *Meaning and the Moral Sciences*. Boston: Routledge & Kegan Paul.

Putnam, H. (1981). *Reason, Truth and History*. New York: Cambridge University Press.

Putnam, H. (2001). "Was Wittgenstein Really an Anti-Realist about Mathematics?," in T. McCarthy and S. C. Stidd (eds.), *Wittgenstein in America*. Oxford: Oxford University Press, 140–194.

Putnam, H. (2004). *Ethics Without Ontology*. Cambridge, MA: Harvard University Press.

Quine, W. V. (1948). "On What There Is." *Review of Metaphysics*, 2: 21–38.

Quine, W. V. (1960). *Word and Object*. Cambridge, MA: MIT Press.

Quine, W. V. (1966). "On Carnap's Views on Ontology," in his *The Ways of Paradox and Other Essays*. New York: Random House. (Originally published in *Philosophical Studies*, 2 (1971): 65–72)

Quine, W. V. (1970). *Philosophy of Logic*. Englewood Cliffs, NJ: Prentice-Hall.

Quine, W. V. (1981). *Theories and Things*. Cambridge, MA: Harvard University Press.

Ramsey, F. (1978). "Truth and Probability," in D. H. Mellor (ed.), *Foundations*. London: Routledge & Kegan Paul.

Ramsey, F. (1990a). "General Propositions and Causality," in D. H. Mellor (ed.), *Philosophical Papers*. Cambridge: Cambridge University Press, 145–163.

Ramsey, F. (1990b). "Facts and Propositions," in D. H. Mellor (ed.), *Philosophical Papers*. Cambridge: Cambridge University Press, 34–51.

Ramsey, F. (1990c). "Mathematical Logic," in D. H. Mellor (ed.), *Philosophical Papers*. Cambridge: Cambridge University Press, 225–244.

Ramsey, F. (1990d). "Causal Qualities," in D. H. Mellor (ed.), *Philosophical Papers*. Cambridge: Cambridge University Press, 137–139.

Ramsey, F. (1991). *Notes on Philosophy, Probability and Mathematics*, M. C. Galavotti (ed.). Naples: Bibliopolis.

Rée, J. (1998). "Strenuous Unbelief." *London Review of Books*, 20 (Oct. 15): 7–11.

Romanos, G. D. (1983). *Quine and Analytic Philosophy*. Cambridge, MA: MIT Press, ch. 3.

Rorty, R. (1981). *Philosophy and the Mirror of Nature*. Princeton: Princeton University Press.

Rorty, R. (1991). "Pragmatism, Davidson and Truth," in *Objectivity, Relativism and Truth: Philosophical Papers*, Vol. 1. New York: Cambridge University Press, 126–150.

Rorty, R. (1998). "Is Truth a Goal of Enquiry? Donald Davidson versus Crispin Wright," in *Truth and Progress: Philosophical Papers*, Vol. 3. New York: Cambridge University Press, 19–42.

Rosen, G. (1994). "Objectivity and Modern Idealism: What is the Question?," in M. Michael and J. O'Leary-Hawthorne (eds.), *Philosophy in Mind: The Place of Philosophy in the Study of the Mind*. Dordrecht: Kluwer, 277–319.

Russell, B. (1931). "Critical Notice of Ramsey's *The Foundations of Mathematics and other Logical Essays*." *Mind*, 40: 476–482.

Ryle, G. (1938). "Categories." *Proceedings of the Aristotelian Society*, 38: 189–206.

Ryle, G. (1949). *The Concept of Mind*. London: Hutchinson.

Sahlin, N. (1997). ""He is no good for my work': On the Philosophical Relations between Ramsey and Wittgenstein," in M. Sintonen (ed.), *Knowledge and Inquiry: Essays on Jaakko Hintikka's Epistemology and Philosophy of Science, Poznan Studies in the Philosophy of the Sciences and the Humanities*, 51: 61–84.

Schilpp, P. (ed.), (1963). *Library of Living Philosophers*, Vol. XI: *The Philosophy of Rudolf Carnap*. La Salle, IL: Open Court.

Searle, J. (1962). "Meaning and Speech Acts." *Philosophical Review*, 71: 423–432.

Searle, J. (1969). *Speech Acts: An Essay in the Philosophy of Language*. London: Cambridge University Press.

Skorupski, J. (1980). "Ramsey on Belief," in D. H. Mellor (ed.), *Prospects for Pragmatism*. Cambridge: Cambridge University Press, 71–89.

Smith, B. (1992). "'Understanding Language," *Proceedings of the Aristotelian Society*, 92: 109–141.

Smith, M. (1987). "The Humean Theory of Motivation." *Mind*, 96: 36–61.

Smith, M. (1988). "On Humeans, Anti-Humeans and Motivation: A Reply to Pettit." *Mind*, 97: 589–595.

Smith, M. (1989). "Dispositional Theories of Value." *Proceedings of the Aristotelian Society*, 62 supp.: 89–111.

Soames, S. (1989). "Semantics and Semantic Competence." *Philosophical Perspectives*, 3: 575–596.

Stich, S. (1996). *Deconstructing the Mind*. New York: Oxford University Press.

Strawson, P. (1949). "Truth." *Analysis*, 9: 83–97.

van Fraassen, B. (1990). *Laws and Symmetry*. Oxford: Oxford University Press.

Weyl, H. (1921). "Über die neue Grundlagenkrise der Mathematik." *Mathematische Zeitschrift*, 10: 39–79. Reprinted in Weyl, H. (1968). *Gesammelte Abhandlungen* (Vol. II), ed. K. Chandrasekharan. Berlin: Springer Verlag, 143–180: page references are to the reprint. English translation "On the New Foundational Crisis of Mathematics," in Mancosu, P. (ed.), (1998). *From Brouwer to Hilbert*. New York: Oxford University Press, 86–118.

Weyl, H. (1927). *Philosophie der Mathematik und Naturwissenschaft: Handbuch der Philosophie* 5. Munich and Berlin: R. Oldenburg. English translation (1949) *Philosophy of Mathematics and Natural Science*. Princeton: Princeton University Press.

Weyl, H. (1928). "Discussionsbemerkungen zu dem zweiten Hilbertschen Vortrag über die Grundlagen der Mathematik." *Abhandlungen aus dem Mathematischen Seminar der Universität Hamburg* 6, 86–88. Reprinted in Chandrasekharan, K. (ed.), (1968). *Gesammelte Abhandlungen*, Vol III. Berlin: Springer Verlag, 147–149. English translation in van Heijenoort, J. (ed.), (1967). *From Frege to Godel: A Sourcebook in Mathematical Logic*. Cambridge, MA: Harvard University Press, 480–484.

Wiggins, D. (1976). "Truth, Invention and the Meaning of Life." *Proceedings of the British Academy*, 62: 331–378.

Williams, B. (1973). "Consistency and Realism." Reprinted in *Problems of the Self*. Cambridge: Cambridge University Press, 187–206.

Williams, M. (1980). "Coherence, Justification and Truth." *Review of Metaphysics*, 34: 243–272.

Williams, M. (1999). "Meaning and Deflationary Truth." *Journal of Philosophy*, 96 (11): 545–564.

Williamson, T. (2004). "Past the Linguistic Turn?," in B. Leiter (ed.), *The Future for Philosophy*. Oxford: Clarendon Press, 106–128.

Wilson, J. (1832). "Tennyson's Poems." *Blackwood's Magazine*, 31: 721–741.

Wittgenstein, L. (1968). *Philosophical Investigations*, 3rd ed. English edition. Oxford: Basil Blackwell.

Wittgenstein, L. (1980). *Culture and Value*. G. H. von Wright (ed.), P. Winch (trans.). Chicago: University of Chicago Press.

Wright, C. (1988). "Realism, Antirealism, Irrealism, Quasi-realism." *Midwest Studies in Philosophy*, 12: 25–49.

Wright, C. (1992). *Truth and Objectivity*. Cambridge, MA: Harvard University Press.

Wright, C. (1993). "Realism—the Contemporary Debate: Whither Now?," in J. Haldane and C. Wright (eds.), *Reality, Representation and Projection*. Oxford: Oxford University Press, 63–84.

INDEX